NATURE, CULTURE, AND THE ORIGINS OF GREEK COMEDY

Aristophanes' *Birds, Wasps,* and *Frogs* offer the best-known examples of the animal choruses of Greek comedy of the fifth century B.C., but sixth-century vase-paintings of men costumed as cocks, bulls, and horses indicate that the comedies were only the last phase of a longer tradition. This book suggests that although the earlier masquerades may have had ritual origins, they should be seen also as products of the culture of the archaic aristocratic symposium. The animal choruses of the late fifth century may have been conscious revivals of an earlier tradition. Moreover, the animals of comedy were not the predators found in other literary genres; they were, instead, social animals who showed that nature and culture could coexist. *The Birds,* which tells the story of a city foundation, parodies fifth-century philosophical accounts of the origins of human civilization. Also discussed are the *Wasps, Frogs,* and fragments of lost comedies.

Kenneth S. Rothwell, Jr., is associate professor of classics at the University of Massachusetts, Boston. He is the author of *Politics and Persuasion in Aristophanes' "Ecclesiazusae."*

NATURE, CULTURE, AND THE ORIGINS OF GREEK COMEDY

A STUDY OF ANIMAL CHORUSES

KENNETH S. ROTHWELL, JR.

University of Massachusetts, Boston

CAMBRIDGE
UNIVERSITY PRESS

CAMBRIDGE UNIVERSITY PRESS
Cambridge, New York, Melbourne, Madrid, Cape Town, Singapore, São Paulo

Cambridge University Press
32 Avenue of the Americas, New York, NY 10013-2473, USA

www.cambridge.org
Information on this title: www.cambridge.org/9780521860666

First published 2007

Printed in the United States of America

A catalog record for this publication is available from the British Library.

Library of Congress Cataloging in Publication Data

Rothwell, Kenneth S. (Kenneth Sprague)
Nature, culture, and the origins of Greek comedy: a study of animal choruses/Kenneth S.
Rothwell, Jr.
p.   cm.
Includes bibliographical references and index.
ISBN-13: 978-0-521-86066-6
ISBN-10: 0-521-86066-0
1. Greek drama (Comedy) – History and criticism – Theory, etc.   2. Drama – Chorus (Greek
drama)   3. Aristophanes – Criticism and interpretation.   4. Animals in literature.   I. Title.
PA3166.R76   2007
882′.0109–dc22   2006007801

ISBN-13   978-0-521-86066-6 hardback
ISBN-10   0-521-86066-0 hardback

Coniugi carissimae

CONTENTS

LIST OF ILLUSTRATIONS

ABBREVIATIONS

AA	*Archäologischer Anzeiger*
ABV	J. D. Beazley, *Attic Black-Figure Vase-Painters.* Oxford, 1956.
Add.	Carpenter, T. H., with Mannack, T. and Mendonca, M. *Beazley Addenda.* 2nd ed. Oxford, 1989.
AK	*Antike Kunst*
AJA	*American Journal of Archaeology*
AJP	*American Journal of Philology*
AM	*Mitteilungen des deutschen archäologischen Instituts, Athenische Abteilung*
ANS	American Numismatic Society
*ARV*²	J. D. Beazley, *Attic Red-Figure Vase-Painters.* 2nd ed. Oxford, 1963.
BCH	*Bulletin de correspondance hellénique*
BICS	*Bulletin of the Institute of Classical Studies*
CJ	*Classical Journal*
CP	*Classical Philology*
CQ	*Classical Quarterly*
CR	*Classical Review*
CVA	*Corpus Vasorum Antiquorum*
DK	Hermann Diels and Walther Kranz, edd. *Die Fragmente der Vorsokratiker.* 6th ed. Zurich, 1951–1952.
FGrH	Felix Jacoby, ed. *Die Fragmente der griechischen Historiker.* Berlin/Leiden 1923–1958.

G&R	*Greece and Rome*
GRBS	*Greek, Roman and Byzantine Studies*
HSCP	*Harvard Studies in Classical Philology*
IG	*Inscriptiones Graecae*
JdI	*Jahrbuch des deutschen archäologischen Instituts*
JHS	*Journal of Hellenic Studies*
LIMC	*Lexicon Iconographicum Mythologiae Classicae*
Para.	J. D. Beazley, *Paralipomena*. Oxford, 1971
PCG	R. Kassel and C. Austin, eds. *Poetae Comici Graeci*. Berlin and New York, 1983–
PCPS	*Proceedings of the Cambridge Philological Society*
QUCC	*Quaderni Urbinati di Cultura Classica*
RA	*Revue Archéologique*
RE	*Realenzyklopädie der Klassischen Altertumswissenschaft*
REA	*Revue des études anciennes*
RhM	*Rheinisches Museum*
SBAW	*Sitzungsberichte der Bayerischen Akademie der Wissenschaften, Philosophisch-historische Abteilung*
TAPA	*Transactions of the American Philological Association*
TrGF	*Tragicorum Graecorum Fragmenta*. B. Snell, R. Kannicht, and S. L. Radt, eds.
WS	*Wiener Studien*
ZPE	*Zeitschrift für Papyrologie und Epigrafik*

ACKNOWLEDGMENTS

For illustrations I have had assistance from many quarters, and I would like to thank the following for their help in procuring prints and transparencies of the vases and statuettes: Rüdiger Splitter (Staatliche Museen Kassel, Antikensammlung); Dr. Nikolaus Kaltsas (National Archaeological Museum, Athens); Michael Slade (Art Resource, for the Antikensammlung, Staatliche Museen zu Berlin); Horst Getter of the Staatliche Museen, who allowed me to inspect the "Berlin Cocks" firsthand; Jan Jordan (American School of Classical Studies at Athens, Agora Excavation); Corinne Emery (Ashmolean Museum, Oxford); Alex Truscott (London, British Museum); Jacklyn Burns (Malibu, J. Paul Getty Museum); Elena Stolyarik (American Numismatic Society); Natasha Derrickson (University of Chicago, Smart Museum of Art); Nadia Perucic (Michael and Judy Steinhardt Collection, New York); Eileen Sullivan (New York, Metropolian Museum of Art); Jutta Stroszek and Michael Krumme (German Archaeological Institute, Athens); Erin Schleigh (Museum of Fine Arts, Boston). Dr. Claire Lyons (Getty), and Dr. Carmen Arnold-Biucchi (Sackler Museum, Harvard). Prof. H. A. G. Brijder and Dr. Ellen Reeder helped me locate crucial pieces of information. I would also like to acknowledge my debt to the online Beazley Archive Pottery Database (http://www. beazley.ox.ac.uk).

This book has been longer in gestation than I care to remember. I have not, however, forgotten that it has been aided by many friends and colleagues. I am grateful to Charles Mercier and Rachel Kitzinger for inviting me to present some of my findings at an APA panel on animal noises in Greek Comedy 1992. Ken Kitchell asked me to contribute to a session on animals at the Classical Association of the Middle West and South 2002. Other aspects of this project were presented at annual meetings of the Classical Association of New England. Colleagues at the various schools that I have taught at since I conceived of this project have offered encouragement and advice: I thank Deborah Boedeker (then at Holy Cross College, now Brown University), Mary Lefkowitz (Wellesley College), Ted Ahern (Boston College), and Emily McDermott and Frank Nisetich at the University of Massachusetts, Boston. A sabbatical year in 2002–03 granted to me by UMass Boston allowed me finally to pull the manuscript together. I have been especially fortunate that Jeffrey Henderson has been nearby, at Boston University, willing to serve as a sounding board and to offer suggestions. Other friends and colleagues – Phil Ambrose, Kellee Barnard, Fiora Bassanese, John Marincola, Vince Rosivach, and Gretchen Umholtz – have, over the years, alerted me to various pieces of information and posed thoughtful questions. The book has benefited enormously from the input of its readers, and I would like to express my deepest thanks to Prof. John Oakley and Prof. Frank Romer, who read it for Cambridge University Press and offered both learning and sound judgment. They are of course not to blame for my more unfounded conjectures.

A longer-term debt is owed to two mentors in graduate school. Prof. L. E. Rossi, visiting Columbia from Rome, asked us to consider the context of performance of everything we read; Prof. James Coulter kindled my interest in the intellectual life of the fifth century B.C. This book, which falls roughly into halves, reflects precisely those two concerns. Readers will join me in thanking my father, Kenneth S. Rothwell, Sr., professor emeritus of English at the University of Vermont, who read the entire manuscript and identified some twenty or thirty pages' worth of dispensable verbiage. Beatrice Rehl of Cambridge University Press has been patient and encouraging. Thanks also go to Maggie Meitzler of Techbooks, whose expertise aided the copyediting.

Much of the time spent writing this book would otherwise have gone to my wife and children; my gratitude for their support and forebearance cannot be measured.

INTRODUCTION

O scar Wilde said of his prison warden, "He had the eyes of a
ferret, the body of an ape, and the soul of a rat."[1] Projecting
animal qualities onto a human being, as Wilde did, and human qualities
onto an animal, are near-universal customs. After all, animals furnish
us with ready-made symbols of every aspect of human life. What is
notable about the ancient Greeks, however, is that they elevated this
familiar practice into a sophisticated literary form, the genre of Old
Comedy, which flourished in Athens in the fifth century B.C. Rarely
have symbolic projections come to life as vividly as they did on the
Greek stage.

An "animal chorus" is a chorus in comedy whose dancers were costumed as animals and assumed many animal characteristics, including
animal voices and behavior. If we apply strict criteria we can name
only a few: Aristophanes' *Birds* and *Frogs* (although it is possible that
the frogs only sang off stage); it also seems certain from fragments that
Crates' *Beasts*, Eupolis' *Nanny-Goats*, and Archippus' *Fishes* had animal
choruses. Moreover, vase-paintings such as those in London, Berlin,
and Malibu representing men costumed as birds probably show animal
choruses; each of these three vase-paintings includes an *aulos*-player,
which is a clear sign that a performance is depicted.

If we use broader criteria, however, there are other plays and vase-
paintings that come into consideration. Aristophanes' *Wasps*, for example, has a chorus of Athenian citizens who though human have dis-
tinctly vespine traits. A number of vase-paintings depict men riding
dolphins, horses, and ostriches; presumably the riders were the members of the chorus, yet it is by their various mounts that they are

remembered – Aristophanes' *Knights* is an example – and these mounts may have been other dancers acting the part of animals. Whether or not such animals speak and sing, they need to be considered. I have not limited my inquiry to choruses. Even a terracotta statuette of an actor dressed as an animal can shed light on ancient costuming conventions. This book, then, offers a study of the literary fragments, complete comedies, and vase-paintings that pertain to animal choruses in Greek Comedy.

An invaluable guide has been the chapters on animal choruses in G. M. Sifakis's *Parabasis and Animal Choruses* (London, 1971), which lucidly sets forth the essential evidence, yet the approach taken here is to set the tradition in a wider social, religious, and intellectual context. A central theme developed in this book can be stated as follows: animals were important not because they represented forces of nature but because they made contributions to human culture. Their position as "natural" creatures has been overstated.

This may seem counterintuitive. After all, at the risk of making an "essentialist" statement about transcultural significances of animals, it is usually assumed that people have often dressed and danced as animals out of a desire to draw on the powers of nature. Animals represent the forces of fertility and procreation in the world around us, and for that reason were associated with gods such as Dionysus, Artemis, and Poseidon. We should bear in mind, of course, that "nature" is a deeply problematic and paradoxical concept, meaning different things at different times. For some the "state of nature" refers to the complete absence of any redeeming or civilizing force. The sharp division between the two realms – the natural world of animals and the cultured world of human beings – is the premise of a much-quoted anecdote about Thales: "Hermippus in his *Lives* refers to Thales the story told by some about Socrates, namely, that he used to say there were three blessings for which he was grateful to Fortune: 'First, that I was born a human being and not one of the animals; next, that I was born a man and not a woman; thirdly, a Greek and not a barbarian'" (DK 1 A11).

Nevertheless, although the distinction between "self" and "other" is fundamental to this study, matters rarely fit into this binary framework in a tidy way, for the "self" frequently contains seeds of the "other" (and *vice versa*). The gulf between nature and culture, and

2

between animals and human beings, can be bridged and even obliterated. In fact, Aristophanes and other comic playwrights could so tame and anthropomorphize non-human creatures that it is misleading to peg animals in comedy as representatives of an unsettling "other." One could argue that comedy's cavalier sense of control masks what is actually a profound sense of unease with the animal world, but evidence for this unease is scant in comedy. Far from being unsettling, animals can serve as the basis for society, in which case "nature" simply means "pre-civilized."

Therefore, although we conventionally think of animals as representatives of the state of nature, what may be more significant is that we find precisely the opposite tendency at work: animals can leave nature behind and contribute to human civilization. This, too, will work in paradoxical ways: either nature is superseded and left behind, or nature becomes the basis for civilization. One recurrent motif studied here is the role that animals play in the foundation of cities and other cultural accomplishments. Comedy in this respect offers parallels with the Native American mythological tradition of the animal as culture hero, a feature not especially prominent elsewhere in the Greek tradition. Apollo, a quintessential god of civilization, was associated with dolphins in such undertakings. Moreover, animals can be "discovered" to be social creatures. What this reflects, of course, is a human desire to project ourselves onto animals.

The first two chapters, which analyze the evidence on vase-paintings of pre-comic performances from the sixth and early fifth centuries, take up the question of the possible ritual origins of animal choruses. It may be possible to argue that tragedy bears no relation to ritual practices at Athens, but these vase-paintings imply that ritual masquerades contributed to comedy in a significant way. I will suggest, however, that the contribution of ritual was at best an indirect one; we simply do not have sufficient evidence to identify with confidence any ritual costumed performance that would have been transformed into comedy. Instead of stressing the religious aspects of the *komoi* ("revels") in which comedy probably originated, we will look at the social dimension. As I will explain in Chapter 2, the cocks, cavalrymen, and dolphin-riders that we see on vases make best sense if seen as the products of the symposium culture of the archaic aristocracy.

It will emerge that some animals in the comic tradition occupy "liminal" positions in Greek thought (dolphins, for example, stand on the taxonomical line between fish and mammal). There are, moreover, hints that the animals here studied were associated with rites of passage. The choruses may reflect, or may have grown out of, rituals of initiation that raise questions of personal identity and growth. Moreover, the animals of the chorus were not always shown as ordinary animals; frequently some blurring of categories is found, such as of animals and satyrs, or of animals and human beings. In this regard the god Hermes is perhaps present.

The plays themselves – Aristophanes' *Birds*, *Wasps*, *Frogs*, *Knights*, and the fragments – are discussed in Chapters 4 and 5. I correlate these not only with patterns in myth and ritual but with other types of evidence as well (laid out in Chapter 3), such as satyr-plays and fifth-century speculation concerning nature and culture. Greek folklore and zoological writing also yield clues about the animals we encounter. We will see, for example, that the concept of the "social animal" emerged at an opportune time. Appendix A provides the essential textual evidence for the fragments.

My methodology is somewhat eclectic – necessarily, given the different types of evidence I am marshalling – but I am in general attempting to reconstruct different volumes of the "cultural encyclopedia of the viewer."[2] Evidence for this encyclopedia, which is unfortunately largely lost to us, is contradictory and ambiguous (as evidence often is), though I have suggested some ways in which sense can be made of the material at hand. In a few instances cross-cultural comparison offers some possible solutions. In other matters, such as descriptions of animal behavior, we must use sources such as Aristotle, Pliny, and Aelian as evidence for much earlier periods. This is reasonable where we can assume that there was some continuity of attitudes and practices in the ancient world, and where no evolution can be shown to have occurred.

The evidence for animal choruses in vase-painting poses its own methodological problems. Vase-paintings are an important source of evidence for performances in Greece, yet they must be used with caution. Painters were almost certainly selective in choosing what performances and what aspects of performances to illustrate. Writes

Sparkes, "We are not being presented with a direct copy of reality: these images are not actual tracings of life, not photographic documents, they are social statements, constructs, symbols; a conscious choice of figures and compositions has been made by the artist."[3] The number of vases is modest. We still have only a dozen or so paintings of animal choruses; by contrast, a recent study of animal sacrifice in Greece could survey a corpus of evidence that included 674 reliefs and vase-paintings, students of satyrs can examine at least 3,000 depictions of them from archaic and classical times, and by one count Dionysus appears 4,343 times on vases.[4] For some of the choruses studied here, such as the "Knights" and ostrich-riders, we do not have a single exact parallel and are unable to establish any secure iconographical tradition. Even when we have a group of related images, such as the dolphin-riders, we cannot be sure that we understand their significance. In no case are we able to point conclusively to a specific story or myth that is illustrated in these vase paintings.

Fortunately, we can identify in these images some familiar conventions in depictions of *komoi* and choruses, such as the presence of an *aulos*-player and dancers in regimented order, and we will examine these in Chapter 1. Students of comedy at least have an advantage over students of tragedy in that painters of scenes from tragedy tended to create an illusion of reality by omitting clues of a theatrical performance, so that we are unable to distinguish depictions of myth from depictions of performances of myth. By contrast painters of comic scenes, at least in the fifth century, did not attempt to be illusionistic and were willing to show masks, the *aulos*-player, and other theatrical paraphernalia; thus comedy is more likely to be shown as theater.[5] A further advantage is that the uses of the vases themselves are surely relevant to what is depicted on them. As we will see, this is most striking in the case of the psykter, a special type of cooler that had a short life span in Greek history and functioned specifically in the context of the symposium.

KOMOS, SYMPOSIUM, AND PERFORMANCE

Asurvey of Attic Old Comedy reminds one of a visit to a zoo: these creatures delight, instruct, and live together in contrived harmony, yet are of different species and trace their origins to disparate places. Key features of comedy were said to have been invented by Megarians, Sicilians, and Athenians; plots revolved around myth, fantasy, and political satire; and the comedies had choruses of every imaginable type: peasants, foreigners, women, cities, islands, personified abstractions, satyrs, and animals.

This diversity was not simply the product of imaginative fifth-century playwrights: the heterogeneity of fifth-century comedy, certainly the types of choruses, was anticipated by costumed performances in the sixth century.[1] This chapter reviews the various venues of performance in archaic Greece, including symposia, *komoi*, ritual masquerade, and formal choruses; also presented here is the evidence for pre-comic choruses, including padded dancers, phallic dancers, satyrs, men wearing animal ears, and foreigners. An examination of these non-animal performers establishes a context for the archaic animal choruses studied in the next chapter. It will emerge that they share several features with one another: an interest in the vigor of the world of nature (unlike the more easily tamed aspects of nature in fifth-century comedy), possible connections with the cults of specific gods, and a lack of clear distinction between human and non-human beings. In fact, a recurrent issue is the extent to which these choruses were composed of "outsiders."

KOMOS, SYMPOSIUM, AND PERFORMANCE IN ARCHAIC GREECE

Aristotle derived the word "comedy" from the word *komos*, and the *komos* is a reasonable point of departure for any inquiry into the origins of comedy and animal choruses.[2] After all, the sixth-century vase-paintings of animal choruses can, with good justification, be seen as representations of *komoi*.

The Komos

The *komos*, or "revel," was a ritualistic, drunken procession.[3] The participants, komasts, were frequently on their way to or from a symposium, and hence vase-paintings showed them carrying drinking cups. That music and dance were significant parts of the *komos* is suggested by literary evidence and by vase-paintings that show komasts dancing and carrying musical instruments.[4] Torches were also carried, as a *komos* could take place at night.[5] A *komos* was not an occasion for quiet, disciplined behavior; in the *Acharnians* "War " is described as an unwelcome, drunken komast "who has committed every kind of outrage."[6] Costumes or masks could be part of a *komos*: in the fourth century, Demosthenes criticized Kyrebion, the brother-in-law of Demosthenes' enemy Aeschines, for not wearing his mask at a *komos* at the Dionysia, thus transgressing ritual practice.[7]

Although *komoi* were frequently associated with symposia, there was in fact no single occasion for them. The earliest instances of the word refer to private gatherings, such as a wedding (Hesiod, *Shield* 281), or to general opportunities for song and dance (*Homeric Hymn to Hermes* 481). Other *komoi* were public activities, independent of private symposia, that had established roles in city festivals and were performed with the care accorded to a sacred cult. They were held in honor of various deities, including Apollo,[8] Zeus,[9] Artemis,[10] and Heracles.[11] *Komoi* thus need not have been exclusively or intrinsically Dionysiac. Nevertheless, it was with Dionysus that the *komos* was most frequently associated. He was, after all, the god of wine, and drinking was a virtual premise for the *komos*. His own Great Dionysia had some sort of scheduled *komos*, perhaps performed on the evening of the first day.[12]

The *komos* can be distinguished from a chorus and a *pompe*. A chorus (χορός) entailed highly coordinated dancing and singing. Here music was a *sine qua non* and drunkenness only optional. Members of a chorus behaved less spontaneously than komasts, were more rehearsed, probably followed a leader (ἐξάρχων, to borrow Aristotle's term), and even sang from a composed script. The chorus performed more for the enjoyment of an audience than for their own pleasure. Poets such as Alcman had been writing lyrics for choruses since the seventh century B.C. Nevertheless the *komos* and chorus are not immediately distinguishable on vase-painting and the choice between the two is often a subjective one. The *pompe*, like the *komos*, entailed a procession but was more formal and dignified.[13] For example, the *pompe* on the first day of the City Dionysia consisted of a procession that escorted victims, traditionally bulls, to the sacrifices in the sacred precinct of Dionysus. Various ritual participants, such as *choregoi*, would parade in colored robes and evidently *phalloi* were carried in honor of the god.[14] A *komos*, by contrast, was raucous and disorderly; moreover, whereas the *pompe* was directed toward a specific goal (the sacrifice), participants in a *komos* were either lost in the enjoyment of the moment or at most moving on to another symposium (as illustrated in Plato, *Symposium* 212c–d and 223b).

The Symposium

Komasts, therefore, were frequently symposiasts who had moved into the street in a drunken carousal.[15] In other words, the *komos* could be a continuation of, or extension of, the social event that began with the symposium. I propose, therefore, that any inquiry into *komoi* and costumed dancers should take into account the social and cultural milieu of the archaic symposium. It was this context that produced *komoi*, themselves a source for animal choruses. In fact entertainments at the symposium itself may have been a venue for animal costumes, and Chapter 2 will explain how the specific animal masquerades depicted on vase-painting make sense as an expression of symposium culture.

The symposium was a central institution of the archaic aristocracy.[16] Although Homer's elite warriors ate and drank together, it was not until the end of the seventh century, when the Greeks adopted dining practices from the Near East, such as reclining on couches, that these gatherings became a social ritual in the lives of aristocratic men.[17] Through the symposium the Athenian elite shaped their group identity and social values. "The symposion became in many respects a place apart from the normal rules of society, with its own strict code of honor in the *pistis* [mutual trust] there created, and its own willingness to establish conventions fundamentally opposed to those within the polis as a whole ... It became a 'spettacolo a se stesso'."[18] Consequently the symposium became an occasion for educating and initiating youths into the world of adult, male society. Elegies in the tradition of military sympotic poetry by Archilochus, Mimnermus, Callinus, and Solon would inculcate in individual youths patriotism and a sense of duty.[19] Narrative poems on the achievements of the community were evidently recited at symposia; these might have included a work by Ion of Chios concerning the *ktisis* (foundation) of Chios, Mimnermus on the colonization of Smyrna, and Xenophanes' poem on the *ktisis* of Colophon and colonization of Elea in Italy.[20] This transmission of traditional military and social values made sense in an institution that originated in a warrior group.[21] Furthermore, some sympotic poetry was explicitly addressed to boys, and vase-paintings seem to show that the symposium had become a locus of pederastic activity.[22] The drinking cups and mixing jugs were themselves decorated with scenes showing the refined interests of this social class, such as symposia with participants who are reclining on couches, drinking, listening to recitals, and enjoying their conviviality. Painters also produced vases with scenes reflecting wider cultural interests of the elite, such as horse-riding, hunting, and athletics.

The symposium had its own protocols and table manners. After finishing a meal, participants would wear garlands, sing *skolia* (drinking songs), play a game of *kottabos*, in which wine lees were tossed at a target, and mix their wine.[23] A presiding *symposiarchos* determined the proper measure of wine. Different types of drinking vessels were developed for specific needs. In fact proper behavior at a symposium was felt to distinguish a civilized Greek from a barbarian or monster.[24] That said, one of the fashions at the symposium, especially from ca. 510–480 B.C., was to wear the dress of a foreigner: vases show symposiasts wearing a floppy oriental hat known as the *kidaris*, a vogue that

1.1. Attic black-figure skyphos attributed to the White Heron Group, showing symposiasts with headgear. Ca. 500 B.C. Athenian Agora, P 32413. Photograph courtesy of the American School of Classical Studies at Athens: Agora Excavation.

reflected Athenian interest in luxury goods from the East and served as an "effective statement of elitism."[25] Thracian garb was also popular among well-born Athenians.[26] In this way Athenians liberated by wine could experiment with *altérité* and seek a new temporary identity.[27] Perhaps the costumed figures anticipate the clique of young men in classical Athens who, flouting conventional behavior, dubbed themselves "Triballoi" after the savage Thracian tribe of that name.[28] An outlandish or even barbarian outfit may therefore have been a popular affectation in the sophisticated milieu of the symposium.

An enigmatic recent find illustrates this practice. A black-figured, Heron-class skyphos of ca. 500 B.C., found in the Athenian Agora in 1995 (Figure 1.1), is described as follows:

Side A: A group of two banqueters with a flute player between them share a single large mattress. The banqueters wear unusual headdresses. The one on the right is clearer, with two elongated animal ears between curving horns. The figure on the left has three large projections off the front of his headdress, with an elongated bulge at the back.

Side B: A similar scene, less well preserved, with a female lyre player as the central musician. Framing the main scenes and clustered under the handles are numerous large, plump, long-necked birds, in pairs or threesomes. Several stand on stumps, the landscape element perhaps suggesting an outdoor banquet, as does the single bird in flight on side B. There are thirteen birds in

I.2. Attic red-figure hydria attributed to the Nikoxenos Painter, showing symposiasts. Early fifth century B.C. Staatliche Museen Kassel, Antikensammlung ALg57. Photograph © Staatliche Museen Kassel.

all. The birds, the outdoor picnic, and the headdresses are all hard to parallel, and it is not clear whether these are scenes taken from drama or cult ritual.[29]

Although the vase was discovered in a well ten meters from the late archaic altar of Aphrodite, no material in the well can be specifically connected with cult activity there. The group of vases to which it belongs seems to represent the pantry of a single household that was thrown into the well as debris from the Persian destruction of Athens. Several of the scenes painted on pottery are, as Camp observes, "related to the symposium: preparations for the party, banqueting, and the after-effects of too good a time." Because all participants in the vase-painting, including the flute-player, are reclining rather than dancing, the scenes more likely represent a symposium than a *komos* or performance. Curiously the event occurs in the open air, though Lynch suggests that the extraordinary location may be a way of defining group identity.

A further example, Figure 1.2, is an Attic red-figure hydria of the early fifth century, attributed to the Nikoxenos Painter and now in Kassel. Between two reclining symposiasts stands a black-figure hydria decorated with a dancing satyr and containing a pyskter. The older symposiast, reclining on the left, wears an effeminate, Oriental Anacreontic-style turban or headdress; he looks to his left at a youthful, beardless symposiast who is doubtless his *eromenos*.[30]

Vases show also that symposia provided opportunities for entertainers to perform dances and play music. On a Siana cup by the Heidelberg Painter (ca. 550–540 B.C.) a dancer and *aulos*-player in the center of the composition entertain symposiasts reclining on the left and right.[31] More elaborate entertainment is recounted in Xenophon's *Symposium*: tables are removed to make room; music is performed with the lyre and *aulos* (2.1–2); a girl dances with hoops and does somersaults (2.8, 2.11); a buffoon burlesques dances of a girl and boy, making his body grotesque (γελοιότερον) and getting a laugh from his fellow guests (2.22–23); a girl juggles while standing on a potter's wheel (7.2); and near the end a mime, relying mostly on dance and music but also including short dialogue, enacts the myth of Dionysus and Ariadne (9.2–7).[32] A private symposium was generally held in a special room, the *andron*, that contained seven to eleven *klinai*. It might seem too tight for anything more than a small performance, though Xenophon recorded that tables would be removed (2.1). Some hosts would have had more spacious rooms. "Outsiders" also performed for the guests; these might be the "uninvited" (*akletoi*) who did not belong to the social milieu but performed in order to be laughed at – and fed.[33] Black-figure vase-paintings, such as Figure 1.3,[34] show fat, padded dancers who are apparently clowning around to the amusement of the elite spectators. Cavorting satyrs are shown walking on their hands and thus symbolizing an "upside-down world."[35] Paradoxically, then, indecent behavior was appropriate at an elite event.[36] The continuum between the refined symposium and the riotous *komos* is illustrated by an oinochoe in Athens that depicts komasts clowning around: one is carrying another on his back, while the rider evidently breaks wind; a krater is set in the middle of the composition with the carefully drawn figure of a horse. "Despite the crass behavior, it is worth noting the delicacy of this drawing... the horse recalls the aristocratic class of knights," remarks Lissarrague.[37]

1.3. Corinthian bowl by the Medallion Painter, showing symposiasts and padded dancers. Ca. 600–575 B.C. London, British Museum, 61.4–25.45. © Copyright The Trustees of The British Museum.

Elite symposiasts may have participated in these antics and entertainments themselves.[38] One thinks of the anecdote told in Herodotus of Hippocleides son of Teisander, said to be the wealthiest and most handsome man in Athens in the early sixth century B.C. Hippocleides, along with other aristocrats from all over the Greek world, from Magna Graecia to the islands, was a suitor for the hand of the daughter of Cleisthenes, the tyrant of Sicyon. At a symposium Hippocleides was expected to compete in music; after drinking too much, however, he began dancing in excess and finished by standing on his head. Cleisthenes was so disturbed that he told Hippocleides that he had "danced away his marriage" (Herodotus 6.126–29). The degree of exhibitionism cost Hippocleides dearly, yet it is clear that, although he crossed the line of propriety, some performance was appropriate. Furthermore, the episode reveals the international nature of the symposium-class of Greece. There was an aristocratic, pan-Hellenic network that could expose elite guests to local performances.

With the advent of democracy at Athens at the end of the sixth century and the victories over Persia in the early fifth century, the symposium became increasingly democratized and lost the exclusive role it had once held among the aristocracy.[39] Innovations appear that may be linked to the social and political changes around the symposium. In this period some defensiveness on the part of symposiasts can be detected; Neer, writing of the Anakreontic vases popular in these decades, suggests that this was "precisely the time at which the luxury-loving elite was at its weakest politically. The pictures seem to be compensating for the failings of political reality."[40] Most of the animal masquerades on vase-paintings were produced at this cultural moment, and by the second decade of the fifth century comedy had emerged as an autonomous genre.

The Birth of Comedy

The historical development of comedy from its pre-comic period to its official recognition in 486 B.C. followed a course that we can only guess at.[41] The "Parian Marble" reports that the first comic chorus was introduced by Susarion between 581 and 561 B.C. at Ikaria, a deme of Attica.[42] Although Susarion's very existence is doubtful, padded dancers appeared on vases in Attica from ca. 575 to 540 B.C. (these owe an iconographical debt to vases painted at Corinth ca. 625–550 B.C.), and the earliest vase showing an animal costume (men costumed as horses, in Berlin) is from ca. 540–530 B.C. The correspondence of dates may be coincidental, but it is a fair surmise that around the middle of the sixth century someone, if not Susarion, began shaping *komoi* (or symposium entertainments) into choruses. Vase-painters took notice. Some sixth-century vases suggest that the choruses may even have broken into rival semi-choruses and competed with one another. True drama crystallized when actors took roles and engaged the chorus in song or dialogue, although it is unclear whether actors emerged from within or outside the chorus.[43] Scenes on a few Corinthian vases appear to have narrative elements and may be the ancestors of plot-features of later comedy, perhaps including myths of the gods for whom the *komos* was performed. Actors may have been imported into Athens from Dorian cities such as Megara and Corinth, although assessing the degree of influence on Attic comedy from Dorian Greek cities such as Corinth and Megara has long been the subject of scholarly contention. Fortunately the debate has focused more on the origin of actors than of choruses, so we need not linger over it yet. Some choruses were probably derived from indigenous Attic *komoi*, although the Corinthian padded dancers or other types of performers may have contributed.[44]

Dionysus

Virtually all *komoi* entailed a degree of drunkenness and thus fell into the domain of the god of wine.[45] Of course other reasons exist for considering pre-comic *komoi* as Dionysiac. Above all, Dionysus was the patron of drama: official performances of Attic tragedy and comedy were at the Rural Dionysia, Lenaea, and Great Dionysia. A statue of Dionysus was present in the theater.[46] Indeed his function as the god of drama is the premise of Aristophanes' *Frogs*.[47] The fact that *phalloi*, which were closely associated with Dionysus, were part of the costume of comic actors and possibly of chorus members points to a Dionysiac source. The role of masks in the cult of Dionysus – illustrated by the "Lenaean vases," depicting actual masks that are attached to poles and that are the focus of cultic attention – further reinforces his affinity with drama.[48] The mask, in turn, is an aspect of Dionysus that has received much scholarly attention in recent years, for his cult lends itself to the obliteration of distinctions between self and other, male and female, foreign and citizen, gods and men, and wild and civilized.[49] Dionysus, who was thought to have had foreign, eastern origins, was sexually ambiguous.[50] It is an easy step from being exotic to being dangerous, and the destructive power of Dionysus is also an important feature in myth, above all in the myth of Pentheus in Euripides' *Bacchae*, in which his vitality disrupts the orderly polis.[51]

And yet, notes Henrichs, "The myth of the *Bacchae*, like many other myths, portrays a worst-case scenario ... By contrast, the practice of religion in cult is designed to circumvent the sinister element highlighted in myth; cult regards the gods as beneficent and proceeds on the expectation of a mutual beneficial reciprocity between the divine and human realms."[52] The Dionysus that Greeks actually worshipped,

15

then, was a god of wine and festivity whose cult brought fertility and renewal. These blessings are conspicuous in comedy. For example, a well-known scene in *Acharnians* (241–79) reenacts a *phallophoria*, a ritual of the Rural Dionysia in which a *phallos* pole was carried in procession. This *phallophoria* has been seen as a relic of the sort of primitive fertility ritual that might have led to comedy.[53] Needless to say as the god of wine Dionysus was equally at home in the civilized, orderly world of the symposium.[54]

The cult of Dionysus could have, at least in theory, fostered animal *komoi*. In addition to the importance in his cult of masks, of natural fertility, and of the ambiguities of wildness versus civilization – all of which offer a hospitable setting for animal choruses – Dionysus is unmistakably associated with the animal world itself. Notes Lada-Richards, "It is Dionysus par excellence who annihilates the frontiers between beast and god."[55] Vase-painters showed him riding or in procession with lions, bulls, and goats; in depictions of the Return of Hephaestus he sometimes rides a donkey and, in miscellaneous other episodes, rides a sea-monster or griffin. The panther (*pardalis*) eventually becomes the dominant animal in this motif.[56] Satyrs, his ubiquitous companions, embody both beast and human, and Chapter 3 will show that animal choruses can be profitably compared with satyr choruses. The violent side of Dionysiac imagery manifests itself when maenads tear a roe in two, and their ecstatic wildness is visually intensified by the presence of animals such as panthers and snakes.[57] Dionysiac figures wore animal skins, with initiates at Dionysiac ceremonies clothed in fawn-skins[58] and maenads or even Dionysus himself wearing the skin of the *pardalis*.[59] In the *Homeric Hymn to Dionysus* (44) he is transformed into a lion and in the *Bacchae* he takes on the appearance of a bull.[60]

Nevertheless, despite these suggestive associations between Dionysus and animals, it requires a leap of faith to trace our animal choruses back to a specifically Dionysiac source. A primary reservation is that the animals that appear in animal choruses are rarely the ones we find associated with Dionysus in art or literature.[61] No evidence for a comic chorus of panthers, lions, or fawns has survived. Bulls and goats are discussed in chapters that follow (vases show bull-headed dancers and Eupolis wrote a *Nanny-goats*), but neither creature was exclusively Dionysiac. Both of these animals were standard sacrificial offerings in other cults as well. Of the thousands of surviving vases documenting the myths and cult of Dionysus, not a single one establishes an unambiguous connection with any surviving animal chorus. Although the possibility that *komoi* and animal choruses were related to Dionysus is deeply satisfying, no automatic assumptions should be made.

Furthermore, as important as it is that comedy was eventually included in the City Dionysia, it is reasonable to ask why comedy was *excluded* for as long as it was (and even longer from the Lenaea). Was it regarded as too unsophisticated until 486 B.C., as was conventionally thought? Aristotle spoke of the early choruses as being performed by "volunteers" (*Poetics* 1449a37–b9). Or was it felt to be insufficiently Dionysiac? The choruses of surviving Aristophanic comedy were sung in honor of a variety of gods and divinities, only directly invoking Dionysus twice.[62] Scullion, challenging the orthodoxy that drama is intrinsically Dionysiac either in its origins or in surviving texts, has pointed out that elsewhere in the Greek world dramatic performances could occur at festivals to Apollo, Zeus, Nike, and Hera.[63] Is there a possibility that animal *komoi* performed for other gods, such as Artemis, Demeter, Poseidon, or Apollo (who will be considered in the next chapter), inspired some of the choruses of pre-comedy? Non-Dionysiac masquerades could have been drawn into the comic orbit shortly after (or even before) comedy was admitted to the Dionysia in 486 B.C., and evidence need not be squeezed into a Dionysiac pattern, particularly when alternatives are available.[64]

Demeter, Artemis, and Animals

An apparent masquerade or *komos* related to Demeter was performed by the animal dancers sculpted by Damophon, probably in the early second century B.C., at the shrine of Despoina at Lycosura in the Peloponnese (Figure 1.4).[65] The dancers – eleven female figures with animal masks and hoof-like footgear – were carved in relief on the border of the dress of Despoina. She was part of a sculptural group that also included her mother, Demeter; Anytus, a Titan who raised Despoina; and Artemis, wrapped in a deerskin. The masked dancers are believed to represent primitive cults characteristic of Arcadia.[66] The masks seem to represent a horse, ass, hare or cat, sheep, and pig – generally domesticated animals, perhaps an indication of interest in agricultural husbandry.[67] Some, running in procession, are playing the lyre and *aulos*. An animal-headed figure is visible on Anytus' breastplate.[68] Excavations at Lycosura also yielded terracotta figurines of human beings with animal heads, such as a woman with a sow's head and others with rams' heads. Stiglitz, suggesting that they were initiates dedicated to the goddess, interprets them as an expression of the forces of nature driving animals and human beings alike.[69]

The cult of Artemis also exalted animals.[70] Her most distinctive role was *Potnia Theron*, "Mistress of Animals," and as such she could be found flanked by animals on vase-paintings.[71] One of the most ambitious events in the Athenian sacred calendar was the sacrifice of five hundred she-goats to Artemis Agrotera in fulfillment of a vow made at the Battle of Marathon.[72] In myth Artemis transformed Actaeon into a stag and Callisto into a bear.[73] Although a huntress, she was a protector of young animals as well as an agent for guiding boys and girls to maturity. She presided over the transitions of boys to citizenship, yet she was more concerned with women's transitions, especially in childbirth and in the passage from *parthenos* (virgin girl) to woman.

Artemis' cult, like that of Dionysus, was linked with the use of masks. Excavations in the sanctuary of Artemis Orthia at Sparta revealed a large number of dedicatory masks.[74] Classified by type, they include realistic human faces as well as grotesque caricatures, comprising masks of old women, satyrs, and Gorgons. The cult of Artemis Orthia was organized for ephebes, young men undergoing military training, and conceivably the ephebes themselves wore the masks found in her precinct. If so, wearing the masks exposed the youths to aspects of marginality, such as feminine reserve and animal ferocity, so that the youths would internalize rules that they would have to keep.[75] Carter, who thinks that the masks were part of an initiation ritual for young women, proposes that the masks were influenced by Sumerian hymns about the marriage of Inanna, possibly known to Spartans through their Phoenician contacts. The masks would represent Inanna's bridegroom and an opponent.[76] On either interpretation, then, the masks were related to transitional experiences.

More relevant, because it involved animals, was the festival of the Brauronia. Young girls between ages five and ten served Artemis as

1.4. Sculptural fragment from Lycosura by Damophon, showing dancers with animal masks. Probably early second century B.C. Athens, National Archaeological Museum 1737. Photograph © National Archaeological Museum.

Arktoi ("Bears") at the sanctuaries at Brauron and Munichia in Attica.[77] Playing the part of a bear, according to Vernant and Frontisi-Ducroux, helped the girls overcome their latent wildness, so they could live safely with their husbands.[78] They do not appear to have worn bear costumes, but one fragmentary vase shows two adults – one male, the other female – with bear heads and human bodies. These may be masked priests, though it is also possible that we see figures from mythology at the moment of their metamorphosis into bears.[79] A further ritual animal costume is attested for Artemis Lyaia at Syracuse; in this *komos* the participants, who seem to have been farmers, wore stag's horns on their heads while singing and making libations.[80]

One could speculate that these rituals inspired animal choruses, but it is difficult to anoint these as the "origins" of comic choruses, in part because of the same objection to the theory of Dionysiac origin:

they are the wrong animals. We know of no comedies or choral performances of bears or stags. Furthermore, I am aware of no theater dedicated to Artemis. At best one can point to an underlying function of Artemis, which she shares with Dionysus: the cults of both divinities, like animal choruses, offered a spectacle of the grotesque and bestial. This, in turn, brings the discussion to the related phenomenon of festive inversion.

Festive Inversion

Role-reversals and carnivalesque inversions, in which we find that authority figures are deposed or humiliated and that representatives of marginalized members of society triumph, have always been among the most powerful engines driving the genre of comedy. Aristophanic comedy has its share of uncrownings; one can think of Lamachus, Cleon, and Socrates. Aristophanic comedy is also notorious for the degree to which, by allowing uninhibited vulgarity and obscenity, it put on stage the popular grotesque.[81]

Furthermore, festivals are fitting models for comedy in that both operate by temporarily violating proper decorum and overturning the conventions of everyday life. Dionysiac festivals, the sole venue for the performance of drama in Athens, sanctioned behaviors that contravened social norms. During the Great Dionysia, prisoners were released, legal proceedings banned, and the assembly adjourned.[82] The first night of the Dionysia saw *komoi* that were evidently marked by unrestrained drunkenness and obscene humor.[83] The Anthesteria, to choose another festival of Dionysus, celebrated the arrival of spring as well as the opening and drinking of the new wine. On this festival's second day ("Choes"), Dionysus, perhaps impersonated by an actor wearing a mask and accompanied by others masked as satyrs, was apparently brought into Athens on a ship-chariot. In the procession those riding in carts abused and mocked bystanders. Slaves and foreigners were allowed to participate, giving a Saturnalian mood to the occasion.[84] The "world-turned-upside-down" motif was, however, not restricted to Dionysiac festivals. At the Kronia, a festival sacred to Kronos, state business was banned and slaves were given free rein to enjoy a banquet.[85]

For human beings to take on the roles of animals would seem to conform readily with the principles of festive inversion, but a caveat is in order. Although the humiliation of a political or social superior constitutes an overturning of a hierarchy, wearing an animal costume does not have any single significance. It could be seen as degrading – one thinks of Falstaff dressed as a stag in Shakespeare's *Merry Wives of Windsor* – but it could just as easily be empowering. Certainly this is the case for Peisetaerus, who becomes a bird and usurps dominion for himself.

Of course much of what occurred in these festivals and on stage was infused with playfulness and imaginative creativity. There was surely an element of sheer fun involved in *komoi*, as in comedy, no doubt heightened when the participants wore masks and costumes.[86] The entertainment derives from several roots.

Laughter can be a collective experience that unifies a group and that is generated at the expense of an outsider or misfit, or at least at someone costumed as a misfit. Enjoyment can also stem from the temporary release from social control that sanctions someone to wear a costume.[87] The details, then, of these costumed *komoi* (and comedy) need not have been determined solely by specific ritual practices. Nevertheless it is difficult to imagine a carnival world that is autonomous and completely unrelated to its social or ritual context.[88] I also hesitate to resort to appeals to "pure humor" as an explanatory device simply because we cannot easily trace performances to obvious rituals or *komoi*. We should try to read these choruses with the vocabulary that Athenians themselves used, and our knowledge of myth, ritual, literature, and philosophical evidence constitutes our best hope of achieving this goal.

We can now turn to specific types of costumed performance.

PRE-DRAMATIC PERFORMANCES IN ARCHAIC GREECE

Padded Dancers

A series of vases painted in Corinth between 625 and 550 B.C., and then in Attica between 575 and 540 B.C., depict "padded dancers," figures who wear padded chitons that give them exaggerated bellies and posteriors (Figure 1.3).[89] On rare occasions they wear masks or display *phalloi*. The padded dancers may be the ancestors of actors in Attic comedy who, beginning around 430 B.C., appeared on vases wearing padding and dangling *phalloi*.[90] Significantly, the Attic padded dancers functioned as forerunners not only of actors but also of the comic chorus. Moreover their exaggerated, absurd appearance – so primitive that they can be confused with satyrs – suggests that they fell into the category of "outsiders." They may also have been related to the cults of Dionysus and, in cases where dancers are women, Artemis.

These dancers, although sometimes referred to as komasts in scholarly literature because so many are drinking and dancing, often more closely resemble a chorus. Only one-sixth of the padded dancers on Corinthian vases dance solo; the others, although not dancing in close synchronization, usually appear in pairs or threesomes.[91] The frequent presence of an *aulos*-player suggests organized dance. Attic versions differ in that they lack the *aulos*-players, and the dancers are nude rather than costumed, yet their stances and movements clearly stem from the Corinthian counterparts.[92] There are similar dancers on proto-Attic vases that antedate the Corinthian ware, so perhaps Attic artists simply adopted Corinthian conventions to depict performances that had already been occurring in Attica,[93] though Attic vases tend to omit the *aulos*-player, who would decisively establish these as dramatic performances.[94] Susarion (if he existed) was said to have introduced a comic chorus ca. 581–561 B.C., and, although it exceeds the evidence to suggest that the Attic padded dancer vases represent Susarion's choruses, it is conceivable that they and their performances inspired him or served as his model. Actors may therefore not have been imported from Dorian cities but evolved directly out of an indigenous Attic chorus.[95]

The types of pottery on which these images, especially Attic dancers, were painted were usually intended for a drinking party, and the dancers were often painted on drinking cups.[96] To satisfy the taste of sophisticated symposiasts, some of the artists who painted padded dancer pottery were also producing other vases decorated with images of athletes, horses, hunts, and symposia themselves.[97] In a few instances one finds reclining symposiasts on one side of a vase and a corresponding number of horsemen on the other, as if to emphasize the connection of these spheres of life.[98] On the Attic cups, at least those by the Heidelberg Painter, smartly dressed upper-class Athenians watch the entertainment offered by padded dancers.[99]

These padded dancers were undignified caricatures of human beings and glaringly stood out among the refined participants at a symposium. The fact that some vases show symposiasts as onlookers only highlights the distance between the two realms (Figure 1.3). The padded dancers drink in excess and use sticks and stones as weapons. Sometimes shown imbedded in animal friezes,[100] they invert the values of the civilized symposiasts. Fehr has suggested that they should be understood as the *akletoi*, the "uninvited" guests at a symposium, who were trying to get a meal or outdo one another in their exhibitionism. "In every particular they are a negation of the symposion code."[101] They are coarse, unattractive, deformed, and yet for precisely these reasons they entertained the refined symposiasts, who could laugh derisively at them. Thus, the padded dancers may have been conceived of as social misfits or laughable foreigners. Alternatively they may be symposiasts who, like the "Triballoi," have donned costumes to mimic indecent or barbaric behavior.[102]

Whether the padded dancers were related to a cultic ritual is possible but unproven. Their pinguid proportions and primitive antics could link them with vegetation daemons of a supposed seventh-century Dorian fertility cult.[103] More likely, however, the dancers depicted on the vases were not daemons but human beings dancing in a *komos*. As Schöne observed, their occasional nudity on Attic paintings endows them with human traits.[104] Of course, if drinking and raucous behavior alone confer Dionysiac status, they have achieved it. A further potentially Dionysiac feature is their resemblance to satyrs: some dancers squat frontally, with their genitals occasionally exposed, a posture which approximates that of satyrs. Moreover, a few Corinthian vases show Dionysus accompanied by padded dancers. The dancers were evidently being substituted for the satyrs that usually appear in depictions of the "Return of Hephaestus," a role that would indicate a Dionysiac function for the dancers.[105]

Another possible cultic connection arises from the fact that the women on these vases may have been performing a ritual devoted to Artemis. The indecent behavior might be appropriate for the worship of a goddess who oversaw the fertility of plants, animals, and human beings. Artemis could have been a patroness of these female dancers, as well as of male padded dancers involved in the same festival.[106] The irreverent padded dancers return us to an earlier question: was comedy invented by Athenians or Dorians? That so many padded dancer vases came from Corinth, a Dorian city, certainly gives weight to the Dorian claim, particularly since later Attic actors inherited this costume.[107] Aristotle wrote that Megarians, themselves Dorians, claimed to have invented comedy and that developed "plots" were introduced into comedy from (Dorian) Sicily by Phormis and Epicharmus, who were active in the late sixth and early fifth centuries.[108] Similarly, a painting on a krater in the Louvre depicting an *aulos*-player, a padded komast who may be wearing a mask, and several other characters carrying a wine-bowl, may represent a comic episode.[109] Perhaps, then, actors and plots of Athenian comedy owed a debt to Dorian Greece: Megara, Sicily, and Corinth.

Dorian influence should, however, be set in a larger context. Although some local ritual practices could be expected to maintain traditional continuity in Attica, cultural interaction among the various city-states must have played a key role in archaic Athens, especially in the time of Peisistratus and his sons. In fact it would be surprising if Athenian drama flowered without some cross-pollination. Economic, religious, and cultural exchange, especially among aristocratic circles, was an important component of sixth-century Greece.[110] Cleisthenes of Sicyon, who is known to have transferred tragic choruses from the cult of Adrastus to Dionysus (Hdt. 5.67), married his daughter Agariste to the Athenian Megacles (Hdt. 6.126–31, the occasion of Hippocleides' drunken disgrace). Cultural and social relations among the "international aristocracy," quickened by activities such as intermarriage and athletic contests, were part of the symposium culture of sixth-century Greece.[111] Megara, which abuts Athens, was probably a source of farce. As important to the symposium as lyric poetry was, we can also imagine a pan-Hellenic stock of ritual dances, songs, and costumes that were adapted for private consumption at a symposium or *komos*.[112] The seeds of comic choruses could have been sown here. The notion of comedy emerging out of a "spontaneous ritual generation" by which local cults naturally evolve into sophisticated

24

performances may be true,[113] and may be truer of comedy than of tragedy, but other sources for Athenian drama, from Megara, Corinth, Sparta, Sicily, or even Lycosura should be considered. As Stone has put it, "Undoubtedly, many different kinds of performances and sub-literary genres were combined in the early, less formal stages of Old Comedy."[114]

As has been outlined here, then, an iconographical tradition in which dancers were depicted with an *aulos*-player had originated in the sixth century. In some instances the context was explicitly symposiastic. The grotesque costumes of komasts and chorus-dancers marked them as outsiders. The *phallos* was rare but still part of the paraphernalia for performance; it and the padding lived on into the next century as the actor's costume. At the same time rudimentary narrative plots were probably taking shape. Connections with Dionysiac cult are plausible, appropriate, but unproveable. A relationship with Artemis or even a non-Attic source cannot be excluded. The padded costume itself seems to have led directly into animal choruses in that it is worn by characters who also wear horse costumes (on the Berlin vase, examined in Chapter 2). The padded dancer vases thus offer a useful model for understanding the dynamics of performance.

Phallika

Aristotle thought comedy grew "out of the leaders of the phallic songs (φαλλικά)."[115] On the face of it this statement is consistent with the phallic songs or costumes that actually appear in Old Comedy. The *phallophoria* in the *Acharnians*, for instance, included a song to Phales, and a dangling *phallos* was part of the regular costume for actors (and on occasion the chorus) in Old Comedy.

There are grounds for supposing that the *phalloi* of comedy derived from some Greek ritual practice. We know of the *ithyphalloi* and *phallophoroi*, Dionysiac groups described by Semus of Delos (second century B.C.).[116] The *ithyphalloi*, wearing masks of drunkards and long chitons, entered a theater orchestra with a *phallos*-pole and announced the presence of the god.[117] The *phallophoroi* went without masks but wore caps and thick cloaks; in procession they sang to Bacchus and jeered bystanders. They may have resembled the figures depicted on a sixth-century Attic black-figure cup in Florence who carry a ritual *phallos*-pole in a procession.[118] The *phallophoria* was part of the Rural Dionysia, as the *Acharnians* testifies, and appears to have been part of the *pompe* of the fifth-century City Dionysia.[119]

Whether these can be linked with comedy, though, is another question. Aristotle may have made inferences about phallic songs based on little more evidence than we have today. Semus' report, which is three centuries later, offers nothing specifically about Athens;[120] and the *phallophoroi* on the Florence vase have no known connection with comedy. In sum, neither Aristotle, Semus, nor the vase constitute sound evidence for the source of the comic *phallos*. Because the *ithyphalloi* and *phallophoroi* wore long chitons or cloaks, it is not clear that they even had *phalloi* themselves. In fact, the majority of sixth-century vase-paintings of pre-comic choruses or of *komoi* do not show phallic chorus members. Many vases, however, are of animal choruses and non-phallic costumed men, and on padded dancers *phalloi* appear only rarely.[121]

Although we can say nothing with certainty about the origins of the comic *phallos*, the evidence concerning actual performance is sufficient to indicate that the wearing of the *phallos* was, at the very least, an option available to members of the chorus and that there are "no adequate grounds for denying that in Old Comedy a chorus representing men wore *phalloi*," as MacDowell has put it.[122] For instance, the chorus members of *Wasps* seem to refer to their *phalloi* twice.[123] The men of the chorus in *Plutus* are told by Carion to follow him "with erections" (ἀπεψωλημένοι, 295), implying that they are ithyphallic. The "Getty Birds" on the late fifth-century krater in Malibu are unmistakably ithyphallic and may represent an animal chorus.[124] Moreover, one of the figures wearing a bird costume on an oinochoe in London also seems to have an erect *phallos*. Taken together this evidence demolishes a premise of many scholarly discussions in the last century: that animal and phallic origins for the chorus were mutually exclusive alternatives.[125] More likely, in practice, the costumes of pre-comic choruses were eclectic.

Taplin, who saw no reason to doubt that male chorus-members wore a *phallos*, pointed out that most *phalloi* are not erect but limp, indicating that they are not vestiges of a fertility ritual but are gender-signs consistent with the indecency of the genre.[126] This would account for the hints that the chorus wore *phalloi* without insisting on a phallic *komos* as the sole origin of comedy. Yet the bird vases attest to the Greeks' unflinching acceptance of the potency of human fertility and their readiness to connect it with the animal world.

Phalloi certainly link comedy more closely to Dionysiac cult, but they also lead us to a further issue: the possible influence of satyrs.

Satyrs

Aristotle wrote that tragedy passed through a satyric stage as it developed (τὸ ἐκ σατυρικοῦ μεταβαλεῖν, *Poetics* 1449a20) and the satyr play found a home in the tragic "tetralogy." Yet satyrs possibly contributed to the emerging comic chorus as well. There was evidently some seepage between the different genres in the fluid, early period of development.

In vase-painting satyrs sport beards, squat noses, equine ears, tails, hooves, and, frequently, erect *phalloi*.[127] Although they may have had a prior existence independent of Dionysus, possibly as fertility spirits,[128] they are conspicuous in myth and vase-painting as his companions.[129] Satyrs also appeared in satyr-plays beginning ca. 520–510 B.C., when new scenes began to appear on vases.[130] Some scholars, however, have attempted to push the date of satyr performances farther back into the sixth century. Brijder has identified a cup in Amsterdam from ca. 560 B.C. (on which more below) as a representation of a satyr performance.[131] Hedreen has also made a spirited case for seeing earlier paintings of myths such as the Return of Hephaestus as representations of satyr performances.

Establishing the earlier date depends on proving that the vases depict not just the myth but a performance of the myth.[132] Evidence includes the presence in a painting of masks, costumes, or an *aulos*-player. Also suggestive are motifs that are foreign to their traditional roles in myth, including satyrs with musical instruments, sports equipment, and other tools that are known from literary evidence to have been used by them in satyr-plays. These clues are largely absent from vases from before 520 B.C., but Hedreen identifies certain padded dancers as satyrs. For example, on the "Dümmler krater" the padded dancer facing the *aulos*-player appears to be wearing a mask with a satyr-like face and to act like a satyr.[133] Moreover, although it was satyrs who accompanied Dionysus in most depictions of the Return of Hephaestus, in some instances padded dancers seem to take on this task.[134] If so, the distinction between satyrs and padded dancers was not rigid.[135] Hedreen also points to vases that seem to depict early satyr choruses. Among these is Berlin 1697, a black-figure amphora of ca. 540–530 B.C., which shows silens and nymphs formally arranged before an *aulos*-player as if preparing for a performance.[136]

If Brijder and Hedreen are correct, and performances by satyrs occurred earlier in the sixth century than previously supposed, then satyr performances must be considered among the influences that comedy was exposed to. Such influence would be surprising, for it was not in comedy but in the tragic tetralogy that satyr-plays eventually found a home. As will be shown in the next chapter, however, there are hints of satyr costumes on vase-paintings of early comic choruses. Furthermore, because the titles of several fifth-century comedies indicate that they had satyr choruses, it seems reasonable to conjecture that there were sixth-century precedents. At the very least, their semi-human status and their close association with Dionysus serve as important benchmarks in evaluating animal choruses.

Costumed Non-Phallic Dancers

Several vase paintings from ca. 560 B.C. to ca. 490 B.C. show costumed men involved in various types of dances or *komoi* that are possibly related to pre-comic performances. Although none is of an animal chorus, a few dancers have animal ears and all are in some way either grotesque or alien. The dancers depicted on these vases are more formally organized and dance in tighter coordination than did the padded dancers, so they seem to constitute a chorus or rehearsed entertainment rather than a *komos*. Moreover, they are generally accompanied by an *aulos*-player, which becomes standard in the iconography of dramatic or pre-dramatic choral performances.[137] They fall into four categories: men wearing ears, walking on stilts, swathed in cloaks, and standing on their heads.

Dancing Men Wearing Ears

On two vases are men with animal ears who appear to constitute a
chorus. Their buttocks are less exaggerated than those of the padded
dancers, so they should be considered a distinct group or at least a
variant.

I. The first vase, in the Allard Pierson Museum, is a black-figure
Siana cup of ca. 560 B.C. by the Heidelberg Painter.[138] On side A
are seven bearded figures wearing caps and ankle-length chitons.
An *aulos*-player stands in the middle; there are three dancers to his
left and three to his right. Each group of three dancers maintains
its own specific dance posture and they seem to constitute a semi-
chorus. Side B has a similar group of seven figures, consisting
of an *aulos*-player surrounded by two semi-choruses of three
members each. All fourteen figures are dressed almost identically,
differing only in their dance postures and headwear.

Once thought to be choruses of men wearing women's clothing, more recent studies suggest that they are men wearing short
tunics over long chitons. Boardman suggested that the wearing
of chitons follows the fashion in East Greece and Lydia.[139] Their
headwear, too, may be Lydian in origin, though Brijder sees a
resemblance to caps worn by Thracians.[140]

The cap of the piper and left semi-chorus on side A have
vertical protrusions, which Trendall and Webster took to be
feathers.[141] Brijder, arguing for a specifically theatrical association, points out that their costume can be found on tragic
actors in later vase-painting.[142] He also suggests that the "ears"
are equine and, because they are similar to ears of satyrs on a
Rhodian vase, concludes that these are padded dancers imper-
sonating satyrs, perhaps performing a dithyramb.[143] Acknowledging that their appearance is unusual, Brijder also suggests that
they are "refined and humanized" satyrs.[144] If so, the ears can
be paralleled, but one expects more markers in order to identify
them as satyrs. A further possibility is that the dancers were themselves ambiguously costumed, and the vase simply demonstrates
that the categories of padded dancers and satyrs were not rigidly

drawn in this period. If Brijder is right, the vase shows a performance that antedates any distinction between tragedy and
comedy. In other words, they may be padded dancers, whom
we tend to associate with comedy, dressed as satyrs who are
wearing costumes that we associate with tragic actors.

2. The second vase is a black-figure hydria, attributed to the Manner of Lydos, of ca. 550 B.C. (Figure 1.5).[145] On the left is an
aulos-player in a chiton; facing him from the right are four men
dancing and wearing white feathers or ears in headbands similar
to those on the Amsterdam vase. Trendall and Webster saw them
as feathers (and regarded this as decisive evidence that the Amsterdam vase discussed above also has feathers).[146] For Brijder,
this vase depicts men dressed in female robes wearing the white
ears of mares or she-donkeys; that is, they are stage nymph-
satyrs.[147]

Men on Stilts

A chorus appears on a black-figure amphora by the Swing Painter
of ca. 530 B.C.[148] Five bearded men, wearing corselets and pointed
hats, walk on stilts. There is no *aulos*-player, but, with their identical
postures and similar costuming, "the identification as a comic chorus
seems certain."[149] The stilts may be a way of imitating Titans; Trendall
and Webster suggest that the pointed caps look Scythian and would suit
Titans if they were visiting Prometheus in the Caucausus, an episode
staged in Aeschylus' *Prometheus Lyomenos*.[150] But Titans were also the
chorus of Cratinus' *Ploutoi*. If this vase does depict a chorus of Titans,
it may offer further evidence of a pre-comic chorus of non-human
figures.

Men in Cloaks and Men Standing on Their Heads

Two sides of a black-figure skyphos in Thebes of ca. 480 B.C. also seem
to illustrate comic themes.[151] On side A an *aulos*-player is followed by
six old men in cloaks holding walking sticks; on side B six old men are
standing on their heads; the piper is to the right. Green speculates that
side B parodies a representation of Antipodeans; Trendall and Webster
compare the scene to the story of Hippocleides, who lost the chance

1.5. Attic black-figure hydria attributed to the Manner of Lydos, showing dancers possibly wearing ears. Ca. 550 B.C. New York, Metropolitan Museum of Art 1988.11.3. All rights reserved, The Metropolitan Museum of Art.

to marry a tyrant's daughter when he stood on his head, the story that Fehr cited to illustrate the *akletoi* at a symposium.[152]

Walking Warriors

Four vases from the early fifth century show walking men dressed as warriors. The case for considering them representations of pre-comic *komoi* is weak, yet they are worth consideration because they do seem to be dancing in choruses and even resemble the men riding dolphins (discussed in Chapter 2).

1. Black-figure skyphos, Guarini collection, ca. 500 B.C., attributed to the workshop of the Athena Painter.[153] Each side shows four dancers with helmets, striped mantles, dotted chitons, and *krotala* like those on the Brooklyn and Würzburg vases. They move from the left, in tight coordination, toward an *aulos*-player on the right; on side A the four lean forward and look down

31

while those on side B look back over their shoulders. Fedele suggested that the dancers on Side B were *"figure femminili."* Nevertheless, although two of the dancers in the middle of side B are beardless and evidently young, the other two seem to have beards, and in any event there is nothing else to signal their femininity. Fedele identified the four dancers on Side A as satyrs and the snub noses and protuberant ears make it hard to disagree.[154]

Webster suggested that these warriors were running in during the parodos of a performance.[155] That they are helmeted might remind us of the pyrrhic dance, in which armored men held shields and leaped into the air.[156] Lawler, however, suggested that the dance was performed by youths as part of their training, and to judge from vases of graceful youths marching precisely, armed with helmets, shields, and spears, at Athens the emphasis was on grace, which is missing from this vase.[157] Thus this vase does not depict pyrrhic dancers, for none seem to wear body-armor or carry shields and spears. Could they instead be comic satyr-warriors?

2. Black-figure oinochoe in Würzburg, toward 490 B.C. by the Painter of Villa Giulia M. 482. Three helmeted men, who seem to be bearded, hold up their cloaks with their left hands but carry no weapons. The one on the right looks back at those behind him. Their movement suggests a chorus, though there is no *aulos*-player.[158]

3. Black-figure amphora, in Brooklyn, said to be from Thebes, toward 490 B.C. Side A: Two pairs of helmeted men with long hair and beards move right and hold up decorated *himatia*; side B: two similar figures. None seems to carry a weapon.[159]

4. Black-figure lekythos in London by the Beldam Painter, from the second quarter of the fifth century. Three men wearing helmets, short chitons, and greaves walk to the right in a dance file, each carrying a severed head still in its helmet. Green, while acknowledging that there is no *aulos*-player, thought the movement suggests a chorus. Brommer believed that in this and the Würzburg vase "the comic element is at its clearest." Vermeule, however, related it to the threat of keeping severed heads as

ornaments and says that it "seems to allude to a common element in the traditional repertory of torture and taunting."[160]

CONCLUSIONS: PATTERNS IN SIXTH-CENTURY PRE-COMEDY

The archaic festivals and performances here cited were the primordial soup out of which the comic chorus emerged. A few summary remarks are in order before moving on, in the next chapter, to animal choruses themselves.

Performance and Iconographical Conventions

On a practical level, the vase-paintings show that conventions were being established for the representation of choral performance. Clues include the presence of the *aulos*-player, often in a long, elaborate robe, and dancers in coordinated dance postures. On the Allard Pierson cup they even form semi-choruses.[161] Actors do not appear in this period.

Otherness

No vase depicted choruses that were composed of what one might call "ordinary" Athenians.[162] Choruses of men wore Scythian, Lydian, or Thracian hats.[163] Their appearance in the sixth century may be part of an infiltration into Athenian symposiastic and komastic culture of East Greek habits, in which Lydian fashions played a large role, culminating around 520 B.C. They anticipate the Anakreon type of komast that becomes popular on vase painting in the early fifth century. Other dancers were possibly costumed as Antipodeans and even subhuman creatures such as satyrs and Titans. The padded dancers were too grotesque to claim close semblance to humanity. Some of the Guarini Collection warriors may have been satyrs. To judge from this limited evidence, then, "otherness" – the alien and the unknown – was a prerequisite for these *komoi* and choruses. Such incongruous costumes might be fun for any audience but would have been especially amusing for Greeks. By the fifth century choruses of barbarians were part of the comic repertory. In fact Chionides, the victor in the first comic competition at the City Dionysia, was credited with a comedy titled *Persians or Assyrians* (*PCG* IV.73).[164]

Staging the "other" is a useful means through which human beings may reflect on their own values and conventions.[165] What Bowie has written about the use of peasants from outlying demes as Aristophanic heroes is apposite: "The centre is asked to look at itself from the margins, and *vice versa*."[166] It is unclear whether foreigners on vases were meant to be spoofed, as they were in late fifth-century comedy, where a more conscious antithesis between Greeks and barbarians predominates. Attitudes toward barbarians changed considerably in the early fifth century,[167] but even in the sixth century some of these dancers would have been the antitypes to sophisticated society.

The status of those who wore these costumes needs to be considered as well. Fehr thought aristocratic youths might costume themselves in a symposium; if so, we would be remiss not to note the similarity to the apparent use of costume in the cult of Artemis, where masks were associated with initiation rituals in Sparta and Brauron. (I say "associated" because the evidence does not go as far as to indicate that the initiates themselves wore masks.) Costuming oneself as a foreigner, fat man, or satyr could invite derision – or may be empowering to the wearer in a liminal phase.[168]

We observe, then, that few of these chorus types had any sort of fixed, well-defined identity. What instead predominates are fluid boundaries: men with animal ears who are still clearly men; padded dancers with human features so grotesquely exaggerated that they are almost inhuman; dancers whose costumes hint at a foreign origin; men dressed as satyrs, the ultimate hybrid; and satyrs apparently dressed as warriors. One remembers that a significant theme in Dionysiac cult is the blurring of natural or conceptual boundaries.[169] If the choruses were not composed of "ordinary" Athenians, neither were they representations of any other ordinary creature.

Performance Context

Nothing examined here precludes the possibility that these dances were performed at cultic *komoi* of, for example, Dionysus or Artemis. Indeed, there are reasons to expect that they were. Dionysus was associated not just with animals but with drama and masks. It is surely correct to assert that "the true home of masks is in ritual."[170]

Nevertheless, the evidence of these early Greek cults is too slender for a satisfactory explanation of how masks and costumes were used or how the masks entered drama. There were certainly no *necessary* reasons for the cults to generate them. Moreover, no evidence has survived to prove that animal costumes were a part of these cultic *komoi*. Demosthenes' anecdote about Kyrebion is the only solid hint that a mask was used at a *komos* and, as noted, that anecdote may describe a *pompe* rather than a *komos* proper. Moreover, the dance movements in depictions of performances are coordinated and accompanied by an *aulos*-player, thus resembling not spontaneous *komoi* but self-conscious *choruses*. Thus the influence of ritual practice on animal masquerades, though plausible, can only be said to be indirect or remote.[171]

The symposium, however, offers an alternative source. Antics seen in a *komos* might have originated there, and the symposium was the driving force behind fashions such as the wearing of outlandish dress and head-gear. It may not be irrelevant that rhyta and moulded vases used at the symposium were given the shapes of heads of every animal, wild and domesticated (lion, eagle, stag, board, dog, donkey), and of all types of human beings, including women and Africans, with a sole exception: "ordinary" white males. The rhyta defined the drinker by opposition.[172] Xenophanes had discouraged the telling of stories about Titans, Giants, or Centaurs (DK 21 B1), yet this advice made most sense if in fact men had been telling such stories.

Performances of poetry, music, and dance were expected at symposia. It would go beyond the evidence to assert that costumed performances like the cabaret in Xenophon's *Symposium* took place at archaic symposia, yet neither can this be ruled out.[173] In any event, the larger point is that costumed dancers of a *komos* are often the same men who, shortly before, were symposiasts, and the *komos* is part of the culture of the symposium that preceded it. Symposia, as a point of contact for elites from different Greek cities, would have served as a natural venue for the introduction of costumes and dance movements from other Greek or non-Greek cities. If we needed a mechanism for explaining how Dorian padded dancers entered Attica, these gatherings, which could include the pan-Hellenic elite, might just be it.

2

ANIMAL CHORUSES: THE EVIDENCE
OF VASE-PAINTING

The sixth- and fifth-century vase-paintings that depict performances of men dressed as animals foreshadow plays like Aristophanes' *Birds* and *Knights*. Chronologically, the vases range from the
"Knights" vase from ca. 540–530 B.C., and to the bull-headed dancers
from ca. 510 B.C. and to the cocks, dolphin-riders, and ostrich-riders
from ca. 500–480 B.C. Of concomitant importance are the "Getty
Birds" of ca. 415 B.C.

Several interlocking themes and motifs will emerge from this study
of these vase-paintings. There are clues that these performances arose
from the elite milieu of the archaic symposium, not popular agricultural or fertility rituals as is often assumed. Some costumed dances
also evoke coming-of-age transitions and may reflect ritual practices.
Significantly, the species of animals were often hybrid creatures. The
bull-men or cock-satyrs, for example, combine the physical characteristics of two creatures, but even some of the "pure" animals that are
ridden (dolphins and ostriches) were hybrid in that as "dualizers" they
did not fit any single taxonomical category. In contrast to the animals
of the late-fifth-century comedies to be examined in Chapters 4 and
5, most of these animals (horses, bulls, and cocks) are domesticated;
though capable of violence none is "wild." Finally, in the case of bulls
and dolphins, we find animals associated with myths of city foundations, a motif that anticipates the dominant motif of the *Birds*. This
bears directly on a central theme of this book: animals are important
not just because they represent nature but because they contribute to
human civilization.

The vase-paintings offer powerful archaeological evidence that animal choruses played a role in the genesis of comedy, but they have had
to compete with other accounts of its origins. Reich and Herter, who
followed Aristotle and believed the phallic *komos* to be the principle
source of comedy, deemphasized the role of the animal chorus.[1] Giangrande suggested that the origins of the comic chorus lay in a native
tradition of fertility divinities who manifested themselves as satyrs in
Attica and as padded dancers elsewhere. At a later stage, as the genre
lost its religious nature, the Dionysiac costume of the satyrs yielded to
versatile animal costumes in order to distinguish comedy from other
genres.[2] Others have seen the animal chorus as the prototype for all
subsequent comic choruses, though conceding that comedy eventually
branched out in other directions. Körte believed that the comic chorus
originated in a native Attic chorus with animal motifs; he limited any
role for *phallika* to actors, who derived from the Corinthian dancers.[3]
Pickard-Cambridge also gave more weight to the animal *komos* than
to phallic dancers.[4]

A more defensible position, I believe, is to assume that the comic
chorus stemmed not from a single tradition but from many that co-
existed and occasionally intermingled with one another from the sixth
century on.[5] The "Getty Birds," showing two men who are *both* phallic
and costumed as birds – assuming, for the moment, that they are a
chorus – dramatizes the complexity of the problem. Fifth-century
playwrights had more than one tradition to choose from.

"KNIGHTS" ON A VASE IN BERLIN

An Attic vase-painting in Berlin depicts young riders mounted on the
shoulders of men who are dressed as horses. I will suggest here that
(a) this spectacle originated in the culture of the symposium, (b) the
"horses" were padded dancers, and (c) the activity relates to a male
rite of transition.

The vase, a black-figure amphora of ca. 540–530 B.C., shows an
aulos-player on the left and, facing him, three men wearing horse
costumes with three other men straddling their shoulders (Plate I).[6]
The "horses" wear horse-tails and horse-head masks, although their

bearded faces peep out below. Their short red chitons resemble those of the padded dancers.[7] The young riders – of small stature and beardless[8] – hold the horses' manes with their left hands and raise their right hands up in the air. With this gesture they may be about to strike their horses, they may be raising their arms as part of a dance or celebratory gesture, or they may have just hurled javelins.[9] In any case, the young riders wear short chitons, breastplates, and helmets with unusual crests. The helmet on the left sports what appear to be ears; the helmet in the middle a crescent-shaped projection resembling narrow horns or a *meniskos*; and the helmet on the right a circle intersected by four spokes (best visible in a line drawing in Poppelreuter 1893). The letters EIO+EO++, which appear between the *aulos*-player and the "knights," have been thought to be the equivalent of "giddy-up" – wrote Pickard-Cambridge, "the horses doubtless understood it" – but Beazley showed that these same letters (esp. EIO) occur on contemporary vases that depict completely different genre scenes or episodes from myth, and are merely nonsense words.[10]

The presence of the *aulos*-player identifies this as a representation of a performance. The reverse side of this amphora, which shows three satyrs and two nymphs, indirectly confirms the dramatic context, in that these five face another satyr who prepares to play an *aulos*.[11] Although we cannot tell whether these are satyrs or men dressed as satyrs, the scene on the reverse side seems to represent a chorus at the moment before a performance. Conceivably the horse-riders and satyrs were involved in the same performance. At the very least the propinquity of these two images on one vase points to the knights being part of an actual performance, not a purely imaginary scene.[12]

The Horse and Cavalry in Ancient Greece

If the exact occasion of this performance is uncertain, the cultural significance of the horse is reasonably well known. In Greek religion, horses were associated chiefly with Poseidon. As the god of the sea he embodied the raw power of nature, a quality notable in horses. He was worshipped as Poseidon Hippios at the sanctuary at Kolonos, where

Athena was also worshipped as Hippia since it was she who was credited with the invention of the bridle and bit. Thus Poseidon was linked with the power of a horse and Athena with the ability to transform that power into something useful.[13] Poseidon was credited with siring various horses. Areion, for example, was the progeny of Demeter's rape by Poseidon.[14] A cult statue in Phigaleia showed Demeter with the head of a horse.[15] The animal dancers on the cloak of Persephone/Despoina at Lycosura included one wearing a horse head.[16]

With rare exceptions, such as Patroclus' funeral (*Iliad* 23.171–72), the Greeks neither sacrificed nor consumed horses in the archaic or classical period.[17] This was unthinkable, for Greeks, who thought horses were devoted and intelligent, felt a special kinship with them. In the *Iliad*, for example, the horses of Achilles had the gift of speech and prophesied his death (19.404–19). Plutarch later embellished the theme of the equine intelligence.[18] Xenophon so elevated the horse in the animal hierarchy that his Cyrus imagined an ideal of a union of man and horse (*Cyr.* 4.3.17), which combined speed and strength as emblems of elite *kalokagathia*.[19] This aristocratic fondness for horses found an outlet in chariot and horse races, which were notoriously expensive elements of the four panhellenic games and the Panathenaea.[20]

In practical terms, by contrast, the horse had only limited value in sixth-century Athens. Of negligible use as a draft animal, it was largely removed from the working realities of peasant agricultural life. Hesiod, for example, only mentioned it twice.[21] The horse had no significant military function in sixth-century Athens. Although the second-highest of the Solonian classes of citizens were called "Hippeis" ("Knights") and although one might expect such a classification to involve cavalry duties (the word, somewhat ambiguously, could refer either to the class of citizens or to cavalry),[22] very few military engagements involved Athenian cavalry in the sixth century. The evidence for cavalry in sixth-century Athens is so sketchy that one scholar concluded that there was no formal cavalry at all, only mounted hoplites (infantry warriors), though some studies suggest that vase-paintings do in fact depict cavalrymen in this period.[23] It would be later, in the fifth century, that the Athenian cavalry was organized systematically, although there was still a prevailing democratic bias in favor of hoplites.[24] A horse was therefore little more than a status symbol in sixth-century Athens.

Symposium, Komos, *and Horse Society*

The social status of the riders helps explain the performance depicted on the vase. The horse-and-rider masquerade, inexplicable as an agricultural ritual, would be hypothetically appropriate for the worship of Poseidon Hippios, yet no such ritual is known. The masquerade does make good sense, though, as part of an upper-class *komos* or the symposium preceding it.[25]

As noted, Corinthian ware depicted coarse padded dancers who evidently entertained refined symposiasts. These vases also showed symposiasts in conjunction with other images designed to appeal to aristocratic viewers, such as horses, athletics, and hunting. The Berlin vase compresses the padded dancers and horses into one scene. The older men playing "horse" wore the chiton that was the costume of the padded dancer, and although the padding is less exaggerated than in Corinthian ware, this aligns them with the tradition of Corinthian and, later, Attic komasts.

The helmet crests are not without parallel on black-figure vase-painting. Deer-antlers and four-spoked wheels appear atop Chalcidian and Corinthian helmets on a few vase-paintings, and a fragment of a black-figure Ionic amphora from Rhodes shows helmet crests with animal (donkey?) ears, *meniskoi,* and feathers attached in various combinations.[26] They also resemble crests on helmets of contemporary warriors from the hill country of central South Italy.[27] These distinctive helmets, of which many examples have survived from the sixth to the fourth centuries B.C., typically had feathers or crests inserted into metal prongs. The prongs by themselves recall, in miniature, the stylized, geometrical features of the crests on the Berlin Knights. With the feathers inserted, the crests seem fuller and resemble the "donkey ears" on the Berlin vase.[28]

Nevertheless, they remain unusual, and one might wonder whether they share in the tradition of the odd headgear worn at a symposium, such as shown on the Agora skyphos.[29] On that vase the banqueter on the right of side A wears what seems to be an amalgamation of donkey ears and antlers, the components of the crests of the left and center riders on the Berlin vase. Of course those banqueters seem not to have attached these crests to helmets. Nevertheless, the parallels are suggestive. Furthermore, the exotic headdress of the horsemen is in keeping with the rest of the costume: spots on the Berlin riders' skirts, although perhaps simply reflecting the elaborate decoration of the performers' costumes, could also recall spotted barbarian dress.[30] The riders might be foreigners or, more precisely, Athenians masquerading as foreigners.[31] The possibility should be entertained that what is in question here is a symposium at which participants wore idiosyncratic, possibly non-Greek headdresses, and the "Knights" vase shows the *komos* following the symposium, or even a masquerade in the course of the symposium itself, which entailed (literally) horse-play and helmets with alien crests.

As noted in the last chapter, outlandish performances probably had a place in the symposia shown on sixth-century Corinthian ware. Fehr suggested that although such antics were initially performed by *akletoi*, young aristocrats also sometimes behaved in a similar manner.[32]

Ephebeia?

The fact that the riders on the Berlin vase are evidently young (possibly in their teens, though it is impossible to give an exact age), while the "horses" are older men, calls attention to another pertinent pattern: not only were horsemen generally aristocratic, they were almost always thought of as youthful. Many examples from the fifth century, including the chorus members of Aristophanes' *Knights*, look young.[33] Hippeis were overwhelmingly depicted on paintings and reliefs as youthful.[34] "Riding was therefore associated with the education of rulers and aristocrats and this must have been reinforced by the sight of young men of the leisured classes exercising their horses or practising their riding at the exercise grounds."[35]

At an age when they were ready to begin military training, they were also at an important transitional stage. Many societies mark this transition in life with formal rituals.[36] Such ritualistic transitions from one status in life to another are often distinguished, either literally or symbolically, by an intermediate state of marginality. This marginal status might include isolation, trials, inversion of lifestyle, or symbolic death, before the initiate returns to a new place in the community. In various cultures young people making the transition from one stage in society into a new one are symbolically considered not quite human and occasionally assume animal disguises. In the Andamese turtle dance initiates imitate the motions of the swimming turtle, and girls who have reached puberty among the Kalahari Bushmen participate in a dance in which they paint their faces white with the markings of the gemsbok. We should note, however, that some animal masquerades were not performed *by* the initiates but *for* them. In Australia, for example, the initiates were witnesses to the Red Kangaroo Dance, the Hawk Dance, and the Bat Dance. At the Kalahari Gemsbok Dance the girls must encounter a male Bushman – the most honored and sexually potent of the tribe – who wears antelope horns and proceeds to "seduce" them.[37]

No evidence suggests that animal costumes were worn by initiates in Greece.[38] Although girls at Athens were "Bears" in the cult of Artemis at Brauron, the costumes appear to have been worn not by the girls but by the adults supervising them.[39] Might it not be the case, then, that the "Knights" vase illustrates the custom in the Kalahari, Australia, and Brauron whereby the older supervisors don costumes?

At Athens the rite of passage that saw young men through to adulthood and citizenship at age eighteen was the *ephebeia*. They underwent a careful inspection (*dokimasia*), were registered, swore an oath of citizenship, spent a year being trained in hoplite warfare under the tutelage of older men, were presented with a shield and spear, and served a second year on patrol in frontier posts, as guards (*peripoloi*), where they wore a black cloak. Upon completion of the two-year duty they were granted full citizen rights.[40] Such, at least, was the procedure followed by ephebes in the 330s B.C., which was evidently the product of fourth-century reorganization. Parts of it were almost certainly present in the fifth century, although Pericles seems to disavow any formal role for the state in military training.[41] With what procedures young Athenian men had been introduced to society in earlier periods is a much-debated topic. In the sixth century they would have been initiated into their phratry ("clan") at the festival of the Apatouria. The occasion, at the age of sixteen, was marked by the cutting of the young man's hair, a sacrifice, and feast.[42] There is no evidence for a ritual of isolation or inversion, but a myth derived "Apatouria" from *apate* ("deception"): a dispute over the border between Athens and Boeotia was settled by a single combat in which Melanthus ("Black Man"), fighting for Athens, killed Xanthus ("Fair Man"), a Boeotian, by deception.[43] Because this incident, which occurred in a border area, seems to validate deception over the fair play that was esteemed in normal hoplite combat, it can be interpreted as expressing the marginal, inverted status of the ephebe, who would graduate to become a hoplite.[44]

The *ephebeia* in the fourth century, of course, focused on hoplite training and had no provisions for cavalry. In fact, the values of the hoplite – cooperation, courage, and forthrightness – were regarded as antithetical to those of the cavalryman, who relied on stealth and manoeuvre.[45] Although there were signs already in the fourth century of increasing respect for the cavalry, it generally played a minor role in military engagements. Hoplite warriors were more representative of the democracy; cavalrymen were associated with oligarchies.[46] The "Knights" vase is from the middle of the sixth century, long before the triumph of the democracy of Cleisthenes and at a time when hoplite training was not assumed to be the only appropriate art of warfare into which a young man would be initiated. We would not expect to find in the sixth century the *ephebeia* attested for later periods, and the Berlin vase may have nothing to do with any formal initiation, but there are signs that the young cavalrymen were subject to some degree of oversight. An early red-figure cup in Basel of ca. 510–500 B.C. shows three youths carrying two spears each, leading horses, and wearing *chlamydes* and *petasoi* or *chitones* and *alopekides*.[47] Apparently about to join a procession, they are moving toward a man holding a writing tablet.[48] The vase in Basel on one level depicts a genre scene ("youths with horses"),[49] but on another level underscores the specific place youths with horses had in sixth-century Athenian society and culture.[50] The scene may illustrate a *dokimasia*, an examination of the fitness of horses and cavalrymen. The procedure as done later in the fourth century is described by the *Athenaion Politeia* (49.1–2), but the Basel vase offers evidence for some degree of regulation in the sixth century.[51] This occasion surely did not have as much ritual import as the later *ephebeia* or other rites of passage, yet it documents the importance of young Hippeis.

These activities square with the function of the symposium and *komos* by reinforcing the identity of male companions as a military group. In this respect the symposium overlaps with the *syssition* (shared military mess hall). This social context makes sense as an expression of hoplite values,[52] but what does one make of a cavalry group? The Berlin Knights may reflect the military function and origin of the symposium but reinforce the values of a smaller, elite segment of society that maintained enormous social clout in the sixth century. They probably had political influence even under Peisistratus, but later, in the age of the democracy and of hoplite warfare, their military function was an anachronistic relic. Yet this would make sense, for one function of the symposium was to become a place apart from society and "to establish conventions fundamentally opposed to those within the polis as a whole."[53]

To sum up: The horse masquerade may have been part of a cultic *komos*, though the case for that is speculative. The cult statue of Despoina at Lycosura bore figures wearing horse masks, but those were women, and there is no reason to link them with a male masquerade at Athens. More relevant might be the cult of Poseidon Hippios at Kolonus, which would have been a fitting venue for the Berlin Knights, but nothing known about that cult gave rise to horse costumes. Riders escorted the *pompai* of other festivals,[54] but none entailed disguises.

The Berlin vase appears to show us a *komos* in a different sense: a procession, with song and dance, preceding or following a private symposium. The head-gear may be sympotic, the costume of the horses is that of the padded dancers, and the vase reflects the milieu of upper-class Athenians who could afford horses. All of this points to the culture of the elite symposium, not the animal mummery of coarse, popular entertainment. Although no direct evidence connects the Berlin Knights with the Apatouria or *ephebeia*, it is possible that this spectacle was related to a coming-of-age occasion in which "marginality" or at least a carnivalesque spirit was expressed by the odd-looking helmet crests, with the older men literally and symbolically in a position to guide and support the younger.[55] Because of the early date of the vase and presumed social class of the participants, there is no trace of the hoplite-oriented *rite de passage* of the late classical period.[56]

BULL-HEADED DANCERS

Two vases from the end of the sixth century show figures with the bodies of human beings and the heads, hooves, and tails of bulls. Long thought to be Minotaurs, they have more recently been identified as river gods. Both possibilities will be considered.

One is an Attic black-figure hydria in London of ca. 520–500 B.C. (Figure 2.1).[57] On the shoulder of the hydria are three figures who move to our right, with hands near their hips, looking back to the left. They appear to be holding stones in their hands. Nothing indicates that they are wearing costumes, and there is no *aulos*-player. The second vase is a black-figure cup (Droop cup) in Oxford from ca. 510–500 B.C. (Figure 2.2).[58] On one side are three figures, again with the heads, hooves, and tails of bulls, positioned between two sphinxes. They are dancing right in a kind of conga-line, each apparently holding the hip or tail of the one in front, though more likely their hands are drawn overlapping the hip or tail of the one in front, a conventional way in black-figure to indicate depth.[59] On the other side are two similar dancers, though the one behind does not seem to be holding the hip of the one in front. The torsos, again, are those of men, but the bodies (or costumes?) are spotted.

Neither vase shows an *aulos*-player, and it is possible that these are not costumed men in a performance but mythological creatures drawn either from the imagination of the painter or from other images; nevertheless, the coordinated movement suggests a chorus. Green thought that the painter of the Oxford cup tried to show that masks were

2.1. Attic black-figure hydria, showing dancers in bull costumes. Ca. 520–500 B.C. London, British Museum B 308. © Copyright The Trustees of The British Museum.

being worn.[60] Furthermore, the simple fact that these two vases should appear within a decade of one another, and that both had three dancers, could indicate inspiration from a particular performance.

The Bull in Greece

The bull's strength and procreative powers were valued by nearly every Mediterranean culture, yet such was its impetuous violence that it could barely count as "domesticated." Only by being castrated and becoming an "ox" could it be used as a draft animal. If anything, one of the most important functions of the bull was to breed more oxen. Fittingly, the bull was used as a symbol of agricultural fertility on coinage, primarily in Magna Graecia.[61] Both the fertile and violent sides of the bull are reflected in myth: Zeus' disguise as a bull in abducting Europa is a transparent symbol of its sexual potency, whereas

46

2.2. Detail of Attic black-figure cup (Droop cup) attributed to perhaps Wraith Painter, showing dancers in bull costumes. Ca. 510–500 B.C. Oxford, Ashmolean Museum 1971.903. Photo copyright The Ashmolean Museum.

the stories of Dirce and the Marathonian bull attest to its terrifying power. The bull had an important place in Greek religion from the second millenium B.C., as attested by the bull-jumpers of Crete, until the end of antiquity, when the bull-slayer Mithras became central in his own cult.[62] Throughout antiquity it was the sacrificial animal par excellence, more expensive by far than sheep or goats.[63] In the archaic and classical period, the bull was not linked exclusively to any single god or goddess. Both Demeter and Artemis had the cult title Tauropolos ("drawn by the bull"?).[64] A stronger association was with Dionysus, himself a god of fertility whose epiphanies in the form of a bull were a recurrent motif in the *Bacchae*.[65] It was Poseidon who sent the bull that terrified Hippolytus' horses, causing the young man's destruction in the *Hippolytus* (1214). At a festival of Poseidon Taureos in Thessaly young men of noble families would wrestle bulls to the ground.[66] Moreover, young unmarried men bearing *oinochoai* at sacrifices to Poseidon in Ephesus were called "Tauroi."[67]

We do not know whether these "Tauroi" wore bull masks or costumes, but if they did they were not unprecedented. Bull-men have been identified on seals from Bronze-Age Crete, though it is difficult to establish whether they are mythical animal-human hybrids or priests wearing masks.[68] Terracotta priest figures wearing bull masks have been found at Agia Irini and Kourion on Cyprus from the second millennium B.C.[69] Figurines with bull masks have also been found at Kourion from ca. 650–600 B.C., suggesting the possibility of cultic continuity through the Dark Age.[70] When bull-headed figures appear in art of the Greek mainland in the eighth century B.C., usually in figurines, seals, and gems, they initially follow the iconography set in

47

Syrian and Cypriot seals of the second millennium B.C.,[71] though this may reflect artistic imitation and experimentation, not a shared cultic practice, or they may have served as apotropaic monsters.[72] A painted plaque from Penteskouphia shows a bull-headed man who is striding to the left; since these plaques were dedicated to Poseidon, we would expect it to be connected with him.[73]

Furthermore, bull-headed creatures, or dancers with bull masks, might simply have been meant to assume the fertile powers of the bull.[74] The vases may also depict a ritual, for which other evidence is lost, in which the bull's violence was somehow channeled into dance, possibly in honor of Poseidon or of Dionysus. Dowden speculated that the Tauroi of Ephesus were a liminal class of "Bulls" passing from one status to another.[75] Similarly the Tauropolia, the festival of the cult of Artemis Tauropolos held at Halai Araphenides, involved dances for girls but may have been a male innovation. Lloyd-Jones associates the bull, an obvious symbol of virility, with the initiation of males: "Fritz Graf has pointed out that all cults of Artemis Tauropolos . . . were linked with the incorporation of young persons into the adult world by means of *rites de passage*, like the ordeal of the ephebes in the allied cult of Artemis Orthia [at Sparta]."[76] The London hydria or Oxford cup may reflect such practices.

Minotaur?

The resemblance of the Oxford and London bull-headed dancers to contemporary depictions of the Minotaur is striking. Closely comparable to the London hydria is the rendering of the body of a Minotaur on a cup in Paris of ca. 520–500 B.C.: although this Minotaur's arms are raised up (not held at his hips, as in London), he runs to the right but looks back to the left.[77] A further iconographical clue is that the Minotaur, like the London dancers, was frequently shown holding stones.[78]

The Minotaur played no role in any myth other than that of Minos and Theseus.[79] The myth of Theseus was especially popular from the middle of the sixth century until the early fifth century, and one could speculate that the myth inspired a performance that required a chorus of multiple Minotaurs.[80] Perhaps a triple challenge had been set for the young hero of Athens. We can only guess at what a performance of dancing Minotaurs would mean to an audience. A chorus of them might, be ominous or apotropaic – or quite comic. Mythological parody may have had an older ancestry than previously thought.

There are, however, hurdles to identifying these figures as Minotaurs. Above all, mythology knew only one Minotaur, in the company of Theseus; no parallel for multiple Minotaurs exists.[81] To compound our uncertainty a bull-headed dancer could represent another figure in archaic Greece – the river god.[82]

River Gods

River gods were portrayed as bulls, as bull-headed human figures, or, later in the fifth century, as human figures with horns.[83] The closest iconographic parallel to the London and Oxford vases is a depiction of the river Achelous on a silver stater from Metapontum of about 490–450 B.C. He is shown as a nude man with a bull-like head, hooves, and tail, standing frontally and holding a phiale.[84] The inscription clearly gives his identity. Other river gods were depicted in the same way on coins and vases; although their features became more humanized throughout the fifth century, they retained at least vestigial horns and a hint of their bull nature.[85] The earliest literary source for this description of their hybrid form is Archilochus, who likened Achelous to a bull (ὡς ταῦρον) when it fought Heracles.[86] In Sophocles' *Trachiniae* Deianeira described Achelous as taking on three shapes: "in visible form as a bull (ἐναργὴς ταῦρος), then as a shiny, winding serpent, and then bull-faced with the body of a man (ἀνδρείῳ κύτει βούπρῳρος, 10–13)."[87] Thus, although there was no uniformity in descriptions of river gods, their bull attributes remained unquestionable. These inconsistencies, together with the fact that there are weaknesses in the case for seeing the dancers as Minotaurs, make the identification of the figures on the Oxford and London vases as river gods more compelling. It is plausible to imagine that Greek comedy, which had choruses of islands and clouds, harbored a chorus of rivers among its ancestors. But what would a river-god dance mean?

The Fertility of Rivers

Because the bull symbolized growth and procreative power in ancient Greece, the enriching power of a river's fresh water was naturally associated with the animal.[88] Hesiod said that the river gods, along with Apollo and the nymphs, belong to the Kourotrophoi, who nourish the young and bring fertility to women.[89] For successful nurture young men ritually trimmed their hair and dedicated it to a local river or nymph.[90] Moreover, the stones the bull-headed dancers are shown holding on the vases may be general symbols of fertility.[91] Thus, this bull-man composite could represent an aspect of nature that is far more benign than the Minotaur, even compatible with civilized pursuits such as the foundation of a city, which was another prerogative of river gods.[92]

Indeed, the motif of river fertility appeared in later comedy: Athenaeus (268e–270a) quoted a series of passages from Old Comedy on the abundant food flowing from the rivers in exotic and imaginary places such as the Underworld, Persia, and Magna Graecia. The *Thuriopersai* of Metagenes, for example, described the rivers Crathis and Sybaris as literally flowing with barley-cakes, cheesecakes, and meat (fr. 6 K-A).[93]

Colonization and City Foundation

Colonists sought arable land, a harbor, and fresh water; hence many cities in Sicily and Southern Italy were built at or near the mouths of rivers, and many river gods are attested there.[94] The temple and temenos of a river god was located at the river itself.[95] The river, which nourished the land and its inhabitants, could become the protective deity and emblem on a city's coinage. Agrigento was named for the river Akragas, the river Taras was honored as the eponym of the city Taras,[96] Gela was depicted on coins,[97] and literary sources (especially Aelian) cite still more.[98]

2.3. Silver tetradrachm from Selinus, showing Selinus making an offering. Ca. 467–445 B.C. American Numismatic Society 1957.172.624. Photo courtesy of The American Numismatic Society.

A series of coins from the fifth century depicting the eponymous river Selinus and the river Hypsas illustrates the role of rivers specifically in the establishment of a city. The city Selinus, a colony of Megara Hyblaea, was founded in the seventh century between the two rivers. On tetradrachms beginning around 480–450 B.C., and ending when the city was destroyed by Carthage in 409 B.C., the rivers Selinus and Hypsas are represented as young men with bull horns on their heads (Figure 2.3).[99] Selinus, while holding a phiale, makes an offering to an altar that has a cock on it. Behind him is a bull on a podium. Hypsas, who appears on didrachms, stands in front of a heron, a bird of good omen that was associated with Apollo and Artemis at the foundation of Zancle.[100] Apollo *archegetes* presided over the domain of colonization, of course, and consultation with Delphi was a virtual prerequisite for departing colonists.[101] The coins, then, can be interpreted as depictions of Selinus and Hypsas making offerings to Apollo on the occasion of the city's foundation.[102]

The bull-headed dancers, I propose, represent the assembled rivers of the colonies of Sicily and Magna Graecia. It is those rivers that are best represented in the archaeological record from the sixth and fifth centuries, and the rivers were multiple in number. The linking of a bull-headed chorus with celebrations of city foundations interestingly foreshadows Aristophanes' *Birds*, in which birds, who turn out to have resources essential for urban life, establish a new city.

BIRD CHORUSES

Several vases, some from early in the fifth century and another from later in the century, depict human beings wearing bird costumes with wings and crests. All of these deserve special attention because they illustrate a trend found in literature: in addition to Aristophanes' *Birds* (414 B.C.), there was Magnes' *Birds*. I will suggest that (a) the costumes of the birds, who are usually cocks, have affinities with satyr costumes and (b) these masquerades make best sense as the product of the symposium-attending class of Athenians. (For some other bird vases, see Appendix B.)

London Birds

Two bird dancers appear on an Attic black-figure oinochoe in London, painted by the Gela Painter ca. 500–490 B.C. (Plate II).[103] To their left is an *aulos*-player wearing a long himation; two men dressed as birds are at center and right, striding to the right but with heads turned to the left. Trendall and Webster suggested that this is the entrance of the chorus.[104] The costume of the one on the left only partially covers his body, which allows the viewer to see how the wings are attached to his arms and shoulders. Both men wear feathered tights with "feet" attached to their knees. When dancing the birds would look as if they were flying, and when resting the men could bend on their knees.[105] The men wear cockscombs on their heads and have red beards. There can be no doubt that they are cocks, for the cock was the only bird known to the Greeks with a permanently erect crest.[106] Since ὄρνιθες could mean "cocks" and since the date is about right, the London oinochoe just may commemorate Magnes' *Birds*.[107] Because comedy entered into the City Dionysia in 486 B.C., it is possible that this is not simply a *komos* or symposium masquerade but an authentic chorus of comedy.

This group is somewhat difficult to interpret but possibly shows satyrs, or at least men costumed as satyrs, who in turn wear bird costumes. The beards may simply indicate that they are adult male dancers, but they also resemble beards worn by other satyrs of the Gela Painter.[108] Moreover, Trendall and Webster call attention to the resemblance of the tights with feathers to those on satyrs by the Gela Painter.[109] Finally, the dancer in the middle may have an erect (horizontal, at least) *phallos*, which is so lightly silhouetted against his left thigh that it is not immediately obvious. This protuberance cannot be easily explained as a fold in his costume.[110] Although the image may be only of bearded dancers with tights, the possibility of a satyric element should not be dismissed out of hand, especially with the presence of vines of ivy, which, although a common motif in late black-figure, could reinforce a Dionysiac context.[111] These vines are virtually identical to others by the Gela Painter, such as on a black-figure lekythos also of 490–480 B.C., which depicts satyrs playing lyres and processing from a Herm to an altar,[112] and on a lekythos depicting a satyr playing an *aulos* for Dionysus and Ariadne.[113]

Berlin Birds

Two bird-dancers appear on one side of an Attic black-figure amphora of ca. 480 B.C. (Plate III).[114] The "bird chorus" is on side A: two men in large cloaks (*himatia*) and cock-masks are being led by an *aulos*-player who is marching to the right. On side B is a running Heracles. Although the figures on side A have not yet removed their cloaks to reveal their bird costumes, the cockscombs on their heads and the wattles hanging below their chins prove that they are disguised as cocks. They too, although in a different way from the figures on the London vase, possibly resemble satyrs. The Berlin figures have pig-faces with snub noses and protruding lips, a detail that may have been borrowed from the iconography of the faces of satyrs.[115] To judge from Aristophanic comedy, choruses made their entrance wearing cloaks;

once the action had begun they would discard these cloaks to reveal their costumes and dance.[116] In short, this vase may depict the stately entrance of the cloaked chorus members.[117]

"Getty Birds"

On a red-figure calyx-krater from the later fifth century, now in Malibu,[118] are two men dressed as birds, facing one another and flanking a piper, who stands in the center and faces the viewer (Plate IV). The two men, who strike dancing poses, have masks with hooked beaks and crests. Wings project from their shoulders and spurs from the backs of their ankles. They wear *perizomata*, shorts that have cocks' tails attached in back and erect *phalloi* in front. The large decorative circles on the shorts they wear resemble those on the dress of satyr-players.[119] Green suggested a date near, but not at, the end of the fifth century B.C., and wrote, "The equation of the obverse with the *Birds* of Aristophanes is, to say the least, difficult to avoid. It is one of the plays for which we have a firm date, 414 B.C."[120] An alternative view, however, is that they are the two Logoi of the first version of Aristophanes' *Clouds*, who, according to scholia, were exhibited in wicker cages fighting like cocks.[121] Several points stand in favor of this. The various members of the *Birds* chorus seem to be differentiated from one another by species and gender (female as well as male birds are named in the chorus), whereas the vase shows two nearly identical figures;[122] the costume *phallos* of comedy was not normally erect and the *Birds* offers no specific reason for their having erect *phalloi*; and nothing in *Birds* would account for their facing one another with aggressive stances. Above all the figures' resemblance to cocks tips the scales against the *Birds*. In the chorus of the *Birds* there are no cocks or even domesticated birds (see the inventory of chorus birds at *Birds* 297–304). Nevertheless, whether they are a chorus or simply a pair of characters, they are clearly involved in *some* kind of animal performance, and interesting questions about animals and human beings remain to be addressed.[123]

The Cock in Greece

On all of these vases the birds have features too characteristic of cocks for any other species to be considered. A closer look at them is in order. The cock (ἀλεκτρυών) was a relative newcomer to Greece and was absent from Homer and Hesiod. An early seventh-century depiction exists from the Athenian agora,[124] by the early sixth century it began turning up on Corinthian ware,[125] and from then on it appeared with increasing frequency on Athenian pottery. Cocks appeared on Panathenaic prize amphoras from around 540 B.C. until the 390s.[126] Interest in them intensified at the time of the Persian Wars when the cock came to be called the "Persian bird."[127] The cock was regarded as a *psychopompos*, leading souls to the beyond, so that it has been found on funeral stelai.[128] It could be sacrificed to Aesclepius, but this is not attested before Plato's *Phaedo*, and evidence for the cock's association with other divinities is often from the Roman period.[129] The cock, demonstrably a newcomer, played no visible role at all in archaic Greek religion, so that it is highly improbable that a cultic *komos* entailed a cock costume at the time of these vases, from the first decade of the fifth century.[130] Therefore, the costumed dances on these vases were not vestiges of an ancient rite, as the bull-masks may have been, but a newly contrived masquerade either for a private or public entertainment.

The cock, if lacking known religious significance, nevertheless had important social connotations in archaic and classical Athens.[131] It was known foremost for its aggressiveness in the cockfight. Fittingly, the fighting cock was used as a motif on shields and on the cock columns of Panathenaic amphoras.[132] Themistocles was said to have established an annual cockfight in the theater to commemorate the victory over the Persians.[133] It was precisely this competitive nature that made the cock suitable for the *agon* of the *Clouds*, which the Getty birds may depict; the cock was so aggressive that it would even fight its own father. The cock was therefore held up as a model of warrior courage for young men.[134] Although no cock was a member of the chorus of the *Birds*, the fearsomeness of the cock ("a child of Ares," 833–35) made it a suitable tutelary deity for Nephelococcygia.[135]

It is a short step from war to love. The cock's competitiveness manifested itself in sexual ways, and the ithyphallic Getty Birds, whatever else they may be, illustrate that marvelously. The cock was associated with Zeus in the context of the abduction of Ganymede.[136] The triumph of the cock over its opponent in combat harbored an erotic element to it.[137] Accordingly, cocks appeared as love-gifts given by men to youths on Attic black-figure vases by the sixth century.[138] A Corinthian alabastron of ca. 600 B.C. shows two cocks confronting one another, and because alabastra were used to carry scented oils, this one would be a "suitably suggestive gift for a young man from his lover."[139]

In both its martial and erotic aspects, therefore, the cock is associated with the young man on the point of coming of age.[140] Winkler pointed out that the reverse of the Getty Birds vase shows a young man receiving his armor while his parents look on – that is, an ephebe who presumably would be learning precisely the virtues of manhood that the cocks exemplify – so that the vase illustrates two *topoi* of manhood.[141] It is also significant that the cock, whose crowing at dawn is one of the features most noted in fifth-century literature,[142] was regarded as a liminal creature, suited for marking transitions such as birth, death, and rebirth.[143]

This is not to say that the vases in London, Berlin, or Malibu illustrate a step in the *ephebeia*. After all, unlike the Berlin Knights none of these vases has young men on them, but a cock masquerade might have played a symbolic role in the education of young men. In view of their antagonistic and individualistic nature, it is hard to imagine just what a chorus of cocks would do except fight with one another, and that is precisely what is called for by the Logoi in the *Clouds*. Moreover, a feature of choruses in Aristophanic comedy is the occasional tendency to fall into semi-choruses and fight among themselves.[144]

The venue of the performances of the London and Berlin cocks remains a mystery, but in the light of the absence of evidence for the cock in Greek religion at the beginning of the fifth century, the performances were unlikely to have been ritual masquerades. Rather, we should consider them in the context of the social elite at Athens. As Vickers put it, "flute-playing, cock-fighting, and sodomy [were] three occupations of the *symposion*-attending classes."[145] Cocks adorned drinking cups.[146] Conon, the well-born defendant in Demosthenes 54, was a member of elite clubs like the "Ithyphalloi" and "Autolekythoi," and was said to have flapped his arms and crowed like a cock over the prostrate body of a beating victim (54.9, 14, 34). A conversation in Xenophon's *Symposium* casually alludes to the technique of giving garlic to fighting cocks (4.9). Like other features of the symposium – exotic garments, headdresses, reclining poses – the cock was imported from the East. The London vase could plausibly be understood as a costumed mime at a symposium. Furthermore, the dates of the two earlier vases (500–490 and 480 B.C.) correspond to the time of the Persian Wars and the introduction of the public cockfight by Themistocles. The vases probably reflect the culture of the cockfight at Athens in these decades.

The Berlin vase, however, shows birds still wearing cloaks, which, as noted, marked the conventional entrance of the chorus in drama. Because comedy entered the Dionysia in 486 B.C., this vase, which is dated to ca. 480 B.C., may well represent a known comic chorus. Magnes, who won his first victory in 472, was credited with a *Birds*, and the date of the Berlin vase is quite close. Moreover, the evidence for his *Birds* rests in part on the word πτερυγίζων (Ar., *Knights* 522), which seems to mean "flapping wings," precisely what Conon did in his cock imitation.[147]

Cock-Satyrs?

As noted, the Malibu and London vases, and perhaps the Berlin vase, appear to depict satyrs wearing bird costumes. With their beards, tights, squat nose, and *phallos*, each of these birds has a feature that belongs not to cocks but to the repertory of the satyr costume.[148] This hybrid nature suggests that dancers in these masquerades felt free to transgress the boundaries of genre.

One reason for this is practical: the satyrs' loin-cloths, being made of stiffer material than the dramatic skins, were suitable for the attachment of the *phalloi* of the birds' costumes.[149] Alternatively, one might envision a metamorphosis in progress, although there is, as Taplin points out, no precedent for a theriomorphosis or ornithomorphosis in comedy. What seems to be portrayed is what Taplin calls a *satyralektryon*; he conjectures, "Could some comedian have invented the *satyralektryon*, and produced a whole chorus of them? This might explain the puzzles of the Getty Birds, but we have no evidence of any such thing, and it does seem very far-fetched."[150] And yet the hints I have pointed to suggest that the invention was not unprecedented.

THE DOLPHIN-RIDERS

"Don't be surprised, Poseidon, that we're kind to men. We were men ourselves, before we became fishes," says a dolphin in Lucian.[151] The transformation he alludes to, which was told first in the *Homeric Hymn to Dionysus,* was one way of explaining the special affinity of the dolphin for human beings. The creature was regarded as a companionable aquatic counterpart to the horse. A series of vases painted between 510 and 480 B.C., which show armed men riding dolphins, illustrates exactly this relationship and signals a special interest in the dolphin-rider theme. It is likely that, because they ride in an orderly procession and because many of them are accompanied by an *aulos*-player, a now-lost performance involving dolphin-riders had occurred at Athens. I suggest here that Phalanthus and his companions, who were rescued by dolphins on their voyage to establish the city of Tarentum, were the subjects of the performance. Moreover, I propose that dolphins evoked Poseidon, Apollo, accounts of city foundations, and themes of transitions. I will also describe how the dolphin-rider carried Dionysiac and symposiastic significance.

In chronological order, the vases are:

1. **New York Dolphin-Riders**. A red-figure psykter in New York of ca. 510 B.C. by Oltos shows six bearded men riding dolphins (Plate V).[152] Arrayed as if they were cavalry, they are hoplites in full armor, each wearing a breastplate, Corinthian helmet, and greaves, and carrying a spear and shield.[153] All are shown in profile riding to the left. The words ΕΠΙΔΕΛΦΙΝΟΣ (ἐπὶ δελφῖνος, "on a dolphin") are written retrograde next to the head of each rider. There is no *aulos*-player, but very similar vases

do depict one. Moreover, the very phrase ἐπὶ δελφῖνος may echo an origin in drama: although Greifenhagen thought this was simply an emphatic caption explaining what they were doing or an echo of the title of the piece,[154] the words, as Sifakis pointed out, seem to be coming from their mouths and could be the lyrics of their song. They are in anapestic dimeters, appropriate for an entrance song.[155] The functional and aesthetic aspects of this vase blend in a satisfying way: the psykter, which was designed to be filled with wine and then set into a krater filled with snow or ice water, would sink far enough that, as the ice water melted, the dolphin-riders would seem to be riding through waves.[156]

2. **Los Angeles Dolphin-Rider**. A lone rider is on the interior tondo of an Attic black-figure kylix of ca. 500 B.C. in Los Angeles.[157] He wears greaves, a cloak (a *chlamys*), and helmet. He carries no shield or spear and his arms are invisible. He is thus costumed more like an armed cavalryman than a hoplite. No beard is visible on the reproduction that I examined. This cup is attributed to the Leafless Group; the subject "is unique among the several hundred cups attributed to this late group." There is no *aulos*-player, and nothing indicates that this is a performance, but his similarity to the other riders is notable.

3. **Basel Dolphin-Rider**. A fragment of an Attic black-figure cup of ca. 500–490 B.C., in Basel, depicts one dolphin-rider with helmet, two spears, and a cloak over his arms.[158] He may be bearded, but his helmet's cheek guard obscures it. The letters Α Δ Ε are written in front of him.[159] Like the rider in Los Angeles, he is alone on a tondo.

4. **Athens Dolphin-Riders**. An Attic black-figure lekythos by the Theseus Painter (ca. 490–480 B.C.) depicts two bearded dolphin-riders with an *aulos*-player between them (Figure 2.4).[160] The riders wear breastplates, helmets with high crests, and cloaks decorated with red. Each carries two spears with one hand while extending the other arm. The riders face the *aulos*-player, who is shown in profile, facing right.

5. **Palermo Dolphin-Riders**. Two armed men are depicted riding dolphins on an Attic black-figure lekythos (of ca. 490–

480 B.C.) by the Athena Painter, found near Selinus and now in Palermo.[161] As on the Athens lekythos, each is bearded, wears a helmet with a high crest, a cloak (a *chlamys*), and carries two spears with his left hand. Unlike the Athens lekythos, both are riding to our left, toward the bearded *aulos*-player, with the rider in the middle looking back to the one on the right, who in turn seems to raise his arm in greeting. Letters visible between these human figures are scarcely legible and do nothing more than fill space, suggests Tusa.

6. **Paris Dolphin-Riders**. On the side of an Attic black-figure cup in the Louvre of ca. 490–480 B.C. are eight bearded dolphin-riders.[162] They wear helmets and breastplates, though not cloaks, each carrying two spears, with left arm upraised; there is an *aulos*-player standing in their midst. They ride to the right; none turns his head back. The dolphins' heads appear to overlap with the tails of the ones preceding, possibly suggesting that they moved in a row, not in single file. In the tondo of this cup a dancing satyr holds a kantharos.

7. **Boston Dolphin-Riders**. One side of a black-figure skyphos in Boston (ca. 490–480 B.C.) shows six dolphin-riders; like the Los Angeles rider they wear helmets and have cloaks over their arms (Plate VI).[163] Although the detail of the painting is obscure, they seem beardless. The helmet crests appear to have white, flowing tails that reach down to waist-level. They ride to our right, toward an *aulos*-player who faces left. The first four dolphins have especially high dorsal fins. On the other side of this skyphos are six ostrich-riders, apparently unbearded, facing a small bearded figure and an *aulos*-player (discussed below).[164]

Performance or Illusion?

The painter of the Berlin Knights made no attempt to hide the fact that the "horses" were costumed men. In the case of the dolphin-riders, however, three painters omitted the *aulos*-player and all seven erased many hints of a performance. Those omitting the *aulos*-player were the earliest. The fact that explicit signs of performance are missing, and the serious, ceremonial feel to the movement of the riders,

2.4. Attic black-figure lekythos by the Theseus Painter, showing two men riding dolphins. Ca. 490–480 B.C. Athens, Kerameikos Inv. 1486. Photograph courtesy of the Deutsches Archäologisches Institut, Athens.

led Bielefeld to suggest that the earliest scenes were more suited to dithyramb than to comedy. If so, the painters probably did not reproduce the performances exactly as they occurred, for it is thought that, as a general rule, costumes or masks were not used in dithyrambic performances.[165] Possible exceptions include two late-fifth-century dithyrambs, one about Arion and the other Philoxenus' *Cyclops*,[166] and dithyrambs may have been performed by men in satyr costumes.[167] Nevertheless, none of these exceptions is compelling in the case of the dolphin-riders: Arion's dancers are conjectural, Philoxenus' work was a century later and experimental, and there is no question here of satyrs. Bielefeld's solution was to suggest that the heroes were shown as described in the myth (and as painted in a votive offering dedicated by the winner of the contest at which a chorus had performed the story) along with the *aulos*-player as seen in the performance.[168] But of course this would constitute an unparalleled, selective juxtaposition of myth and performance. Moreover, these dolphin-riders may seem serious and ceremonial, but the outlandish ostrich-riders on the reverse side of the skyphos might imply that both sides were meant to be humorous and hence comic, not dithyrambic.[169]

The fact that the earliest vases omitted the *aulos*-player could plausibly indicate that they illustrated the myth prior to any performance. Alternatively, a visually appealing art-work such as a votive-offering or at least a story of dolphin-riders may have struck a chord in the last two decades of the sixth century, when it was initially painted or sculpted (statues of dolphin-riders dedicated at Tarentum, Taenarum, Isthmia, and Delphi are discussed below). Perhaps the later vases, which included the *aulos*-player, depicted a subsequent choral performance of the theme early in the fifth century.

Yet other clues commend the view that the depictions were of a performance. For example, the bodies of the dolphins may in fact have been stage-props that the dancers wore around their waists. The Boston vase could reveal traces of this, for, as Csapo and Slater have pointed out, the painter seems unsure whether to depict the illusion of men riding dolphins or the reality of performance. On this vase the first and third riders from the right are clearly shown to have legs and are straddling the dolphins; the second, fourth, fifth, and sixth are shown without legs so that their torsos end where they meet the dolphin.[170] This inconsistency perhaps betrays its origins in a performance. Furthermore, the Boston riders are not entering in single file but in formation: the head of the third dolphin from the right overlaps with the tail of the one in front of it and the tail of this third dolphin overlaps the head of the one behind, while all others simply have heads overlapping the tails of the ones in front. What seems to be shown, then, are two rows of three, which increases the odds that this depicts the entrance of a chorus.[171] Also favoring the theory that these vases depict a performance is the possibility that the cloaks on some of the riders were those conventionally worn during the entrance of a chorus, a practice followed by the Berlin cocks.[172]

Moreover, the painters who omitted the *aulos*-player in earlier versions may have done so because of the nature of the space available. The psykter's use (floating in ice water) precluded the more realistic portrayal of a performance on the vases in Boston, Paris, Athens, or Palermo. Sifakis pointed out that, given the illusion achieved on the psykter, an *aulos*-player would look ridiculous floating on the wine.[173] Likewise, the tondo of a cup was not generally used for multi-figural images, a convention that would require the painter to omit an *aulos*-player. Such an omission is precisely what we find in Basel and Los Angeles. The sides of the tall, slender lekythoi are adapted to showing only two riders (as in Athens and Palermo), whereas the side of the cups (as in Boston and Paris) are better suited for illustrating six to eight members of a chorus in a frieze-like row, with an *aulos*-player. In other words, conventions of painting vases of different shapes dictated what the painter was able to include. Therefore, the lack of an *aulos*-player does not preclude the depiction of a performance.

The Dolphin in Greece

The status of the dolphin raises a set of problems that we did not encounter with the horse, bull, or cock.[174] According to Aristotle the dolphin was a "dualizer" (ἐπαμφοτερίζων), sharing the characteristics of more than one animal species, in that it lives in the sea like a fish, yet like a land animal it has no gills and breathes through a snout.[175] Other dualizers include the seal, a water animal that has "feet"; the bat, who has wings but a ground animal's feet; the ape, which is a biped and quadruped; and the ostrich (on which more below).[176] These dualizers, falling into no single taxonomical category, held anomalous positions in the order of nature. Although no writer before Aristotle explicitly described the dolphin as a dualizer, literary references prove that the Greeks were quite familiar with the animal's peculiarities.[177] Furthermore, although there was technically no taboo against eating dolphins, in practice they were rarely eaten or sacrificed, and killing a dolphin was seen as barbaric.[178] They were moderately social animals, swimming together in schools, and parents appeared to protect their young.[179]

The dolphin, being a marine creature, was associated with Poseidon; in fact the presence of a dolphin was an important identifying attribute of the god of the sea, although he never seems to ride one.[180] Dionysus, too, was closely linked with dolphins when, in a well-known myth, he was captured by Tyrrhenian pirates; to defend himself Dionysus turned into a lion, caused the pirates to jump overboard, and transformed them into dolphins.[181] The metamorphosis, in which we usually see dolphins with human legs, was shown on vases already ca. 540 B.C. and on the frieze of the Lysicrates monument.[182] A painting by Exekias in Munich may illustrate the aftermath: Dionysus is seen reclining on a ship whose mast is entwined with vines while dolphins sport in the sea around him.[183]

It later became a topos for dolphins to trace their sense of kinship with human beings back to this metamorphosis, as did the dolphin in Lucian quoted above.[184] This unselfish affection shown by dolphins to men was also reflected in the many anecdotes told of their willingness to rescue people lost at sea or to convey them from one place to another. These take on folktale dimensions and form a small genre in their own right.[185] Perhaps the earliest is the story of Arion, the poet who was forced to leap into the sea while returning from Tarentum to Greece but was carried back to land by a dolphin.[186] In one tale the dolphin rescued the dead body of a boy and returned it to land: Melicertes, for example, was flung into the sea and carried to

Isthmia, where he was renamed Palaemon and where the Isthmian games were established in his honor. A statue of him riding a dolphin was seen there by Pausanias.[187] Phalanthus was rescued by a dolphin and carried to Italy, where he founded Tarentum.[188] Icadius, the son of Apollo, was shipwrecked on the way to Italy, rescued by a dolphin, and carried to Delphi, where he dedicated a temple to his father.[189] Further examples of dolphin-riders abound,[190] allowing identification of recurrent patterns.

a) Not surprisingly, Poseidon and Dionysus are important presences. In "The Return of the Dolphin," a chapter in *Homo Necans*, Burkert suggested that legends about dolphin-riders were shaped by a "polarity of Dionysus and Poseidon."[191] One of the boys rescued by a dolphin was named Dionysius; Dionysus was shown on the exterior of the Dechter cup; and Koiranus was rescued near Naxos, an important island in Dionysiac myth.[192] A few were sons of Poseidon.[193]

b) Several were involved with the establishment of some sort of cultural or religious institution: the dithyramb, the Isthmian games, temples to Poseidon and Apollo, and the city of Tarentum. Since the dolphin was thought to share certain human qualities, it is not surprising that the dolphin was given a role in legends of human cultural accomplishments. Appropriately, the dolphin was said to love music and the *aulos*.[194] A black-figure cup in the Villa Giulia shows a dolphin who has grown arms in order to play an *aulos*.[195]

c) The dolphin was seen to function as a mediator. Burkert noted that in Greek myth "again and again the path from destruction to a new beginning leads through the sea" and that the path was traced by "the nimblest, the most nearly human of all the inhabitants of the sea – the dolphin."[196] In the tale of the boy of Iasus the dolphin transported the body of an ephebe who was accidentally killed; in other stories it conveyed living people from one place to another. The dolphin is thus liminal not only in that it is a "dualizer" in taxonomical terms but also because it served a role between the living and the dead, the young and old.

Phalanthus and Partheniai?

In attempting to identify the dolphin-riders depicted on the vases in question, several of those listed above can be eliminated: Arion, at least in Herodotus' version of the story, did not have any companions riding with him, and the Arion myth does nothing to explain why the riders are armed warriors. Moreover, no vase characterizes any of the dolphin-riders as a dithyrambic poet. Most of the dolphin-rider legends involved youths – an interesting fact in itself – but the vase-paintings usually show bearded, grown men. Beazley related these scenes to Theseus' trip to Amphitrite,[197] and the cult of Theseus (a son of Poseidon by some accounts) seems to have been promoted in the years of the establishment of the democracy, so it would be appealing to imagine the vase celebrated him in some way. But there was no reason for Theseus to have any companions. Furthermore, when the trip to Amphitrite was represented in art, Theseus was carried not by a dolphin but by a Triton.[198] A few scholars have assumed that the myth of Dionysus and the pirates was alluded to, but dolphin-riders played no part in that episode.[199]

The myth of Phalanthus and the Partheniai, however, is a more promising possibility for the theme of the vase-paintings. Accounts of the foundation of Tarentum relate that Phalanthus was expelled from Sparta along with the Partheniai, men who were considered illegitimate. With the encouragement of an oracle at Delphi, they sailed to Italy to settle a new city, but were shipwrecked on the way and saved by dolphins.[200] The final conquest depended on Phalanthus' wife, Aethra, fulfilling an oracle given at Delphi. If married, Phalanthus was no longer a youth. Phalanthus was thus the only adult dolphin-rider in Greek myth who was accompanied by others.[201] Bielefeld thought that the uplifted arms of several of the dolphin-riders were a gesture of prayer by these men saved from death.[202]

Other evidence supports the identification suggested by Bielefeld. Tarentine coins, often labelled ΤΑΡΑΣ (the Greek name of Tarentum), begin showing Phalanthus riding a dolphin around 520 B.C., around the time that our series of vase-paintings commences. Coins of ca. 520–500 B.C. depict him as a bearded man (Figure 2.5),[203] coins

66

2.5. Silver Didrachm from Tarentum, showing Phalanthos riding a dolphin. Ca. 520–500 B.C. American Numismatic Society 1967.152.17. Photograph courtesy of The American Numismatic Society.

in the decades following (500–450 B.C.) show him as a young man astride a dolphin with arms upraised,[204] and coins minted around 420 B.C. depict him carrying a shield and holding a helmet.[205] Although no single coin shows him both bearded and armed, these are the closest parallels one can find to the vases (the New York dolphin-riders have shields) and considerably increases the odds that the vases depict Phalanthus and his companions.[206] Furthermore, fragments of a votive plaque from Penteskouphia seem to depict him en route to Italy. These fragments, which date from the sixth century and are dedicated to Poseidon, show a man at the stern of a ship that has spears stacked on it and hoplite shields hanging from its side. Visible are the back of a man's head, with hair apparently flowing down to his shoulders, and the letters -ανθος (possibly preceded by a lambda) written boustrophedon above him. One or two men are on the prow. The scene is probably Phalanthus guiding the Partheniai to Tarentum with their weapons of war.[207] Pausanias (10.10.6) reported that when they arrived in Italy, they defeated the natives in battle and captured the place, so we must expect them to be warriors.[208]

Apollo and the Dolphin

This city-founding dolphin-rider leads us not just to Italy but to the realm of Apollo. Although one might think of Apollo as the god of Delphi and of oracles, his purview also included music, archery, and medicine, all of which associate him with higher civilization. Apollo was also, as described above, the patron god of city-founders.[209] Typically, colonists would consult the oracle of Apollo before embarking on their journey. By the sixth century A.D. Stephanus of Byzantium could write that the name "Apollonia" belonged to twenty-five cities.[210]

This function is consistent with Apollo's role in myth as a "coming" god, characteristically arriving from a visit to the Hyperboreans and thus representing the transition from nature to the world of human culture. Apollo, suggested Versnel, controlled the division between the inner region of order and the outer region of wildness.[211] His role as a guide for colonists followed logically from this. Colonization, because it necessarily entails the creation of a city in a barbaric place, is an act of transformation between the worlds of nature and culture.

Apollo's role as a civilizing force corresponds to many of the functions of dolphins, and his status as a transitional god complements the dolphins' path to a new beginning.[212] Foundation myths, for example, connect Apollo and Delphi with the dolphin. We noted above that Icadius, who was shipwrecked, was saved by a dolphin and went on to found a temple at Delphi. In the *Homeric Hymn to Apollo* the god took the form of a dolphin and guided Cretans on a journey that led to the foundation of Delphi itself.[213] The cult name "Delphinius" would seem to be derived from *delphis*, the Greek word for dolphin, but the etymology is more suggestive than conclusive, for dolphins play no other role in the cult of Apollo Delphinius.[214]

The cult of Apollo Delphinius may be relevant for the dolphin-riders in another way. Apollo Delphinius, who oversaw citizenship oaths, has been seen as a patron of ephebes. From the earliest times, Apollo was depicted as unbearded and youthful, almost an ephebe himself. Just as his twin sister, Artemis, was responsible for the initiation of young girls, Apollo, in the form of Apollo Lykeios, was associated with a tribal group of young men, a "Männerbund."[215] As an example of this, Graf adduces the Aeginetan contest held for Apollo at the Hydrophoria, said to have been established at the landing of the Argonauts.[216] The landfall after a sea journey concludes a period of isolation.[217] The Athenian festival of the Hydrophoria offers a parallel to the Aeginetan festival in that it was said to have originated at the end of the flood of Deucalion, another period of isolation and the beginning of a lasting new order.[218]

A journey by dolphin, itself a creature ambiguously set on the zoological divide between fish and mammal, and a social intermediary between the human world and the animal world, is an appropriate vehicle for (a) representing the transition from the savage or natural world to the human world and (b) returning young men from a marginal period. Achilles' education at the hands of another taxonomically anomalous creature, the centaur Cheiron, himself a subject of later comedy, is comparable.[219] On the model of the Männerbund associated with Apollo Lykeios, Graf raised the possibility of a "Delphinbund" (dolphin-band), related to Apollo Delphinius and analogous to the wolf-band.[220] Could the dolphin-riders depicted on the vases constitute a kind of "Delphinbund"? If so, we can think of the dolphin-riders as a group that has just left ephebic status and arrived at manhood. Apollo has guided these *oikistai* who, having been expelled from Sparta, would found a new society, just as he would guide ephebes who had been expelled and would be reintegrated into society after a liminal period.[221] Such a status might be reinforced by the fact that some wear the *chlamys*, a garment of, among others, ephebes.[222]

Although Phalanthus, like most young men of "ephebic" status, was often shown on coins as a young man, on at least four of the seven vases the riders were bearded men. Depicting these dolphin-riders as bearded men would be a conscious decision, not simply a product of the iconographical tradition of the cavalcade, in which cavalrymen were shown as youthful. Yet the suggestion that they are ephebes can be reconciled with the visual evidence if one imagines that the painters (and perhaps the original performance) portrayed the re-entry of the ephebes, now become adult citizens, into their new society: they are armed for war. After all, notes Jameson, Apollo was a "god of the initiated, not of the initiants."[223] Similarly, Versnel observed that a man depicted as being bearded can be an ephebe who, having completed his transition, is just now re-entering society as an adult citizen.[224] Of course this opens the door to anointing any bearded male an "ephebe," but in the case of Phalanthus, where the early iconographical tradition seems to be either inherently ambiguous or in the process of evolution in the late sixth and early fifth centuries – showing him either bearded or unbearded – we might make allowances.[225]

Whether ephebes or not, perhaps it is transition enough that Phalanthus and his companions leave their native land, cross the sea under the tutelage of the dolphins and Apollo, and found Tarentum. It is uncertain how a band of dolphin-riders whose patron is Apollo would appear in a pre-comic performance, but there were comedies featuring Cheiron, animals as guides for *oikistai* (as in Aristophanes' *Birds*), and animals accompanying characters crossing water (Aristophanes' *Frogs*). Thus a thread connects Apollo, dolphins, transitions, and *oikistai*. The meaning of these dolphin-rider vases resides in this tapestry.

Symposium

Whether the performance we are shown occurred as a masquerade at a symposium or *komos* is impossible to say, but it is clear that dolphins, the sea, ships, wine, and the symposium were intertwined with one another in ancient Greece.[226] We have already noted the association of Dionysus and dolphins. Symposiasts cast themselves as "sailors of the symposium and rowers of the cup," as the fifth-century B.C. poet Dionysius Chalkous wrote (fr. 5 West). Cups could be conceived of as ships and were even molded in the shape of ships; guests at a symposium could think of themselves as a ship's crew; and nautical themes were painted on the interior of drinking vessels. On a red-figure cup in the Louvre of ca. 500 B.C., satyrs ride through the sea on casks of wine.[227] Likewise Oltos' dolphin-riders were contrived to give the illusion of riding on the waves of wine. Theatricality was subordinated on that vase to the demands of sympotic illusion.

The psykter, it should be remarked, was a rare type of vase that seems to have been developed only ca. 530 B.C. and disappeared after ca. 460 B.C. It was a luxury item created at the high-water mark of the aristocratic symposium culture at Athens, when the tyranny gave way to democracy and when red-figure painting was introduced.[228] The dolphin-rider may have been a self-projection of upper-class Athenian symposiasts. "The circle of drinking guests, citizen soldiers of Athens, is met by its own image," suggests Lissarrague; "The community of men reasserts itself again and again by means of two collective actions, the symposion and warfare."[229] These riders thus express the solidarity of the fellow citizen-symposiasts.[230]

THE OSTRICH-RIDERS

On the reverse side of the Boston dolphin-rider skyphos (490–480 B.C.) are six riders mounted on ostriches (Plate VII). They ride to the right clad in cloaks with stripes or folds and circles;[231] on their heads they wear wreaths or helmets without crests. They hold spears (or possibly long sticks). The third rider from the right is shorter by a head than the others and was probably meant to be youthful, but even his taller companions seem to be beardless. The leading ostrich opens his mouth as if crying out. Facing the riders, on the right, are a bearded *aulos*-player and, standing before the player, a very short bearded figure who has either horns like a goat's[232] or hair combed high on his forehead.[233] He raises an arm under his cloak and looks up at the ostrich-riders.

The short bearded figure has been described as a "dancing dwarf" reminiscent of the sons of Carcinus at the end of Aristophanes' *Wasps*[234] and as a "Pan."[235] Sifakis suggests he is a pygmy.[236] At least he is our one hint that the performances at this date were not entirely choral.[237]

Ostriches in Greece

Ostriches were rarely mentioned in literary sources from the classical period.[238] Like cocks, ostriches seem not to have had any mythical role or religious function.[239] Their chief attribute in folklore was that they were exotic. Eubulus (fr. 114 K–A) implies that captured ostriches were held in Athens. Aristotle considered ostriches "dualizers" in that they were feathered, had wings and were two-footed, but, like tetrapods, were large, had eyelashes and cloven hooves, and did not fly.[240] Their meat was forbidden to Jews,[241] and although there is no hint that eating it was taboo for Greeks and Romans, there is little indication that Greeks or Romans ever did so. The few descriptions we have of human beings riding ostriches tend to be extravagant and derive from the Ptolemaic court: according to Athenaeus, eight teams of ostriches were harnessed in a procession for Ptolemy Philadelphus.[242] We have a single anecdote of Oppian (ca. A.D. 200) about an ostrich that carried a boy on its back.[243] There are depictions of Amor riding ostriches.[244] Ostriches seem not to have been especially social animals; reports of their unkindness to their children appear in Job 39.16 and Lamentations 4.3, but Aelian (NA 14.7) wrote that an ostrich feels great maternal affection. Thus, there is very little that we can say about the cultural significance of ostriches themselves or the ostrich-riders depicted on the Boston vase.

In view of the apparent lack of any role for the ostrich in classical Greek religion or myth, it is difficult to see how the *komos* or performance depicted here could have any connection to an Attic festival or ritual; in other words, it is possible that this vase, which has dolphin-riders on the other side, marks a stage at which a performance of a comedy was uncoupled from the *komos*, and offers a forceful reminder that myth and cult will not always help us interpret a performance. The vase is dated to 490–80 B.C., the point where we are more likely to be viewing comedy than pre-comedy, though we have no way of knowing what sort of a comedy would involve an ostrich chorus. Surely it is difficult to imagine that a procession of ostrich-riders would be a serious subject suitable for dithyramb, as has been suggested of the dolphin-riders. In this instance we even need to consider the possibility that the painter, out of sheer silliness, is parodying the reverse side of his own vase.

An alternative view is that there may have been a semi-chorus of dolphin-riders appearing in a comedy with a semi-chorus of ostrich-riders.[245] If there is a relationship between the two sides of the skyphos, what might its meaning be? Humor, of course;[246] but the juxtaposition could be silly for a specific reason. These two animals, in the context of one another, might have made sense to an audience in that both are dualizers, occupying ambiguous positions in Greek taxonomy. Because the one shares features of sea and land animals while

the other shares features of land animals and birds, they complement one another. Other oppositions may be at work as well: dolphins were surely familiar to many Greeks, whereas ostriches would
have been highly exotic; dolphins are relatively social, ostriches not.
The fact that both ostriches and dolphins are ridden reminds us that
they can be subordinated and harnessed, yet neither is a conventional
domesticated animal. Thus the two sides of the vase, or of the performance, would have spanned the ambiguities of the human/animal
boundary.

CONCLUSIONS

Although much about these images was surely Dionysiac and komastic,
it would require a lack of curiosity to leave matters at that. I have
come to regard these performances as the products of disparate sources.
Comedy, after all, had a history of appropriating other forms for itself
and putting them to her own use.

Animal Categories

We noted above that Aristotle recognized taxonomical differences
among various animal species and that the Greeks were aware of "dualizers." Animals were also grouped according to their social behavior:
some naturally congregate in flocks or herds, while others tend to live
and act in isolation (a matter we return to in Chapter 4). One can
categorize animals by the degree of their distance from human beings,
which in turn often corresponds to whether or not they are considered
edible. A typical gradation might be: (i) pets living in the house, such
as the cat and dog, which are usually not eaten; (ii) tame livestock, such
as pigs, sheep, chickens or oxen, which can be eaten; (iii) wild animals
of the forest, such as deer or hare, which are also edible; (iv) powerful
and dangerous forest animals, such as lion or tiger, which are often
considered inedible. Thus, edible animals are intermediate. Moreover,
in many cultures the eating of animals is described with euphemisms
and subject to taboo. Cultural norms dictate the treatment of animals.
In China, to take a famous example, the dog has been edible since at
least 800 B.C.; as late as 1983 – dog-keeping being seen as a bourgeois

affectation – dogs in Beijing were purged and beaten to death in front of their owners.[247]

Not surprisingly, animals that fit the categories imperfectly, like Aristotle's dualizers, attract the greatest attention of contemporary anthropologists. Leach found that categories of animals could be correlated to types of verbal abuse.[248] Tambiah, in a study of Thai villagers, showed that animal categories corresponded in symbolic fashion to household arrangements and marriage customs.[249]

One need not accept these categories as universally valid to see that they are useful as heuristic, descriptive tools. I would suggest slightly different emphases for archaic and classical Greece. The division between domesticated and wild is surely appropriate, although any given animal might not fall into the same category in different cultures. Specific Greek cults had prohibitions, but there were no universal food taboos in Greece (save perhaps human flesh), and a list given in the Hippocratic corpus of foods that can be eaten includes cattle, goats, pigs, sheep, donkeys, horses, dogs, wild boar, deer, hares, foxes, and hedgehogs.[250] Not that all of these would be equally desirable: the Sausage-seller in Aristophanes' *Knights* describes how his successor will be mixing dogs' with asses' meat (1399). That piece of sausage may have been unappetizing, but not ritually unclean. The animals most likely to be eaten in Greece were domesticated livestock, which were killed in a sacrificial ritual. Some animals of course were particularly "sacred" to certain gods.

The animals adopted by dancers in the performances or *komoi* studied here were the horse, bull, cock, dolphin, and ostrich. The ostrich is unique and exotic, for reasons discussed above, but we may note some similarities among the others. The bull and cock were domesticated animals, neither was hunted, and both could be sacrificed and eaten.[251] The dolphin, not being livestock, was rarely eaten, but could be thought of as a surrogate horse; after all, the dolphin was famous for letting human beings ride on it, and the dolphin-riders resembled cavalry. For that matter, the ostrich was also treated this way. Thus three of the chorus animals were subordinated to human beings. Although dolphins tended to frolic together, none of the rest is a particularly social animal. Left to their own devices, they stay by themselves, not in easily tended flocks.

Sacred Animals?

There is no clear pattern in these *komoi* of the use of sacred animals. When Dionysus was accompanied, it was frequently by animals such as panthers, leopards, or a phallic donkey.[252] The bull was associated with Dionysus, but not exclusively. One might have expected Artemis, the "Mistress of Animals," to be linked with animal *komoi* at Athens, but the animals under her care were wild and the young "Bears" of Brauron were evidently not costumed as bears at all.

Poseidon's association with the horse, bull, and dolphin is notable, but no evidence attests to a festival of Poseidon in Athens with a ritual *komos* that required masquerades, perhaps similar to the "Tauroi" of Ephesus. There may be a hint of interest in Theseus, whose popularity was rising in Athens at this time.[253] Also significant is the possible role of Apollo as a patron of colonists, who may be pertinent to river gods and dolphins. Dolphins and cocks were associated with leading the souls of the dead to the next world – a highly transitional activity – but evidence for these activities tends to come from a period later than our vases. The current state of the evidence is suggestive only.[254]

Hybrids

Of course the creatures that appeared on the vases were not simply bulls, horses, or cocks, but hybrids. The bull-headed dancers are both bull and human being; the Berlin cocks flaunt satyr-like noses; one of the two London birds may have a phallos and neither makes any attempt to disguise his face and beard;[255] the Getty Birds seem to be cocks with satyr-waists; dolphins and ostriches, being dualizers, are hybrids even in their natural state. To complicate matters further, dolphins were thought to resemble satyrs because of their snub-noses. The horses on the Berlin vase are perhaps a better instance of a serious attempt by men to disguise themselves, but they fall so short of creating the illusion that one scholar took them for centaurs.[256] This willingness to blur the boundaries of animal species sets a precedent for Old Comedy, which eschewed the realism of tragedy. Several comedies even had choruses composed of satyrs, the most familiar hybrid.

Although fabulous beasts and hybrid creatures had been introduced into Greek art during the orientalizing period, they were especially popular in sixth-century art even apart from the dancers already studied: representations of the cock-horse (Hippalektryon), as well as panther-cocks and boar-cocks, are examples. Perhaps significantly, these exotic creatures all existed for the use of human beings, for by the middle of the sixth century they were ridden by youths who acquire "some of the trappings of the Athenian Hippeis, sometimes carrying spears, at other times wearing a Thracian cloak or a petasos."[257]

Ephebes

Several of the vases may be connected with the *ephebeia*. The youthful Hippeis riding older men dressed as horses may have been young men of ephebic status, though, as the debate concerning the young riders on the Parthenon frieze illustrates, this identification is more speculative than conclusive. The reverse side of the Getty vase depicted a young man receiving his arms, which many would agree shows an important transition in a young man's life; whether there is a message here for the cocks on the other side is, while beyond proof, at least a plausible notion. Some of the dolphin-riders in the choruses may have been youthful (certainly many of the dolphin-riders in folklore were young), and an association with Apollo would be appropriate. If the vases show the journey of Phalanthus and the Partheniai from Sparta to Italy, the symbolic and literal nearly correspond. Did these animal costumes originate in marginal periods of people's lives? If so, these choruses would act as a counterpart to Winkler's tragic chorus of ephebes.

City Foundations and the Western Greeks

If the bull-headed men were meant to be river-gods, the colonies of Magna Graecia and Sicily offered the best sources for them. If the conjecture that the dolphin-riders were Phalanthus and the Partheniai is correct, then they are headed for Tarentum. The helmet decorations worn by the Berlin Knights may resemble the crests of helmets from Italy. We can only speculate as to why *komoi* and choruses in Attica in the late sixth century, and vase-painters in their wake, would turn to myths and legends pertaining to Dorian settlements in the West, but we noted in Chapter I that poems about foundations and colonizations may have been sung at symposia. These stories may have made entertaining choruses and Athenians were willing to exploit them. In any case, the trend was not without parallel; Aeschylus' *Aetnaeae* was composed, in the 470s, in honor of the foundation of the Sicilian city of Etna.[258] Many dolphin-riders were involved with the establishment of some cultural or religious institution, and a theme on that topic may have been intended. There was, of course, the tradition that comedy was a Dorian invention, but it has been assumed that this pertained primarily to actors and had little if anything to do with choruses. An Attic choral interest in the Dorian West might suggest that the influence was broader.

Tyranny and Democracy

The period in which these animal choruses first seem to have arisen (ca. 560–540 B.C.) coincided with the tyranny of Peisistratus, and it is possible that he had encouraged a festival at which dancers wore costumes of animals and hybrids. As a Neleid, Peisistratus may have wished to promote interest in the cult of Poseidon, and the Hippeis, river-gods, and dolphin-riders were all connected with that god as well. Then again, aside from the Berlin Knights, no vase is demonstrably from before 510 B.C. Could the interest in animals have been triggered somehow by the emergence of the democracy, established in 508–507 B.C.? It is often supposed that Theseus was the hero of the new democracy, since there seems to be a special interest in him around the last decade of the sixth century.[259] It is conceivable that the bull-headed men were the Minotaurs of his exploit and the dolphin-riders were Theseus with otherwise unattested companions. Moreover, many dolphin-riders are from 490–480 B.C., the decade of the Persian Wars; could the popular dolphin-riders be related to the naval victory at Salamis?[260] A specific connection would require circular argumentation. Perhaps the vogue for these dancers stemmed from an audience that was taken with all of the themes mentioned above.

Symposium and Komos

The democracy may have been responsible for these masquerades in a less direct way. The vases under consideration — all from ca. 510 to ca. 480 B.C., except for the Knights — coincide precisely with epoch-making events in Athenian political and cultural history: the shift of power from the aristocracy to the *demos* and the dramatic victories of the Greeks over the Persians. The cessation of animal vases corresponds closely with the introduction of comedy into the Dionysia, in 486 B.C.[261] It was in just these years that the privileges of the elite must have faced challenges from other socioeconomic groups. The social and political pressures of the day have been cited to explain contemporary changes in symposium practice, such as the diminution of pederastic themes beginning in the fifth century. Challenged by the new climate, as other institutions were democratized, the symposium became a refuge in which the *kaloi kagathoi* were able to express their identity as a select group. Neer sees vase-paintings of the time as representing the role-playing, especially the practice of wearing Lydian hats, that was characteristic of the sympotic milieu. "By and large, vase-painting comes out squarely on the side of the Panhellenic aristocracy."[262]

This, I suggest, is the context of animal masquerades. We saw in the last chapter that some entertainments might have been performed by the padded dancer *akletoi*, the "uninvited," who parasitically sought a meal; the chitons worn by the "horses" of the Berlin vase were those of the padded dancers, and padded dancers in turn performed in the presence of reclining symposiasts. Although one hears of professional musicians and dancers, songs and dances could also be performed by elite symposiasts themselves, of whom the best-known example was Hippocleides. Misrule was thus institutionalized: symposiasts enjoyed a vogue of wearing foreign-looking head-gear, and as noted in Chapter I in later generations aristocratic drinking clubs called themselves "Triballoi," affecting an exotic identity. That the symposium was an institution open to upper-class Greeks from other cities would account for the transmission of cultural customs from one city to another in a period when the dramatic genres were crystallizing and when artists were attracted to Athens by its festivals.

78

Thus the themes evoked by our vases coalesce around the archaic symposium class: Equestrianship, for instance, was an elite endeavor. Straddling dolphins was iconographically similar, especially because the dolphin-riders were linked with Dionysus, wine, and the symposium. The use of the psykter was limited to this period, and the fact that dolphin-riders should appear on one is probably not a coincidence. Just as the symposium was a venue for male bonding and the education of young men, so too the horse-riders and dolphin-riders may have signified the transition to adulthood. The values of aggression and courage that cocks embodied would also have been imparted.

The spectacles as recorded look more like rehearsed, organized performances than the drunken *komoi* often depicted on vases. Of course it is not impossible that these animal masquerades derived from cultic worship of rural fertility divinities, in which men either drew on the powers of animal nature by wearing theriomorphic costumes or, in a carnivalesque spirit, used the disguises to mock authority (one thinks here of Susarion's peasants),[263] yet a role for Dionysus must remain indirect and Apollo and Poseidon, gods who are at least as relevant, are hardly agricultural. Cultic or religious resonances can not be excluded from these scenes – in fact I have tried to show what they might be – but we would do better to consider the *social* dynamics of these masquerades. If I am right that they emerged from the world of the symposium, then they were not expressions of popular culture (ot at least not directly) but of elite group solidarity.[264] The *akletoi* were surely present to be laughed at, yet the fact that elite youths wore animal costumes may have yoked together entertainment and something more serious: social acceptance. Animal costumes could facilitate such a transformation.[265]

The disappearance of the animal masquerades from vase-painting around 480 B.C. may be due to the institutionalization of the comic chorus in 486 B.C. – the coincidence is difficult to overlook – but the exact process behind it remains hidden from view. It seems reasonable to suggest that the *demos* appropriated comedy for itself and used it to make carnival attacks on the wealthy and powerful in the early democracy.[266] Once institutionalized as a democratic practice, performances of animal disguises may have ceased; vase-painters, at least, lost interest. Having left the symposium culture for the theater, the animal costumes no longer drew the painters' attention. There were many other types of choruses available to comic playwrights. Chapter 4 will show that the only literary evidence for an animal chorus before ca. 440 B.C. is that of Magnes, so the practice either continued unrecorded on vases or was neglected altogether, only to resurface fifty years later. But that is a story for subsequent chapters.

3

ANIMALS AND SATYRS IN CLASSICAL GREECE: AN EXCURSUS

Before turning our attention to Aristophanic comedy and the surviving fragments, we need to examine the new attitudes toward animals that were emerging in the fifth century. We will see that, in contrast with animals in genres such as tragedy, epic, and historiography, the animals of comedy were less hostile to human beings, though more vulnerable to exploitation. This unthreatening view of animals made comedy a more hospitable place for anthropomorphism, a phenomenon that was itself facilitated by sophistic ideas of the fifth century and disseminated in new adaptations of familiar myths. Although these new conceptions marked a discontinuity between the worlds of the sixth-century vase-paintings and of fifth-century comedy, other features, particularly the fact that animals are shown to be part both of culture and of nature, suggest a continuous tradition. Moreover, the paradigm of the satyr, who straddled the boundary of civilization and nature, continues to offer a parallel to themes of comedy.

Except for the exotic ostrich, the Greeks were familiar with the animals discussed in the last chapter. Horses and dolphins are swift, capable creatures that can be harnessed and tamed; even cocks and bulls (if I am right that they represent river gods), although potentially dangerous, have powers that can be turned to human use. All, save probably the cock, played a part in the cults of certain gods, notably Poseidon and Dionysus. None was a wild predator, but neither were any used as pets. To dress up like one of these animals and enlist its powers would work to human advantage. By contrast, the species of animals that appear in comedy of the late fifth century are different and presuppose an alternative approach to the animal world. As we will see, several of them are "social" animals, neither harnessed nor invoked for presumed natural or cultic powers but serving as parallels to human society. This exceeds simple anthropomorphization, and vase-paintings (which, incidentally, are virtually useless for tracing the history of comedy in the fifth century) cannot fully express it.

NATURE, CULTURE, AND ANIMALS IN CLASSICAL GREECE

Greek ideas, like our own, were shot through with contradictions and paradoxes. There was no single "Greek" view of the animal world, but their heterogeneous ideas need to be delineated and analyzed.

Animal Savagery

Aristophanes and other comic playwrights, viewing animals as essentially benevolent or at least easily controllable, selected animal species that fit their bias. In other authors and genres, however, animals were seen as more volatile and naturally prone to savagery. A look at some examples from epic, tragedy, and historiography confirms this pattern.

The pets, insects, birds, fish, herds, and predators who inhabit the similes of the *Iliad* bear striking resemblances to human beings – otherwise the similes would be pointless – and are capable of beauty, courage, and intelligence. Nevertheless, these similes have been contrived for a specific reason: to illustrate the violence of warfare. The most frequent subject of Iliadic similes is the marauding lion, which preys on herds of livestock.[1] This choice is understandable in an epic about war, but the reader is also aware that there is a level of social behavior that lions are incapable of attaining. The world of nature is essentially adversarial. "The hostility between man and beast is part of a larger theme setting nature against people."[2]

This dark view of the animal world found its way into fifth-century tragedy. The *Oresteia* mobilizes dangerous animals, such as eagles, lions, snakes, and vultures, and pits them against their prey, such as the innocent young of the hare, prey of eagles (*Agam.* 109–15). As Heath has noted, when Aeschylus conflates animal and human, it is to the disadvantage of the latter: the pervasive imagery in the *Oresteia* casts human

82

beings as creatures defined by instinctual, predatory impulses. Only at the end of the trilogy, where with the help of Athena the spheres of human and animal are separated, do domesticated field animals contribute productively. In this Aeschylean world "culture, not nature, provides our salvation."[3]

Nature poses a threat in Euripides' *Bacchae*, as a simple tabulation can show: whether in simile or analogy, animals are mentioned seventy-one times, of which the largest category entails predatory violence. The animals most often cited are snakes (fourteen times), lions (eight times), bulls (seven times), and hunting dogs (four times); frequent too is the appearance of θήρ ("wild beast," fifteen times). When non-predatory animals appear, such as when women are compared to doves (*Bacchae* 1090) or a swan (1365), they are vulnerable. The benefits of nature are not entirely absent – one could point to the nectar of the bee (142–43) – but these benefits sit forlornly in a harsher world. In the climax of the play Pentheus is violently dismembered when he is mistaken for a lion (1142).

The *Oresteia* and *Bacchae* are extreme examples,[4] but the patterns tend to reappear in other tragedies as well. Animals play a much smaller role in Euripides' *Hecuba*, for example, but it famously ends with the transformation of Hecuba into a dog. The five other animals mentioned are used as metaphors or analogies for characters in the play, all either hunters or hunted.[5] Apparently animal qualities have entered into the human genetic stream. The *Ion*, surely one of the least violent of all Greek tragedies, never directly compares any human character to an animal, instead using animals in more diffuse ways (e.g., birds that sing and are agents of the gods, gods taking animal shapes, animal ornaments), yet nearly one third of the thirty-one instances, the largest single category, involve predator, prey, or sacrificial victim.

Herodotus' canvas, being much broader than that of tragedy, shows animals in a variety of contexts, but the trend is similar. Smith identified 111 different animal terms in the *Histories*, used for a total of 804 instances,[6] and called attention to anecdotes in Herodotus in which animals show strong emotional reactions in ways disturbingly parallel to human behavior: male Egyptian cats kill their children out of desire for the female (2.66–1–3) and the female flying snake of Arabia kills her mate but is killed by her child in revenge (3.109.1–2).[7] Animals thus exhibit the fierce family attachments found in human beings, and are to that extent anthropomorphized. Paradoxically the violence is beast-like when performed by human beings: Orestes, famously, was likened to a snake in the *Choephoroe* when he killed his own mother (527–34, 549).[8] Herodotus believed that this ruthless behavior is divinely sanctioned: "It seems likely that divine providence (τοῦ θείου ἡ προνοίη), in its wisdom, has made prolific every kind of creature which is naturally timid and preyed upon, so they would not become extinct by being eaten, while troublesome and savage animals have very few children" (3.108). Hares, for example, are prolific, whereas a lioness (thought Herodotus, mistakenly) produces only one cub. The same divine providence governs human behavior, and the will of the gods is revealed to human beings through animals. This is especially common when animals are part of portents. At Herodotus 7.57–58, to cite one instance, a mare gives birth to a hare, which was understood to mean that Xerxes might lead his mighty army into Greece but would later flee for his life. Animals were thus visible intermediaries of the design of the gods.[9] That human beings should be so well informed by portents offers little comfort if animals represent forces beyond human control.

To anticipate the more benign view of animals to be proposed in Chapters 4 and 5, a look at the *Acharnians* (to take a comedy without an animal chorus) is in order. Forty-four different animal terms appear, several used repeatedly for a total of ninety-nine instances; of these, twenty-eight animals (and forty-seven of the ninety-nine instances) serve as food.[10] No mention of their being hunted, caught, or sacrificed appears; they are simply meat for consumption. In a further twenty-three instances their only role is as commodities. Other animals are pets, prizes, ornaments, or status symbols. In two instances Dicaeopolis is compared to a bird (he is figuratively "winged" at 970 and 988), but no animal analogy is made with any other major character in the play.[11] Some animals mentioned are pests, such as various insects, but in not one instance can it be said that they are dangerous or predatory. In tragedy the animal taint manifested itself violently, yet even Aristophanic figures like the wasp chorus or Peisetaerus, who "becomes" a bird, are less savage than are characters in tragedy, who are merely compared with animals.[12] This is not to say that Dicaeopolis and Peisetaerus are not capable of stunningly callous behavior; the point is that they feel no fundamental threat from animals and are ready to control or eat them.

Civilization as a Rejection of Animal Savagery

The similes and imagery of Homer, tragedy, and Herodotus are powerful because they reveal a dark truth: human beings can and do act like animals. Yet a more optimistic school of thought had it that human beings could rise above animal savagery. Hesiod, for all his pessimism, had observed that human beings at least do not eat one another (*Works and Days* 276–78). Later Greeks advanced this notion even farther. In the fifth century, when questions concerning nature and culture were treated in more complex and self-conscious ways, a number of writers offered accounts of the progress made by human beings in leaving behind a primitive, animal-like existence and gradually forging the institutions of society.[13] Versions of this "Theory of Progress," which begin to appear in fifth-century poets and sophists, typically included specific steps toward civilization: human beings, who were in constant danger of being eaten by beasts, had been forced to dwell in caves, live like nomads, and eat acorns and grass. Gradually they learned how to use fire, mine minerals, use metals, develop agriculture, create languages, build houses and cities, find ways to defend themselves, and coalesce into a society. More steps followed, including the establishment of religion, law, and institutions of government; finally, humanity perfected higher, non-essential cultural accomplishments such as music and literature. This account was more historically plausible and rational than the mythological alternatives that had been circulating (on which more below), and it became influential in the fifth century. The following chapters will show that this anthropological or evolutionary scheme can be detected in comedies with animal choruses, above all in Aristophanes' *Birds*.

The fifth-century intellectuals who agreed on the principle of the historical approach nevertheless disagreed about its implications for problems such as the exact relationship between nature and culture, the basis of justice, and the line between human nature and animal nature.[14] A sketch of two central questions can illustrate the issues.

1. *What is the "natural life"?* The progressivists agreed that life in the state of "nature" had been a squalid, disorganized existence that was best left behind. Nostalgia or idealization of a past Golden Age are absent. The fact that the phrase "beast-like existence" (θηριώδης βίος) recurred in fifth-century descriptions of this life suggests that there was a single source for this notion, or that there was widespread agreement about it. For example, an excerpt from the satyr-play *Sisyphus* by Critias (or perhaps Euripides) characterized the life of the earliest people as "disordered and beastlike, enslaved to force" (Critias DK 88 B25.1–2).[15] Thucydides saw the earliest people as living in complete disorganization, lacking commerce, communication, and protected cities, and suffering both civil war and attacks from pirates; agriculture was unknown, although food for day-to-day existence seems to have been available (1.2). The *Savages*, a comedy by Pherecrates, depicted the "natural" existence as squalid and primitive.[16] Pherecrates' savage society was cited in Plato's *Protagoras* as the antitype to the just society that Protagoras believed was evolving over time (327d). In the raw state of nature human beings were naked, unshod, and unarmed (321c5); instead of having fixed dwellings, they lived scattered about (σποράδην, 322b1). Many of these writers would have agreed that human government did not exist in nature (φύσις) but was an artificial convention (νόμος) created perhaps through a social contract.

2. *Was culture created by human beings or given with divine assistance?* In some accounts the earliest human beings were guided by a culture hero or assisted by the gods. In the *Prometheus Bound* (443–506) Prometheus took credit for instructing human beings in a large number of technical skills.[17] The myth as told in Plato's *Protagoras* (320d3–323a2) has Prometheus give fire and technological skill (ἔντεχνος σοφία) to helpless men, but the assistance of the gods is later needed to ensure a measure of safety and political tranquillity.

But other fifth-century accounts of the rise of civilization suggest that human beings were able to create civilized life without assistance. Another fragment of Critias (DK 88 B2) credits specific peoples with technological inventions: the Phoenicians invented writing, Carians the merchandise ship, and Marathonians the potter's wheel. The chorus in Sophocles' *Antigone* (333–75) credits human beings with many collective qualities and accomplishments, omitting any higher force or assistance. Similarly in Thucydides' "Archaeology" (esp. 1.2–15) the evolution of political units occurred in response to the stimuli of the circumstances at the time and thus owes nothing to divine or heroic intervention. None of the fragments of Democritus indicates that his version of civilization included divine direction; in fact his accounts cling to a causal sequence, with one step allowing for the next.[18] Some, like Anaxagoras, accounted for human advances by pointing to unique endowments, such as the use of the hand, which makes a human being the wisest of all creatures (DK 46 A102).

The picture that emerges from a review of these two questions is one of contentious debate about human society and its origins. At least all agreed that animals were inferior to human beings and needed to be conquered, not emulated. It was, however, also possible to take an entirely different approach – fifth-century intellectuals being quite willing to problematize any orthodoxy – and assert a fundamental similarity of animals and human beings.

Human-Animal Kinship

The notion of kinship between the two did not, of course, originate in the fifth-century; it was a precondition for the simile in Homer. Although benevolent animals were in the minority in Homer, their voices could be heard. In the *Iliad*, for example, Achilles' horses grieve for Patroclus (17.426–40, 23.279) and can even speak prophecies (19.399–423, 23.276). Odysseus' dog Argus famously recognizes his master on his return to Ithaca (*Odyssey* 17.301).

Also dependent on the notion of kinship was the state of harmony among living creatures that was imagined to have occurred in the Golden Age. The earliest version of this in Greek literature is Hesiod's Myth of the Ages (*Works and Days* 106–201), wherein the human condition gradually declines through a succession of "races" or "generations" (γένη), which are (save one) named for metals: gold, silver, bronze, a heroic age, and iron.[19] The ideal existence of the golden race, in the "Age of Cronus," was a peaceful one, when mortals lived in harmony with the gods and food came forth automatically (αὐτομάτη), without need for work. Thereafter, however, human beings were afflicted with increasingly oppressive ills.[20] This conception of history as a degenerative process obviously runs counter to the "Theory of Progress." Some fifth-century comic poets fantasized about a return of the Golden Age and brought earlier generations of politicians back to life in the hope of recovering long-lost civic stability. In the *Cheirones* of Cratinus of 425 B.C., Solon returns to offer guidance to the present (fr. 246 K-A), and in the *Demes* of Eupolis of ca. 412 B.C. Solon returns with Miltiades, Aristides, and Pericles (cf. frr. 102, 104 K-A).[21]

An amusing premise of animal choruses can be found in the notion that there was an original state of nature in which animals and human beings could speak the same language and live together harmoniously.[22] "It was a time when birds and fish and quadrupeds conversed, just like the mud-pies of Prometheus," wrote Callimachus.[23] Although this conceit has the feel of a primitive myth, evidence for it does not appear before the fifth century – Empedocles, ca. 492–432 B.C., being the earliest source – and it may be the product of fifth-century speculation about nature and culture.

Regrettably (for animals), these warm feelings of kinship were not enough to override the ugly reality that the Golden Age was long past and that both animals and people had become carnivores. Some even saw virtues in this fallen state: the comic poet Athenio claimed that cooking and flavoring meat released human beings from an animal-like existence (*Samothracians*, fr. 1 K-A). Of course in Greece, as in many cultures, the act of killing an animal for sustenance was viewed with a degree of ambivalence,[24] though by performing it as a ritual act of sacrifice the violence can be ameliorated and the ingestion of animals could thus be made acceptable or even civilized.

A peaceable kingdom for human beings and animals logically requires a vegetarian diet. Hesiod appears not to have thought of men as meat-eaters, but by the early fifth century the doctrine of vegetarianism was associated especially with Pythagoras.[25] Our earliest evidence for Pythagoras' position is Xenophanes' statement that Pythagoras recognized the voice of a friend in a dog (DK 21 B7). This may tell us more about Pythagoras' concern for his friends than about any feeling of kinship with animals per se, but it marked a significant point of reference in ancient thought about animals.[26]

Social Animals and Anthropomorphism

It was hard not to conceive of animals as living in their own societies, exhibiting organized political behavior resembling that of human beings. They built dwellings, lived in groups beyond their immediate family, and appeared to have social hierarchies. This is an aspect of the animal world that is evident even to casual observers, but fifth-century Greeks began to define and elaborate on it. Democritus observed, "All creatures associate with their kind: pigeons with pigeons, cranes with cranes, and so on" (DK 68 B164).[27] He implied that there was even a continuity between human beings and animals: "We learn from the animals in the most important things: in spinning and mending we imitate the spider; in building we imitate the swallow; and we imitate the songsters, the swan and nightingale, in singing" (DK 68 B154), though of course the exact technical skills needed by human beings and animals may differ.[28] The chorus in Sophocles' *Electra* noted that birds wisely care for their parents, who in turn nourished them (1058–62). This view was voiced more explicitly in the next century. Xenophon saw bees as a model for an orderly if hierarchical society: the queen bee presided over the little ones, who obeyed her; she apportioned work to them and once grown the offspring were sent forth to found a colony.[29]

It was not obvious that all animals were inferior. Plato, describing the kinds of bodies that certain souls will inhabit when they return to the world for a second time, thought that a soul that cultivated gluttony, selfishness, or drunkenness was likely to assume the form of a donkey; those persons who preferred a life of irresponsible lawlessness and violence would become wolves or hawks or kites; but the happiest, who cultivated self-control and integrity (σοφροσύνη τε καὶ δικαιοσύνη), would "pass into some other kind of social and disciplined creature like bees, wasps and ants (πολιτικὸν καὶ ἥμερον γένος, ἤ που μελιττῶν ἢ σφηκῶν ἢ μυρμήκων), or even back into the human race, becoming decent citizens" (*Phaedo* 82b). Aristotle echoes this when he divides animals according to whether or not they

89

are "social animals" (πολιτικά, "meant to live in a *polis*"; the phrase is also used of human beings at *Politics* 1253a3):

> The social animals (πολιτικά) are those which all have some one common activity; and this is not the case of all the gregarious animals (ἀγελαῖα). Examples of social animals include: the human being, bee, wasp, ant and crane. Some of these live under a ruler while others have no ruler; for example, the crane and bee live under a ruler, but ants and a very large number of others do not. (*HA* 488a8–13)

Aristotle distinguishes these from tame or domesticated animals, such as horses, oxen, swine, sheep, goats, and dogs, and from the ferocious and wicked animals, such as boars, serpents, wolves, and foxes.

Perhaps the most radical approach was that taken by the Cynics. Diogenes (ca. 400–325 B.C.) rejected the validity of any city or country on the grounds that it was artificial.[30] He insisted on the superiority of animals and felt that Prometheus' introduction of civilized life was disastrous for humanity.[31] Plutarch's *Gryllus* reaches the logical conclusion to this Cynic line of thought when one of Odysseus' crewmen, who had been turned into a pig by Circe, explains that animals were happier, more courageous, and more naturally skilled than men, and refused to be turned back into his human form.[32] In short, animals were more civilized and human than human beings.

A parallel trend of anthropomorphization can be detected in fifth-century art. The monsters and hybrids that were popular in art of the sixth century gradually disappeared in the fifth century. In their place arose a trend toward naturalism and anthropomorphization: "the tendency is to expunge the monstrous and exotic."[33] The hippalektryon, for example, vanished from art after 480 B.C. As the century progressed river gods were portrayed in an increasingly human way, with their bull features reduced to a pair of horns growing out of the forehead of an otherwise normal human being.[34] The practicalities of stage costuming may have contributed to the increasingly anthropomorphic depiction of creatures of mythology.[35] Io, traditionally a cow in mythology, was described in the *Prom.* as a "maiden with a cow's horns" (βούκερως πάρθενος, 588), and she first appeared that way on later fifth-century vase-painting.[36] This humanizing tendency has been observed also among satyrs and centaurs, whose faces became so indistinguishable from those of human beings that they began to be shown in family groups.[37]

The preceding survey has been selective, but a more exhaustive study would not change one essential conclusion: there was no such thing as a neutral representation of animals. A comic poet's decisions about the choice of animal species, the degree of anthropomorphism, the state of nature, and even what to eat for dinner, could carry significant implications in the context of late fifth-century debates.

HYBRID CREATURES: NATURE AND CULTURE IN THE SATYR-PLAY

No animal chorus was "pure"; in other words, all had at least some hybrid quality, combining human and animal features. A small yet significant number of comedies had choruses of part-human, part-beast creatures that were traditionally known from myth and art, including satyrs, centaurs, griffins, Cyclopes, and Cheirones.

Mythological and Hybrid Comic Choruses

Date	Playwright	Title	PCG
445–440	Ecphantides	Satyrs	V.127
437	Callias	Satyrs	IV.49
436	Cratinus	Cheirones	IV.245–57
434	Callias	Cyclopes	IV.42–45
430	Cratinus	Dionysalexandros	IV.140
425–420	Phrynichus	Satyrs	VII.414–16
424	Cratinus	Satyrs	IV.232
414–385?	Plato comicus	Griffins	VII.438–39
410–370s?	Nicophon	Sirens	VII.70–71
410–370's?	Theopompus	Sirens	VII.732–33
late 5th century	Apollophanes	Centaurs	II.520
4th century	Ophelio	Satyrs	VII.97
4th century	Timocles	Ikarian Satyrs	VII.766–69
4th century	Timocles	Demosatyroi	VII.757–58

Although several of these comedies are discussed in the following pages, because the surviving fragments for most cast only a dim light on animal-human concerns, I have not included fragments or testimonia for them in Appendix A.[38] Information abounds, however, for the allied genre of the satyr-play, which offers a counterpart for the study of animal choruses.[39]

Chapter 2 offered evidence that vase-paintings of *komoi* or performances allowed for some overlap between the "comic" and the "satyric"; the Getty Birds, for instance, wear the breeches of satyr costumes and several comedies had choruses of satyrs. Conversely, a large number of satyr-plays dealt with mythological subjects that also appeared in comedy. These formal similarities correspond to a more substantive convergence: both animal choruses and satyr-plays, by putting non-human or semi-human creatures on stage, encouraged their audiences to reexamine the relationship between animals and human beings and to reconsider what institutions are exclusively human in origin. Specifically, satyr-plays tended to cast satyrs as participants in human cultural advances and were "a means to explore human culture through a fun-house of mirrors."[40] Chapters 4 and 5 will present the case that something comparable is at work in animal-chorus comedies.

Nature and Civilization in Satyr-Plays

Although vase-paintings began to show satyric performances by at least 520 B.C., it was probably not until 502/501 B.C. that they were added to the tragic trilogy at the City Dionysia.[41] On one level, satyr-plays offered "comic relief" to distract the audience from the severity of tragedy.[42] According to another interpretation, satyr-plays were introduced into the City Dionysia in order to restore a religious dimension that had been waning in tragedy by the end of the sixth century.[43] If so, satyrs may have represented an older, Dionysiac form of social solidarity that was being lost as Athens became more sophisticated and urban. Writes Seaford, "In an urban culture the pre-urban *thiasos* acquires a sharper symbolic significance."[44] The rustic settings of many satyr-plays – as many as twenty-seven plays may have been set in caves, mountains, or seashores – would have reinforced this pastoral ambience.[45] In Aeschylus' *Diktyoulkoi*, for example, Silenos imagines that the baby Perseus will "take pleasure in martens and fawns and porcupines."[46] In the earlier fragments there are themes "taken up into a specifically satyric world, rustic, self-sufficient, and still very much alive," where the civilized *polis* does not impinge.[47] This may have appealed to Athenians who had been brought up in the countryside and were nostalgic for their native rustic haunts.[48] In the light of the association of satyrs with nature and the countryside, it is no wonder that in vase-painting their chief preoccupations are the "natural" ones of sex and wine.

Paradoxically, however, satyrs perform more civilized activities in art and drama. An important feature of satyr-plays and myths about satyrs was the depiction of a discovery of a culturally significant object or skill.[49] As early as Aeschylus satyrs were associated with the discovery of artefacts such as fire, wine, the *aulos*, and the lyre, or with skills such as metal-working, athletics, archery, and spelling. On vases, similarly, they were fishermen, athletes, nurses, pedagogues, trackers, shepherds, heralds, and thaumaturges.[50] Satyrs were not only present at the discovery of human tools and skills but also took an active role in using them, as shown in a range of activities itemized below, some rudimentary but others more refined. These were not necessarily indebted to sophistic theories of progress, but there is an affinity with those theories insofar as one detects a self-conscious awareness of human culture as something that advanced in discrete steps, discoveries, or inventions.

Fire

A fundamental step toward civilization was the gift of fire from Prometheus. Fragments of Aeschylus' *Prometheus Pyrkaios* (472 B.C.) show that the novelty of fire was welcomed with delight: Prometheus warns a satyr not to burn himself with fire (fr. 187a *TrGF*),[51] and satyrs celebrate Prometheus' gift (fr. 204b *TrGF*). One of the most popular themes in depictions of satyr-plays was of Prometheus holding torches, surrounded by satyrs who seem astonished at the marvel of fire.[52]

Hunting

In Sophocles' *Ichneutai* the tracking ability of satyrs was described as a kind of skill or art. Silenus asks, "What's this skill you've discovered (τίν' αὖ τέχνην σὺ τήν[δ' ἄρ' ἐξ]ηὗρες)? What's the trick, hunting while you lie like this on the ground?" (fr. 314.124 *TrGF*). Sositheos seems to have written of the invention of archery in a satyr-play.[53]

Metal-Working

In Aeschylus' *Theoroi or Isthmiastai*, satyrs are perplexed by certain
"new toys" (νεοχμὰ ἀθύρματα, fr. 78c.50 *TrGF*) made with adze and
anvil, and hesitate to use them; their interlocutor encourages them,
saying they are part of the skill (τέχνη) they have taken up (fr. 78c.56
TrGF).[54] Dionysus fears that satyrs will criticize him for not being
good at working with iron (fr. 78a.67 *TrGF*), which perhaps implies
their own dexterity with it.[55] Hephaestus, the god of iron-working,
appeared in several plays.[56] Vases show satyrs at work at the forge.[57]

Wine

As befits companions of Dionysus, satyrs were associated with the
discovery or invention of wine. Sophocles' *Dionysiskos* showed satyrs
delighting at their discovery of wine, evidently just invented by the
infant Dionysus (ηὗρον, fr. 172 *TrGF*). In fifth-century vase-painting
satyrs were shown treading on grapes.[58]

Athletics

In the fragments of Aeschylus' *Theoroi or Isthmiastai* satyrs are apparently attempting to escape from Dionysus in order to adopt the "skill"
(τέχνη, fr. 78c.56 *TrGF*) of athletics, which Dionysus frowns on as
"new ways" (τρόπους καίνουμς, fr. 78a.34 *TrGF*).[59] Seaford speculates that this reflects the satyrs' contempt for ritualistic Dionysiac
"mountain-wandering" (*oreibasia*), which they might regard as primitive, and their preference for participation in athletics, which civilizes
the satyrs.[60] Several vases depict satyrs with athletic equipment.[61]

Statues and Portraiture

In Euripides' *Eurystheus* an old man was frightened by some speaking
statues made by Daedalus.[62] The presence of Daedalus, the legendary
craftsman, may suggest that these were newly invented. In Aeschylus'
Theoroi or Isthmiastai satyrs express delight at likenesses of themselves
that could have been created by Daedalus (εἴδωλον . . . τὸ Δαιδάλου
μίμημα, fr. 78a6–7 *TrGF*); these appear to be painted and, to judge
from the emphasis on their newness, are a recent invention.[63] A vase
in Boston shows a satyr working as a sculptor.[64]

Spelling

In the *Omphale* by Achaeus (fr. 33 *TrGF*) satyrs discover reading, which had been invented by Palamedes, and the name of Dionysus. In Euripides' *Theseus*, which may have been a satyr-play, an illiterate shepherd describes the letters that spell out the name "Theseus."[65] How this was related to the satyrs of the play remains murky.

Music

Satyrs were associated with the discovery of musical instruments. On a vase in Berlin Marsyas picks up the *aulos*, which has been invented by Athena.[66] Satyrs show consternation at the *syrinx* in Sophocles' *Inachos*, which suggests that it has just been invented,[67] and in his *Ichneutai* satyrs fear but then are fascinated by the sound of the lyre, which has been created out of a tortoise shell by the infant Hermes.[68] A vase-painting in New York, on which satyrs are holding large concert citharas, is interpreted by Froning as linking satyrs with the establishment of the Panathenaea; at the very least it shows them playing at the festival in a self-conscious way.[69]

Paidotrophia

Satyrs, especially Silenus, are present and participate in the care or education of young heroes and divinities.[70] Pearson thought the centaur Cheiron, the teacher of Achilles, was a character in Sophocles' *Achilleos Erastae*, which was evidently set at Mt. Pelion (fr. 154 *TrGF*).[71]

A Compendium of Skills

In a fragment from a satyr-play by Sophocles, satyrs tell their interlocutor that they are ready to participate in an athletic contest for the hand of Oeneus' daughter: "Every worthwhile skill is embodied in us (πᾶσα δ' ἥρμοσται τέχνη πρέπουσ' ἐν ἡμῖν): fighting with spears, contests of wrestling, horsemanship, running, boxing, biting, grabbing men's balls; in us are musical songs, prophecies entirely unknown but not contrived, discriminating knowledge of medicine, the ability to measure the heavens, to dance, and to make the parts below speak" (lines 8–16).[72] This amusing little *tour de force* invokes a range of sophisticated skills beyond those described in the previous paragraphs and recalls (or anticipates – we are not sure of its date) the words of Prometheus in the *Prometheus Bound*, "All skills come to mortals from Prometheus" (πᾶσαι τέχναι βροτοῖσιν ἐκ Προμηθέως, 506).

Satyrs were therefore much more than beasts. By nature they were partly human, a fact increasingly stressed in fifth-century vase-painting. On the earliest vases satyrs were shown to be aggressive (they can be found assaulting divinities)[73]; within a generation their wildness had been tamed and they were depicted with families or engaged in music and the other inventions described above.[74] In red-figure vase-painting they start wearing clothes, such as the chiton, and when standing still they can look like respectable citizens.[75] One underlying reason for this civilizing of satyrs is a subtle trend in archaic red-figure by which scenes from myth were replaced by scenes from everyday life, such as industry, commerce, sports activities, entertainment, and women at domestic work.[76] This trend, which had nothing intrinsically to do with satyrs, nevertheless affected the depiction of satyrs and put them into "human" contexts.[77] Furthermore, they are occasionally credited with having a divine parentage that allows them access to hidden knowledge.[78] Thus there are anecdotes from antiquity about a silen being captured and brought to a king or leader who would try to benefit from the knowledge that the satyr instinctively drew from the world of nature.[79]

Nevertheless, their bestial potential, not their civilized behavior, remained an ever-present factor even in the fifth century. In Sophocles' *Ichneutai*, satyrs, compared to hedgehogs and monkeys (127–28), are several times called "beasts" (θῆρες 147, 153, 221). On vase-paintings they exchange roles with animals by pulling chariots, and they couple with animals in dance and sexual relations.[80] Satyr costumes in drama included furry breeches with an erect *phallos* of the sort worn by the "Getty Birds." When in motion, they seem "incapable of controlling their bodies."[81] For Seaford, a Dionysiac *thiasos* of satyrs was united by a sense of kinship and shared animality, which was "antithetical to the *polis*."[82] Even when portrayed as "human," some "otherness" slipped out, as when they wear Thracian boots.[83] On a vase in Berlin anatomical variations in the portrayal of satyrs can be discerned, animal hooves appearing on one, and human feet on two others.[84] Confronted with the satyr, human beings would catch a glimpse of themselves and be forced to acknowledge their own animal-like qualities.

What needs to be accounted for, however, is not the predictable animality of satyrs but the unexpected juxtaposition of the subhuman satyr with civilized skills and inventions. Seaford has suggested that the association reflects earlier cultic practice and that the satyr's evident surprise at the appearance of these inventions was a relic of pre-dramatic Dionysiac celebrations at which cult objects such as wine, masks, or musical instruments were revealed to an initiand who was perhaps at first confused about the objects.[85]

One can easily imagine the humor intrinsic in juxtaposing crudeness and refinement. The comic incongruity of inferior creatures like satyrs working as skilled specialists must have been a source of amusement to the audience, who would feel superior to the ignorant chorus. The satyrs are like "naifs who discover what the spectator knows too well."[86] Indeed what strikes one about their encounters with civilized skills is that, though they may celebrate these skills, they stumble across them through no cleverness of their own. Of the inventions and skills described above almost none can really be credited to satyrs. The satyrs in turn depend heavily on the inventions of heroic or divine agents such as Prometheus, Daedalus, Orpheus, Palamedes, Athena, Hermes, Hephaestus, and Dionysus. When first confronted with unexpected discoveries such as fire, the *aulos*, lyre, portraits, and athletic gear, they express surprise or even fear. Prometheus worries that they might burn themselves with fire.[87] When, as we see in vase-paintings, they cause a living being to rise out of the earth, as if to resurrect life, it turns out to be Pandora, who brought mixed blessings with her.[88] In addition to the civilized accomplishments listed in *P.Oxy.* 1083, the satyrs claimed expertise in farting and grabbing men's testicles. As for the other skills in this fragment (medicine, measuring the heavens), there is no independent evidence associating satyrs with them, and their claims would probably have been seen by the audience as hollow bravado. The cultural discoveries that they point to are achieved only inadvertently or unconsciously.

Accordingly Nietzsche wrote of satyrs: "In their presence the audience could feel its civilized surface annulled and replaced by a

97

consoling sense of unity with nature" (*Birth of Tragedy* §7).[89] Yet, paradoxically, the encounter with the satyrs leads not to "annulment" but to a reconstitution of various features of civilization. To be more specific: satyrs reveal that civilization is not to be understood as an artificial creation, as many sophists might have seen it, but as an outgrowth of nature (wine, clearly, or music from a tortoise shell); alternatively, institutions and skills that are clearly artificial (iron-working, perhaps) have the sanction of the satyrs, creatures of nature. Therefore unity with nature need not obliterate civilization but be a precondition for it or even assist it. Notes Seaford, "Satyrs belong to the wild, and to the very point indeed at which culture is created out of nature: when wine is for the first time ever extracted by a god from the grapes, or the sound of the lyre from a dead tortoise, they are there as the first to enjoy the invention. This position gives them a special perspective on mankind."[90] I would qualify this slightly: satyrs themselves have too little insight and awareness to possess any special perspective themselves, but their presence calls attention to the creation of culture and allows the audience a new perspective. If they behave like children inadvertently discovering the human world for the first time, the response suggests a renewal of the world and culture.[91]

Their list of accomplishments is, however, a selective one, and the omissions may be significant: we hear nothing about several social skills that are necessary for a civilized life, such as the creation of homes, language, commerce, or government. After all satyrs tend to exist in a *thiasos*, an unordered collectivity.[92] It was these social skills that exponents of the "Theory of Progress" emphasized and that play a role in Aristophanes' *Birds*. The satyrs' *thiasos* resembles in some ways the pre-civic state of the birds in the *Birds*, although the birds are more organized, more anthropomorphized (although purely "animal"), and more aggressive. The satyrs, by comparison, are less inspired, yet neither do they pose any danger to the social order.[93] Satyrs never go to war with the human race as do the birds, fishes, and beasts of comedy. Satyrs are more human and less potentially threatening than horses, cocks, and bull-headed river gods. Whereas satyrs remained firmly embedded in a *thiasos* of Dionysus ("antithetical to the *polis*"[94]), animal choruses seem to have played a role in social contexts or performances that went beyond the Dionysiac; similarly in drama they could represent a more disciplined social order.

As a *tertium quid* one should also compare centaurs.[95] These hybrid creatures, who are not associated with any divinity, inhabit the extreme ends of the spectrum. On the one hand, Cheiron at least had access to divine wisdom. Knowing about both wilderness and culture, he taught Achilles, Jason, and Asclepius, and was as famous a tutor as existed in mythology.[96] On the other hand, centaurs virtually embodied barbarism and far exceeded the satyrs in violence, the Centauromachy so popular in classical art being a prime example.[97]

Euripides' Cyclops: *Polyphemus and Human Society*

The single satyr-play that survives in its entirety is the *Cyclops* of Euripides. The date of performance, although uncertain, falls in the last two or three decades of the fifth century.[98] Possible allusions to the Sicilian Expedition would put it at 414/413[99] or within a year of Aristophanes' *Birds*.[100] More pertinent is the fact that it has not only a chorus of satyrs but another semi-human creature, a cyclops, who demarcates the line between animal and human behavior.

Polyphemus considers himself a god (231, 345; he is a son of Poseidon), yet Odysseus refers to him as a beast (θήρ, 442, 602).[101] How short he falls of human standards can be gauged by his propensity for cannibalism, which marks him as an animal in the eyes of the Greeks. Matters are, however, complicated by the fact that, whereas in Homer Polyphemus ate Odysseus' men raw and whole ("like a mountain-bred lion," *Odyssey* 9.292), in Euripides his dining habits are more refined: he prepares a cauldron, butchers the men, roasts them, and finally boils them (382–404).[102] The cook in Athenio's *Samothracians* (discussed above) claimed that ὀπτᾶν (roasting or grilling) and the institution of sacrifice rescued human beings from primeval cannibalism. Polyphemus' cookery has the added dimension of being described as a sacrifice (cf. θύω, 334; θυσία, 365; σφαγεῖα, 395), which is simultaneously both more civilized and more horrifying.[103] Paradoxically, then, this care in preparing his food defines Polyphemus as a cannibal with sophisticated flair. Euripides has humanized, and even Hellenized, Polyphemus. At the end of the play, when Polyphemus has become the victim, some commentators have even found him sympathetic, a "likeable buffoon" whose blinding is an outrage.[104]

One aspect of this Euripidean "Hellenization" is that Polyphemus speaks as if he is up-to-date on contemporary intellectual developments, though the strand of sophistic thought that he represents is one that justifies indulging appetites and seeking self-interest. Particularly remarkable is the speech Polyphemus gives at lines 316–47, in which he offers materialistic explanations for the phenomena of the world and gives priority to physical needs. The best way to satisfy his soul (ψυχή, 340), he says, is to eat. The natural power of the earth to grow food for his flocks is conceived of as a necessity (ἀνάγκη, 332). Not only does he have contempt for those who "embroider" human life by establishing laws (τοὺς νόμους ἔθεντο ποικίλλοντες ἀνθρώπων βίον, 338–39), he thinks that Zeus is no stronger (κρείσσων, 321) than he and he is not afraid of Zeus; the gods he worships are wealth (316) and eating and drinking (336). In so doing he implies that "smart" people (σοφοί, 316; cf. σώφρονες, 336) can see that religion is merely a construct made of "fancy words" (λόγων εὐμορφία, 317). Polyphemus' little exposition echoes Callicles' argument that laws were contrived by the weak to constrain those who were naturally strong, though Polyphemus does not, like Callicles, conclude that the rule of the naturally strong is just.[105]

In Euripides' play he lives alone in a cave and has at most brothers scattered about the mountains, a condition that constitutes a pre-social horde. Konstan suggested that the contrast with the collectivity of the Bacchic horde of satyrs reinforces the sense of Polyphemus as an isolated individual, and both of these are set in contrast to the companionship of Odysseus and his comrades, who respect the reciprocal, social responsibilities of life in a *polis*.[106]

Exponents of the "Theory of Progress" would recognize in Polyphemus' life the savage state of nature in which men lived in caves like animals; this was overcome as they invented laws, housing, and a proper diet. In Euripides the Cyclopes live in caves and are isolated (μόναδες, 120).[107] The one golden-age feature of Polyphemus' life in the *Odyssey* – the spontaneous growth of cereals – has been omitted by Euripides in the *Cyclops*, where they are pastoral and eat flesh. Wine, too, is a novelty for Euripides' Polyphemus, unlike Homer's. Thus the life of Euripides' Cyclops fits into the "progressive" view of the savage past.[108]

It was uncharacteristic of the Greeks to allow such bestiality into their mythology and religion. Although gods could briefly take on animal shapes or have animal attributes, there were no animal gods per se: the quality that distinguished Greek myth and religion was not theriomorphism but anthropomorphism.[109] Metamorphosis stories are found in Greece, but once the transformation had occurred the creature's identity remained stable; moreover, these stories were not numerous before the Hellenistic period. In general, then, the "boundaries may be crossed, but they are not obliterated."[110] Yet this is what we see comedy doing: "regularly blurring the boundaries" by giving a human voice to animals and animal features to human beings.[111]

Comedies probably had choruses for decades after Aristophanes' career ended in the early fourth century,[112] but if the surviving evidence is representative, animals played little role in them. The animal choruses belonged to a particular historical moment. In the late fifth century comic poets capitalized on a convergence of ideas and gave new life to an archaic masquerade. As we have seen, certain sophists and Presocratics, interested in identifying the natural advantages of men and animals, had begun to find analogies between their lives and the lives of animals, and established an organic connection between nature and human society.[113] In the fourth century, however, this balance was no longer sustained. On the one hand, Aristotle denied reason to animals;[114] on the other, Cynics and poets of New Comedy found animals to be superior and devalued human life.[115] Even in Plato we hear of those who, in their next lives, would choose an animal life over a human life (*Rep.* 620a). Either way, parity was lost and anthropomorphism became more difficult. Eventually, Greek poets began to use features of the natural world in a more artificial way, as symbols of abstract notions, no longer as "ambiguously fertile or destructive powers."[116] The conditions that enabled a dramatist to play creatively with natural boundaries, and to stage a comedy with a chorus of such creatures, ceased to exist.

4

THE LITERARY FRAGMENTS
AND ARISTOPHANES' *KNIGHTS,*
WASPS, AND *FROGS*

Animal choruses, which had disappeared from the archaeological and literary record around 480 B.C., returned in force to
the stage in the last third of the fifth century before completely van-
ishing in the early fourth century. In this relatively short span of time
appeared Aristophanes' *Knights, Wasps, Birds, Frogs,* and the fragments
or titles of at least sixteen other comedies. It is to these that we now
turn. The *Birds,* which has the best and purest example of an animal
chorus, deserves the more extended discussion that it will receive in
Chapter 5.

These choruses differed in kind from those depicted on archaic
vases because, in part, of the new attitudes toward animals described
in Chapter 3. For example, the tendency in the classical period to
anthropomorphize animals and hybrids of all kinds inevitably affected
animal choruses. The species of chosen animals began to include insects
and other "social" animals. Moreover, some fragments made it plain
that the killing and eating of animals was a volatile issue.

In other respects, however, late-fifth-century comedies formed a
continuous tradition with the earlier animal masquerades: For example, the use of some animals presupposed the fertility and potency of
the natural world. Although the context of the performance of these
comedies is not a matter of speculation – they were performed at
festivals of Dionysus – one can still detect some resonances with the
earlier possible venues of animal masquerades at aristocratic symposia
and *komoi.* Certainly Aristophanes' *Knights* echoes the chorus on the
earliest surviving vase.

Assessing the Fragmentary Evidence

Many of these comedies are known only from fragments, and a few words about using this evidence are in order. The weakest sort of documentation is a simple assertion by a scholiast that, for example, Magnes wrote a play with the title of *Birds*. Without fragments or corroborating epigraphical testimonia the very existence of his *Birds* is open to doubt. But even when one has fuller documentation one faces the well-known pitfalls of reconstructing plots and themes. Had only the titles and a few fragments of Aristophanes' *Wasps* and *Frogs* survived, no one would know that wasps and frogs played a secondary role in those comedies.[1]

Furthermore, when fragments did survive it was not because a later scholar wanted to preserve representative selections of a comedy but because he wished to offer a specimen of proper diction or to summon up images of food at a banquet. In this latter category we find Athenaeus of Naucratis (ca. A.D. 200), whose *Deipnosophists* was devoted to learned dinner-table conversation. Because animals are vital sources of food, Athenaeus quoted lengthy passages from several animal comedies.[2] The danger, of course, is that fragments might trick a reader into thinking that the playwrights of lost comedies were as concerned with food as was Athenaeus. There is virtually no way to control for this, though it is worth recording that food and feasting (and animals) are fundamentally important for the protagonists of Aristophanes' complete comedies.[3] Moreover, the discussion of fish in the *Comoedia Dukiana*, which has survived only in papyrus and was thus not filtered through Athenaeus, potentially offers independent confirmation of the importance of animals and food in lost comedy.[4] Other biases, too, may govern the selections. A passage from Eupolis' *Nanny-Goats* (fr. 13 K–A) is a good fifth-century specimen of an anthropomorphizing portrayal of animals, but it was quoted by Plutarch, who was prone to anthropomorphism himself. The passage from *Nanny-Goats* may be more revealing of Plutarch than representative of Eupolis. Then again, a glance at Aristophanes' *Birds* confirms that anthropomorphization could run rampant on the classical stage. Therefore the fragments, which were plucked from context and survived by chance, can at best give only a distorted view of the plays.

TABLE 4.1. Comedies with Animal Choruses

Dates	Playwright	Title	PCG
470s–40	Magnes	*Birds, Fig-Wasps, Frogs*	IV.626–32
430s–20s?	Pherecrates	*Ant-men*	VII.161–67
430s–20s	Callias	*Frogs*	IV.42
early 420s?	Crates	*Beasts*	IV.91–96
429–23	Eupolis	*Nanny-Goats*	V.302–14
425–22	Plato	*Ants*	VII.468
420s–10s?	Cantharus	*Nightingales, Ants*	IV.57 & 59
424	Aristophanes	*Knights*	
422	Aristophanes	*Wasps*	
414	Aristophanes	*Birds*	
405	Aristophanes	*Frogs*	
410–380?	Diocles	*Bees*	V.20–22
401–400?	Archippus	*Fishes*	II.542–49
		(+ *Comoedia Dukiana*?)	VIII.473–77
390s?	Aristophanes	*Storks*	III.2.239–44
370s or later?	Antiphanes	*Knights*	II.368–69
4th Cent.?	Crates II	*Birds*	IV.111

Nevertheless, they are clues that are simply too important to be ignored. As long as it is clear where the evidence leaves off and speculation begins, judicious inferences should be entertained. Moreover, the fragments can usefully be compared with the comedies of Aristophanes that survive in their entirety. In order to minimize the tedium induced by reading discontinuous, not-always-illuminating fragments, their full texts, with translations, appear in Appendix A. This chapter includes only the most relevant passages.

In Table 4.1, in roughly chronological order, are the titles of comedies that appear to have had animal choruses.[5]

Assuming that the evidence of the vases and the literary fragments is representative, animal choruses thrived in what was barely more than a single generation of playwrights.[6] The popularity of animal choruses reached a peak around 510–480 B.C., declined for a few decades (we only know of Magnes' comedies, whose dates are uncertain), but then saw a revival in the last third of the century, reaching a crescendo in the 420s and 410s B.C. It seems, then, that the tradition of animal choruses, active ca. 510–480 B.C., had died out for a generation or two, only to be consciously revived around 440–410 B.C. They were apparently not archaic relics, dusted off every spring and kept in the repertory by sheer force of inertia. There may have been positive reasons for a new generation to revive them (or, if they remained a constant though invisible presence throughout the century, for continuing to use them). Comic poets like Aristophanes – who, after all, had to compete for the audience's favor – must have found them worthwhile. Whatever the original ritual or komastic impetus for animal choruses had been in the sixth century, fifth-century playwrights would have dropped them if they proved unpopular with audiences. (Indeed, by the beginning of the fourth century they disappeared.) In short the challenge is to determine what the animal choruses may have meant to a contemporary Athenian audience in the last three decades of the fifth century.

The material that follows is discussed not by date or author but by animal species. This, it seems to me, is the more illuminating approach. Insects can be profitably discussed as a group; the *Beasts, Goats, Birds,* and *Fishes* are "edible choruses" and share common themes; and frogs constitute their own order of amphibians. These are certainly not a representative cross-section of the animal kingdom but, as will be clear, the principles of selection are significant.

INSECTS

Aristophanes' *Wasps,* Magnes *Fig-Wasps,* Diocles' *Bees,* Pherekrates' *Ant-Men,* Plato's *Ants,* and Cantharus' *Ants*

None of the earlier evidence we examined from Greek theater, religion, or vase-painting would have led one to expect insect choruses. Wasps, ants, and bees are strikingly new entrants into the comic theater and their presence reveals something crucial about fifth-century animal choruses.

The animals in sixth-century vase-painting – cocks and bull-headed men, as well as horses and dolphins ridden by others – could in theory be associated with cults of various gods (although in practice it cannot be shown that any one performance was dedicated to any particular god). Animals in the sixth-century paintings were on balance domesticated, and two, bulls and cocks, could be sacrificed. When we turn to the fragments and plays of the later fifth century, however, little of this can be found. The *Knights* of Aristophanes and of Antiphanes may have used horses as illustrated on the Berlin "Knights" vase (Plate I), and *Knights* 595–610 also shows that they could be endowed with human characteristics, but domesticated and sacrificial animals disappear from the record, the exceptions being Eupolis' *Nanny-Goats* and, very likely, the Getty Birds (Plate IV).[7]

In the late fifth century, simply to judge from surviving titles, a disproportionate number of plays were named after what Aristotle in the *Historia Animalium* considered "social" animals, including bees, wasps, ants, and cranes.[8] Remarkably every single one of these social animals is represented in Old Comedy: bees were the chorus of Diocles' play; wasps, in Aristophanes and Magnes; ants appear twice as ants and once as "ant-men." Cranes figure in Aristophanes' *Birds*. Being mostly insects, they were neither domesticated animals nor sources of food.

Moreover, animals that one might not consider social are treated as if they were: in the *Beasts, Fishes*, and (as we will see) *Birds*, the animals are evidently presented as so humanized and sophisticated that, had they acted that way in nature, anyone would thought them social. After all, since "beasts," "fish," and "birds" are broad categories of the animal world, one could project onto them whatever one wished. The most salient feature of storks was their sense of duty to children or parents and, evidently, their concern for social order. Because other choral animals such as goats and frogs do not fit this Aristotelian category without Procrustean distortion, these patterns should be thought of as general trends, not hard-and-fast rules. This was a challenge comic playwrights met creatively.

Conversely, playwrights appear to have avoided animals that Greeks singled out as unjust or anti-social. Plato, as we will see shortly, saw wasps as creatures of justice, whereas donkeys, hawks, and wolves were unjust (*Phaedo* 82b); for that matter comic choruses were generally not composed of most of the animals that Semonides compared to bad women in his misogynistic poem (pigs, foxes, dogs, asses, monkeys, mares, and the like). Nor were there choruses of domestic pets such as dogs or cats, which were considered inedible. Playwrights apparently also ignored some of the animals depicted on archaic vase-paintings, since no literary evidence exists for a chorus of bulls or bull-headed men. Whether cocks formed a chorus in the late fifth century is uncertain: they are not named as chorus-members in Aristophanes' *Birds*. The Getty Birds vase seems not to depict that chorus. Bulls, being earlier and therefore closer to possible roots in cultic ritual, embodied growth and fertility yet also represented the more aggressive and volatile side of the natural world.

By comparison the choruses of the late fifth century were unthreatening. Obviously the wasps of Aristophanes' comedy could be potent animals, and Reckford is right that using them would have the effect of drawing on "daemonic" powers of the tradition.[9] At the same time wasps were thought to be just and social and thus embodied the tension between wildness and civilization.[10] There are still (we can guess) horses on stage in the *Knights*, but the chorus of young men does its best to describe them in human terms. Moreover the word "savagery" hardly applies to frogs, wasps, goats, ants, storks, or nightingales. Even the *beasts* of the *Beasts* sound more plaintive and defensive than aggressive. The only really threatening passage is in the *Fishes* when certain human beings are to be handed over to the fish to be eaten (fr. 28 K–A), although even this threat is embedded in the terms of a formal peace treaty. We will see that Aristophanes' *Birds* also has, in its opening scenes, a pitched battle between birds and human beings, but the two sides eventually achieve a reconciliation, however ambiguous: Peisetaerus becomes a bird and the birds become virtual human beings.

In the late fifth century, then, playwrights chose animals less for their "wildness" or "daemonic" powers than for potential social qualities and their ability to be humanized. This is not to say that the wilder aspects of animals were suppressed, but that other features counted for more. The general trend was toward choosing animals that illustrated what human beings and animals shared.

Aristophanes' Wasps *(Σφῆκες), 422* B.C.

The Wasp in Greece

Wasps are prime specimens of social creatures.[11] Wasp societies seem to follow a division of labor, including workers (ἐργάται), leaders (ἡγεμόνες), and drones (κηφῆνες). From a small nest of four cells, with tidy hexagonal holes, wasps construct larger habitations and colonies where their offspring are raised.[12] Their sense of domestic collectivity was common lore in Homer, who compared the tenacity of the Achaeans in battle to "quick-waisted" (μέσον αἰόλοι) wasps or bees "who make nests by the rocky road, and do not leave their hollow home, but stay and fight off hunters for the sake of their children" (*Iliad* 12.167–70). That wasps had a keen sense of justice was enunciated in Plato's statement that citizens who have cultivated self-control and integrity will have the happiest souls, passing into some other kind of "social and restrained creature, such as bees, wasps, or ants" (*Phaedo* 82b).

But Plato's view that wasps were "restrained" would have seemed to many Greeks to be too generous, for more commonly wasps were marked by their belligerence. Another Homeric simile describes wasps who, provoked by young boys, come out to defend their children but then attack innocent passers-by (*Iliad* 16.259–65). This irrational anger was proverbial. Aelian reported that wasps drew poison for their stingers from snakes and Aelian thought that antidotes were needed for the wasp's sting.[13] A nuisance of a different sort annoyed Dicaeopolis, who compared the raucous music of pipers to wasps (*Ach.* 864).[14] That said, Aristotle distinguished "wild" (*agrioi*) and "tame" (*hemeroi*) wasps (*HA* 627b23–28a11). Wasps must not be thought of as one-dimensional creatures. They are simultaneously irascible and social, as Aristophanes' comedy will show.

The Chorus in the *Wasps*

The chorus is composed of retired Athenian men who devote their spare time to serving as jurors. One of their fellow-jurors, the elderly Philocleon, has been detained at home by his son, Bdelycleon, in an attempt to cure Philocleon of his obsession with serving on juries. Early in the play Philocleon tries to sneak out of the house by riding underneath a donkey, just as Odysseus escaped the Cyclops' cave by clinging to a ram.[15] The old jurors aid and abet this attempt. Despite the title of the comedy, then, the chorus members are not primarily wasps but human beings. Whereas the choruses of *Fishes* or *Birds* were essentially animals with human characteristics, these are citizens of Athens with wasp characteristics. One might say that instead of an "anthropomorphizing" tendency in this comedy, there is the reverse:

a "theriomorphizing" tendency, in which obviously human characters take on the features of animals. The boundary between "human" and "animal" being porous, it is not the pure specimen but the hybrid that is staged.

That they are human beings is clear, for many reasons: they are aging veterans of military service, seemingly from lower classes (230–35); their concern about the lack of rain suggests that they are farmers (259–65); they have sons who have no obvious wasp features (248ff., 408);[16] the members of the chorus have been carrying staves (727); they have white hair (1064–65); and call themselves "men" (ἀνδρῶν, 454). They enter wearing cloaks that covered their wasp costume and the audience's initial impression was probably that they were human beings. The text leaves no explicit buzzing noises.

Their waspish nature is, however, more than a casual metaphor and should not be minimized. They are called "wasps" (σφῆκες) by Philocleon (430), by Bdelycleon (456), by themselves (1072, 1090, 1103, 1106), and are collectively thought of as a "wasps' nest" (σφηκιά, 224, 229, 404; cf. ἀνθρήνια 1080, 1107) or a "swarm" (σμῆνος, 425; ἑσμούς, 1107). When they are packed into their seats in court, they crouch down "like larvae in their cells" (1111). In the parabasis they give a full description of their waspish features (1060–1121, on which more follow). Whether they are "wild" or "tame" wasps is not clear. The most visible sign of their nature is the stinger that each one wears as part of his costume.[17] Bdelycleon, speaking to his slave Xanthias, describes them this way:

You idiot! Old men like that become a virtual wasps' nest if someone gets them angry. You see, they have a very sharp stinger coming out of their rumps (ἔχουσι γὰρ καὶ κέντρον ἐκ τῆς ὀσφύος) which they use as intended. They buzz around, leap up, and strike you as if they were sparks of fire. (223–27)

When they realize that they will have to mount an attack on Bdelycleon's slaves in order to rescue Philocleon, they think as wasps would:

Tell me, why should we delay stirring up that wrath which we rouse when someone irritates our wasps' nest? Now, *now*, that easily angered stinger (κέντρον), which we use to punish people with, must be braced for sharp action. (403–07)

These stingers were probably not visible when the chorus-members first arrived on stage (230), for they were wearing cloaks (*himatia*). But the jurors now have removed these cloaks, fully revealing their costume to the audience and to Bdelycleon's slaves, who suddenly see what they are up against. Says Xanthias, "Heracles! They really do have stingers (κέντρ)! Master, don't you see!?" (420). Later, at 1072, wasp-jurors say that they are "wasp-waisted," so their costume must have conveyed the impression of a wasp's segmented body.[18] They may have worn tunics with black and yellow stripes and perhaps even a wasp mask.[19] In the fray with the slaves the chorus members fight as would wasps – by extending their stingers and attacking vulnerable parts of the body such as fingers, eyes, and rear ends (422–32) – and are defeated as wasps by being forced by smoke to withdraw (457–60). Therefore, although we should not overemphasize the animal nature of the chorus, it is worth bearing in mind that the chorus members first appear dressed as men but reveal themselves to be animals. This second identity emerges in the course of the play and will complement their human identity. "Nothing is more manly than an Attic wasp," they will assert (1090), their waspishness and virility easily coexisting and their animal identity thus seeming perfectly natural and uncontrived. Perhaps it is no coincidence that Philocleon, when trying to escape his captors early in the play, invokes the name of Cecrops, the mythical first king of Athens who was literally born of the Attic soil and was thought to have had the body of a serpent from the waist down (438). There is nothing inauthentic about a half-animal, half-human creature.

After the wasps retreat they take on the task of judging a debate between Philocleon and his father. Philocleon speaks in defense of the life of the juror, although it emerges that his true interest is less in justice than in the sadistic humiliation of virtually every defendant brought before him (548–635). His disposition should be no surprise, the chorus having already said that he was the fiercest of the jurors, incapable of being persuaded and showing mercy to no one (276–80, cf. 319–22). But it is Bdelycleon who wins the day by persuading the chorus that jurors are actually being exploited by politicians. When the chorus in turn urges Philocleon to follow his son's advice (725–49), he does so and agrees to act as a juror in a mock trial, to be held at home, of a dog accused of stealing cheese.

Nothing in this debate or in subsequent episodes requires that members of the chorus behave as wasps, but if their wasp nature is seldom acted out, it is strongly asserted. In the parabasis, especially in the antepirrhemata (1071–90 and 1102–21), they confirm and refine their wasp identity. As wasps, they are quick to anger, but their role is not limited to irrational, unprovoked attacks. The relevant passages follow:[20]

1071 εἴ τις ὑμῶν, ὦ θεαταί, τὴν ἐμὴν ἰδὼν φύσιν
      εἶτα θαυμάζει μ' ὁρῶν μέσον διεσφηκωμένον,
      ἥτις ἡμῶν ἐστιν ἡ 'πίνοια τῆς ἐγκεντρίδος,
      ῥᾳδίως ἐγὼ διδάξω "κἂν ἄμουσος ᾖ τὸ πρίν."
1075 ἐσμὲν ἡμεῖς, οἷς πρόσεστι τοῦτο τοὐρροπύγιον,
      Ἀττικοὶ μόνοι δικαίως ἐγγενεῖς αὐτόχθονες,
      ἀνδρικώτατον γένος καὶ πλεῖστα τήνδε τὴν πόλιν
      ὠφελῆσαν ἐν μάχαισιν, ἡνίκ' ἦλθ' ὁ βάρβαρος,
      τῷ καπνῷ τύφων ἅπασαν τὴν πόλιν καὶ πυρπολῶν,
1080 ἐξελεῖν ἡμῶν μενοινῶν πρὸς βίαν τἀνθήνια.
      εὐθέως γὰρ ἐκδραμόντες "ξὺν δορὶ ξὺν ἀσπίδι"
      ἐμαχόμεσθ' αὐτοῖσι, θυμὸν ὀξίνην πεπωκότες,
      στὰς ἀνὴρ παρ' ἄνδρ', ὑπ' ὀργῆς τὴν χελύνην ἐσθίων.
      ὑπὸ δὲ τῶν τοξευμάτων οὐκ ἦν ἰδεῖν τὸν οὐρανόν.
1085 ἀλλ' ὅμως ἐωσάμεσθα ξὺν θεοῖς πρὸς ἑσπέραν.
      γλαῦξ γὰρ ἡμῶν πρὶν μάχεσθαι τὸν στρατὸν διέπτατο.
      εἶτα δ' εἱπόμεσθα θυννάζοντες εἰς τοὺς θυλάκους,
      οἱ δ' ἔφευγον τὰς γνάθους καὶ τὰς ὀφρῦς κεντούμενοι,
      ὥστε παρὰ τοῖς βαρβάροισι πανταχοῦ καὶ νῦν ἔτι
1090 μηδὲν Ἀττικοῦ καλεῖσθαι σφηκὸς ἀνδρικώτερον.

Spectators, if any of you sees my appearance and then wonders, when you see that I am wasp-waisted, what our stingers are for, I will easily enlighten you – even those of you who didn't know about it until now. We who have this rump attached to us are the only truly native-born, aboriginal men of Attica, the bravest race of men and the one that most aided this city in its battles, when the barbarian came, smoking out and setting afire the entire city, eager to destroy our nests by force. Rushing out right away, "with spear and shield," we engaged them in battle, after finishing a bitter drink of spirit,[21] standing man next to man, biting his lip out of anger. You couldn't see the sky because of their arrows. But we forced them back by evening, with the help of the gods; for an owl had flown across our army before we fought. And then we pursued them, harpooning them in their baggy trousers, and stung in the jaws and eyebrows; some were in full flight, so that among the barbarians everywhere, even still today, nothing is called more courageous than an Attic wasp. (1071–1090)

Then they recall sailing over to recapture cities from the Persians and take credit for the tribute that was brought back to Athens. Thereafter they resume the description of themselves as wasps:

1102 πολλαχοῦ σκοποῦντες ἡμᾶς εἰς ἅπανθ' εὑρήσετε
τοὺς τρόπους καὶ τὴν δίαιταν σφηξὶν ἐμφερεστάτους.
πρῶτα μὲν γὰρ οὐδὲν ἡμῶν ζῷον ἠρεθισμένον
1105 μᾶλλον ὀξύθυμόν ἐστιν οὐδὲ δυσκολώτερον.
εἶτα τἄλλ' ὅμοια πάντα σφηξὶ μηχανώμεθα.
ξυλλεγέντες γὰρ καθ' ἑσμοὺς ὥσπερ εἰς ἀνθρήνια
οἱ μὲν ἡμῶν οὗπερ ἄρχων, οἱ δὲ παρὰ τοὺς ἕνδεκα,
οἱ δ' ἐν Ὠιδείῳ δικάζουσ', ὧδε πρὸς τοῖς τειχίοις
1110 ξυμβεβυσμένοι πυκνόν, νεύοντες εἰς τὴν γῆν, μόλις
ὥσπερ οἱ σκώληκες ἐν τοῖς κυττάροις κινούμενοι.
ἔς τε τὴν ἄλλην δίαιτάν ἐσμεν εὐπορώτατοι·
πάντα γὰρ κεντοῦμεν ἄνδρα κἀκπορίζομεν βίον.
ἀλλὰ γὰρ κηφῆνες ἡμῖν εἰσιν ἐγκαθήμενοι
1115 οὐκ ἔχοντες κέντρον, οἳ μένοντες ἡμῶν τοῦ φόρου
τὸν γόνον κατεσθίουσιν οὐ ταλαιπωρούμενοι.
τοῦτο δ' ἔστ' ἄλγιστον ἡμῖν, ἤν τις ἀστράτευτος ὢν
ἐκροφῇ τὸν μισθὸν ἡμῶν, τῆσδε τῆς χώρας ὕπερ
μήτε κώπην μήτε λόγχην μήτε φλύκταιναν λαβών.
1120 ἀλλά μοι δοκεῖ τὸ λοιπὸν τῶν πολιτῶν ἔμβραχυ
ὅστις ἂν μὴ 'χῃ τὸ κέντρον μὴ φέρειν τριώβολον.

If you look at us from different angles, you will find that we are very similar to wasps in many details, in our ways and lifestyle. First of all, no animal is quicker to anger or grouchier than we are when provoked. What's more, we work everything else out in the same way that wasps do. We gather for jury duty as if we were swarming into wasps' nests: some of us go to the court where the archon presides, others to where the Eleven preside, and yet others in the Odeon, squeezed in tightly along the walls, like this, bending down to the ground, like larvae moving in their cells. We are also very resourceful at making a living: you see, we sting everyone and provide a livelihood. In spite of that, drones are sitting among us who have no stinger, and they stay at Athens and eat up the produce of our tribute without doing any work. It is most painful for us if someone avoids military service and gulps down our pay – someone who's never taken up an oar or a spear or a blister on behalf of his country. As far as I'm concerned, in the future, any citizen who doesn't have a stinger should not receive three obols. (1102–1121)

These speeches establish their temper as an inbred trait. No animal is "quicker to anger" (ὀξύθυμος, 1105, also 406 and 455; cf. ὀξυκάρδιοι, 430),[22] and they generate more instances of ὀργή ("anger") and ὀργίζω ("become enraged") than any other comedy of Aristophanes.[23] If they "sting everyone" (1113), they are, as in *Iliad* 16, indiscriminately attacking innocent and guilty alike. Of course this motif was established in the first half of the play, where it seemed a foregone conclusion to the wasp-jurors that Laches deserved punishment (240–44).

We should be careful, however, not to conflate the chorus with Philocleon and impute to them his arbitrariness. Philocleon had described, with relish, the satisfaction he derived from convicting all and sundry, without being held accountable to anyone (ἀνυπεύθυνοι, 587). The chorus had never shared this fixation and distinguished themselves from him when they singled him out as the "fiercest" of the jurors (277). That comment may have been meant as praise, but they did not follow his example. These wasp-jurors can be reasoned with. They listened carefully to the debate between Philocleon and Bdelycleon, and voted against their fellow-juror. This is not to say that their judgement in court was objective and impartial, and Bdelycleon succeeded in the debate by appealing to their self-interest, showing them that by serving on juries they were being exploited. But at least it was persuasion, not violence, that decided the issue and convinced them to "slacken their anger" (727). Near the end of the play, they praise Bdelycleon for his *philopatria* (ambiguously, either "filial love" or "love of country") and for his arguments in debate (1462–73). They congratulate Philocleon on his good fortune, but say that he may be unable to change his nature (1450–61), a remark that is perhaps intended to contrast his self-indulgence with their own willingness to relent and side with Bdelycleon.[24]

Even when they were physically attacking Bdelycleon and his slaves at the beginning of the play, they were responding to provocation, for Philocleon had been imprisoned and the chorus was there to free him. As in both similes in the *Iliad* the wasps are protecting their own; unlike the simile in *Iliad* 16, their anger is not arbitrary. The chorus is acting to right a wrong committed against a friend. Perhaps, therefore, these are not the "wild" wasps who come from the mountains but "tame" ones described by Aristotle.

The wasp-jurors continue to see themselves as agents of justice even after they have been won over to Bdelycleon's point of view, but their actions are now broadened to include service to the state as a whole: Athens was the "nest" that was threatened with smoke by the barbarians (1080), though they fought as hoplites, in a phalanx with shield and spear (1080–83). All of this was designed to cast the juror-wasps as hoplite infantrymen in the Persian Wars, probably at the Battle of Marathon. The tactics in the skirmish with Bdelycleon and his slaves were those of hoplites (cf. 422–25). Because the *orge* of the wasps is not purely destructive, they deserve credit for their willingess to sacrifice themselves for a larger good. The aggressiveness of the wasps is what is needed in combat (though they comically speak of this quality as "manliness": ἀνδρικώτατον, 1077; ἀνδρικώτερον, 1090). By adopting the Persian Wars as an arena in which to exhibit the irascibility of the wasp, Aristophanes has chosen something that all citizens would look to as a laudable and politically neutral goal. The 420s B.C. saw the rise of politically divisive issues, ranging from the controversial leadership of Cleon in the Peloponnesian War to the problem of frivolous speech-making in the courtrooms (1095–96), so by recalling the non-partisan defense of the country earlier in the century, Aristophanes falls back on a slogan that unifies rather than divides.

The conciliatory disposition of the chorus is probably overdetermined: the pattern of a hostile chorus being won over by persuasion and reconciled with an antagonist was a device that Aristophanes had used before and would use again; their change thus follows, to a certain degree, the requirements of the genre. The nostalgic appeal to a period of unity is also not unique to the wasp chorus but is a device Aristophanes has used before.[25] Here, however, it underscores the fact that their fierce waspishness can coexist with social solidarity.[26]

Notably the wasps do not, as did Philocleon, entirely renounce the life of the juror. They proudly describe, in the parabasis, how they go to different courts of Athens – the Archon's court, the Eleven, the Odeion – and squeeze into their seats as they settle down to work. The wasp-jurors then contrast their courtroom activities with the life of certain drones who have no sting and are able to avoid the sacrifices of public service, especially military service. Our wasps are at least able to provide a livelihood (1103). Although Bdelycleon had appealed to the jurors by showing that they stood to benefit from his suggestions, they later say that they agreed with him because he had the best interests of the Athenian people (*demos*, 888) at heart. Whatever their true motivations, they viewed serving on a jury, like serving in the military, as a socially responsible activity.

There may be further levels of significance to the wasp nature of the chorus. In the late fifth century the word "sting" (κέντρον) was taking on a figurative meaning in the law courts. The "sting" they inflict can of course be the vote of conviction.[27] Thus at *Wasps* 420 Xanthias exclaims, "Look at the stingers (κέντρα)!" to which Bdelycleon responds that it was with stingers that the wasp-jurors destroyed a certain Philippos, someone active in the law courts and associated with Gorgias the rhetorician. A "sting" was thus a point that was driven home with forceful, perhaps devastating, effect by a speaker or someone rendering a verdict in court. In the *Clouds*, of 423 B.C., Worse Argument says that Better Argument will be "stung (κεντούμενος) by my arguments, as if by hornets" (947). Sommerstein has called attention to Euripides' *Suppliants* 240–43 "where it is said that the poor, 'giving too much rein to envy, unloose evil stings [*kentr'*] against the wealthy, being deceived by the tongues of wicked leaders.' Since Euripides' *Suppliants* may have been produced at the City Dionysia of 423, it is not impossible that this phrase may have helped to inspire Aristophanes with the idea of presenting jurymen as human wasps".[28] Other striking usages of the word, with more positive connotations, appear within a few years. In a well-known passage from the *Demes* of Eupolis (412 B.C.), the persuasiveness of Pericles was likened to a *kentron* that he left in his hearers (fr. 102 K-A); a few decades later Plato spoke of Socrates as a bee who left a sting (*Phaedo* 91c). However painful the sting may be, its effectiveness in debate is acknowledged.

Thus a wasp quality can be of service to the polis. Bowie has drawn attention to an analogue in the *Plutus*, where "Poverty" took credit for creating citizens who were "lean, wasp-like and painful to their enemies" (561). These are necessary qualities; there is, as Bowie writes, "a tension in man between wildness, which helps him defend his soci-ety, and civilisation, which lets him do this in an ordered and rational way."[29] Of course this is not to suggest that wasps were meant to be a model for human society, for despite their positive qualities – a keen sense of justice and patriotic solidarity – they embody militaris-tic regimentation. They could never accommodate the individualistic Philocleon.

This discussion of the *Wasps* would be incomplete without some consideration of the world of animals as it marks Philocleon. He is probably compared to more different types of animals than any char-acter in Aristophanes.[30] This variety alone suggests volatility in his characterization and instability in his identity. Moreover, Bowie has suggested that Philocleon can be seen as undergoing a reverse *ephebeia* in which he will shed an old identity and take on a new one; several of the animals associated with Philocleon can be taken as symbols of liminality or marginality: the dog, whose trial he judges, is a marker of margins; the wolf, which symbolically presides over the trial, is a creature that withdraws from society; the crab, with whom he dances, is a marginal animal.[31] It is unlikely that he is a wasp. The jurors con-sider him to be the "fiercest of us" (278), but they never say that he is a wasp and there is no indication that he wore a wasp costume. In the skirmish with the slaves he is isolated and unable to join his fellow wasp-jurors as they prepare a hoplite-like assault. Aristophanes was probably careful to compare Philocleon with a variety of other ani-mals so that the audience would not pigeonhole him with the wasps, which are not particularly marginal creatures. Their own identity is not really unstable; when they remove their cloaks they are not trans-forming themselves but unmasking themselves and revealing who they were in the first place. Far from being isolated or at the margins of society they form a society of their own. In their consistent wasp-juror identity they complement Philocleon's individualism and provide the structure that Philocleon may be truant from. Hence the choice of a social animal adds an important resonance to this comedy.

Why are the wasps in the *Wasps* Attic wasps (1076)? At *Plutus* 561 "Poverty" had praised the Athenians for being "wasp-like" and a scourge to enemies. The notion that Athenians were an indigenous people was a commonplace at the time (*Lys.* 1082; Eur. *Ion* 589–90;

etc.), but the special identification with Attica remains a mystery. A possible answer is that, since the fig was an important product of Athenian agriculture, the wasps of the *Wasps* are fig-wasps.[32] If so it might explain Magnes' choice.

Magnes' Fig-Wasps, ψῆνες *470s–440s* B.C.?

Magnes is thought to have won a victory at the City Dionysia in 472 B.C., making him a member of the first generation of comic playwrights. Our evidence for his animal comedies, as well as for his *Lydians* and *Barbitistai*, rests entirely on the parabasis of Aristophanes' *Knights* (520–25) and scholia for these lines. Aristophanes has been remarking on the willingness of Athenian audiences to turn their backs on playwrights deemed too old, and cites the case of Magnes.

τοῦτο μὲν εἰδὼς ἅπαθε Μάγνης ἅμα ταῖς πολιαῖς κατιούσαις,
ὃς πλεῖστα χορῶν τῶν ἀντιπάλων νίκης ἔστησε τροπαῖα,
πάσας δ᾿ ὑμῖν φωνὰς ἱεὶς καὶ ψάλλων καὶ πτερυγίζων
καὶ λυδίζων καὶ ψηνίζων καὶ βαπτόμενος βατραχείοις
οὐκ ἐξήρκεσεν, ἀλλὰ τελευτῶν ἐπὶ γήρως, οὐ γὰρ ἐφ᾿ ἥβης,
ἐξεβλήθη πρεσβύτης ὤν, ὅτι τοῦ σκώπτειν ἀπελείφθη.[33]

He knew what Magnes endured as his hair started turning grey – Magnes, who set up the largest number of victory trophies over rival choruses, yet though sounding off in every voice, plucking the lyre, flapping wings, speaking Lydian, acting like a fig-wasp, and dyeing himself frog-green, he did not last, but finally in old age – not as in his youth! – the old man was driven off stage because his jokes had lost their bite.

The scholia (text from Koster 1969, 129–30) on line 522 are:

ψάλλων· τοὺς Βαρβιτιστὰς ἂν λέγοι· δρᾶμα δέ ἐστι τοῦ Μάγνητος. ἡ δὲ βάρβιτος εἶδος ὀργάνου μουσικοῦ, "πτερυγίζων" δὲ ὅτι καὶ Ὄρνιθας ἐποίησε δρᾶμα. ἔγραψε δὲ καὶ Λυδοὺς καὶ Ψῆνας καὶ Βατράχους. ἔστι δὲ χρώματος εἶδος. τὸ βατράχειον. ἀπὸ τούτου καὶ Βατραχὶς ἱμάτιον. ἐχρίοντο δὲ τῷ βατραχείῳ τὰ πρόσωπα, πρὶν ἐπινοηθῆναι τὰ προσωπεῖα τὸ "Ψηνίζειν" δὲ εἶπεν ὡς πρὸς τοὺς Ψῆνας ἀναφέρων.

'Plucking the lyre': he would mean the *Barbitistai*, which is a drama by Magnes. The *barbitos* is a kind of musical instrument. 'Flapping': because he also wrote a drama with the title *Birds*. He also wrote *Lydians, Fig-Wasps* and *Frogs*.

Batracheion is a kind of [greenish] color from which comes the name of a garment, the *batrachis*. They smeared their faces with *batracheion* before masks were invented. He spoke of *psenizein* since he was referring to *Fig-Wasps*.

Thus the scholiast thought that the participles in *Knights* 522–23 (ψάλλων καὶ πτερυγίζων καὶ λυδίζων καὶ ψηνίζων καὶ βαπτόμενος βατραχείοις) alluded to plays with specific choruses and interpreted the passage as meaning, "Magnes, in his *Barbitistae, Birds, Lydians, Fig-Wasps* and *Frogs*." Unfortunately no independent sources survive to support the scholiast's commentary and it is legitimate to wonder whether these animal comedies even existed.[34] Spyropoulos suggested that the participles denote actions and gestures that were performed on stage not by a chorus but by Magnes himself; after all, there is some evidence that in early comedy the poets acted as protagonists in their own plays.[35] These participles would simply be in apposition to the earlier participial phrase, "sounded off in every kind of voice" (πάσας δ᾽ ὑμῖν φωνὰς ἱείς), which might more naturally refer to an individual actor. He points especially to other uses in Greek of -ίζω verbs, which do not denote "offering a comedy with a chorus composed of. . . ."[36]

Nevertheless, nothing precludes the possibility that these participles refer to titles and that, despite the parallel usages in Greek (which are helpful but not conclusive), we have in the *Knights* unique meanings for these participles, a figurative way of alluding to comedies that were familiar to many in the audience. Furthermore, we can be fairly certain that he wrote a *Lydians* because two lines have survived (frr. 3, 4 K-A), and it is reasonable to suppose that, despite the lack of independent evidence, the other participles refer to the titles of actual comedies as well. The existence of these as animal comedies cannot therefore be rejected out of hand; it seems sad that Magnes, who won more victories than any other comic playwright, should be deprived of these titles. At the very least, even if these were not plays with choruses of animals, they must have presented animal mimicry on the Greek comic stage.

How Magnes, whether as actor or producer, would have used fig-wasps in a comedy is unknown, but a number of observations can be made. The fact that Aristophanes introduced his list of Magnes' choruses or stage routines as ways in which Magnes had "produced every kind of sound" (πάσας δ᾿ ὑμῖν φωνὰς ἱεὶς) suggests that what was striking for Aristophanes was the aural or verbal element of these theatrical productions.[37] This emphasis suggests that the animal spectacle was not limited to costumes but extended to allowing the animals to speak in their various voices. Thus to translate ψηνίζων as "buzzing like a gall-fly" (Sommerstein, *inter alios*) cannot be entirely off the mark. But the choice of the fig-wasp (sometimes translated as "gall-fly" or "gall-wasp") as a role for a chorus, or even for an individual actor, raises interesting possibilities.

This type of wasp was known chiefly for its role in pollinating figs. In a process known as "caprification" the fig-wasp carried pollen from the male flowers of the wild fig tree to the female flowers of the cultivated fig tree. Farmers would purposely place wild figs or fig trees near the cultivated ones in order to facilitate this pollination. Exactly how much Magnes knew about this symbiosis of plant and insect we do not know. Aristophanes seems not to have understood it, for at *Birds* 590 Peisetaerus apparently believes that fig-wasps were pests who ate the fig and, not realizing that they were essential to cultivation, trumpets the ability of thrushes to clear fig-wasps out of trees. Herodotus, however, had a grasp of the essential procedure, and many members of the audience no doubt were keenly aware of the fig-wasp's role.[38]

If fig-wasps played a part in Magnes' comedy it would be surprising if caprification, their paramount task in the world of nature, were not somehow alluded to. Magnes could have cast them as destructive pests (as mistakenly believed by Peisetaerus) or as making their contribution to agriculture. In fact the verb ψηνίζειν, taken more precisely, seems to refer not to buzzing but to the role of the fig-wasp in fertilizing female figs. Tellingly, in virtually the only other occasion the verb is used in Greek, it was applied to pederasty: the proverbial οὐδεὶς κομήτης ὅστις οὐ ψηνίζεται ("There is no long-hair who is not pollinated like a gall-fly").[39] Thus the primary denotation of the verb must have been for the act of pollinating, and ψηνίζων would, in the first instance, refer to fig-wasps performing this activity.

That being the case, the chorus (if it was one) of this comedy would have been composed of animals that were known for their potent fertility. As previously noted, these themes were implicitly present in the choruses of horses and bull-headed dancers and explicitly in the case of the Getty Birds.[40] We do not know whether any social qualities of the fig-wasps were emphasized, but these qualities were not much written of anyway.

Diocles' Bees (Μέλιτται), 410–380 B.C.?

All that has survived of this play are the title and seven uninformative fragments, none longer than two lines. This is a pity, for given the key role of bees in Greek life and religion it would be illuminating to see how a comic playwright treated them. Aristotle, for example, devoted a disproportionate amount of attention to bees in the *Historia Animalium.* Bees attracted interest for their hives, sting, buzz, honey, and communication, but a few items of bee lore were especially important.[41]

Aristotle ranked the bee only slightly below human beings in its degree of social organization (*Politics* 1253a7-9), and bee society would be used as a parallel for human society in literature throughout antiquity. Aristotle noticed that there seemed to be a division of labor among bees (*HA* 625b17 and 627a20). For example, as noted in Chapter 3, young bees would be sent out by the queen to establish a new colony (Xenophon, *Oec.* 7.34).

Owing perhaps to the bee's reputation for purity and chastity, various priestesses were sometimes known as "Melissai" (female bees).[42] The priestess of Apollo at Delphi was called *Delphis Melissa* (Pindar, *Pythian* 4.60). In the classical period the bee appears in association with Artemis on coins of Ephesus in the classical period, and a line of Aeschylus quoted in the *Frogs* invokes "Melissonomoi" who are "present to open the home of Artemis."[43] In the cult of Demeter some "Melissai" were credited as a civilizing force: "The Melissai stopped men from eating meat and persuaded them to eat nourishment from the trees at the same time that one of them, Melissa, was the first to discover honeycombs."[44] Unfortunately we know of no evidence for these cult titles (much less for any cultic bee mask or costume) being used at rituals in Athens.[45] Semonides, satirizing women as various animal types, regarded the "bee" woman as the only virtuous wife (Semonides 7 Page, 83–93). There was also a long tradition in antiquity associating bees with poets and poetry.[46]

None of these issues arise in the surviving fragments of Diocles' comedy. Schmid suggested that fr. 8 K-A (καὶ διὰ τετρημένων ἀθέλδεται τύπων "And it is filtered through perforated impressions") referred to the preparation of honey.[47] In 1706 Hemsterhuis wrote, "Perhaps he portrayed the ingenuity and diligent industriousness of bees, an industriousness that reproduces a well-organized republic, just as Aristophanes did in the *Birds*, using a different approach but on a closely related theme" (cited in *PCG* V.20). One can add very little to this.

Pherecrates' Ant-Men *(Μυρμηκάνθρωποι), 430s–420s* B.C.?

Plato Comicus' Ants *(Μύρμηκες), 425–422* B.C.?

Cantharus' Ants *(Μύρμηκες), 420s–410s* B.C.?

No fragments survive for the *Ants* of Plato comicus or the *Ants* of Cantharus; all we have are the titles, listed in the *Suda* along with other comedies by Plato. We can only guess that the roles of these choruses reflected one of the salient characteristics of ants, such as the organization of their society. Aristotle of course included them with the "social" animals.[48] Their homes in anthills have quarters designated for seemingly specific uses and tunnels so elaborate that in the *Cheiron* Pherecrates compared them to the twists and turns of contemporary music.[49] Through its collective efforts an ant colony could accomplish prodigious tasks of gathering and storing grain. It was even thought that they could forecast the seasons and weather.[50] The ant does not seem to have been associated with any divinity or cult, but did have roles in several myths. In one, a young maiden of Attica named Myrmex tried to steal credit from Athena for the invention of the plow, and Athena punished her by transforming her into an ant.[51] There was a local tradition in Attica about ants protecting gold on Mt. Hymettus.[52] Hesiod said that Zeus changed ants into men and women so that Aeacus, the ruler of Aegina, would not be alone; Hesiod went on to say that the Aeginetans were "the first to build ships that curved at both ends and the first to use sails, the wings of a sea-going ship."[53] According to some traditions these new human beings traveled to Thessaly, where they were called the "Myrmidons" (derived from *myrmex*, "ant").[54]

Pherecrates' *Ant-Men*, of which fifteen fragments have survived, perhaps drew on the Aeginetan myth. The title suggests the chorus was made up either of creatures who were half-ant and half-man or who were at least men created from ants, such as the Myrmidons had been on Aegina. Fr. 126 ("by scraping they will heap up a mound of earth from the roof onto your head") might describe the building activity so characteristic of ants,[55] or it could refer to men behaving like ants, just as the *Wasps* of Aristophanes is more about men behaving like wasps than about wasps proper.

And yet the fact that it is Deucalion who is spoken to in fr. 125 ("Don't ever offer me fish, Deucalion, not even if I ask for it") suggests a role for the Myth of the Flood, in which the human race, save for Pyrrha and Deucalion, was obliterated. Humanity was created anew when Deucalion and Pyrrha threw stones, which turned into human beings. Frr. 118 ("Alas, woe is me, a hurricane, a hurricane is coming") and 119 ("But as quickly as you can, set up the spindle as a mast") would perhaps allude to Deucalion and his wife Pyrrha crossing the flood aboard ship; an exchange about fish in fr. 117 might have occurred during the voyage (A: "What are you blabbering about? They say that a fish most certainly does not have a voice." B: "By the goddesses, no other fish does except the *boax*").[56] An ancient treatise on comedy recorded that Pherecrates was "highly regarded for the introduction of new subject matter and for his creativity with plots,"[57] but exactly how he assimilated the myth of Deucalion and Pyrrha to the myth of the Ant-men of Aegina is a mystery.[58] Whittaker thought that Pyrrha and Deucalion made landfall at Aegina, where the population had been wiped out by the flood, though the usual versions of the myth have them land elsewhere.[59] Dover suggested that the creation of men out of ants was substituted for the stone-throwing motif.[60] Kaibel speculated that Aeacus, a leader of the age of heroes, was juxtaposed with a new age of petty men established by Deucalion. Conceivably the ship-building skill of the ant-people from Aegina was somehow connected with the sea-faring of frr. 118 and 119, quoted earlier.

EDIBLE ANIMALS

The ingestion of animals is pervasive in Old Comedy; many animals are introduced or mentioned for the sole reason that they were hunted, fished, raised as food, sacrificed, skewered, roasted, stewed, boiled, served with a garnish, and consumed. After all, one of the most important aspects of the relationship between animals and human beings is that animals are eaten. It is the most common use of animals in Aristophanes.

Killing animals may or may not have been a source of anxiety for human beings, but it certainly was for several animals in comic choruses. In Crates' *Beasts*, Archippus' *Fishes*, and (as we shall see) Aristophanes' *Birds*, this fear is what brings animals and human beings into conflict. (The *Nanny-Goats* and other bird comedies do not directly indicate that the issue was raised.) The articulate, anthropomorphized creatures in *Beasts* and *Fishes* saw the eating of meat for the threat it was. Yet what was at stake may be more than the simple need for self-preservation; as we saw in the last chapter, animals and eating had wider cultural implications. Thus these comedies illustrated the consequences of anthropomorphization: if the animals are humanized, human beings will cease to eat meat (as in the *Beasts*) or fish (as in *Fishes*), causing potential disruption in society.

Crates' Beasts *(Θηρία), early 420s* B.C.?

Θηρία, a generic word for "beasts" or "wild animals," being in form a diminutive of θήρ (the common expression for "beast" in epic and tragedy), was more at home in prose and comedy. *Therion* could be a general term for animals,[61] used to distinguish land and sea animals from birds and human beings,[62] from plants,[63] or from men and gods,[64] but could also be more specific: *theria* tended to be wild animals, either hunted or carnivorous.[65] If applied to a human being it was an insult.[66] *Theria* were by no means particularly social or pleasant animals.

Four fragments of Crates' play survive. The first three describe a life of miraculous leisure, with conveniences that defy the laws of nature but are imaginable in a utopian Golden Age. The speaker of fr. 16 claims that it is possible to lead a comfortable life without slaves: kitchen utensils will magically perform their tasks and fish will obligingly allow themselves to be cooked. In the next fragment a speaker describes how he will create an indoor plumbing system that can bring hot water right into the bathtub; after the tub has been filled a bottle of myrrh will arrive "all by itself" (*automatos*, fr. 17.7). The third fragment is only a few words: "Having an easy life and substantial property" (fr. 18). It was probably the theme of the "life of ease" that caught the attention of Athenaeus (our source for frr. 16, 17, and half of 19), and these first three fragments offer a reasonably consistent vision of it.[67] The fourth fragment (fr. 19) seems to introduce an animal who says, "You should boil some cabbages, and roast fish, fresh and salted, and keep your hands off us," to which a second speaker replies, "So, as you would have it, we won't eat any meat at all? We can't get anything from the marketplace, and we aren't supposed to make rissoles or black puddings for ourselves?"[68]

We know nothing about the significance of these fragments in the context of the comedy. Who was promising the life of ease? Was this life related to the animals' insistence on the abstention from meat? How were human beings persuaded to stop eating meat? What was the plot? We can only speculate. There is enough here, however, to see that issues of the day were raised.

Although the life of ease described in the fragments is one set in the immediate future, they also look to the past and draw on the myth of the Golden Age. The notion of a life without labor may be traced to Hesiod's Myth of the Ages, although the only verbal overlap here is the use of the word αὐτόματος ("by itself") in Crates fr. 17.7 (cf. καρπὸν δ᾽ ἔφερε ζείδωρος ἄρουρα / αὐτομάτη πολλόν τε καὶ ἄφθονον, *Works and Days* 117–18). Other elements of the Golden Age can be detected, such as vegetarianism, the notion that food was spontaneously offered by the earth, and the possibility of communication between animals and human beings.

The Golden Age motif is also echoed in fr. 16, which states that slaves will not be necessary. In fact what prompted Athenaeus to quote frr. 16 and 17 was his desire to show that the primitive times described in Attic comedy lacked slaves.[69] It is possible that this theme in the *Beasts* found further expression in the Attic festival of the Kronia. This was an agricultural festival held in midsummer for Kronos, who was originally a god of the harvest, and although the Kronia seems not to have derived specifically from the notion of an "Age of Kronos," it included a banquet at which slaves were allowed to dine with their masters, as if social restrictions had been erased.[70]

This return to a Golden Age should not be confused, however, with a "natural life."[71] The comforts described in the fragments were the products of Golden Age magic and of human contrivance, not of nature. The common desideratum of the first three fragments is to enhance human comfort and civilization, and hot baths, utensils, bread, and cooked fish are not compatible with a straightforward understanding of nature. This is a minor but significant point, for as noted earlier, animals in comedy tended not to be hostile to human beings but were often socialized and humanized. They were not simply alien forces of "otherness" but part of civilization.

Moreover, even if the *Beasts* had been set in the time of Kronos, it should be considered a critique of contemporary Athenian consumption. A mythical tradition was being co-opted by fifth-century intellectual speculation. We noted in Chapter 3 that Empedocles had been an early source for the notion that animals and human beings originally lived in a state of friendship. His version of a lost utopia was an "Age of Cypris" (Aphrodite), when "all creatures, both beasts and birds, were tame and gentle toward human beings" (DK 31 B130).[72] Although this is not inconsistent with the myth of the Golden Age, it is the product of rational, philosophical investigation. His belief in a lost utopia when no god's altar was "drenched with the blood of bulls," because it was considered pollution to eat the meat of an animal (B 128), probably owes something to Pythagoras. This prohibition against eating meat, of course, was deeply problematic.

The beasts of Crates' play follow a less rigid prohibition, since the diet they suggest in fr. 19 includes fish and vegetables.[73] It may be that one of the beasts or their representative is offering the life of ease to human beings in return for not eating meat.[74] Their motivation would then be more a matter of self-interest than of principle. Nevertheless, these animals, however anthropomorphized and on the defensive, were not the potent forces of nature that cocks and bulls seem to have been. Crates' *Beasts*, then, raises incendiary issues – the abolition of slavery and of sacrifice, both fundamental institutions in Greek society – but puts at least the second of these proposals in the mouths of animals.[75]

Archippus' Fishes *(Ἰχθύες), ca. 402–400* B.C.

Crates may have imagined fish compliantly allowing themselves to be cooked; Archippus' fish, however, refuse to play along, and it emerges that one theme in this comedy was their revenge on those who had eaten them. In fr. 28, for example, we learn that Melanthius, a poet who was known to enjoy eating fish, and was ridiculed for it in other comedies (e.g., *Peace* 803–813), was tied up and handed over to the fish to be eaten by them. (The scene, we are told by Eustathius, parodied the myth of Hesione, the daughter of Laomedon who was set out on a rock to be devoured by a sea-monster.) The anger of the fish was also directed at a certain Egyptian fish-seller named Hermaeus who had been flaying monkfish, selling dogfish, and gutting bass (fr. 23). To judge from the surviving fragments, then, the chorus of this comedy was on a campaign to end the consumption of fish.[76] Because fish were rarely sacrificed, there was no ritual provision for eating them – a circumstance that made them, if anything, more readily and savagely consumed.[77] One might wonder, of course, whether fish who were still willing to eat their enemy were morally superior.

Although fish were thought to be of a lower order than land animals and may have seemed unlikely to be staged and anthropomorphized,[78] Archippus clearly enjoyed finding a human element in their existence, or at least contriving one, and much of what happens in this play expresses or presupposes a developed society of fish: fish can make a proclamation (frr. 16, 25), sound a trumpet and earn a seven-obol wage (fr. 16), punish enemies (fr. 28), be priests (frr. 17, 18), and make prophecies (fr. 15). We should not overlook the fact that the fish (like Eupolis' goats, Aristophanes' birds, and no doubt other choruses) spoke Greek perfectly well – surviving fragments have no fish noises – and fr. 15 seems to be a dialogue between an Athenian and a fish. In fr. 30 they are addressed as "Gentlemen fish" (ἄνδρες ἰχθύες), and thus may have been holding a political assembly. The fish are united into a state with all the "statutes, institutions and customs of the Athenian state."[79] This exceeds even the social aspects of the wasps in the *Wasps*.

This fish community can also be credited with diplomatic skills: we have, in appropriately legalistic prose,[80] what appear to be the terms of a peace treaty struck between fish and human beings, no doubt as the resolution of a conflict. In the surviving portion the fish promise to "give back whatever we have of each other's property, namely, that we give up the Thracian women, Atherina the flute-girl, Sepia wife of Thursos, the Trigliai, Eucleides who was archon, the Korakiones from Anagyros, the son of Kobios of Salamis, and the assessor Batrachos from Oreos" (fr. 27). On the surface this seems to be a list of human captives, but behind each of these lies the name of a fish. For example, Sepia, the wife of Thyrsus, could be σηπία, "cuttlefish."[81] Archippus pursues this punning so relentlessly in the peace treaty that we cannot be entirely certain whether the fish are returning Thracian women, Atherina, et al., or herring (*thraittai*), smelt (*atherina*), cuttlefish (*sepia*), mullets (*triglai*) and crowfish (*korakinoi*). At least the presence in this list of Eucleides, whose name corresponds to no known fish,[82] strongly suggests that these are people, not fish. Fr. 27 represents only half of the treaty (note μὲν in line 1); in the other half we would probably learn what the Athenians owed. In fr. 28, of course, it was Melanthius who was delivered to the fish, so conceivably the fish and human beings had identified him as a common enemy.[83] Possibly the sacred fish in frr. 17 and 18 were exempt from the exchanges.[84]

These puns are characteristic of Archippus and the technique reappears in fr. 14. Here a speaker refers to the practice of rejecting but re-approving the same leaders; if they continue this, *"everyone* will be removed from office and then re-elected (παλιναιρέτους)." The adjective παλιναιρέτους, however, could also describe fish who had escaped the net only to be captured once again. Thus we cannot be sure whether this fragment describes the treatment of fish or of human elected officials.[85] Perhaps the re-election of an official was intentionally likened to a fish caught a second time. Some political satire, then, may have been part of the *Fishes.* The treaty in fr. 27 contains a provision for the return of Eucleides, archon of 404/03 B.C.; and in fr. 31 the democratic leader Anytus apparently was ridiculed for being a cobbler.

The creation of an animal society, accompanied by touches of political satire and mythological parody, makes it plausible that the *Fishes* was influenced by Aristophanes' *Birds* of a decade earlier. Just as in the *Fishes*, fish and human beings came into conflict, so too in the *Birds* the two central human characters, Peisetaerus and Euelpides, find themselves in combat with birds and must negotiate a peace; a leitmotif in the *Birds* is the birds' resentment of bird-hunting and threats to make bird-hunters into bird-prey (*Birds* 1076–83, cf. 529), much as the fishmonger Hermaeus is attacked in fr. 23.[86] Several types of fish were mentioned in the *Fishes* fragments; perhaps, as in Aristophanes' *Birds*, the chorus was not limited to any single species. If we had more of Archippus' *Fishes*, we might find that Archippus introduced a human being who became a fish and championed their cause.

This is not to say that fish life would have been shown to be superior to human civilization. It might be noted that there is nothing in the surviving fragments that describes activities that are unique to the lives of fish, and if natural abilities or qualities are mentioned, they are ones that correspond to human abilities or human concerns. The *boax* of fr. 16 was known for its ability to make noises,[87] and the gilthead was already thought to be a sacred fish.[88] In other words, Archippus' concern is not to show that there is anything in the world of nature that is somehow superior to human beings, but that the fish world could form a counterpart to the human world. Of course this is the comic effect: seeing that, amusingly, the fish, as fish, are not dissimilar from human beings. By implication, what is humanly created need not be artificial. But whether Archippus exploited this theme we cannot tell.

"Comoedia Dukiana" (PCG VIII, Adespota fr. 1146)

A papyrus from the late third or early second century B.C., now at Duke University, contains fifty lines of dialogue from a Greek comedy in which two characters discuss the merits of cooking and serving the sheat fish.[89] In the course of this conversation fish are endowed with human characteristics and qualities: the sheat is considered "the wisest, prince of the fish, leader, monarch, commander" (2–4) and a "River Adonis" who wants "to gamble and love" (8). Other fish, including the bass and pigfish, stand like clients by his door at dawn, ready to present petitions when the sheat appears (11–16). Though it is possible that the names of the fish are "punning allusions to their human or mythical counterparts,"[90] nothing compels us to understand them that way – Archippus fr. 27 was far more suggestive, with obviously human names – and the fish may have been treated anthropomorphically without reference to specific human beings.[91] The primary speaker in the fragment then continues to describe, in extravagant terms, the preparation and presentation of the dish, a process likened to a ritualistic initiation into a mystery cult. The experience of eating fish thus becomes a quasi-religious experience.

We do not have conclusive evidence for the date and authorship of this fragment, but it has stylistic affinities with Old Comedy. Archippus' *Fishes* must of course be considered: for example, a reference in lines 17–18 to Isocrates' *Encomium of Helen* (of the 390s?) would suggest that this fragment is from the early fourth century, and an allusion like this would be expected to be recent and "fresh."[92] Other clues, however, point to a later date. The form ἐντετεύχασιν (line 15) and references to a *dioiketes* (a Ptolemaic administrator, 38), Isis (39), and Harpocrates (44) would be expected from an Alexandrian date.[93] Perhaps the passage simply imitates Archippus; it is, after all, a somewhat self-consciously rhetorical display of conceits that would have been familiar by the fourth century (cf. *enkomion*, 6).

Unfortunately, even if the fragment is from Archippus' *Fishes*, it sheds no light on the fish chorus and in fact makes no clear reference to a chorus of any kind. What it does do, however, is to enrich the surviving corpus of ancient comedy with a splendid example of anthropomorphized fish, described second-hand. The sheat is cast as a leader and the other fish are eager to win his attention; to that extent there is a social structure. The sheat (if the *Silurus glanis* correctly identified as the fish in this fragment) was notable for its gigantic size and was said by Pliny to be able to eat a horse (*NH* 9.45). Thompson cites a Bohemian proverb: "One fish is food for another, but the Sheatfish eats them all." But in the papyrus the sheat is a "river Adonis" who wants to "gamble and love" (7–8) and it is this attractiveness that has led to its undoing: it is now surrounded by sauce and ready to be served.[94] If this fragment is from Archippus' *Fishes*, it would make sense early in the play, before human beings had seen the fate of Melanthius and realized the high price of eating fish. Perhaps it was the cruel demise of the princely sheat that triggered the war between fish and Athenians for which fr. 27 constitutes a peace treaty.

Eupolis' Nanny-Goats *(Αἶγες), 429–423* B.C.?

Goats were among the most common domesticated animals in the ancient world.[95] They were less expensive than sheep, and their hides were used for clothing by ordinary people such as shepherds and soldiers.[96] Goats were prized for their meat, cheese, and milk, in fact, drinking goat's milk later became a motif in accounts of Golden Age luxury (Virgil, *Eclogues* 4.2; Horace, *Epodes* 16.49). The he-goat, after the bull and sheep, was a standard sacrificial victim.[97] It was noted for its reproductive power and came to symbolize lewdness,[98] one consequence of which was that, especially in the post-classical period, the satyr was depicted as being part-goat. The goat was sacrificed to Artemis, a practice that has been explained as a vestige of an era before the goat was domesticated, for she is often understood to be the mistress of wild animals.[99] The Spartans sacrificed to Artemis Agrotera before engaging in battle,[100] and the Athenian polemarch sacrificed five hundred goats annually to Artemis Agrotera in thanks for the victory at Marathon.[101] In one myth, an Athenian named Embarus, who was required to sacrifice his virgin daughter to Artemis at Munychia, substituted a disguised she-goat instead.[102] Goats were sacrificed above all to Dionysus, who had the epithets *aigobolos* ("goat-shooter") and *melanaigis* ("of the black goatskin").[103] Of course the word "tragedy" (τραγῳδία) may derive from "song at the sacrifice of a goat" at the Dionysia.[104]

Eupolis' play was composed of *aiges*, female goats, not *tragoi*, which were male goats.[105] This may be significant in one respect: it was he-goats that were more often sacrificial victims; females thus had less to fear, and none of the fragments indicate that being eaten was a concern of theirs. Of the several "edible animals" who constituted choruses, these are the least likely actually to have been consumed, at least from what the few fragments suggest.

It was eating, not being eaten, that was their concern. Fr. 13, an excerpt from the parabasis of *Nanny-Goats* that was quoted by Plutarch, is simply an exhaustive list of their own diet. "We feed from material of all sorts, nibbling off young tender shoots of fir, prickly-oak and strawberry-tree...," they say, going on to list altogether twenty-two plants that they eat. This list of items in their vegetarian diet might be part of a longer critique of carnivorousness. But Plutarch, who harbored reservations about the eating of meat, might have raised this point; instead, he excerpted it for the narrower purpose of showing that it was wrong to think that animals have a simple diet.[106] Wilkins thought that the only references to human consumption in the frag- ments of this play were to small fish (frr. 5 & 16) and tripe (fr. 34).[107] The goats thus have a rich variety of foods and are, in their own eyes, sophisticated gourmands who have demonstrated that naturally occurring nourishment is, in variety, not inferior to humanly prepared foods. As Schmid suggested, Eupolis' aim may have been to diminish the gulf between the worlds of animals and of human beings.[108]

The effect, however, is not simple "anthropomorphizing" – making animals resemble human beings – for the foliage that was presumably so desirable to goats is unappetizing to human beings.[109] Nor do the goats claim, in the surviving fragment, that these plants are attrac- tive to human beings. This list of naturally available foods cannot be understood as a description of the abundance available in the Golden Age.[110] Similarly, in the *Agrioi* or *Savages* (420 B.C.) Pherecrates refuted the myth of the noble savage and the desirability of a primitive exis- tence by exposing the harshness of its diet, which included wild olives and wild pears, but also chervil, weeds, and acorns.[111] Those, at least, are conceivable as human foods.

In the *Nanny-Goats*, however, the question of whether or not the goats' nourishment is desirable or even edible is not raised: the nat- ural diet was seen as a self-sufficient good. This runs counter to the tendency we have seen in other choruses (in the *Fishes*, for example, and *Beasts*, where, although meat was forbidden, the consistent trend was to assimilate tastes to human standards): although the criterion of "variety" might be one that emulates human diet, the world of nature is found to have its own offerings and can be self-sufficient. Nature can stand on its own, without artificial human intervention, independent of whether or not it offers anything to human beings.[112] This attitude is unusual in the animal choruses. Possibly this valuation of nature is related to the fact that this chorus was decidedly female.[113]

Other fragments of this play, however, exhibit interest not in nature but in the very human arts of writing, poetry, and dance. We learn in fr. 18, which is a scholion on an unknown work of Old Comedy, that Eupolis referred in the *Nanny-Goats* to the one-time unity of the art of writing and the arts of the Muses (viz., poetry and music). This unity was mentioned also by Quintilian (fr. 17), who reports, in what was surely in reference to the *Nanny-Goats*, that Prodamus appeared as a teacher of both these arts. We know nothing else about Prodamus, and some have wanted to emend this to "Prodicus," the sophist, or "Pronomus," a music-teacher and *aulos*-player of the late fifth century. In fr. 18 we also learn that a rustic was being taught to dance in a "fluid" (μαλακῶς) manner.[114] This rustic may be the same person who was ignorant of the arts of the Muses in fr. 4, and perhaps also the goatherd in frr. 1, 3, and 12. The motif recalls the attempted education of Strepsiades in the *Clouds*.[115] But the word μαλακῶς is ambiguous, usually meaning "effeminate" but here plausibly meaning "fluid." Eupolis fr. 18 is thus open to two possible interpretations: that the rustic should be taught to dance μαλακῶς either satirizes the rustic for his lack of sophistication, or satirizes the teacher for teaching someone to dance effeminately.[116] Accordingly, Bergk considered fr. 326 as part of the *Nanny-Goats* because it referred to music and fr. 388 because it addressed a sophist (though K-A subsume these both under *incertae fabulae*).[117]

What this had to do with the goats we do not know. Dover asked, "Did the goats 'take over' rural Attica and try to improve their quality of life by having their boorish herdsmen educated?"[118] There is nothing to suggest that the goats themselves were associated with these higher cultural accomplishments, but we might guess that the natural foliage of the goats, the rustic life of herdsmen, and the sophisticated arts were all contrasted.

Magnes' Birds (Ὄρνιθες), 470s–440s B.C.?

Crates II's Birds (Ὄρνιθες), Fourth century?

As noted above, the existence of Magnes' *Birds* has been inferred from a single participle (πτερυγίζων, *Knights* 522), which means "flapping wings." It was also used in Aristophanes to denote a winged adulterer able to fly out of the theater for a tryst (*Birds* 795), an informer being told to fly away (1466), and "Poverty" insisting that, in debate, Chremylus is simply flailing away uselessly (*Wealth* 575). Conceivably Magnes' play involved a memorable scene of flapping wings, perhaps as part of a dance. It might not be irrelevant that the birds on the London oinochoe discussed in Chapter 2 (Plate II), painted at approximately the time Magnes began his career, are doing precisely that: flapping their wings.[119] The list of Magnes' activities at *Knights* 520–25, cited earlier (p. 117), was preceded by the statement that he was "sounding off in every voice," which implies that there was a striking aural aspect to this and his other comedies.

Two poets with the name Crates existed: the author of the *Beasts*, active in the fifth century, and a second Crates, who was perhaps active in the fourth century, though only the title of his *Birds* is reported.

Aristophanes' Storks (Πελαργοί), 390s B.C.?

Although storks played an insignificant part in any cult or myth,[120] in the *Birds* they help build a wall for the new bird city of Nephelococ-cygia, a role that depends partly on a pun on the name of the wall (Pelargikon) and the stork (Pelargos), and perhaps on the fact that they were familiar with mud.[121] Because they nested on roofs, their domestic life was visible. Storks were known, deservedly, for caring for their children. They also had a reputation (undeserved, apparently[122]) for caring for their parents (e.g., *Birds* 1353–57). By Aelian's day a stork at a man's house was even credited with punishing the man's adulterous wife.[123]

Aristophanes' *Storks*, of which fourteen fragments have survived, is thought to have illustrated the bird's good reputation.[124] Goossens suggested that the chorus of storks arrived to supervise the application of their moral standards to Athens; hence several fragments – including those mentioning various social pests ("I sealed up the houses of the malefactors," fr. 447[125]; "For if you prosecute one unjust man, twelve parasites will testify against you for the others," fr. 452), the politician Neocleides (fr. 454), and the poets Meletus (fr. 453) and Patrocles (fr. 455) – would have been from scenes in which notorious Athenians were put on trial. In fr. 445 ("For you are not offering anything for your father to wear") the speaker reprimands someone insufficiently solicitous of his father.[126] Aristophanes has thus chosen one of the most "social" of bird species for a chorus, one with as much a sense of justice as the wasp though more concerned with the family than with the *polis*.

Cantharus' Nightingales (Ἀηδόνες), *420s–410s* B.C.

The nightingale was celebrated for its mournful song, and poets likened themselves to these birds (Alcman fr. 25, Bacchylides 3.98). Democritus thought that all human beings, as students, learned music from the swan and nightingale (fr. DK 68 B154). The foremost nightingale of myth was Procne, who served up her son as a meal to her husband Tereus in retaliation for the rape of Philomela. As Tereus pursued them he was changed into a hoopoe, Procne into a nightingale, and Philomela into a swallow. (Later poets made Philomela the nightingale.) The story was told in Sophocles' *Tereus*, where Tereus was evidently cast as a savage barbarian, and Aristophanes used the story in the *Birds* (414 B.C.), where against all expectation the couple seems to live contentedly as birds.[127]

Since no fragments of Cantharus' *Nightingales* exist, nothing is known of its content, but it is difficult to imagine a play on the subject of nightingales that did not entail either song or the Procne myth. Cantharus is also credited with a *Tereus*, and it would be interesting to know how the myth was treated in these two comedies, as well as their relationship to Sophocles' and Aristophanes' versions.

A LIMINAL ANIMAL?

Magnes' Frogs (Βάτραχοι), *470s–440s* B.C.?

Callias' Frogs (Βάτραχοι), *430s–420s* B.C.?

Aristophanes' Frogs (Βάτραχοι), *405* B.C.

Probably produced in the 430s or 420s B.C., only the title of Callias' *Frogs* survives. Aristophanes wrote of Magnes "dyeing himself frog-green" (*Knights* 524), and the scholiast remarked that, before masks were invented, performers smeared their faces with *batracheion*, a green-ish color. Whether the scholiast was right about this practice we cannot say; it is clear, though, from the evidence of the vase-paintings that animal disguises were already in use in the sixth century and that masks were surely available to Magnes. Perhaps comic actors or choral dancers were still using face-paint in the middle of the fifth century, or perhaps the scholiast was projecting onto comedy a practice said to have occurred in tragedy.[128] Nevertheless, whatever historical realities lurk behind *Knights* 524 or the scholiast's comments, in this case it was the *visual* component of Magnes' performance that was remem-bered. Aristophanes' frogs, which we return to shortly, are by contrast notable for their *aural* performance.[129] That play, of course, survives in its entirety, and we return to it shortly.

The Frog in Greece

Zoological knowledge of frogs was spotty in antiquity, though Aris-totle reported on matters such as their manner of living (*HA* 487a) and reproduction (510b35, 540a30). Their greenish color attracted comment.[130] They were not thought to be particularly social animals, though they were at least "gregarious," and their croaking certainly constituted some mode of communication.[131] Aristotle also remarked on their noisiness (536a8), which was what many in antiquity associated it with. The racket could be annoying, even to the point of interrupt-ing sleep. Indeed the presence of frogs in great numbers could be an omen of an unhealthy season, and they were credited with magical powers, such as being able to forecast rain.[132] Abilities such as these suggest that frogs were associated with Apollo, the god of prophecy.[133] A further link between Apollo and the frog is the myth of Leto and the Lycian peasants: the peasants refused to let her drink from a lake when she was wandering with the new-born Artemis and Apollo; as punishment she turned them into frogs, to live in marshes and lead quarrelsome lives.[134] According to the Ovidian Pythagoras frogs orig-inated in mud and slime, so on at least that level they are "chthonic" creatures.[135]

Frogs' habitats in poorly defined regions like marshes and swamps made them liminal creatures. Although they were not treated as "dualizers" by Aristotle,[136] a folk taxonomy of frogs might well have

135

been that these amphibians, neither fish nor fauna, fell outside the boundaries of what was normal. Even their habitat, the marsh, is ambiguous and ill-defined, being neither completely water nor completely land. In Aristophanes' comedy they dwell in a marsh that is part of the Lake of Acheron, where they accompany with song the souls who row across the lake with Charon en route to their final destination. A more liminal role would be hard to find.[137]

Aristophanes' *Frogs*

This comedy actually has two choruses, a fact that gives it considerable notoriety in literary history. Frogs constitute a brief, preliminary chorus, first heard at line 209 and disappearing after 262. At 316 a new chorus, composed of the souls of initiates in the Eleusinian Mysteries, enters and remains to the end of the play.[138]

There is no doubt that these frogs were more frog-like than the chorus of *Wasps* was wasp-like: their refrain, "Brekekekex koax koax," mimics the sound of a frog, and they stay in character throughout their short role.[139] About their costume, however, nothing can be said, for we do not even know whether they appeared on stage. Doubts about their visibility stem principally from a scholion that states that the frogs did not appear in the theater.[140] Indeed, there is no reference in the text to their physical appearance, which sharply contrasts with the *Birds* and *Wasps*, where costumes are described or physical attributes such as stingers are invoked. Moreover, the frogs are largely identified with aural activity: Charon tells Dionysus and Xanthias, who are rowing across the Lake of Acheron on their way to the Underworld, that they will "hear the frogs' loveliest songs" (205–06). Dionysus later says, "You are nothing but 'koax'" (227), which may imply that he cannot see them either.[141]

Nevertheless, the theory that any chorus of Aristophanes could have been invisible is not entirely compelling.[142] Were it not for the scholiast's note – itself perhaps inferred from the lack of a specific description of the frogs' appearance – there would be no doubts about their presence. For example, practical difficulties arise in making off-stage music audible.[143] Moreover, the frogs are not identified exclusively with aural activities: they leap through the galingale and reeds (243–44) and their "bubbling splutters" (πομφολυγοπαφλάσμασιν, 249) have a visual as well as an aural impact. One solution to the whole problem may be to imagine that the frogs "swim" where they are visible to the off-stage audience but not to on-stage characters like Dionysus.[144]

Nor does it seem likely that concern for cost-saving kept the frog chorus off stage. It has been suggested that financial problems at Athens in 406/405 B.C. might account for the chorus of initiates' cheap costumes, which were made up of virtual rags; one might further expect the *choregos* to save even more money on costumes by keeping the frogs invisible and off stage.[145] Yet the initiates' frugal costumes may not have been dictated by cost-consciousness at all, for initiates were typically clad in old cloaks. In fact, precisely because of the savings from the inexpensive initiates' costumes, money would be available for frog costumes.[146] Moreover, in view of the financial pressures a *synchoregia* was implemented so that two *choregoi* could share the expense of costuming the chorus.[147] Although the *synchoregia* might be interpreted as evidence of an invisible chorus – the *choregoi* being considered so impoverished that they not only shared expenses but cut back on their costume budget – it could also suggest the opposite: by providing two *choregoi*, the production would be assured of generous financial backing.

Finally, the invisibility of frogs in nature is one of the arguments in favor of the invisibility of frogs in the play, yet the frogs' color was an often-noted characteristic in antiquity. Surely this was an opportunity for a "frog-green" costume. The well-known croaking of the frogs, however, is a tour de force of sound and song.

The frogs appear at a point in the play when Dionysus, en route to the underworld to find a tragic poet who will save Athens, begins to row across the Lake of Acheron. Charon tells Dionysus that, to accompany his rowing, he will hear beautiful songs from Frog-Swans (βατράχων κύκνων, 207).[148]

> βρεκεκεκὲξ, κοὰξ κοάξ.
> βρεκεκεκὲξ κοὰξ κοάξ.
> λιμναῖα κρηνῶν τέκνα,
> ξύναυλον ὕμνων βοὰν
> φθεγξώμεθ᾽ εὔγηρυν ἐμὰν ἀοιδάν,
> κοὰξ κοάξ,
> ἣν ἀμφὶ Νυσήϊον

Διὸς Διόνυσον ἐν,
λίμναισιν ἰαχήσαμεν,
ἡνίχ' ὁ κραιπαλόκωμος
τοῖς ἱεροῖσι χύτροις χω-
ρεῖ κατ' ἐμὸν τέμενος λαῶν ὄχλος.
βρεκεκεκὲξ κοὰξ κοάξ.

Brekekekex koax koax! Brekekekex koax koax! Children of the watery marshes, let us sing, in harmony with the *aulos*, that sweet-voiced song of ours – koax, koax – which we cried out to Dionysus, the Nysean son of Zeus, in the Marshes, when that *komos* of revelers with hang-overs moves, during Chutroi, through my holy precinct in a crowd. Brekekekex koax koax! (209–20)

The sanctuary of Dionysus "in the Marshes" was possibly located on the Ilissus River and would naturally be a home to frogs.[149] Because of their drinking on the second day of the Anthesteria (Choes), the revelers now, on the third day (Chutroi), have hangovers. Dionysus then tells the frogs that he's getting a sore bottom from rowing (221–22), to which they respond, "Brekekekex koax koax!" He retorts, "You're nothing but 'koax'!" Their answer:

εἰκότως γ', ὦ πολλὰ πράττων.
ἐμὲ γὰρ ἔστερξαν εὔλυροί τε Μοῦσαι
καὶ κεροβάτας Πὰν ὁ καλαμόφθογγα παίζων,
προσεπιτέρπεται δ' ὁ φορμικτὰς Ἀπόλλων
ἕνεκα δόνακος, ὃν ὑπολύριον
ἔνυδρον ἐν λίμναις τρέφω.
βρεκεκεκὲξ κοὰξ κοάξ.

And rightly so, you busy-body! For I am cherished by the Muses, who are skilled in the lyre, and by goat-hoofed Pan, who plays the reed pipe; Apollo the *phorminx*-player delights in me too because I tend the reed-stalks that grow underwater in the marsh and that are used in making the lyre. Brekekekex koax koax! (228–35)

Dionysus then complains that he has blisters on his bottom and asks the frogs to stop; they refuse:

μᾶλλον μὲν οὖν
φθεγξόμεσθ', εἰ δή ποτ' εὐ-
ηλίοις ἐν ἀμέραισιν

ἠλάμεσθα διὰ κυπείρου
καὶ φλέω, χαίροντες ᾠδῆς
πολυκολύμβοισι μέλεσιν,
ἢ Διὸς φεύγοντες ὄμβρον
ἔνυδρον ἐν βυθῷ χορείαν
αἰόλαν ἐφθεγξάμεσθα
πομφολυγοπαφλάσμασιν.

On the contrary, we will sing out even more, if we ever leapt about on fine sunny days through galingale and the wool-tufted reed, rejoicing in the verses of song that we sing when diving, or if, escaping the rain of Zeus, we sang in the depths an underwater choral song that was colored with our bubbly splashes. (241–49)

As Dionysus rows off, he begins to cry "Brekekekex koax koax" himself and insists that he will outlast the frogs in this sort of shouting contest. They fall into silence after line 262, presumably beaten.

The scene is one of the most memorable in Aristophanes, abounding in comic incongruities. These ridiculous animals claim to be the musical equals of swans and to enjoy the good graces of various divinities. In the process they act with condescension toward Dionysus, whom they appear not to recognize but merely see as an interloper.[150] It is difficult not to look at these frogs through the lens of Aesopic fable, where frogs had an inflated sense of their self-importance (cf. Phaedrus 1.24). Dionysus, too, is made to look ridiculous as he rows across the lake on his chafed rear end, annoyed beyond due measure by their croaking song.

The song itself is an incongruous mixture of high and low styles, with elevated moments punctuated by low lyric diction. This "hybrid" style is, as Silk has written, characteristic of Aristophanes, although the frog song is particularly marked by pleonasm and low diction (κραιπαλόκωμος, 218) and thus suffers by comparison with the Hoopoe's song at *Birds* 227–36. Silk finds the frog refrain uncomfortably close to "Edward Lear at his most self-sufficiently childish,"[151] and although "Brekekekek koax koax" may be the only line that most of my friends remember from all of Aristophanes, it is remembered as animal noise, not poetry. The burlesque quality has led to imaginative attempts to identify a hidden purpose, of which three examples deserve mention: Defradas thought that the annoying croak was intended to parody the "new music" of dithyrambs such as those by Timotheus.[152] Demand suggested that the frogs may have been meant to ridicule Phrynichus, who was offering a rival comedy, *Muses*, in the dramatic contest of 405 B.C.; Aristophanes was perhaps punning on his name (*phryne* = "toad," indirectly suggesting "frog").[153] Wills saw the whole scene as a contest in flatulation – certainly an Aristophanic activity.[154] Though attractive and entertaining, the evidence for these three views remains circumstantial.

Although their songs may seem like parodies, the frogs take them very seriously. They extol themselves for singing "a sweet-voiced song, in harmony with the *aulos*" and think they are entitled to a special place with Dionysus (209–20), the Muses, Pan, and Apollo (228–35). This may all seem incongruously pretentious, yet it shows that the frogs badly want to assert their musical credentials. Dover observed that many readers have found the frogs' song not laughable but brilliant, and "a culture which could think of the maddening noise of cicadas as the perpetual 'singing' of creatures dear to the Muses (Plato, *Phaedrus* 259BC) could take in its stride and enjoy lyrics founded upon the cries of *Rana ridibunda*."[155]

The audience may have laughed at the thought of frogs singing like swans, but even if the frogs' assertions are to be taken as comic, it is important that they take the form they do. Far from being lowly animals, inferior to human beings, the frogs have a credible claim to respectability: their contributions to cult and music give them a status as minor culture heroes. Frogs claim some credit for the creation of the lyre and the pan-pipe. They nourish the reed-stalk (*donax*) that is used for the construction of the lyre, thus pleasing the Muses who are "skilled in the lyre" (εὔλυροι, 229) and Apollo who plays the *phorminx*.[156] These may be the same reeds that please Pan, who plays "music on his reed pipe" (καλαμόφθογγα, 230).[157] In a small but pivotal role they glorify one of the highest of human cultural accomplishments: music. It may not, therefore, be ludicrous to speak of frogs and swans in the same breath.[158] Aristophanes makes no serious attempt to anthropomorphize them, and their habitat and activities remain those of frogs, but the world of animals is important because it offers something for human culture. Their role as little culture heroes confers on them a status that no wasp could expect, however law abiding he was. The frogs represent special, creative qualities.

The interaction of the frogs with Dionysus is also significant. Diony-sus, after complaining about their "koax," took up the challenge of matching them in tempo, volume, and endurance. He does not com-pete against them by offering lyric passages of greater beauty, but croaks out the refrain himself. "Brekekekex koax koax! I'm taking this over from you" (250), repeating it at 256, 260 and 267.[159] Here then is a protagonist who has, momentarily, assumed the voice of an animal, and in doing so he is more a frog than Philocleon ever was a wasp.[160] Philocleon took on no overt wasp characteristics, whereas Dionysus embraces a froggy persona, perhaps helped by an identity that is famously ambiguous, eluding easy classification. Lada-Richards has demonstrated that Dionysus spans the opposition of self and other by assuming the identity of Heracles, and spans the opposition of male and female by wearing feminine dress (to choose only two examples).[161] To her inventory one might add that he has spanned the opposition of human and animal by assuming the role of a frog and doing it so well that he beats them at their own musical game. The frogs, important in themselves as mini-culture heroes, therefore have a further role as foils against which Dionysus can broaden his persona and incorporate new dimensions. As victor in the contest, he is, possibly, heir to the frogs' own unique musical qualities.

Perhaps the episode can also be viewed in the context of rites of passage and ritual liminality in which the novice or initiate must pass through a period of role-reversal before being reincorporated into society. Lada-Richards suggests that Dionysus' claim not to be able to row would be seen as inversional (not to mention incompetent, since his arrival in a ship was part of his festival). Such a role-reversal could include a change in costume, including an animal disguise. There is no sign that Dionysus has assumed a frog costume – if the frogs themselves were invisible we would not expect him to – but his willingness to appropriate the frog croak can be seen as a momentary step in that direction. Similarly, the rowing and croaking are a kind of ordeal that he must perform in order to complete the crossing of Acheron.[162] He is, in this scene, transformed from victim to winner. Taking on the new identity endowed him with fresh powers.

HORSES AS MOUNTS

Aristophanes' Knights *(Ἱππεῖς), 424* B.C.

The chorus of the *Knights* were "Hippeis," that is, both young members of the Athenian cavalry and citizens belonging to the second
highest of the Athenian property classes. They were also known for
their hostility toward the democratic politician Cleon.[163] This made
them a logical choice for a chorus, for their chief goals in the comedy
are to attack Cleon and to satirize the gullible Athenian Demos who
supported him.[164] Members of this wealthy property class could afford
to serve in the cavalry, which was a more important military force in
the later fifth century than it had been in the sixth. Indeed, it had been
victorious in battle in the year before this comedy.[165]

It is likely that the members of the chorus either rode on other
men who were costumed as horses, as on the "Knights" vase discussed
in Chapter 2 (Plate I), or wore manufactured "horses" attached at
the waist.[166] Two considerations favor the presence of either type of
"horses" on stage. (a) The orders that the slave Demosthenes gives to
individual chorus members ("head for the right wing," "turn around
again and put up a defense," 243–44) are plausible mounted cavalry commands; he then says, "It's plain from the dust-cloud that
they are close at hand" (245), which makes more sense as a reference to cavalry than to men on foot. (b) In the antepirrhema of
the parabasis (lines 595–610) they praise the horses vividly, endowing
them with the human qualities that we find in other animal chorus
comedies.

Unfortunately, neither of these arguments favoring the presence of
horses on stage is conclusive. There is no direct address to the horses
or explicit reference to their presence. Nor are the horses themselves
heard from: they never speak in their own voices. By contrast, in
Nanny-Goats, Fishes, and *Beasts* animals speak in human voices; in
Frogs and *Birds* the choruses even make frog and bird sounds, and in
the *Wasps* and *Birds* there are explicit references to a costume. No
such clues are given in the *Knights.* Nevertheless, the "Knights" vase
in Berlin (Plate I) decisively shows that men could be costumed this
way. At the very least, the degree to which the chorus of Hippeis

has anthropomorphized their steeds in the parabasis should not be overlooked:[167]

595   ἃ ξύνισμεν τοῖσιν ἵπποις, βουλόμεσθ' ἐπαινέσαι.
     ἄξιοι δ' εἴσ' εὐλογεῖσθαι· πολλὰ γὰρ δὴ πράγματα
     ξυνδιήνεγκαν μεθ' ἡμῶν, εἰσβολάς τε καὶ μάχας.
     ἀλλὰ τἀν τῇ γῇ μὲν αὐτῶν οὐκ ἄγαν θαυμάζομεν,
     ὡς ὅτ' εἰς τὰς ἱππαγωγοὺς εἰσεπήδων ἀνδρικῶς,
600   πριάμενοι κώθωνας, οἱ δὲ καὶ σκόροδα καὶ κρόμμυα·
     εἶτα τὰς κώπας λαβόντες ὥσπερ ἡμεῖς οἱ βροτοὶ
     ἐμβαλόντες ἀνεφρυάξανθ'· "ἱππαπαῖ, τίς ἐμβαλεῖ;
     ληπτέον μᾶλλον. τί δρῶμεν; οὐκ ἐλᾷς, ὦ σαμφόρα;"
     ἐξεπήδων τ' εἰς Κόρινθον· εἶτα δ' οἱ νεώτατοι
605   ταῖς ὁπλαῖς ὤρυττον εὐνὰς καὶ μετῇσαν βρώματα.
     ἤσθιον δὲ τοὺς παγούρους ἀντὶ ποίας Μηδικῆς,
     εἴ τις ἐξέρποι θύραζε κἀκ βυθοῦ θηρώμενοι·
     ὥστ' ἔφη Θέωρος εἰπεῖν κάρκινον Κορίνθιον·
     "δεινά γ', ὦ Πόσειδον, εἰ μήτ' ἐν βυθῷ δυνήσομαι
610   μήτε γῇ μήτ' ἐν θαλάττῃ διαφυγεῖν τοὺς ἱππέας."

We wish to commend our horses, whose merits we know full well. They deserve praise for having suffered so much with us in invasions and battles. We do not admire their deeds on land as much as when they manfully leaped aboard the horse-troop-transports, after buying military issue drinking cups. Some of them bought garlic and onions too. Next, they took their oars, just as we human beings do, and as they pulled hard they cried out, "Neigh-ho! Who's going to row? We must pull more! What are we doing? Aren't you going to get it underway, you branded nag?" At Corinth they sprang out of the boat. The youngest of them dug field-beds with their tools and went off to forage for food. Instead of alfalfa they ate crabs that crawled ashore or hunted them off the bottom of the sea, so that Theorus[168] said that a Corinthian crab said, "It's terrible, Poseidon, if I can't escape the Knights either in the depths or on land or on the sea." (595–610)

The horses emerge as vivid personalities, with their own discipline and social habits. They are autonomous creatures, not simply subordinate appendages. Unsurprisingly those habits correspond to human ones. They boarded their ships "manfully" (599; cf. *Wasps* 1090), rowed their own transport boats like sailors (601–03), drank from water cups (600), ate garlic, onions, and crabs (not alfalfa, 606), dug beds and foraged for food (605).[169] Not one of these is a skill exclusively associated with horses. If "horses" were on stage they may have pantomimed the actions described by their riders.

Both in Aristophanes' comedy and on the vase in Berlin the riders appear to be youthful. Cavalry riders were traditionally shown in art to be young, and accordingly the Knights in Aristophanes are indignant that the Paphlagonian tried to flatter them "as if they were old men" (270), devote part of the parabasis to praise of their fathers (565–80), and are called "youngsters" (*neaniskoi*, 731) by the Paphlagonian.[170] This hardly proves that the chorus-members are ephebes – and if they had campaigned in Corinth in the prior year, their period of training was over – though they might have been on ephebic guard duty, patrolling the frontier against troublemakers such as the Paphlagonian. Bowie suggested that we see young Knights acting in tandem with the sausage-seller Agoracritus, who can himself be seen as undergoing a transition.[171]

Although this is not an animal chorus in the strictest definition, they echo the self-praise of the wasps in the *Wasps* or the praise of the sheat in the *Comoedia Dukiana*, and we can consider them an extension of that tradition.

Antiphanes' Knights (Ἱππεῖς), *370s* B.C.?

Antiphanes' career was exclusively in the fourth century, and he is considered a poet of Middle Comedy. Fourth-century choruses may have lacked the same degree of vigor as those of many fifth-century comedies, but if this play was named for the chorus, we can imagine that, on the analogy of the Berlin vase and Aristophanes' *Knights*, these knights entered the orchestra mounted on other men who were costumed as horses.

Neither of the two surviving fragments (frr. 108 and 109) tells us anything about the chorus. The speakers are evidently the Hippeis, not horses, and Nesselrath sees these fragments as attempts by the speaker to portray the soldier's life as a happy one.[172] The soldier type became common in Middle Comedy: cf. Antiphanes frr. 264 and 200. The "horn of Amaltheia" in fr. 108 is the cornucopia, a motif of the Golden Age.

CONCLUSIONS

Some generalizations can be hazarded about the plays and fragments examined in this chapter.

Nature as a Source of Culture

A recurrent theme has been the tendency of animals to represent the qualities of civilization. This is not to say that they do not also act as symbols of the potency and fertility of nature or that they might not embody daemonic powers important for cultic ritual. Goats, of course, were common sacrificial animals. But it is the anthropomorphization of these animals that attracts attention; many of these animals had mini-societies that could prompt or reenact human cultural achievements. One might have expected that bringing animals on stage would somehow lower the level of discourse, but the opposite turns out to be the case: they lead away from, not toward, the "beast-like existence" (θηριώδης βίος).

The *Ant-Men* of Pherecrates, for example, may have depicted the creation of human beings, or at least turned human history back to a new beginning with the myth of Deucalion and Pyrrha. The social solidarity of the wasps in Aristophanes' play gave them the impetus to serve on juries and fight off barbarian invasions. Choruses of bees and ants in all likelihood exhibited traits of social structure and industriousness. Surviving fragments of the *Storks* are consistent with their interest in domestic and political order. That even certain kinds of fish have a sort of voice and can communicate is a notion that appears both in the *Ant-Men* (fr. 117) and in the *Fishes* (fr. 16). In performance no animal is unable to communicate in Greek, though two, frogs and birds, also have animal voices. The chorus members of *Fishes* appear to have a mini-state: they make proclamations, sound trumpets, earn a salary, serve as priests, make political speeches, and seem to have some sort of political structure; they at least are able to establish a formal peace treaty. As Ceccarelli has put it, "Animal choruses ... do not imply a life outside the polis."[173]

In one respect this function works a variation on the familiar theme of the aetiological myth – in which dolphins and river-gods had a role in the foundations of new cities – but the care with which animals have been anthropomorphized surpassed myth and the simple Aesopian talking animals of fable, pointing instead to an awareness of contemporary speculation concerning nature and culture. Chapter 3 showed that human beings were thought to have achieved civilization by leaving a beast-like existence behind; then, endowed with hands and speech, they built shelters, established cities, and made musical instruments. In comedy, however, these achievements, rather than separating human beings from animals, were extended to or even derived from animals. Only rarely can distinctions be made between what is an artificial construct of human society and what is an organic outgrowth of nature.

Music and Dance

This cultivation extends to higher accomplishments, such as music, which would have been an important part of the audience's theatrical experience. The association of animals and music is surely not just a fifth-century innovation. The dolphin was associated with music, the most famous rider of dolphins (although unlikely to be the specific subject of the vases) being the dithyrambist Arion, and vase-paintings linked dolphins with Apollo and the *aulos*.

In the fifth century, however, the topic was raised in a more self-conscious way. Democritus wrote that human beings imitated the swan and nightingale, and one would expect the song of the nightingale to play a role in Cantharus' *Nightingale*. Aristophanes' *Birds* calls attention to the melodies of birds such as the hoopoe, whose song at 227–62 is characterized by an unusual variety of rhythms, and above all the nightingale "of sweet songs" (ἡδυμελῆ, 659; cf. "clear-voiced" or "high-pitched" λιγύφθογγος, 1380 and see 1332; heard off stage at 222). The tragic dramatist Phrynichus, who produced divine songs, was likened to a bee (*Birds* 748–51). It is clear that in Eupolis' *Nanny-Goats* (frr. 4 and 17) one of the themes was the teaching of μουσική (*mousike*), which comprised the "arts of the Muses" in the broadest sense, but especially poetry and music, which were virtually inseparable. Fr. 13 also mentioned dance instruction, though none of this can be specifically connected with the goats themselves. The frogs were called "frog swans" whose songs were beautiful, and by cultivating reeds they were indirectly responsible for the pan-pipe and the lyre.

PLATE I. Attic black-figure amphora by the Painter of Berlin 1686, showing men costumed as horses. Ca. 550 B.C. Berlin Staatliche Museen F 1697. Antikensammlung, Staatliche Museen zu Berlin. Photo credit: Bildarchiv Preussischer Kulturbesitz/Art Resource, NY.

PLATE II. Attic black-figure oinochoe by the Gela Painter, showing dancers costumed as birds. Ca. 500–490 B.C. London, British Museum B 509. Photograph © Copyright The Trustees of The British Museum.

PLATE III. Attic black-figure amphora attributed to the Dot-Ivy Group, show-
ing men wearing cock masks. Ca. 480 B.C. Berlin, Staatliche Museum F 1830.
Antikensammlung, Staatliche Museen zu Berlin. Photo credit: Bildarchiv Preussischer
Kulturbesitz/Art Resource, NY.

PLATE IV. Attic red-figure calyx-krater, showing dancers in bird costumes. Late fifth century B.C. The J. Paul Getty Museum, Villa Collection, Malibu, California, 82.AE.83. Photograph © The J. Paul Getty Museum.

PLATE V. Attic red-figure psykter by Oltos, showing six men riding dolphins. Ca.
510 B.C. New York, Metropolitian Museum of Art 1989.281.69. Photograph © 1992
The Metropolitan Museum of Art, New York, Metropolitan Museum of Art. All
rights reserved, The Metropolitan Museum of Art.

PLATE VI. Attic black-figure skyphos of the Heron Group, showing six men riding dolphins. Ca. 490–480 B.C. Boston, Museum of Fine Arts 20.18. Gift of the Heirs of Henry Adams. Photograph © 2005 Museum of Fine Arts, Boston.

PLATE VII. Reverse of Plate VI, showing men riding ostriches.

PLATE VIII. Terracotta statuette, Attic or Boeotian, of an actor costumed as a bird. Fourth century B.C. Judy and Michael Steinhardt Collection, New York, A1992.20. Photograph courtesy of the Steinhardt Collection.

Aristophanes stressed the variety of "voices" Magnes unloosed; twanging the lyre and buzzing like a fig-wasp (one possible interpretation of the participle) were included in this list, and if the Greeks could find music in the noise of cicadas (as Dover put it), perhaps the fig-wasp's buzzing was soothing as well.[174] Music is the perfect meeting ground between animals and human beings, the innate endowments of animals becoming models for human artistry. Artifice is rooted in nature.

Comedy's Selective View of Nature

To the pattern outlined above – that comic playwrights tended to create animal choruses that mimicked human activities – there was a corollary: activities and creations routinely expected of animals in nature were frequently ignored unless they resemble their human counterparts. Asocial or savage animals do not fit the profile. For example, the sting of the wasps, a potent weapon of the world of nature, was only acceptable because it will be turned for something beneficial, as this aggressiveness was essential against the Persians. This weaponry could also be transferred to human use by analogy when the rhetorical "sting" became a recognized feature of public debate in Athens. Rarely is nature valued for itself; almost never does it or its creatures become a force to be in awe of, as in tragedy. Almost nothing gets out of human control in comedy, for human beings are endowed with the powers of nature, rather than just being at their mercy.

One can find very few exceptions. Fig-wasps, for example, existed to fertilize figs. If they did this in Magnes' comedy, and if one is not inclined to see the fertilization of the fig as an artificial intrusion, they were unusual in that they were not doing something that human beings could do very well on their own.[175]

At least fertilizing figs benefited human beings. In Eupolis' *Nanny-Goats* the diet praised by the goats included a number of items indigestible for human beings. The notion that something that occurs in nature could be valued even if useless for human beings marks a departure from the general tradition. In finding goats that do *not* assimilate themselves to human conceptions of what is helpful, there is a glimpse into the "other," possibly triggered by the fact that this is, unusually, a chorus of female animals.

The status of most animal choruses as male animals, or of inde-
terminate gender, raises a further question. What might be expected
from them is the sexual potency of the cocks and bulls on archaic vase-
paintings. In the literary remains, however, sexual potency has been
suppressed, conceivably as *too* threatening for human beings. Animal
sexuality may have been seen as exclusively in the sphere of what is
"wild" and was thus relegated to silence.

In contrast, human practices were indicted as too savage by animals.
Two animal choruses appealed to human beings to cease their eating
of animals: in fr. 19 of Crates' *Beasts* the animals urged human beings
not to eat animals but instead to eat fish and vegetables (radishes),
and Archippus' *Fishes* involved sanctions taken against human beings
who were notorious fish-eaters (frr. 23 and 28). Appropriately, the diet
praised by the goats (Eupolis, fr. 13) is entirely vegetarian. Once animals
have been anthropomorphized it becomes harder to butcher them. To
contemplate a cessation of eating of meat (as in the *Beasts*) or fish (as
in *Fishes*) would undercut the "civilized" institution of sacrifice.[176]
At the very least, even if the animals were eaten, the animals (or the
playwrights) have forced hypocritical human beings to consider this as
potential for cannibalism.

These may have been motivated by the Pythagorean taboo against
eating animals.[177] Nothing is known of the context of the beasts' and
fishes' requests, and whether they were proven in the end to be legitimate or preposterous remains unknown. Clearly the beasts and fish
are motivated by self-interest. The fish want to eat Melanthius (fr. 28),
an act which could be explained as simple reciprocal justice, though it
shows that they are no better than human beings, perpetuating their
animalistic ways.

Supernatural and Cultic Roles

None of these comedies can be traced back to a common cultic ritual.
In fact most of the animals chosen seem not to have had any cultic association whatsoever. That there were "Melissai" in the cults of
Apollo and Artemis would be a promising example of an association
with a specific divinity, but they were not costumed as bees and are
thus no more useful as evidence than the "Tauroi" of Ephesus. Nevertheless, the existence of the Melissai serves to remind us that the

significance of bees transcended their role as anthropomorphic "social animals."

Several animals were linked with Artemis: bees were depicted on coins with Artemis, there is evidence for fish dances in her honor, goats were sacrificed to Artemis Agrotera, and the Lycian peasants who mistreated her mother Leto were turned into frogs. Nevertheless, none of this adds up to a reason to see cults or rituals of Artemis as a source for any particular animal chorus, much less the genre as a whole.

Likewise, however important Dionysus was as the patron of theater and as a divinity who could straddle the realms of "self" and "other," there is no sign that the cult of Dionysus played any role in the genesis or persistence of animal choruses. None of the animals traditionally included in his retinue had parts in animal choruses. True, Dionysus did briefly take on the voice of a frog, which provided a convenient outlet for him to express his slippery identity, yet this does not establish grounds to think that the cult of Dionysus engendered animal choruses. Moreover, the frogs in Aristophanes' play claimed to have a special relationship with Pan, Apollo, and the Muses. Animals might also be said to play a transcendent role by being present at ritually significant moments in people's lives. Frogs, for example, were associated with liminality. The fact that the mounted men in the *Knights* were young might indirectly point at a rite of transition, as part of the *ephebeia*; if so, however, the play yields few hints of this.

Hence, no coherent pattern emerges to support assumptions of a direct ritual basis for animal choruses.[178]

Politics and Comedy

Chapters 1 and 2 raised the possibility that the pre-comic masquerades on vase-paintings were performed as entertainments at symposia. They could have been pure fun and nonsense, but would also have been meaningful to the *aulos*-playing, cock-fighting, horse-riding class of elite Athenians. Aristophanes' later *Knights* suggests the association continued.

Moreover, the earlier symposiastic themes possibly correlate with the revival (if that is what it was) of animal comedy in the late fifth century. Perhaps the pre-comic masquerades dropped out of public view when comedy entered the public sphere at the Dionysia. Animal masquerades, at least the ones on vases, might have been seen as an aristocratic, symposiastic affectation, and therefore were not featured in the first few decades of comic festivals. Edwards has speculated that in these years Old Comedy was a vehicle for the *demos* to criticize the elite and that at the end of the century comedy became a tool with which the elite attacked the leaders of the *demos*.[179] Is it then a coincidence that the evidence for animal choruses is strongest precisely when comedy was a vehicle for elite expression? We may wish to consider the animal choruses of the late fifth century as a consciously archaizing, creative re-invention of an older genre.[180]

Aristophanes' *Knights* squares with this; the Berlin Knights vase (probably) and Aristophanes' comedy (unquestionably) convey the values of the Athenian cavalry elite. The wasps of the *Wasps*, admittedly, cast themselves as democrats, and it would be difficult to claim that they played a formative or symbolic role for Athenian aristocrats. Nevertheless they do offer a sense of the close solidarity, based on a shared military past, that the wasps speak so proudly of. The chorus of the *Birds*, too, has a corporate disposition. All of these plays, as well, take a critical stance toward the democracy in general and, in the case of *Knights* and *Wasps*, toward Cleon in particular, a view that even the wasp chorus came to accept.

Of course there are other choruses in comedy – the chorus of *Acharnians* was composed of old charcoal-burners from Acharnae (*Ach.* 179–81) and that of *Peace* seems to settle into an identity as Attic farmers (*Peace* 296–97, 345–60) – neither one of which strikes an aristocratic pose. These, conceivably, are the descendants of Susarion's peasants, although it is perhaps significant that there is no clear record of that tradition in vase-painting.

5

ARISTOPHANES' *BIRDS* AND THE RISE OF CIVILIZATION

Aristophanes' *Birds*, the finest surviving example of an animal chorus, can be understood as a parody of the theories that traced the rise of civilization from savagery.[1] The *Birds*, after all, recounts the success of Peisetaerus as he brings creatures out of a beast-like existence (the *theriodes bios*) and persuades them to help him construct a city in the air. This view of the play extends the proposition in Chapter 2 that dolphin-riders and river gods were related to Greek myths of city foundations. Moreover, the *Birds* exploits the notion of the "social animal" encountered in other fifth-century comedies. The play shows that the new society is built on *physis*, since it was composed of birds, yet the social traits of animals make the process plausible. Notably the chorus, whose members never drop their bird-masks, permeate virtually every phase of the plot.[2] I will also suggest in this chapter that the advances sketched out in the *Birds* most resemble those in the "Archaeology" of Thucydides.

In a further Thucydidean touch, this chapter will also present evidence that Peisetaerus was following the footsteps of an earlier empire-builder, Minos. Peisetaerus, like Wilde's prison-warden, is thus a composite: he is a bird, a Hesiodic usurper, an energetic *ktistes*, a persuasive demagogue, and an ambitious King Minos.

FROM NOMADS TO CITY-DWELLERS: THE FOUNDATION OF NEPHELOCOCCYGIA

The birds' life, which at the beginning of the comedy left them vulnerable to predators, bears a remarkable resemblance to the view of early humanity taken by the Greek "anthropologists." In some reconstructions of early history, advances out of vulnerability were ascribed to individual benefactors or to divine intervention; in others, human beings made these advances on their own, independent of gods or heroes. Some rejected the notion of divine providence but saw developments as natural responses to material conditions or physical necessity. Yet others emphasized the contrived status of social institutions. Although Aristophanes was a poet, not an anthropologist or sophist, the *Birds* reflects these contemporary ideas. More specifically, he accepts some but seems to reject others, following his own comic logic. How Aristophanes shaped these disparate notions into an eclectic new synthesis is traced here.

The Primitive Life of the Birds

Some of the progressivists agreed that existence in the original state of nature was unsettled, lacking permanent habitation. In the *Prometheus Bound* Prometheus described human beings living underground in caves like ants.[3] In Plato's *Protagoras* human beings were "without clothes, shoes, beds or arms" (321c5–6); human beings lived scattered about (ᾤκουν σποράδην, 322a8–b1); social skills were not innate and would only come later. Thucydides, while agreeing that in ancient times there had been no settled population in Greece (οὐ πάλαι βεβαίως οἰκουμένη, 1.2.1), and that it lacked commerce, communication, agriculture, fortified protection, or permanent homes, seems to have thought of the earliest stage of existence as already involving socially cohesive groups or tribes, not scattered individuals.[4]

In Aristophanes the birds seem to lead a nomadic existence in fields, thickets, and trees. Tereus and Procne have settled in a thicket (λόχμη, 202, 207, 224, 265), but a pun – when we expect to hear Tereus say to his servant, "Open the door (πύλην)," he says instead, "Open the glade (ὕλην, 92)" – reminds us that they live, after all, in the wild. Birds are "unstable" (ἀστάθμητος, 169) and have no fixed abode, "never staying in the same place" (170). They are scattered far about: Tereus invokes his fellow birds, calling on all those who live in country plough-lands (ἀγροίκων γύας), in the hills (κατ᾽ ὄρεα), in the marshy valleys (ἐλείας παρ᾽ αὐλῶνας), and over the sea (ἐπὶ πόντιον οἶδμα θαλάσσης, 230–50).

This life, as several scholars have pointed out, bears a strong similarity to that in the Golden Age.[5] These brief but moving glimpses of the meadows, trees, and mountains where the birds live, as well as the availability of food and the fact that they had no apparent need for clothing, fire, or shelter,[6] suggest that this is not a savage state of deprivation but an Edenic existence.[7]

According to this reading, the birds enjoyed the benign and fertile forces of nature. For example, the thicket of Tereus and Procne, which may have been rolled out on an *ekkyklema* as a kind of visual accompaniment to the nightingale, conveys an ambience of song and fertility. This is the "life of newly-weds," remarks Euelpides (161).[8] Auger points out that the birds live without money (157), feeding on sesame and myrtle (159), and offering birds' milk (729–36). The hints of Pythagoreanism – they do not eat one another – are also reminiscent of the Golden Age.[9] Auger cites, as an illustration of Golden-Age harmony, the announcement that human laws will no longer be valid (755–56) and suggests that two uses of the word *nomos* ("melodies," νόμους, 745, and "pasture," νόμον, 1287) show that artificial convention has been superseded by nature. At 615–18 the birds claim that, as gods, they will live in bushes, saplings, and olive trees. The song at 1088–1101 celebrates their freedom from the extremes of climate and their praiseworthy natural self-sufficiency. Nature thus has its benign qualities, which lessens the impact on the birds of harsh necessity (*chreia*).

The "pastoral" moment is significant yet relies on a selective and sanitized view of nature that needs to be balanced against other aspects of the *Birds*. The state of nature as found by Peisetaerus and Euelpides, far from a life of newly-weds, resembles the existence described in the "progressivists" and depicted in the *Savages* of Pherecrates. The stage set of the *Birds* had its greenery, but was also rocky (54) and may even have been the same craggy set used in Sophocles' *Philoctetes*.[10] Peisetaerus, by demonstrating the dangers and inadequacies of the existence that the birds have been living, succeeds in persuading them that they are not self-sufficient after all but are subject to harsh necessities (*Birds* 465ff.). Peisetaerus is *not* "in love with" the life of the birds as he comes to see it. Edenic peace may have sounded alluring, but he turns his back on it and loses little time in creating a new city.

One harsh necessity of life in the wild (as the "anthropologists" saw it) was being vulnerable to wild animals.[11] At Plato's *Prot.* 322b2–4 men were devoured by wild beasts (θηρίων) because they were weaker, and Critias spoke of early men as living a "disordered and beastlike existence, at the mercy of brute force" (ἄτακτος ἀνθρώπων βίος καὶ θηριώδης ἰσχύος θ᾿ ὑπηρέτης, DK 88 B25). Thucydides saw the earliest people as living in complete disorganization, lacking commerce, communication, and protected cities, and suffering both civil war and attacks from pirates; agriculture was unknown, although food for day-to-day existence seems to have been available (1.2).

Being preyed on is a harrowing fact of life for the bird chorus. Understandably, they attack Peisetaerus and Euelpides with a military-style charge (364–65). The chorus-leader asks whether they should show any more mercy to the men than they would to wolves and denounces men as ancestral enemies.[12] The birds cast themselves as hunted creatures and human beings as predatory beasts. Once a truce has been settled between the two camps, Peisetaerus reminds the birds of the indignities they have had to suffer at the hands of fowlers: limed twigs, snares, and nets (525–30; hunting is further bewailed at 1076–87). The life of the birds is, therefore, "nasty, brutish, and short" (Hobbes, *Leviathan* 1.13).

The suggestive uses of the word *nomos* as "melody" (745)[13] and "pasture" (1287) may invoke the world of nature, but they are promptly undercut: although the birds may go to pasture in 1287, the lines immediately following bring us back to civilization: what they forage about for are laws and decrees in the bookstalls (1288–89).[14] The birds ask Tranquility (*Hesychia*, resonant of pastoral peace) to settle in their city (1321), but the request is ironically voiced at the moment of frantic sorting of wings.[15] What is most important about pastoral simplicity is how small a role it plays in the *Birds*.

Although at first it seems to be the fate of the birds to be victims, their own complicity in the predatory world eventually emerges. The chorus cheerfully endorses father-beating and adultery (753–800), and Peisetaerus recognizes that vultures and ospreys would steal (890–92).

What persuades the birds to join the two men is Tereus' argument that treating men as friends is in their self-interest (*chresimon*, 382).[16] Though not monstrous crimes, neither are they consistent with a Golden Age of pastoralism. The bird chorus does have positive qualities, but not ones that are pastoral.

The birds' earliest existence, though nomadic and dangerous, was far from the disordered society described by Protagoras, where men harmed one another and lived scattered about (322b7–8), or the "disordered and beastlike life." Tereus, calling them together from furrows, hills, and seas, said, "We are assembling all of the tribes here" (πάντα γὰρ ἐνθάδε φῦλ' ἀθροίζομεν, 253).[17] They thus resemble the wandering tribes in Thucydides and constitute a "pre-civic solidarity."[18] Their attack on Peisetaerus and Euelpides serves as an expression of *philallelia*, or mutual affinity, in that it gives the birds an opportunity to act in a concerted way and coalesce into a fighting force.[19] They had a capacity, perhaps relying both on innate as well as on learned abilities, to dispose themselves into offensive, hoplite-like formations, with one of them acting as a *taxiarchos*. Possessed of this cohesion and unity of purpose, they represent far more than a *tabula rasa* or "zero-grade" existence. Typically of their non-Edenic state, this social cohesion emerges in a militaristic context, on which more shortly.[20]

The Myth of the Birds' Origins

Their cohesion is conveniently reinforced by the myth of their origins. Peisetaerus reveals that the birds are the rightful rulers of the universe, senior to Kronos, the Titans, and Earth itself (465–538). In the subsequent parabasis the chorus-leader gives his own version of the origin of the universe, according to which birds were the offspring of Eros and Chaos; Eros, in turn, had been born of Night, the first of all beings (*Birds* 685–736).[21] The birds' seniority to the Olympian gods validates their claim to a "natural" position of superiority.

Peisetaerus thus views their current existence as artificial and *un*natural: once the most powerful creatures in the universe, they have been wrongly usurped and are now downtrodden prey.[22] Their situation resembles that described by Callicles, in which natural leaders have been artificially subjugated by others (Plato, *Gorgias* 482e–484c). In giving their version the chorus is also evidently rejecting Prodicus' account of the origins of the cosmos. Prodicus, who is dismissed by name ("tell Prodicus to get lost," 692), had apparently proposed that the very notion of "gods" was simply the imaginative creation of human beings who supposed that a higher source was responsible for blessings such as agriculture (DK 84 B5); the chorus members counter that birds are the source of these benefits.[23] Dobrov has pointed out that the parabasis marks a new sign of self-consciousness and confidence on the part of the bird chorus. They can now evolve into a "self-aware *politeia*."[24]

Warfare and Self-Defense

"War is a stern teacher," wrote Thucydides (3.82), and Tereus evidently agreed, exhorting the birds:

ἀλλ' ἀπ' ἐχθρῶν δὴ τὰ πολλὰ μανθάνουσιν οἱ σοφοί.
ἡ γὰρ εὐλάβεια σῴζει πάντα. παρὰ μὲν οὖν φίλου
οὐ μάθοις ἂν τοῦθ', ὁ δ' ἐχθρὸς εὐθὺς ἐξηνάγκασεν.
αὐτίχ' αἱ πόλεις παρ' ἀνδρῶν γ' ἔμαθον ἐχθρῶν κοὐ φίλων
ἐκπονεῖν θ' ὑψηλὰ τείχη ναῦς τε κεκτῆσθαι μακράς.
τὸ δὲ μάθημα τοῦτο σῴζει παῖδας, οἶκον, χρήματα.

But it is from their enemies that smart people learn the most. Vigilance, you see, keeps everything safe. You wouldn't find this out from a friend, but an enemy compels you [to learn]. For example, it was from enemies, not friends, that cities learned to construct high walls and acquire long ships. This lesson keeps children, home, and possessions safe. (375–80)

The birds, who know what it is like to be hunted, explicitly concur (382).[25] The stages of defense that Tereus describes parallel those in Thucydides' Archaeology: proceeding from life in unfortified places (ἀτειχίστων, 1.2.2, 5.1), to carrying arms (1.6.1), creating a navy (1.4.1, 8.2), and building walled cities (1.7.1). The notion that the birds learn best under necessity matches the rationalistic notion that early human societies improved out of necessity.[26] The force of necessity in matters of self-defense is further alluded to in the *Birds* when Tereus, referring to the Carian use of hill-top fortresses, jokes that the birds have crests because, "like Carians, they live on the crests of hills for security."[27] A warrior code is thus not, by itself, a sign of animal savagery but the first step on a path to civilization.

The birds' ability to take up formation as hoplites, which rests on their pre-civic solidarity, stands in contrast to the human beings of Plato's *Protagoras* who could only fend off the attacks of beasts after the gods had granted them the art of politics, which in turn enabled them to learn the art of war (πολεμική).[28] Thus the birds, who already knew how to attack the men, needed no miraculous gift, as Peisetaerus and Euelpides discover to their dismay. The birds, though technologically backward, nonetheless require no one to teach them about self-defense and the quest for the good life. Of course, the next step in the creation of Nephelococcygia results not from anonymous, collective action but from focused leadership.

Leadership

The transformation of Peisetaerus into the leader of the birds is the most striking development in the *Birds*. Tereus may have been the birds' friend and Greek teacher, but it was Peisetaerus who caught their attention: "Aha! I see in the bird race what could be a grand design (βούλευμ') and a mighty power, were you to be persuaded by me" (162–63), he says, and announces to Tereus that the birds should found a city (172). The bird chorus feels threatened, and a scuffle ensues, but Tereus convinces them to listen (434–38).[29] Peisetaerus' visionary speech (465ff.), appealing to their vanity and self-interest, brings the birds over to his side.[30] The chorus-leader soon announces that Peisetaerus is his dearest friend and that the chorus will follow his "intelligent plan" (γνώμη, 628, 637).

That the birds need to be persuaded, and allow themselves to be persuaded, is significant. Although Peisetaerus' leadership may later become authoritarian, he has achieved it by winning their consent. True, one might concede that it seems artificial for a man to become a leader of birds. In fact, Tereus acknowledges that men are enemies

by nature (φύσιν, 371, though adding that they are friends by inten-
tion, νοῦν), and the chorus insists that men are naturally deceitful
(δολερὸν ... πέφυκεν ἄνθρωπος, 451–52). Nevertheless, verbal persuasion (*peitho*) is also a natural component of benevolent leadership. Peisetaerus' leadership is enhanced by his use of contemporary
rhetorical techniques: "Like the sophists, his teaching proceeds by *epi-
deixis* (483), exemplary demonstration."[31] What wins the birds' adher-
ence is the appeal to their self-interest (χρήσιμον, 372 and 382). He
also flatters them with the myth of their origins, after which they
accept his friendship and pledge assistance with their physical might
(ῥώμη, 636).

A subsequent event renders his leadership less artificial and cements
Peisetaerus' role as the birds' leader: he grows wings. With his altered
physical form nature can catch up with artifice. Peisetaerus and Euelpides are invited to eat a root (ῥίζιον, 654), which will cause them to
grow the wings that are visible when they reappear after the parabasis
(801 ff.). Whether eating the magical root is a natural process or an artificial intervention is ambiguous – eating a vegetative substance might
be less artificial than the divine command that transformed Tereus[32] –
but suffice it to note that from here on Peisetaerus seems to settle into
the role of natural leader of the birds and that the birds are comfortable
with it.

At the same time, he plays the role of a *ktistes*, a legendary city-
founder. After all the comedy reenacts the foundation of a city, by
tracing the myths invoked and rituals performed when a new city was
established. The founder is driven to a new home, performs sacrifices,
and imposes new political order on chaos.[33]

Curiously, several fifth-century reconstructions of the emergence
of civilization omitted any reference to human leadership. The chorus of the *Antigone* presupposes an anonymous collectivity (ironically,
given that play's focus on the leadership of Creon); in the *Prometheus
Bound* the role of Prometheus renders human leadership redundant.
Yet Archelaos DK 60 A4 sees leaders at the earliest stage of the *polis*.[34]
Democritus seems to have accepted that some would emerge as superiors ("Rule by nature belongs to the stronger" DK 68 B267).[35] The
version that most closely resembles *Birds*, however, is Thucydides'
account of Minos, who was induced, at least in part, by a desire

to maximize revenues; he is said to be the first to organize a navy and drive out pirates, thus easing communication and commerce (1.4.1, 8.2).[36]

Prometheus

Prometheus had a history in Greek literature that antedated sophistic accounts of the rise of civilization. Despite efforts in the *Theogony* and *Works and Days* to help humankind, his cleverness was deemed misguided and the result was suffering for himself and humankind.[37] By comparison, in the *Prom.*, which appears to be the first account to make him a "bringer of civilization,"[38] he was portrayed sympathetically and his gifts were positive ones ("All skills have been given to mortal men by Prometheus," πᾶσαι τέχναι βροτοῖσιν ἐκ Προμηθέως 506), with an emphasis on calculation, technology, and reason. Plato's *Prot.* followed this tradition when Prometheus gave people vital social skills.

The *Birds* shows signs of direct influence from the *Prom.*[39] The comedy stages not only a similar revolt against Zeus but personal intervention by Prometheus himself. He tells Peisetaerus that the blockade on Olympus is succeeding and recommends that Peisetaerus insist on getting Zeus' scepter and Basileia.[40] An unambiguous benefactor, he nevertheless is also a ridiculous, fearful figure in this comedy, hiding from Zeus under a parasol and trembling lest his name be mentioned. As Dunbar pointed out, Prometheus retains his love of humankind ("I've always been well-disposed toward human beings!" 1545) but comically overlooks the bird-costume of Peisetaerus and the chorus.[41]

Prometheus' advice is welcome, yet the city has already been built by the time he arrives. The creation of Nephelococcygia, and the social skills of the birds, are independent of his intervention. Moreover, Prometheus cannot play too large a part because Peisetaerus has assumed a Promethean role for himself. What Peisetaerus does for the birds resembles Prometheus' gifts to human beings, as recounted in Prometheus' speech at *Prom.* 450–506, with the qualification that the birds were less dependent on Peisetaerus than human beings were on Prometheus. The effect of Prometheus' appearance in the *Birds* is to sanction Peisetaerus' advantageous position and give his blessing to Peisetaerus' undertaking.

Avis Faber: *Building Houses, Cities, and Walls*

All fifth-century accounts included building as a step in human progress, though they differed in explaining how this came about. In the *Prom*. Prometheus claimed that human beings could not make brick-built houses until he gave them the intelligence to do so (450–53). In the *Prot*. Prometheus gave human beings technical skill (ἔντεχνος σοφία, 321d1), which they used to build houses (οἰκήσεις, 322a6) and to found cities (κτίζοντες πόλεις, 322b6, though these did not survive until they had learned the πολιτικὴ τέχνη). The *Prom*. and *Prot*., as often, affirmed a need for guidance; Thucydides, however, seeing men as rising to the challenge on their own, offered a utilitarian account of how, needing defenses against pirates, walled cities were initially built inland, but when conditions later favored commerce walled cities were built on coasts (τείχεσιν, 1.7.1; τείχη, 1.8.3).

The new wall of Nephelococcygia is not merely defensive but is an act of aggression against the gods, whom Peisetaerus and the birds will encircle and besiege (φάρξητ̄, 183, περιτειχίζειν, 552). It is a technology conceived of by Peisetaerus and directed by him, neither some sort of haphazard discovery nor a defensive response to natural necessity, as one finds in Thucydides and as Tereus suggested at 379. And yet once work begins it develops that the birds are, by nature, well suited to building a city wall.[42] At *Birds* 1122 a messenger describes the new wall, which was wide enough for two chariots to pass and some six hundred feet tall (ἑκατονορόγυιον, 1131).[43] Birds already know what to do. Cranes carried stones with their bills, storks made bricks, thick-knees and river birds brought water, herons brought hods, ducks laid on bricks, swallows carried mortar, other birds were carpenters, and nuthatches made gates (1135–57). That this is built by the collaboration of all birds, with an effective division of labor among the species, makes it seem a process more natural than artificial and, once begun, their efforts require no further prompting.[44]

Only in comic fantasy could this come true. But this concern with the ability of the birds to build has precedents. Democritus, as noted, thought that human beings were students "of the swallow in building" and thus formulated a rationalistic argument for seeing nature as the source of human invention.[45] Men can be said to be self-taught in this matter (as they had been in Thucydides), even though they had an example to follow. Walls were therefore less artificial than might be supposed. What in other versions might have been a gift of Prometheus was converted here into a natural ability of the birds, who are well suited to building. The birds' fortification therefore serves not only the dramatic purpose of blockading the gods but also symbolically shows that technology is a natural trait of birds.

Hands, Feet, and Wings

The messenger reports that the birds built the wall "with their own hands" (αὐτόχειρες, 1135). This is of course nonsense, as birds do not have hands, but the notion of physical endowments as aids to civilization is an old *topos*. Anaxagoras offered a mechanistic view: hands are what make men wise.[46] When geese use their feet as shovels, Peisetaerus asks, "Is there anything that feet can't do?" (1147), adapting what the scholion says is a proverb about hands.[47] Hands and wings fall into comparable categories, and Aristophanes' comedy exploits this when the chorus-leader says at the end of the *parabasis*, "There's nothing better or more pleasurable than to grow wings," and then offers a humorous list of the advantages that accrue from having wings (*Birds* 785–800). Birds' wings enable them to fly, whereas human beings, who only have hands and merely stand upright, are at a disadvantage. This reinforces the notion that construction skills are innate, not artificial.

In a key respect the *Birds* reverses what would later appear in Plato: at *Prot.* 320d8–321b6 hands were not one of the natural endowments mentioned when Epimetheus allotted powers to the different species – Protagoras wishes to emphasize the absolute helplessness of the human species[48] – but at 320e3–4 Epimetheus gives "winged flight" (πτηνὸν φυγὴν) as a source of protection for small creatures, just as he gives size or speed to others. The creatures in this comedy are his beneficiaries.

Language

For the Greek "anthropologists" language enabled men to communicate and create new social values.[49] Euripides' Theseus thought the power of speech was granted by an unnamed god, and Plato's Prometheus gave men the skill they needed to become articulate.[50] In yet other accounts human beings created language on their own, without intervention: speech has been learned, evidently unassisted, at *Antigone* 353, and Democritus DK 68 B26 indicates that words arose by human convention.[51]

Although there is no explicit theory of the origins of speech in the *Birds*, the process of language acquisition is reenacted. In the opening lines of the play (1–8) it was precisely the difficulty of communicating with birds that had brought Peisetaerus and Euelpides to an impasse.[52] But the fact that the birds of the chorus have learned to speak Greek is pointedly brought out early in the comedy. Tereus says, "I've lived with them a long time and have taught them language (φωνήν), since they were inarticulate (βαρβάρους) before" (*Birds* 199–200, cf. 229–315).[53] He performs an act of human benevolence, possibly recalling a *sapiens* making a paternalistic gift. The choice of Tereus as their language instructor is surely significant. In Sophocles' *Tereus* he had cut out Philomela's tongue but, apparently illiterate, was undone by a message she wrote to Procne. Thus although Tereus' role in Sophocles was to suppress communication, here he is a teacher of Greek and encourages communication between the birds and the Athenians. The comic Tereus "has restored the severed tongue."[54]

Yet this learned language ability does not preclude inborn aptitude. The transition from their pre-articulate stage is illustrated by choral outbursts in which natural bird sounds blend with human speech: ποποποποποποποπο ποῦ μ' (310) and τιτιτιτιτιτιτιτι τίνα λόγον ἆρα ποτὲ (315).[55] These outbursts, which might be simply for comic effect or intended to poke fun at Tereus for incompletely teaching them Greek, can also be read as an indication of concord between bird sounds and human language; the birds already had, by *physis*, the elements of language.[56] Logically this might be at odds with the notion that the birds had to be taught – in other words, that language did not exist until it was given to them – but the two notions can be reconciled by assuming that an innate ability was perfected through instruction.

Fire

Traditionally fire was the invention of Hermes or Hephaestus,[57] and Prometheus stole it to give to mortals. The gift was celebrated in the *Prom.* (esp. 252–54); likewise at *Prot.* 321d1–322a2 he steals fire and artful skill from Hephaestus and Athena (τὴν ἔντεχνον σοφίαν σὺν πυρί). But in the fifth century material or rationalistic explanations were developed, perhaps by Democritus, if Democritus was the source for Vitruvius, who thought fire first occurred in nature when trees rubbed together (2.1.1), or for Lucretius, who wrote that fire was sparked by lightening strikes (5.1091–1104).[58] Fire is absent from the accounts of Sophocles' *Antigone*, Euripides' *Suppliants*, and Thucydides, and is curiously lacking from Prometheus' great speech in the *Prom.* (443–506).

In the *Birds* fire was a gift from Prometheus: "Because of you, alone of the gods, we can cook with charcoal" (1547), said Peisetaerus. Fire is associated with other objects: Zeus' thunderbolt is guarded by Basileia (1538) and wielded by Peisetaerus (1709–14), and Zeus' lightening is "fire-bearing" (πυρφόρον, 1750, the epithet of Prometheus).[59] There it is certainly an emblem of power and a gift from Prometheus. Fire is neither a necessary preliminary step from which the bird city arises nor an essential component of the progression.[60] Fire was essential for cooking and was thus, from the birds' perspective, an ambiguous gift.

Agriculture and Cooking

The skills of agriculture and viticulture, which had been given to mortals by Demeter and Dionysus, were stock examples of a divine gift of technology.[61] Thucydides makes no reference to the human discovery of agriculture, but notes that originally "everyday food was available everywhere" (1.2.2). In some versions men were given guidance in plowing and cultivation (*Prom.* 454; Eur., *Suppliants* 205–06; *Prot.* 322a7); in the *Antigone* agriculture is developed strictly by human efforts (337–40). A carnivorous diet would be cast as an advance in civilization,[62] but the birds, like the beasts in Crates' *Beasts*, would demur.

The *Birds* itself mirrors the evolution of food preparation. In the opening scenes the birds are eating fare as found in the wild: white sesame, myrtle-berries, poppies, and water-mint in gardens (159–60). Their availability has a "Golden Age" ring to it, particularly because some were associated with festive occasions.[63] Later they consume locusts, ants, and fig-wasps (588–91 and 1061–65). These dishes are not appealing to human beings, and in that respect resemble the diet of Eupolis' goats, but at least no one could claim that scarcity of food was a problem.[64] As the play proceeds, however, references to cooked food appear with greater frequency: sacrificial sheep to Poseidon and a ram to Zeus (561–69), the sacrifice of a goat (848–903) in which the birds will share (see 900), a camel-lamb (1560), charcoal cooking (1546), roasting dissident birds (1583 and at 1688–90), vow of victim (1618), and cutting of tongue (1705).[65] At 531–38 the birds express indignation that they were caught by hunters and roasted with a garnish. The birds will not celebrate a skill that culminates in an ornithological holocaust.

By growing wheat, figs, and grapes, however, the birds usurp the role of Prometheus and cast themselves as benefactors for human beings who work in the fields.[66] Birds can tell the seasons for sowing (710–11; see below), for shearing sheep (714), and harvesting wheat (505–06). Peisetaerus tells them that men will be grateful to them for wiping out vine-eating locusts, fig-eating ants, and fig-wasps. Men can repay birds by making offerings of wheat and barley (624–26). By encouraging agriculture the birds discourage carnivorous habits.[67] Peisetaerus, sensitive to the birds' concerns, suggests that if one is sacrificing animals to the god (e.g., a sheep or ram), one could make offerings of grain (barley, wheat, loaves) to the bird that accompanies the god. Human beings were at a clear disadvantage without the assistance of birds, for the human way of life fell short of Golden-Age sufficiency. The role of the birds scarcely constitutes artificial intervention.

Divination, Telling Seasons, Shipping, Mining

Birds 588–626 and 709–36 relate four skills that birds revealed to humankind: divination, shipping, mining, and the ability to predict seasons. All rely on the birds' supernatural powers. To some extent these claims resemble the sort of agricultural advice found in Hesiod's

Works and Days,[68] although they are described not as received wisdom but as unexpected gifts. This is the "benefactor" model of the *Prom.*, in which Prometheus reveals things to mortals: (compare ἔδειξα, *Prom.* 457, with δείξουσι, *Birds* 593, or φαίνομεν, 709). The four skills are prominent in Prometheus' speech and appear in other ancient accounts of the rise of civilization as well. The self-conscious awareness of the origins and usefulness of these benefits reflect sophistic teaching about the origins of civilization, as does the methodical exposition: the bird chorus-leader lays out the blessings of the birds in a systematic manner (πρῶτα μὲν... εἶτα... εἶτα..., 709ff.). Some writers had seen these contributions to be the result of human labor, but in the *Birds* they are now revealed to have been done by birds all along, as if the birds were eminently suited to accomplish them and were never as inherently pastoral as believed.

Divination and Omens of Birds

Rationalist accounts, which had no use for divine intervention, predictably said little of the "contribution" of divination, though it was mentioned in Democritus DK 68 A138, where the institution was ascribed to "men of old."[69] But when it was accepted as a valid contribution, divination could loom large: Prometheus "arranged" methods of *mantike*, the skill of interpreting divine signs, and first interpreted dreams.[70] Aristophanes, therefore, departs from rationalistic versions in granting birds access to special mantic knowledge (*Birds* 593, 724, 1332).

Telling Seasons

Prometheus says that human beings had no way of telling seasons, so he taught them about the rising and setting of the stars (*Prom.* 454–58); a fragment of Democritus implies an interest in the calendar; sources indicate that Prodicus wrote a treatise called "Seasons."[71] This interest of the progressivists is reflected in *Birds* when Peisetaerus reminds the birds that they can warn of storms (597). The chorus leader points out that they forecast the arrival of spring, winter, and fall (709),[72] a skill trumpeted as something useful to human beings. For example, a man named Orestes needs to weave a cloak so he won't be cold (712).

165

Shipping

The birds can tell where and when to go on a merchant voyage. Says Peisetaerus, "They will reveal the profitable trading voyages, so that no ship-owner will perish" (*Birds* 594, cf. 718). The value of commerce was noted by other fifth-century writers as well: Eur., *Suppl.* 209–10 seems to be the earliest text to articulate a notion of exchange as a step in human social development.[73] Thucydides noted the lack of trade (1.2.2) and communication (or "interaction," ἐπιμείγνυντες, 1.2.2; cf. ἀμειξία ἀλλήλων, 1.3.4) in early Greece; but Minos' naval empire facilitated these (cf. 1.4.1, 1.8.2). Aristophanes, in acknowledging the importance of shipping, has found a way to insert birds into it.[74]

Finding Minerals

A further example of mantic knowledge is that birds will show diviners where the good mining sites are.[75] The *Birds* thus relies on revelation from a higher authority; similarly Prometheus assisted in the discovery of metals under the earth, which benefited human beings (ὠφελήματα, *Prom.* 501). Alternative traditions gave rationalistic accounts of the development of metallurgy, such as the torturous process described in Lucretius, where it is dependent on fire. Others condemned the use of metals as a mixed blessing.[76]

In all of these four matters, then, human beings are relatively helpless, lacking innate abilities, or skills to discover them. These positive steps in civilization follow precedents from the *Prom.* even though the birds have supplanted Prometheus.[77]

Song

Although few higher cultural accomplishments find a place in Nephelococcygia, the birds remain pre-eminent sources of song. The chorus speaks of Phrynichus, the tragic poet, as "feeding on the fruit of divine songs, like a bee, producing a sweet song" (748–51). The divine songs of the birds invoke the notion that men learn songs from birds, as found in Alcman (frr. 39P and 40P) as well as in Democritus (DK 68 B154).[78]

Gods and Religion

Histories of emerging culture rarely discussed the development of religion or of the gods, the assumption being that the gods, not human beings, came first. For example, at *Prot.* 322a3–5 Plato has Protagoras say that human beings, because of their kinship with the divine, believed in the gods, and set up altars and images of them. The very Prometheus myth presupposes that men are secondary in time. But other fifth-century accounts theorized that gods and religion were human contrivances. Democritus evidently saw belief in the gods as arising from fear of alarming natural phenomena.[79] Critias imagined that the gods had been concocted by some "shrewd man" (πυκνός τις καὶ σοφὸς γνώμην ἀνήρ) who wished to instill fear and reverence in men.[80] Prodicus, as we noted above, saw the origin of gods in (a) the fact that men would conceive of things that are nourishing or useful to them as gods, and (b) the giving to the discoverers of food or shelter names such as Demeter or Dionysus.[81] Of course Thucydides, who emphasized the material side of advancement and minimized the role of the gods, had nothing to say about the beginnings of religion.[82]

A central teaching of the *Birds* is that power is up for grabs; accordingly the power of the Olympian gods will be shown to be transitory. The prominence of Olympian gods was contrived: birds were the children of Eros and Chaos at the beginning of time, preceding the gods. The gods are secondary forces in the universe.[83] What people regard as "gods" can be manipulated: Peisetaerus says to the birds, "But if they [mortals] regard you as their god, as their life, as Mother Earth, as Kronos, as Poseidon, then every blessing will be theirs" (586).[84] The chorus in the parabasis equates birds with other divine things: "Whatever is decisive concerning divination you classify as a 'bird': an ominous utterance is a 'bird' in your terms." (719–20). Of course it is true that even in Homer the equation of names of gods with the objects they were associated with ("fire" was "Hephaestus") was common, but Aristophanes shows a greater, perhaps sophistic, self-consciousness. Certainly the way the birds are predicated with gods and the way divine omens are predicated with birds seem rationalistic and calls attention to the arbitrariness of language in a way that is reminiscent of Prodicus.[85]

A further instance lies in the selection of a guardian deity. Athena Polias is briefly considered as a candidate (*Birds* 828), but the choice is the "fearsome chick of Ares," that is, a cock (834–35). The fact that Peisetaerus should choose a guardian god resembles Critias' view that gods were created by a "shrewd man" for political purposes, useful in preserving order.[86] For all that, the cock was naturally suited to be a protector.

Social Qualities

The need for a glue to keep societies together was commonly recognized. In the *Prot.*, when it became clear that human beings were not able to live in social harmony, Zeus instructed Hermes to let all of them have some share in reverence and justice (*aidos* and *dike*). But social cohesion could also be cast in non-religious terms, as when the chorus of *Antigone* argues that one of the characteristics of man is that he has "instincts for laws that rule a city" (ἀστυνόμοι ὀργαί, 355–56), which evidently are innate.[87]

Other thinkers were not inclined to see human beings as innately endowed with law-abiding instincts; for them, creating social cohesion was a matter of hard work as men emerged from an animal-like, primitive life without external gifts such as those given by Hermes to mortals. Civil society was seen as a matter of self-preservation, not a positive expression of social values.[88] Democritus seems to regard early man as in need of improvement, though neither evil nor good by nature; instruction can "create his nature" (DK 68 B33), implying that men have no fixed qualities.

As suggested above, the birds themselves enjoyed a pre-civic solidarity. Accounts of animals eating one another have been suppressed, apart from the birds' ability to eat insects that ruin crops. The birds appear to be naturally predisposed toward living in a tribe. Yet they may also be in line to benefit from divine dispensations like Hermes' gift of reverence and justice in the *Prot.* Prometheus tells Peisetaerus that when Zeus capitulates Zeus must surrender, along with Basileia, "wisdom, law and order, and prudence" (*euboulia, eunomia,* and *sophrosyne,*

1539–40) – precisely the qualities needed to enhance social organization.[89] It appears, however, that unlike reverence and justice these gifts are not to be shared with all creatures but will be the possessions of Peisetaerus, along with the thunderbolt of Zeus, when he gets Basileia.[90] Furthermore this will occur at the end of the play, *after* the city has been organized.[91]

Respect for Parents

In most accounts of the rise of civilization the family was subordinated to other social groupings. For Protagoras what first brought people together was not affection or common family bonds but shared fear of destruction (*Prot.* 322a–b). Democritus conceded that it was natural that human beings, like other creatures, should have children, but it is only by *nomos* that they rear them and then expect to gain some "advantage from the offspring" (DK 68 B278). Democritus generally stressed the importance of larger social groups (*systemata*). Antiphon pointed to the obverse, suggesting that doing good to parents who have not been good is "contrary to nature" (πολέμια τῇ φύσει).[92] Polybius, on the other hand, possibly following Democritus, saw a positive role for the family.[93]

Although the family plays virtually no role in the *Birds*, these views provide a framework for two incidents in the comedy. During the parabasis the birds announce that what is shameful by human *nomos* is fine with the birds, even if it means that beating one's father is acceptable (755–59). Indeed, among birds, the cock was known for doing just that, and their model was invoked by Pheidippides in the *Clouds* (1427–29), which would appear to give the sanction of *physis* to the parricide who wants to enter Nephelococcygia (1337–71). But he learns from Peisetaerus, who is aware of the behavior of cocks (1350), that storks have an old and different law (νόμος παλαιὸς, 1353–54) that dictates that one must protect parents.[94] Here two arguments from *physis* are in collision, but the latter rule of the storks, asserts Peisetaerus, supersedes the former. That one should not harm parents was evidently in the laws of Solon.[95] Of course this is one of the unwritten *nomoi*: *physis* and *nomos* are thus made to coincide.[96]

The Necessity of Killing Pests and Criminals

At *Prot.* 322d Zeus lays down a law (*nomos*) that those who have no share of *aidos* and *dike* shall be put to death. Democritus also saw the need to kill enemies of *nomos* and social order such as beasts: "As has been written down regarding beasts and reptiles which are inimical, so I think one must do with regard to human beings: one should, according to ancestral law, kill an enemy of the State in every ordered society."[97] Democritus sanctions the killing of pirates and stresses that anyone killing pirates is not liable to punishment (B260). The elimination of pirates, of course, was the foundation of Minos' empire in Thucydides.

In this context the "barbeque" scene near the end of the *Birds* (1583–5) takes on special meaning. The full implications of Peisetaerus' punishment are discussed below, but for the moment it is enough to realize that the killing of trouble-makers was acknowledged as a necessary step in the progress of civilization. It was also a contemporary legal reality. The wording of DK 68 B260 closely resembles a law from Teos that Democritus was probably familiar with, pronouncing the death penalty on pirates or anyone who harbors them.[98]

THE NATURAL CITY OF THE BIRDS

The correspondences between the founding of Nephelococcygia and motifs from the "Theory of Progress" that have been traced here are numerous enough to suggest that Aristophanes drew on these contemporary sources at liberty and that the play should be read in the light of them. The resulting pastiche offers a special vision of nature and society, in which *nomos* and *physis* are contrived to be largely consistent with one another. This city, rather than being an artificial creation, grows organically out of pre-existing natural resources and qualities.[99]

Peisetaerus' natural ambition embodies this: he orchestrates the establishment of Nephelococcygia by exploiting the resources available to him. He even grows wings, though his animality seems to add to his human abilities, not to limit or qualify them.[100] Like Minos he is interested in exercising power and has an unmistakably imperialistic agenda, yet he also creates the conditions for an orderly *polis* that will possess *eunomia, euboulia,* and *sophrosyne.* Birds assist in the establishment of the *polis* and, as comparison will show, they are more social than satyrs.

The Birds *and Theories of Progress*

It would be unlike Aristophanes to depend rigidly on any one source, but similarities to the *Prom.*, Democritus, and, above all, Thucydides' Archaeology do stand out. The *Prom.* or a similar source could account for the presence of Prometheus himself and Peisetaerus' role as a benefactor. Of course the birds, far from being the helpless creatures that Prometheus described in the *Prom.*, turn out to be adept, for example, at brick-making. Moreover, specific skills apparently drawn from the *Prom.*, including divination, finding mines, and telling seasons, are taught or presented as gifts to human beings by the talented birds.

The *Birds* featured other skills that were absent from the *Prom.*, including military tactics, the emergence of a leader, acquiring language, and the facility allowed by wings and feet. For these, Aristophanes seems to have turned to Democritus and to similar explanations that emphasized not benefaction or supernatural intervention but rationally explicable evolution or natural endowment. The skills of warfare are learned out of necessity, feet are suited for building, and language emerges from spontaneous, inarticulate noises. Olympian cult is shown to be an artificial, secondary development, the rule of birds being prior and natural.[101] Democritus also noted that human beings had learned directly from animals. Of course the *Birds* neglects the trademark Democritean notion that the different stages in the development of civilization occurred in a close causal sequence, with all stages occurring in a logical continuum.[102] The *Birds* instead enumerates achievements in no particular order, without indicating any causal connection. In this respect the *Birds* resembles the *Prom.* and *Antigone.* Tereus in the *Birds* is similar to Prometheus in Plato's *Prot.* in that both taught language to their constituencies. A further similarity to the *Prot.* lies in the fact that the birds, in possessing an innate social cohesion, are endowed with qualities similar to *aidos* and *dike*; if such gifts need to be supplemented, Peisetaerus possesses *eunomia.*

In the most important ways, however, the *Birds* is skewed in the direction of Thucydides, where an energetic leader is able to forge an empire out of a dispersed society.[103] Specific steps taken in the Archaeology correspond to Aristophanes' play: the tribes of birds originally lived scattered about (cf. Thuc. 1.2.1), residing in unfortified abodes, without commerce or agriculture, but move about and get everyday food wherever they can (cf. 1.2.2). The birds evidently had no firm awareness of a "national" identity (cf. 1.3.4). Without the protection of walls they were vulnerable to predators (cf. 1.5.1). Finally Peisetaerus began to build his empire: a walled city is established for protection and intruders are fended off (cf. 1.7–8). He did this to enhance his own revenues; subordinates in the empire supported it out of their own self-interest and desire (cf. 1.4.1, 1.8.3).

Thucydides and Aristophanes may simply have borrowed ideas that were circulating at the time; Book 1 of Thucydides was unlikely to be circulating by 414 B.C.[104] Thucydides' interest in the process may also be reflected when, in Book 6, he described Sicily in terms that would be especially meaningful to a potential colonist. Nicias' discussion of the dangers of establishing a city among hostile tribes (6.23.2) resurfaces in the *Birds* (183ff. and 196).[105] The Athenians who are about to embark on the Sicilian expedition were, in Thucydides' description, "confident" (εὐέλπιδες, 6.24.3), recalling the name of Peisetaerus' accomplice, Euelpides.[106]

The parallels between Nephelococcygia and the imperialistic adventure in Sicily in 415–413 B.C. were surely intentional. Yet another adventure deserves closer attention: the Athenian siege and conquest of Melos in the winter of 416/415 B.C., described by Thucydides (5.84–116).[107] The analogy, if not precise – the gods capitulate before being exterminated – has potency. Says Peisetaerus:

ἢν δ' οἰκίσατε τοῦτο καὶ φάρξηθ' ἅπαξ,
ἐκ τοῦ "πόλου" τούτου κεκλήσεται "πόλις"
ὥστ' ἄρξετ' ἀνθρώπων μὲν ὥσπερ παρνόπων,
τοὺς δ' αὖ θεοὺς ἀπολεῖτε λιμῷ Μηλίῳ

But once you settle and fortify it, it will be called a "polis" instead of a "polos"; as a result you will rule over men as you do locusts and you will destroy the gods with a Melian famine. (183–86)

Only later would Peisetaerus justify his empire with an appeal to ancestral rights or the need to correct injustices. Here he seems to be caught up with opportunistic aggression and a desire to "rule where one can" (Thucydides 5.105). As noted earlier, the building of the siege wall at Melos was carried out by a division of labor among various states (5.114), a bird-like approach. The negotiating strategies are also similar: the Athenians and Melians both suggest to one another that they are miscalculating their own self-interest. Likewise Poseidon, urging the birds and Peisetaerus to relent, points out that the gods still control rainwater (1593), while Peisetaerus suggests that if they capitulate the gods will find that birds will help enforce their rules (1606–35). Both Poseidon and Peisetaerus woo Heracles' support by suggesting that his inheritance is at stake (1641–70). Poseidon, like Peisetaerus, strikes a pose of reasonableness, saying that neither side gains by continuing to fight (1591), though Peisetaerus states (falsely!) that they did not initiate hostilities and are prepared to do the right thing (1596). The Athenians as well say that they want the Melians to save themselves (5.91, 93) and even offer the Melians a role in their empire. Significantly, the Athenian general who conducted the final siege and capture of Melos, Philocrates, son of Demeas, has the same name as a reviled bird-seller.[108]

The Athenians' arguments against the Melians have become textbook examples of brutal realism in politics. And yet "it is questionable if [Thucydides] intended to produce the revulsion which most readers of the Dialogue feel."[109] The Archaeology echoed this, reflecting the unsentimental interest in the nature of power that arises throughout the *Peloponnesian War* in general and the Melian affair in particular. Of course the emphasis of the Archaeology differs from the Melian Dialogue in a significant respect: Minos is building an empire that will provide a stable economic and social structure for all. The weaker members of Minos' empire saw that it was in their self-interest to be governed (Thuc. 1.8), whereas the Melians see no benefit in being slaves (5.92). Creating Nephelococcygia, like building a naval empire, is simply another technique for gaining advantages over opponents, and "neither Peisetaerus nor the birds make any apology about their ambition for power."[110] Possibly the birds functioned more as subjects of Minos than as Melians, but more on this below.[111]

The Athenian Empire, then, was a model for Nephelococcygia. Of course the city occasionally departs from the Athenian model in that its citadel god will not be Athena but a fighting cock (*Birds* 826–36); it will not pray for the Chians (880); it refuses to join the Athenian empire (1021ff.); it turns away those attempting to import Athenian laws or customs, considering whatever is unlawful at Athens to be lawful (753ff.).[112] There are even stronger clues, however, that Athens *is* a model. Parallels cited above between accounts of the building of city walls[113] and numerous other details point to an Athenian quality of the new city: it will have an acropolis (836), have laws on *kurbeis* (1534), and Basileia will bring them dockyards and three-obol fees (1537–41).[114]

Nomos *and* Physis

Aristophanes tailored his account to show that there was a basis in nature for nearly every advance toward the *polis* and its institutions. Although one study of the play advanced the view that "founding a *polis* is not particularly a bird affair,"[115] I have come to the opposite conclusion – that it is very much a bird affair, and Aristophanes has gone out of his way either (a) to find innate qualities in birds that make them naturally suited to become citizens or (b) to reveal, with comic assertion, that skills conventionally thought of as artificial actually have a basis in nature or are unnecessary for a city. If Democritus was right to say that human beings learned by imitating animals, then human beings are the defective creatures who must rely on the benefaction of the birds.

The underpinning of their good citizenship is their "pre-civic solidarity." Their cohesion was affirmed by their invocation of ancestral laws and oaths (331–32), and was sanctioned by the myth of their origins. That birds come in different species seems not to matter, for they exhibit interdependence and cooperation over a wide group. Moreover, the political group here takes precedence over the family. There are no families, only the *polis*; there are no claims of kinship – parents, children – apart from the ancestry of all the birds. Peisetaerus certainly has no family or kinship affiliations.[116] Father-beating was raised not to stress the importance of the family as a social unit, but to highlight the contradictory claims of *physis*.

Aristophanes does not miss an opportunity to expose supposedly human contrivances as being, in reality, rooted in naturally occurring skills or endowments. Aristophanes' attempts are, of course, largely preposterous – showing that birds can build a city with their innate abilities is an exercise in comic ingenuity – yet they would not work if there were not already some thread of plausibility: Aristophanes has tirelessly combed through the Greek language for avian metaphors and ransacked ornithological lore to find anthropomorphic skills.[117] For instance, birds are not only able to learn Greek, but have pre-existing abilities to speak it. There are bird species that have just the physical endowments necessary for building walls and for defending themselves. Birds are equipped to assist in agriculture. Even the intervention of a human being, Peisetaerus, is "made" natural when he grows wings. Transparently ludicrous contrivances, perhaps, but in the world of the comedy they should be regarded as natural phenomena.[118]

In general, what is valid concerning skills is also valid for law and social order: the laws that are ultimately sanctioned are those in which both human convention and the benevolent aspects of nature are congruent with one another. Artificial circumstances are identified as such and excluded if they have no natural basis. Above all, the birds are rulers, not prey, in the natural order of the kosmos, and the artificial superiority of the Olympians is undone by the building of Nephelococcygia.

Would-be parasites are sent packing, some with more ferocity than others, including the poet, oracle-monger, Meton, the inspector, decree-seller (903–1057), and opportunists who apply to have wings, such as the young man, Cinesias, and the informer (1337–1469). Turato has characterized the first group as interlopers who are trying to impose their *nomoi* but who are rejected as incompatible with the *physis* of the city; the second group attempts to achieve their notion of *physis* but does not square it with what the city will consider just and *nomimon* ("lawful").[119] The last three imposters are steered toward what is *nomimon*: the youth and Cinesias are actually accepted in one way or another; the sycophant alone is rejected completely, and only after being given a chance. The inheritance laws of Solon, which were of course created by a human being, are cited by Peisetaerus as an impediment to Heracles' claim to Zeus' estate (1660–66). Whether these laws are valid in Nephelococcygia is perhaps beside the point, for Zeus will manipulate matters to suit his purposes (yet another reason for rejecting the gods).

In a few instances the birds express approval of behavior that flouts human custom and unleashes the darker aspects of *physis*. Chief among these is the antinomian outburst made by the birds themselves in the epirrheme and antepirrheme of the first parabasis: "What is shameful by *nomos* with you is fine by us" (755–56).[120] They reject conventional human customs (by endorsing father beating and facilitating adultery: 753–68, 785–800) and embrace a selfish understanding of *physis*.[121] And yet this seldom occurs as the play proceeds. The general pattern, rather, is to invoke laws that are compatible with the more enlightened side of nature. Writes Sommerstein, "In general the bird city proves to be not at all the criminal's and imposter's paradise" foreshadowed in the first parabasis.[122] The *Birds* implicitly conveys the principle that stability requires obedience to laws. Peisetaerus shows careful discrimination in the sorts of laws that should be accepted. In the case of mistreating parents he can espouse laws that are grounded in nature, but he does so by appealing to a different species: storks (1353). The stork laws exist in nature, being the customs of animals, and are also written down on *kurbeis* (1355–57).[123] In the second parabasis (1058–1117), after proclaiming their beneficent effect on agriculture, the birds lay down some of their own laws against atheists, tyrants, and bird-hunters. Admittedly the birds do promise that, if the festival judges award a victory to them, they will help them embezzle public funds when elected to office (1111–12)![124] But other laws prop up social order: we hear, for example, that the crow will peck out the eyes of liars (1612).[125] The laws of Nephelococcygia, evidently, are those based in nature.

Peisetaerus Tyrannos?

Since Peisetaerus' volatile energy, like nature itself, can be as creative as it is destructive, both aspects should receive their due.

The dangers that he poses are easy to identify. His audacity in taking on Olympus has to be unnerving for birds and audience alike. In the course of doing so he displays his formidable skills as a persuader or, one might say, as an amoral manipulator. His techniques are those of a "power politician," relying on the devices of a sophist.[126] There is no small part of the demagogue in him when he promises the birds that he will restore them to a position of leadership but in fact takes leadership for himself. Bird sovereignty, as opposed to the sovereignty of the bird/man Peisetaerus, gets short-changed in the action of the play. All too conveniently, Peisetaerus manages to become a bird, marry Basileia in high style, and become their king. Peisetaerus is even described as a *tyrannos*, a word with dangerous connotations for the Athenians.[127]

In manner he can be imperious. He gratuitously insults the birds for being ignorant and un-inquisitive (471), and his exchange with Iris is unnecessarily coarse (1199–1259).[128] Self-discipline not being a notable quality of his, Peisetaerus may be modeled to some degree on Alcibiades, who shared this trait.[129] Peisetaerus might be said to resemble Polyphemus of Euripides' *Cyclops*, both of whom share animal qualities, have contempt for the power of Zeus, and rely on sophistic arguments about what is really "natural" in order to justify themselves. Paduano saw in Peisetaerus the triumph of egoistic individualism, triggering a crisis in collective values and injuring other individuals; what prevails, in his view, is singular aggression against anything that inhibits his individuality.[130]

The most damning charge against Peisetaerus is that he roasts birds who have been "found guilty of trying to rebel against the bird democracy" (ὄρνιθές τινες ἐπανιστάμενοι τοῖς δημοτικοῖσιν ὀρνέοις ἔδοξαν ἀδικεῖν, 1583–85). His use of this drastic tool to keep his empire together is reminiscent of Cleon's insistence in 427 B.C. that the rebellious Mytileneans be punished (Thuc. 3.40). Auger accuses Peisetaerus of hypocrisy in that, having set out to protect the birds from hunters, he later eats them, like Polyphemus.[131] The *Birds* can be seen as "a classical precursor of Orwell's *Animal Farm*."[132]

Nonetheless, there is perhaps less cynicism in his role than has been thought. No action he takes is presented as an evil undertaking. But even if one were to conclude that he is personally free of or immune to the personal or social bonds expected of a good citizen and especially of a leader,[133] he is nevertheless a visionary who rallies the birds and establishes a powerful and orderly new society. Peisetaerus is the one who creates the *polis* that enables social or personal bonds to exist. Peisetaerus is at heart a creature of the *polis*, unlike Polyphemus, who lives a savage life in a cave. Peisetaerus genuinely enjoys the institutions of the city – so much so that he creates a new one.

On more than one occasion Peisetaerus rejects selfish moral relativism and the ruthless, "law of the stronger" view of nature. He (pointedly, I think) repudiates the view enunciated by the bird chorus, that "everything here considered disgraceful by *nomos* is considered fine by us birds," including the right to beat up one's father (755–59), by urging the young man to obey the benevolent laws of the storks. In fact the three interlopers who arrive after the second parabasis – the young man, Cinesias, and the sycophant (1337–1469) – are not simply rebuffed; rather, Peisetaerus attempts to improve them. The young man is given wings and sent to the Thracian front, Cinesias is kept on to train choruses, and the sycophant is ejected only after Peisetaerus strenuously tries to lead him to something lawful (*nomimon*).[134] He may not exercise conspicuous self-discipline himself, but he does help discipline others. His desire for personal power is balanced by his eagerness to organize the bird city.

Much of what he does is in the birds' interest. Though it is no democracy, he implies that he had consulted the birds on the decision to crush imposters, since the decision had been made unanimously (ὁμοθυμαδὸν . . . δοκεῖ, 1015–16). At line 1600 he claimed to be acting on their behalf, saying that the scepter will be restored to "us birds." Nothing in the immediate context suggests that this is a cynical lie. The fact that Peisetaerus receives assistance from Prometheus, who was a popular god at Athens, would have signalled that Peisetaerus was meant to be seen as a benevolent protagonist.[135]

Even the roasting of birds should not automatically earn him condemnation. One might bear in mind the scandals in the year preceding the production of the *Birds*: three hundred Athenians had been under suspicion for committing sacrilege, of these many were either executed or forced into exile. Athenians were not lenient about such disruptions and in any event the audience would be hypocritical to condemn the roasting of the birds.[136] Moreover, as we have seen, proponents of good rule such as Democritus argued that malefactors needed to be eliminated; execution would not have to be justified to the Athenians.

If there is any irony, it is not in Peisetaerus betraying the birds, but in the fact that they now live by the laws of a *polis* and, if caught in revolt, die by the same laws.

To some degree a comic convention is at work, in which victorious protagonists feast on birds (see *Ach.* 1104 and *Peace* 1197). Peisetaerus "reminds us more of Dicaeopolis or Trygaios than of Alcibiades or Gorgias or the Athenian *demos*," suggests Craik.[137] Certainly no one on stage makes a peep about what he has done. As soon as Heracles says he wants to roast bird meat, a herald, who evidently saw nothing to alarm the birds, tells the chorus, "You who enjoy all good fortune, blessing greater than words can express, thrice-happy winged race of birds, welcome your monarch to his luxurious home" (1706–08). The birds themselves follow this with unreserved approval of Peisetaerus and his marriage; they say the marriage is "most blessed for the city" (μακαριστὸν . . πόλει, 1725), and the chorus-leader exclaims, "Truly great is the good fortune that envelops the race of the birds because of this man" (1726–28). Either Peisetaerus is such a successful manipulator that he has duped the birds completely, or his accomplishments are genuinely welcome to them.[138]

Many in the audience may have opted for the latter of these two choices, and would have left the theater with the impression that the birds were now better off. The birds consented to the new scheme, and it develops that they are educable, have learned Greek, and can construct a city.[139] They have, in short, become "social" animals like those favored in the tradition of animal choruses. Aristophanes affirms that progress is possible: if brute animals, creatures of nature, can coalesce into a community, then (in the world of this comedy) there is hope for human beings as well. The blessings that Peisetaerus will receive – *eunomia, euboulia,* and *sophrosyne* – may not be specifically democratic, yet neither do they indicate that he intends to impose despotism. For the *Anonymus Iamblichi* the quality of *eunomia* was inherent in individuals, and it allowed them to rise up against a strong man attempting to rule unjustly (6.5). Peisetaerus possesses *eunomia*, and although we would like to see him exercise it more, it is difficult to cast him as lawless.[140] As Slater puts it, "Peisetaerus is no Cleon figure, destroying the birds' city by factionalizing it, but a city founder creating order and power out of chaos. While to our modern sensibilities the bird city that devours its own may seem monstrous, it is monstrous in ways unlikely to trouble either Aristophanes or most of his fellow citizens."[141]

Peisetaerus' Urban Ideal

Peisetaerus' goals and pleasures are urban and civilized; it is a life in a *polis* that he builds with the birds. He is not motivated by a desire to return to a pastoral or Golden-Age existence. The first question that Peisetaerus had asked of Tereus was where he could find a comfortable city, "like a soft woolly blanket" (120), and, when asked about his fantasy ideal, Peisetaerus says he would like someone to knock on his door, tell him to bathe, and invite him to a wedding banquet (ἑστιᾶν, 132).[142] Peisetaerus even asks about being directed to a Greek city (147), although none of the suggestions is to his taste. Euelpides fantasizes about being rebuked for not fondling an attractive boy on the way back from the gymnasium (137–42), and it is he who shows interest in the life of the birds (155–61), but only for a few lines, before Peisetaerus cuts in and gives the comedy a new direction when he conceives his plan to build the new city (172). Euelpides is silent about this new city.[143] Henceforth it is Peisetaerus who controls the direction of the play, and Euelpides vanishes shortly after the *parabasis*.

There are hints of idyllic aspects in the *Birds* – we have seen already that the "state of nature" that the birds inhabited contained images of benign nature – but this ideal does not appeal to Peisetaerus. As Konstan says, "It is a city that they are seeking from the beginning: (48, 121, 123, 136); despite the phrase *topon apragmona*, 'trouble-free place,' (44) there is no suggestion of a pastoral ideal."[144] Peisetaerus is largely indifferent to the beauties of the world of nature and probably views the landscape as raw material for the construction of his new city. It is a polis, first and foremost, that he thinks of as a way of defining the undemarcated open space of the sky (πόλος, "sphere," "vault" 179–84). The thicket was where they found Tereus and information about where to go – it was a means, not an end. It is true that Peisetaerus says they are "anti-dicasts" and that such sorts still exist in the countryside (ἐξ ἀγροῦ, 111), but this may simply mean that city-dwellers were more likely to serve as jurors than country-dwellers.[145]

To conclude "that the final triumph of Peisetaerus affirms the idyllic utopia rather than the bellicose Cuckoo City of Peisthetairos' initial masterplan"[146] would be difficult. The play is not about a return to unspoiled, Edenic nature, but about the creation of a new city. This conclusion may minimize what has been for some readers a paradox or contradiction in Peisetaerus' character: namely, the notion that he had set out to find *apragmosyne* but, in a reversal, created a city of *polypragmosyne*.[147] These sorts of paradoxes can be seen as idiosyncratic, endearing, and psychologically plausible in a comic hero, but Peisetaerus' aims are from the very beginning more consistent than have been realized.

By the end of the play Peisetaerus is enjoying a banquet and marriage in his now-peaceful realm. The "life of newlyweds" (161) is fulfilled for him after all.

The Birds *and Satyrs*

The role of the birds is cast into profile if compared with satyrs, the other non-human creatures thought by the Greeks to be appropriate companions in the steps that marked human civilization. Satyrs were of course present when the artefacts and skills of human culture were discovered.[148]

Nevertheless, the differences are significant. The satyrs tend to be passive bystanders and are rarely actively involved in any creation or discovery. Although in theory one might think they have access to hidden knowledge, they are themselves generally not the source of these creations. As we have seen, moreover, their association with some objects may simply have been due to the fact that those had been cult objects. Where we do find them linked with skills and objects, these are certainly marks of civilization: fire, hunting, iron-working, athletics, wine, spelling, music, etc. The birds, although able to teach human beings something about music,[149] are shown in Aristophanes' comedy to pursue different activities: building a city, learning Greek, helping with agriculture, telling seasons, showing where to mine, putting their wings to good use, and offering a model for how to treat one's parents. Their accomplishments, which the satyrs have little to do with, are the ones that are fundamental for a social structure and stable economy, and for the basis of an empire.[150] It is unlikely that the creation of a city or social structure was ever the subject of a satyr-play; or, if it had been, it is unlikely that the satyrs were very helpful in the process.

The birds in this comedy have many of the virtues of human beings, whereas satyrs tended to have only their vices. Initially the birds were hostile and posed a threat to the new human arrivals, yet they become a far more social and cooperative group than satyrs ever were. Although some of the bird species in the chorus were not regarded by the Greeks as "social" animals, they became social in the course of the play; satyrs, however, never became social creatures in a developed way, tending to congregate in an indistinct *thiasos*. Satyrs behaved crudely, indulging in sex and wine. Yet this represents a narrow range of what we might think of as "natural" urges; the bird chorus, by contrast, is associated with a wider range of what can be "natural": the violent, the pastoral, and the social. Birds, being pure animal, are "wilder" creatures than satyrs, and yet ironically they offer more to civilization than satyrs ever did. (Centaurs, similarly, are potentially more violent, yet are also the deeper sources of wisdom.) Precisely because the birds are more creatures of nature than are satyrs, it is easier to project human notions onto them than onto satyrs, who already have well-defined identities in myth.

The rise of Peisetaerus' avian *polis* was thus an Aristophanic adaptation of blueprints developed by the Greek anthropologists. This parody does not mean that Aristophanes denies progress outright or supplants human beings, but that he suggests that "progress" has been too narrowly conceived if animals are excluded.

CONCLUSION

I began this project with the assumption that animal choruses were rooted in some primitive fertility cult. I had imagined also that these costumed dancers represented a world allied with daemonic powers, embodying the antithesis of humanity or revealing a subversive animal world latent in human beings. On both counts my ultimate findings have been different.

To trace the development of animal choruses entirely to ritual would be to overlook an important dimension: the actual masquerades, especially of cocks, horses, and dolphin-riders, make less sense as rituals than as symbolic expressions of the Attic, or even Panhellenic, elite for whom the symposium was a central institution. Horses were status symbols, cock-fighting symbolized the martial spirit that a young aristocrat should have, and dolphins were associated with drinking. Although farmers at Syracuse may have worn stag horns in honor of Artemis Lyaia, there is no persuasive evidence for a similar costumed agricultural ritual at Attica, and if there was such a ritual, it in turn may have been co-opted by the aristocracy before surviving records begin. Of course one can never speak of a purely "secular" symposium or *komos*, for the Greeks would have felt that Dionysus was present on those occasions, but the possibility should be considered that a significant feature of animal masquerades was their association with the elite classes, which casts them in a social or even political light. I have suggested also that if animal choruses were linked with the aristocratic symposium class at Athens, their disappearance from vase-painting around 480 B.C. was no coincidence, for it occurred at

183

just the time when comedy, upon being integrated into the Dionysia, was co-opted by the democracy. In the last decades of the fifth century, when evidence for animal choruses resurfaces, comedy may have been taken up by the elite to attack the demos, and comic playwrights may have revived the genre of the animal chorus in a conscious, almost archaizing way. By then, however, changing fifth-century ideas about animals had brought different species on stage, and the comedies had less to do with symposia than with the social qualities of animals.

I find also that animals in comedy, far from being the predatory and dangerous forces that they were in epic, tragedy, or in Herodotus, where they were antitypes to civilized behavior and represented marginal forces, seem to cooperate with human culture. This is a thread that can be traced throughout the tradition of animal masquerades and choruses, from the archaic vase-paintings into the late-fifth-century comedies. I detect an effort to blur the distinction between animal and human by purging animals of their more threatening features. Long-standing motifs such as the association between dolphins and the dance and between birds and music are certainly important. To some extent this is a simple reflection of anthropomorphization, but more is at work. Animals were shown not only to be capable of functioning as human beings, but to do so in a self-conscious way, even to the point of being associated with the creation of aspects of human civilization. Satyrs were shown in comparable situations, a fact that suggests that this view of animals is not implausible in drama. I have proposed that the dolphin-riders and bull-headed dancers can be connected with Greek myths of city foundations, which were themselves themes of archaic sympotic poetry. Aristophanes' *Birds* is, above all, an account of a city foundation, though I have argued that the way it presents this was filtered through contemporary intellectual understandings of nature and culture. In other comedies, too, animals were marked as often as not by their social or human qualities. One might be expected to turn to animals and draw from them the powers of nature, a common motif in some traditional hunting cultures that adopt animal dress, but in Greek comedy one draws from them the sources of culture. Comedy therefore leads us away from, not toward, the θηριώδης βίος. The animals of these choruses were presented as creatures that, like Dionysus, abolished the difference that separates men from animals, yet unlike Dionysus they do not shatter the social order in so doing; instead, they confirm it.

APPENDIX A

TESTIMONIA AND FRAGMENTS
OF LOST COMEDIES

Collected here are biographical information, Greek text, and translations of the fragments of the animal choruses discussed in Chapter 4.
Translations are mine unless otherwise noted. The Greek texts owe a
great deal to the volumes of *Poetae Comici Graeci*, from which I have
benefited enormously. I would also like to thank S. Douglas Olson
for allowing me to look in advance at his text of selected comic fragments. I have omitted fragments and testimonia that seemed completely unhelpful to appreciating the comedies, though even much
that has been retained may seem only of tangential importance.[1]

T = Testimonia from *PCG*.

ANTIPHANES' *KNIGHTS* ('Ἱππεῖς), 370S B.C. OR LATER?
PCG II.368–69

The *Suda* (2735) says that Antiphanes was born between 408 and
404 B.C. and died aged 74 years, which would put his death between
334 and 331 B.C., but fr. 185 K-A implies that Seleucus already had
the title of king, which did not occur until 307 B.C.[2] On *IG* ii²
2325.146 (= Mette V C 1 col. 3.7) he is credited with eight victories at the Lenaea in the company of playwrights who were active in
the 370s.

Fr. 108 K-A (= 109 K) Athenaeus 11.503b:
πῶς οὖν διαιτώμεσθα; (Β.) τὸ μὲν ἐφίππιον
στρῶμ᾿ ἐστὶν ἡμῖν, ὁ δὲ καλὸς πῖλος κάδος,
ψυκτήρ· τί βούλει; πάντ᾿, Ἀμαλθείας κέρας

A: How, then, are we to lead our lives?

B: The saddle cloth is our mattress, and the pretty felt cap that we use as a jar is our wine cooler. What do you want? [We have] everything – the horn of Amaltheia.

Fr. 109 K-A (= 110 K) Athenaeus 15.700c:

τῶν δ᾿ ἀκοντίων
συνδοῦντες ὀρθὰ τρία λυχνείῳ χρώμεθα

After tying together three of the javelins so that they stand upright, we use them as a lampstand.

ARCHIPPUS' *FISHES* (Ἰχθύες), 401/400 B.C.? *PCG* II.542–49

Archippus won a victory in the years 415–412 B.C. (thus the *Suda*). Fr. 27 of the *Fishes* has a peace treaty that mentions Eucleides, who was archon in 403/402; Anytus, who appears in fr. 31, was also influential in 403 and after, so the comedy would date from this period. Geissler suggested 401/400.[3] If the *Comoedia Dukiana* belongs to the *Fishes*, the date would need to be brought down at least a decade or two since the *Comoedia Dukiana* refers to Isocrates' *Helen*, written in the first decade of the fourth century.

Fish were important enough in the Greek diet that it was probably inevitable that fourteen of the twenty one fragments would survive in Athenaeus' *Deipnosophists*.

Fr. 14 K-A (= 14 K) Harpocration p. 231.13:

αἱρουμένους τε πραγμάτων ἐπιστάτας
ἀποδοκιμάζειν, εἶτα δοκιμάζειν πάλιν.
ἢν οὖν ποιῶμεν ταῦτα, κίνδυνος λαθεῖν
ἁπαξάπαντας γενομένους παλιναιρέτους

... to reject the elected administrators of affairs as unfit for office, and then to approve them again after examination. If we then act this way, there is a danger that, without our realizing it, *everyone* will be removed from office and then re-elected.

Fr. 15 K-A (= 15 K) Steph. Byz. p. 196.21:

(A) τί λέγεις σύ; μάντεις εἰσὶ γὰρ θαλάττιοι;
(B) γαλεοί γε, πάντων μάντεων σοφώτατοι

A: What do you mean? That there are prophets of the sea?
B: Yes, dogfish,[4] the wisest of all prophets.

Fr. 16 K-A (= 19 K) Athenaeus 7.322a:
ἐκήρυξεν βόαξ,
σάλπης δ᾽ ἐσάλπιγξ᾽ ἕπτ᾽ ὀβολοὺς μισθὸν φέρων

The *boax*[5] made a proclamation, and the *saupe*[6] sounded a trumpet, earning a seven-obol wage.

Fr. 17 K-A (= 17 K) Athenaeus 7.315b–c:
ἱερεὺς γὰρ ἦλθ᾽ αὐτοῖσιν ὀρφὼς του θεῶν

For a giant sea-perch,[7] a priest of some god, came for them.

Fr. 18 K-A (= 18 K) Athenaeus 7.328a:
ἱερεὺς Ἀφροδίτης χρύσοφρυς Κυθηρίας

A gilt-head,[8] priest of Cytherean Aphrodite.

Fr. 23 K-A (= 25 K) Athenaeus 6.227a:
Αἰγύπτιος μιαρώτατος τῶν ἰχθύων κάπηλος,
Ἕρμαιος, ὃς βίᾳ δέρων ῥίνας γαλεούς τε πωλεῖ
καὶ τοὺς λάβρακας ἐντερεύων, ὡς λέγουσιν ἡμῖν

A most shameful Egyptian fish-seller, Hermaeus, who violently flays monkfish,[9] sells dogfishes,[10] and guts the bass,[11] as they tell us.

Fr. 25 K-A (= 23 K) Athenaeus 3.86c:
κῆρυξ θαλάσσης τρόφιμος, υἱὸς πορφύρας

A herald,[12] a child of the sea, son of a purplefish.[13]

Fr. 26 K-A (= 26 K) Athenaeus 7.312a:
τοὺς μαιώτας καὶ σαπέρδας καὶ γλάνιδας

The *maiotai*[14] and *saperdai*[15] and *glanidai*.[16]

Fr. 27 K-A (= 27 K) Athenaeus 7.329b:
φέρε εἴπωμεν τίνες εἰσὶν αἱ παρὰ Ἀρχίππῳ ἐν Ἰχθύσι τῷ δράματι
θρᾷτται. κατὰ τὰς συγγραφὰς γὰρ τῶν ἰχθύων καὶ Ἀθηναίων ταυτὶ
πεποίηκεν·

ἀποδοῦναι δ᾿ ὅσα ἔχομεν ἀλλήλων, ἡμᾶς μὲν τὰς Θρᾴττας καὶ
Ἀθερίνην τὴν αὐλητρίδα καὶ Σηπίαν τὴν Θύρσου καὶ τοὺς
Τριγλίας καὶ Εὐκλείδην τὸν ἄρξαντα καὶ Ἀναγυρουντόθεν τοὺς
Κορακίωνας καὶ Κωβιοῦ τοῦ Σαλαμινίου τόκον καὶ Βάτραχον
τὸν πάρεδρον τὸν ἐξ Ὠρεοῦ.

ἐν τούτοις ἄν τις ζητήσειε ποίας θρᾴττας παρὰ τοῖς ἰχθύσιν εἶναι
συμβέβηκεν, ἃς ἀποδοῦναι τοῖς ἀνθρώποις συντίθενταί ἐπεὶ οὖν
ἰδίᾳ μοι συγγέγραπταί τι περὶ τούτου, αὐτὰ τὰ καιριώτατα νῦν
λέξω.

Well, let's explain what "Thracian women" are in the *Fishes* of Archippus, for
in the peace-treaties of the fishes and the Athenians he wrote the following:

To give back whatever we have of each other's property, namely, that we
give up the Thracian women[17] and Atherina[18] the flute-girl and Sepia[19]
wife of Thursos and the Trigliai[20] and Eucleides, who was archon, and the
Korakiones[21] [crowfishes] from Anagyros, the son of Kobios of Salamis, and
the assessor Batrachos[22] [fishing-frog] from Oreos.

Someone might inquire as to who these Thracian women happen to be –
that is, the women who are in the custody of the fishes and whom they agree
to return to the men; and since I have written up a treastise specifically about
this, I will now explain the most important points.

Fr. 28 K-A (= 28 K) Athenaeus 8.343c: (on Melanthius, the tragic
poet)
κωμῳδοῦσι δ᾿ αὐτὸν ἐπὶ ὀψοφαγίᾳ Λεύκων ἐν Φράτερσιν,
Ἀριστοφάνης ἐν Εἰρήνῃ, Φερεκράτης ἐν Πετάλῃ. ἐν δὲ τοῖς Ἰχθύσιν
Ἄρχιππος τῷ δράματι ὡς ὀψοφάγον δήσας παραδίδωσι τοῖς ἰχθύσιν
ἀντιβρωθησόμενον.

Melanthius is ridiculed for eating fish by Leukon in *Phratries*, Aristophanes
in *Peace*, Pherecrates in *Petale*. And in the *Fishes* Archippus has him tied up
because he was an epicure and has him handed over to the fish to be eaten
in revenge.

Eust. In Iliadem p. 1201.3:
ἰστέον δὲ ὅτι παίζων ὁ ποιητὴς Ἄρχιππος εἰς τὸν κατὰ τὴν Ἡσιόνην
μῦθον, ὃς αὐτὴν βορὰν τῷ κήτει ἐκτίθεται, πλάττει Μελάνθιον τὸν
τραγῳδὸν ἔν τινι αὐτοῦ δράματι δεθῆναι, καὶ οὕτω παραδίδωσιν αὐτὸν
τοῖς ἰχθύσιν ἀντιβρωθησόμενον. ἦν γὰρ ὁ ἀνὴρ ὀψοφάγος, κατὰ
ἰχθυοφαγίαν δηλαδή.

It should be known that the poet Archippus, parodying the myth of Hesione, in which she was set out as food for a sea-monster, portrays Melanthius the tragic poet as bound up in one of his plays, and surrenders him thus to the fish to be eaten in turn. You see, the man was an epicure – especially when it came to eating fish.

Fr. 29 (= 7 Dem.) Prov. cod. Par. suppl. 676 apud Cohn CPG Suppl. I p. 68:

ἀγροῦ πυγή· παροιμία ἐπὶ τῶν λιπαρῶς προσκειμένων . . . ὁ δ᾽ Ἄρχιππος ἐπὶ τῶν ἀγροίκων τίθησιν, οἷον ἐν Ἰχθύσιν.

"Rump of the field." Proverbial for things being added richly . . . Archippus applies this to rustics, as in the *Fishes*.

Fr. 30 K-A (= 29 K) Athenaeus 8.331c (cf. 334f):

ἀλλὰ μήν, ἄνδρες ἰχθύες κατὰ τὸν Ἄρχιππον

But, to be sure, as Archippus says, "Gentlemen fishes . . ."

Fr. 31 K-A (= 30 K) Schol Areth. (B) Plato *Apol.* 18b:

Θεόπομος δὲ Στρατιώτισιν ἐμβαδᾶν αὐτὸν εἶπεν παρὰ τὰς ἐμβάδας, ἐπεὶ καὶ Ἄρχιππος Ἰχθύσιν εἰς σκυτέα αὐτὸν σκώπτει.

Theopompus, in his *Stratiotides* ["Soldier-women"] said that he [Anytus] was a "cobbler" because of his shoes, since in the *Fishes* Archippus also ridicules him as a shoemaker.

ARISTOPHANES' *STORKS* (Πελαργοί), 390s B.C.?
PCG III.2.239–44

Fragments 454 and 455 of the *Storks* refer to Neocleides and Patrocles, a politician and a poet respectively, who were active in the 390s; the comedy was probably produced in that decade.[23] It was performed in the same year as the Oedipus trilogy by the tragic poet Meletus (see fr. 453), whatever year that may have been.[24]

Fr. 444 K-A (= 430 K) Scholia *Wasps* 1238a:

ὁ μὲν ᾖδεν Ἀδμήτου λόγον πρὸς μυρρίνην.
ὁ δ᾽ αὐτὸν ἠνάγκαζεν Ἁρμοδίου μέλος

One was singing the tale of Admetus to a myrtle branch, the other forced him [to sing] the song of Harmodius.

Fr. 445 K-A (= 17 Dem.) Phot α 1326:
οὐ γὰρ σὺ παρέχεις ἀμφιέσεθαι τῷ πατρί

For you aren't offering anything for your father to wear.

Fr. 446 K-A (= 405, 441 K) Eust. In Od. p. 1423,4:
τί δὲ τὸν ὀρνίθειον οἰκίσκον φέρεις;

Why are you carrying the little bird house?

Fr. 447 K-A (= 432 K) [Herodian] Philetaerus 83:
ἀπεσημηνάμην
τὰς τῶν κακούργων οἰκίας

I sealed up the houses of the malefactors.

Fr. 448 K-A (= 433 K) Athenaeus 9.387f:
ἀτταγᾶς ἥδιστον ἕψειν ἐν ἐπινικίοις κρέας

The sweetest thing is to boil meat of the francolin [tetrao orientalis] at a victory banquet.

Fr. 452 K-A (= 437 K) Athenaeus 6.247a:
ἢν γὰρ ἕν’ ἄνδρ’ ἄδικον σὺ διώκῃς, ἀντιμαρτυροῦσι
δώδεκα τοῖς ἑτέροις ἐπισίτιοι

For if you prosecute one unjust man, twelve parasites will testify against you for the others.[25]

Fr. 453 K-A (= 438 K) Schol. Areth. (B) Plato Apology 18b:
Μέλητος δὲ τραγῳδίας φαῦλος ποιητής, Θρᾷξ γένος, ὡς Ἀριστοφάνης Βατράχοις, Πελαργοῖς, Λαΐου υἱὸν αὐτὸν λέγων, ἐπεὶ ᾧ ἔτει οἱ Πελαργοὶ ἐδιδάσκοντο καὶ ὁ Μέλητος Οἰδιπόδειαν καθῆκεν, ὡς Ἀριστοτέλης Διδασκαλίαις.

Meletus was a bad tragic poet, Thracian by birth, as Aristophanes says in the *Frogs* and *Storks*, calling him the son of Laius, since in the year that the *Storks* was performed Meletus also produced the *Oidipodeia*, as Aristotle says in his *Didaskaliai*.

Fr. 454 K-A (= 439 K) Schol. Plutus 665:
εἴρηται δὲ καὶ ἐν Πελαργοῖς περὶ αὐτοῦ ὅτι ῥήτωρ καὶ συκοφάντης ἐστίν.

Also in the *Storks* it was said about him [Neocleides] that he is a politician and a sycophant.

Fr. 455 K-A (= 431 K) Schol. *Plutus* 84:

τὸν Πατροκλέα κωμωιδεῖ ὡς Ἀθηναῖον μὲν καὶ πλούσιον, κνιπὸν δὲ καὶ φειδωλόν. ἦν δὲ τραγῳδίας ποιητής, ἄλλως δὲ καὶ κακόβιος καὶ φιλοχρήματος, ὡς καὶ ἐν τοῖς Πελαργοῖς εἴρηται περὶ τούτου . . .

He ridicules Patrocles for being Athenian and rich, miserly and stingy. He was a poet of tragedy, otherwise poor and greedy, as was also said about him in the *Storks* . . .

CALLIAS' *FROGS* (Βάτραχοι), 430S –420S B.C.? PCG IV.42

Callias seems to be the winner at the Dionysia in 446 B.C.: his name is restored[26] on *IG* ii² 2318.78 (= I col. 6.9–11 Mette): Καλ[λίας ἐδίδασκεν. The testimonia below put his activities in the 430s and 420s B.C. as well.

T 1 K-A, Βάτραχοι Suda κ 213:

Κάλλίας· Ἀθηναῖος, κωμικός, υἱὸς Λυσιμάχου, ὃς ἐπεκλήθη Σχοινίων διὰ τὸ σχοινοπλόκου εἶναι πατρός. οὗ δράματα . . . Βάτραχοι . . .

Callias: Athenian, comic playwright, son of Lysimachus, who was nicknamed Skhoinion because he was the son of a rope-maker. His plays include: . . . *Frogs* . . .

T 4 K-A, *IG* xiv.1097.6 = Urb. Rom. 216.6 (Mette VI A 2.6):

. . . ἐπὶ Πυ[θοδώρου - -
- - - - Βατράχ]οις. Ε ἐπὶ Ἀντιοχίδου [

[fourth] in the archonship of Pythodorus . . .
. . . *Frogs*. Fifth in the archonship of Antiochides . . .

This inscription lists several of Callias' victories in the 430s; of the surviving titles βατράχοις is the one that best fits the fragmentary ending]οις. *Frogs* may have come at the end of a list of comedies that placed fourth; if so, it was performed in the archonship of Pythodorus (431 B.C.). Yet Pickard-Cambridge and Mette understand *Frogs* to have been performed in the year of the archonship that *follows* the title of the play in the inscription: that of Antiochides, who was archon in 434 B.C. and whose entry seems to begin a list of fifth-place comedies

(E.) Geissler thought the *Frogs* came after the archonship of Pythodorus and suggests 430–26 B.C.. Dittmer and Schmid suggested even later dates: 427 or 426 B.C.[27] No fragments of this play have survived.[28]

CANTHARUS' *NIGHTINGALES* (Ἀηδόνες) AND *ANTS* (Μύρμηκες), 420S–410S B.C.? PCG V.57 & 59

Cantharus' name has been restored in *IG* ii² 2318.115 (= Mette I col. 8.17) for a victory in 422 B.C. at the Dionysia[29] and restored in *IG* ii² 2325.60 (= Mette V B I col. ii.9), for what is apparently the same victory.[30] Presumably he was active for several years before and after 422 B.C. As to the year of his death, or of the production of the *Nightingales* and *Ants*, we can only guess. No fragments survive for either play. It is possible that Cantharus had been acting as a *didaskalos* for Plato comicus – Cantharus may have done so for a comedy called *Symmachia* – and that Cantharus has been mistaken as the author of the *Ants* that Plato wrote.[31]

T 1 K-A, Suda κ 309:
Κάνθαρος· Ἀθηναῖος, κωμικός. μνημονεύεται τούτου δράματα Μήδεια, Τηρεύς, Συμμαχίαι, Μύρμηκες, Ἀηδόνες

Cantharus: Athenian, comic poet. Plays of his that are mentioned are: *Medea, Tereus, Alliances, Ants, Nightingales.*

"COMOEDIA DUKIANA" (*PCG* VIII, ADESPOTA Fr. 1146)

A papyrus from the late third or early second century B.C., now at Duke University, contains fifty lines from a Greek comedy in which two characters discuss the merits of cooking and preparing various fish, especially the sheat.[32] Consult Chapter 4 for discussion.

> (B.) τί σὺ λέγεις· γλαύκου σίλουρον κρείττον' εἶναι νενόμικας;
> (A.) τῶν μὲν οὖν ὅλως ἁπάντων ἰχθύων σοφώτατον
> φημὶ τὸν σίλουρον εἶναι κοίρανον τῶν ἰχθύων,
> ἡγεμόνα, μόναρχον, ἀρχόν· τοὺς δὲ λοιπούς, ἐπιβάτας,
> ὥστε μὴ ἀξίως ἐνεγκεῖν τῷ σιλούρῳ τὰ δόρατα.   5
> (B.) καὶ τετόλμηκας σιλούρῳ συγγράφειν ἐγκώμιον;

(Α.) ἢ σίλουρος ὄνομ᾽ ἔχων Ἀδωνίς ἐστιν ποτάμιος.
εἰ γὰρ ἤθελεν σίλουρος μὴ κυβεύειν μηδ᾽ ἐρᾶν,
οὐκ ἂν ἤδη δέκα ταλάντων περιέκειτ᾽ ἀρτύματα,
οὐκ ἂν ἤδη πέτασον εἶχε κἂν ἐφήβοις ἤψετο.   10
κᾆτα δή τις ἐστὶν ἰχθῦς ὅστις αὖ πρὸς ταῖς θύραις
ταῖς σιλούρου δόγμ᾽ ἔχων ἔστηκεν ὄρθρου καὶ λέγει·
"εἰ νένιπτ᾽ ἤδη σίλουρος .... ις εἰσπ[ο]ρεύεται·
γέγονεν ἄρα τοῖς μαιώταις πάντα περὶ ὧν ἠξίουν;
ἐντετεύχασ᾽ οἱ λάβρακες ἀπὸ τοῦ πετρηρικοῦ   15
καὶ τὸ τῶν χοίρων μάτευμα τἀπὸ τοῦ σαγηνικοῦ."
(Β.) Ἰσοκράτης ἐγκώμιον τοιοῦτον οὐδεπώποτε
καθ᾽ Ἑλένης εἴρηκεν ὡς σὺ περὶ σιλούρου. πρὸς θεῶν,
ἡ δὲ διατρ[ι]βὴ τίς ἐστιν; θαυμάσαι γὰρ ἄξιον.
(Α.) ὦ πόνηρ᾽, οὐ παντὸς ἀνδρὸς ἐς σίλουρόν ἐσθ᾽ ὁ πλοῦς.   20
ἀλλὰ καὶ προεγγραφῆναι καὶ μυηθῆναί σε δεῖ
τοῖς Σιλουρόθραξι παισὶ καὶ μαθεῖν ὡς ἔψεται.
καταλαβεῖν σε δεῖ δὲ τὴν πλύσιν †δειεκτος μουσικοῦ
καὶ πλυνεῖς, ὡς ἡ γραφή, λεπτοῖς ἁλῶν ἀθύρμασι,
λεπτὰ σωλῆνος πτερίζων αἵματος μελαγχίμου   25
πεντενίκου πεντεκρήνης πεντεπακτωτοῖς ῥοαῖς.
ὡς δ᾽ ἂν ἐκτρίβων ποιήσῃς .ιονη κύκνου πτερὸν
.... η στίλβοντα λαμπρὰ φαλακρὸν ὡς ἀνθήλιον
γίνεθ᾽ ἡ πρόσοψις οὕτως ὡραία τῶν βραγχίων
ὥστε λευκομηρίδος δόκει θεωρεῖν ἰσχίον   30
παρθένου ....ρως. (Β.) τοιαύτης ἄρα τὰ λοιπά, πρὸς θεῶν,
λευκότητος ... ἄνυσον. σὸν γὰρ τὸ νικητήριον.
(Α.) ἡ λοπὰς νῦν εἰσφερέσθω πέντ᾽ ἐφήβων ὠλέναις.
γῦρον αὐλητοῦ ποίησον καὶ κολυμβητοῦ βυθόν,
ἔνθεσιν θρίου τε νεαροῦ πο[ι]κίλων (θ᾽) ἡδυσμάτων,   35
πολυλεπίστων κρομμύων σκόρδων ὀριγάνου κλάδων,
Νηρέως τε χύμα πηγὸν κἀπὸ κρήνης μέλαν ὕδωρ.
καὶ λάβ᾽ ὄξος δριμὺ λεπτὸν ὡς διοικητοῦ νόον.
ἐκ δὲ ληκύθου βαθείας παρθένου ταυρώπιδος
νᾶμα δαψιλὲς πρόχευσον μὴ κακιζούσῃ χερί,   40
ἀλλ᾽ ὅλην μετάρσιον ἄρας τῶν σκελῶν κατάστρεφε.
ὡς δ᾽ ἂν ἐφθῇ σοι γένηται καὶ τὸ πῶμα κουφίσῃς
σεῖε, πρὸς μυκτῆρας ἕλκων πενταδράχμους ἡδονάς,
καὶ ποίησον Ἁρποχράτου θηλάσας τὸν δάκτυλον.
(Β.) Ζεῦ πάτερ, πέφρικ᾽ ἀκούων καὶ δέδοικα μήποτε   45
τὴν κατάζηλον Βοιωτὸν ἡ λοπὰς παρεκβάλῃ.
(Α.) πρὶν δὲ γεύσασθαι τεράμνων κλεῖε λαΐνων μοχλοὺς

καὶ κέλευε τοὺς μὲν ἔσθειν, τοὺς δ᾽ ἐν ὅπλοις περιπατεῖν
μὴ ᾽πανάστασις γένηται τῶν ἀχάλκων γειτόνων,
μὴ κύκνος γενόμενος ὁ Ζεὺς ἐπὶ κρυφαῖον κωμάσῃ.   50

Translation (adapted from Willis 1991)

B: What do *you* say? Are you convinced that the sheat is better than the
    shark?

A: Of absolutely all fish, to be sure, I declare that the Sheat is wisest prince of
    the fish, leader, monarch, commander! The rest (I say are mere) marines,
    such as are not worthy to carry the spears of the Sheat.

B: And have you ventured to compose a eulogy for the Sheat?

A: Surely the Sheat, famous as he is, is a river Adonis! For if the Sheat were
    not wanting to gamble and to love, ten talents of sauces wouldn't now
    surround him. He wouldn't now wear a petasos and broil among the
    cadets. And indeed there is some fish who, in turn, is standing by the
    Sheat's doors at dawn decree in hand and saying, "If the Sheat is now
    washed, he is going into . . . ? Have the Scythian (fish)[33] got all they were
    asking? The seabass[34] from the rockyla[35] and the catch of pigfish[36] from
    the nettyla have presented their petitions."

B: Isocrates has never spoken such a eulogy for Helen as you have about
    the Sheat! But by the gods, what affair is this? It's a marvel!

A: You rogue, not for every man is the voyage to the Sheat! But you must
    register and be initiated into the cult of the Silurothracian[37] children
    and learn how he'll be boiled. You must undertake the washing (you
    must [do it] without a musician?) and you will wash (it), as the writ
    prescribes, with fine adornments of the seas, fledging it with fine blades
    of a dark-blooded razorfish[38] in the five(times)–dammed streams of a
    five(fold)-fountain five(times) victorious. Just as when by polishing you
    make . . . a swan's wing or . . . shining brightly as a bald pate reflecting the
    sun, the aspect of the gills becomes so comely that one imagines he is
    beholding the hip of a white-thighed maiden . . .

B: Of such whiteness, then, by the gods, make all the rest, for yours is the
    victory!

A: Let the dish be carried out now by the arms of five ephebes. Make (it) a
    flute-player's girth and a diver's depth, with mouthfuls of fresh figleaf and
    varieties of side-dishes, much-peeled onions, garlic, sprigs of marjoram,
    and Nereus' salt stream and dark water from the spring. Take vinegar
    sharp as the subtle mind of a finance minister, and from a deep jar of
    (the) bullfaced maiden pour out a generous stream with no cowardly
    hand. But lift the whole pot aloft from its legs and turn bottoms-up.

So when it is cooked for you and you raise the lid, stir (it) and draw to your nose five-dollar pleasure, and do so sucking your finger like (?) Harpochrates.

B: Father Zeus, I shudder to hear it and am afraid that the casserole may ever disdain the envious Boeotian (eel).

A: Before tasting it, shoot the bolts of the marble chambers and invite some to eat, the others to patrol under arms lest there be a riot of our penniless neighbors, and lest Zeus become a swan for disguise and burst in on the revels!

CRATES' *BEASTS* (Θηρία), EARLY 420s B.C.? *PCG* IV.91–96

Crates was said to have gained recognition in 451/450 B.C.,[39] which may mean that he won his first victory in that year. His name has hence been restored in *IG* ii² 2325.52; if this is correct, he won three victories at the Dionysia.[40] Four fragments survive. Athenaeus gave two excerpts from the *Beasts* after quoting a passage from the *Ploutoi* of Cratinus (6.267e), which may have been performed in 429 B.C.,[41] and before quoting from the *Amphictiones* of Telecleides, which has been put between 430 and 426.[42] Assuming that the order of placement in Athenaeus reflects the relative dates of these comedies (reciting passages in chronological order is his stated practice at 268e), the *Beasts* would fall in the early 420s.[43] Aristophanes refers to Crates' career with past tense verbs in *Knights* 537–40 (424 B.C.), so by then Crates was either dead or no longer active.[44]

Fr. 16 K-A (= 14 K) Athenaeus 6.267e–f:

Athenaeus cites this and the following fragment to illustrate how comic poets conceived of a society that had no slaves. Speaker "B" describes to "A" a life of ease.[45]

> (A.) ἔπειτα δοῦλον οὐδὲ εἷς κεκτήσετ' οὐδὲ δούλην,
> ἀλλ' αὐτὸς αὑτῷ δῆτ' ἀνὴρ γέρων διακονήσει;
> (B.) οὐ δῆθ', ὁδοιποροῦντα γὰρ τὰ πάντ' ἐγὼ ποιήσω,
> (A.) τί δῆτα τοῦτ' αὐτοῖς πλέον; (B.) πρόσεισιν αὔθ' ἕκαστον
> 5 τῶν σκευαρίων, ὅταν καλῇ τις "παρατίθου τράπεζα·
> αὐτὴ παρασκεύαζε σαυτήν. μάττε θυλακίσκε.
> ἔγχει κύαθε. ποῦ 'σθ' ἡ κύλιξ; διάνιζ' ἰοῦσα σαυτήν.
> ἀνάβαινε μᾶζα. τὴν χύτραν χρῆν ἐξερᾶν τὰ τεῦτλα.

ἰχθὺ βάδιζ᾽." "ἀλλ᾽ οὐδέπω 'πὶ θάτερ᾽ ὀπτός εἰμι."

10   "οὔκουν μεταστρέψας σεαυτὸν ἀλὶ πάσεις ἀλείφων;"

A: Then no one will possess a male or female slave, but even an old man, all by himself, will have to care for himself?

B: Surely not, for I will make all [of his household utensils] walk on their own feet.

B: And what advantage do they get from that?

B: Each of the utensils will come forward whenever anyone calls them. "Present yourself, Table; get yourself ready for dinner. Start kneading, Bread basket! Start pouring it in, Ladle! Where is the drinking cup? Go rinse yourself. Cake, climb up on the table. The pot should have been pouring out the beets. Hurry up, Fish!" "But I'm not fried on the other side yet." "Well, turn yourself over; then why don't you oil yourself and sprinkle yourself with salt."

Fr. 17 K-A (= 15 K) Athenaeus 6.268a:

Athenaeus says that the speaker of these lines speaks in opposition to the speaker of fr. 16.[46]

> ἀλλ᾽ ἀντίθες τοι· 'γὼ γὰρ αὖ τραπέμπαλιν
> τὰ θερμὰ λουτρὰ πρῶτον ἄξω τοῖς ἐμοῖς
> ἐπὶ κιόνων, ὥσπερ διὰ τοῦ Παιωνίου,
> ἀπὸ τῆς θαλάττης ὥσθ᾽ ἑκάστῳ ῥεύσεται
> εἰς τὴν πύελον· ἐρεῖ δὲ θὔδωρ "ἀνέχετε."
> εἶθ᾽ ἀλάβαστος εὐθέως ἥξει μύρου
> αὐτόματος ὁ σπόγγος τε καὶ τὰ σάνδαλα

But you ought to consider it from another perspective. I, by comparison, will first bring for my friends hot bathwater from the sea on pipes, as is done through the Paionium,[47] so that it will flow into everyone's bathtub; and the water will say, "Enough!"[48] And then a bottle of myrrh will come right away, all by itself, as will a sponge and sandals.

Fr. 18 K-A (= 16 K) Harpocration p. 241, 8:

These lines were saved primarily for the word παρουσία, which here is a synonym for περιουσία. This may come from a *pnigos*.[49]

> ἔχοντες εὐπαθῆ βίον
> παρουσίαν τε χρημάτων

Living a life of ease and having an abundance of property

Fr. 19 K-A (= 17 K) Athenaeus 3.119c and Pollux 6.53:
This "dialogue" is a modern construct: the first two lines, which come from Athenaeus and appear to be spoken by the leader of the animal chorus, were joined by Bergk with the last two, from Pollux, spoken perhaps by a human being. Whether or not "B" spoke immediately after "A," the ideas are certainly complementary and the lines are in the same meter (anapestic tetrameters catalectic).[50]

> (A.) καὶ τῶν ῥαφάνων ἕψειν χρὴ
> ἰχθῦς τ᾽ ὀπτᾶν τούς τε ταρίχους, ἡμῶν δ᾽ ἄπο χεῖρας ἔχεσθαι.
> (Β.) οὐκ ἄρ᾽ ἔτ᾽ οὐδὲν κρέας, ὡς ὑμεῖς λέγετ᾽, οὐδ᾽ ὁτιοῦν ἐδόμεσθα,
> οὐδ᾽ ἐξ ἀγορᾶς, οὐδὲ τάκωνας ποιησόμεθ᾽ οὐδ᾽ ἀλλᾶντας;

A: You should boil some cabbages, roast fresh and salted fish, and keep your hands off us.

B: So, as you would have it, we won't eat any meat at all; we can't get anything from the marketplace, and we aren't to make rissoles or black puddings for ourselves?

CRATES II *BIRDS* (Ὄρνιθες), FOURTH CENTURY B.C.? *PCG* IV.111

The entry in the *Suda* also describes a second Crates.

T 1 K-A, *Suda* κ 2340:
Κράτης· Ἀθηναῖος, κωμικὸς καὶ αὐτὸς τῆς ἀρχαίας κωμῳδίας.
φέρεται αὐτοῦ δράματα τρία, Θησαυρός, Ὄρνιθες, Φιλάργυρος.

Crates: Athenian, he was also a poet of old comedy. Three plays of his are reported: *Treasure*, *Birds*, *Philargyros*.

We hear of five playwrights of Middle or New Comedy who wrote a *Thesaurus* and three who wrote a *Philargyros*; this Crates was perhaps active in the fourth century.

DIOCLES' *BEES* (Μέλιτται), 410–380 B.C. *PCG* V.20–22

The primary evidence for Diocles' career is an entry in the *Suda* that says he was a poet of Old Comedy and a contemporary of the poets Sannyrion and Philyllios, who were active from 410–380 B.C.

Fr. 7 K-A (= 6 K) Athenaeus 10.426d:

(A.) πῶς δὲ καὶ κεκραμένον
πίνειν τὸν οἶνον δεῖ με; (B.) τέτταρα καὶ δύο

A. In what mixture, on the other hand, should I drink the wine?
B. Four parts water to two parts wine.

Fr. 8 K-A (= 7 K) Photius Lexicon α 453:

καὶ καὶ τετρημένων ἀθέλδεται τύπων

And it is filtered through perforated impressions.

Fr. 9 K-A (= 8 K) Pollux 10.99:

ἀπὸ λασάνων θερμὴν ἀφαιρήσω χύτραν

I will remove a pot from its stand

Fr. 10 K-A (= 9, 10 K) Eust. In Iliadem p. 310.30, from Lexicon rhetorikon:

ἡ μίλτος οἶμαι καὶ τὶ τιγγάβαρι
- τιγγάβαρι καὶ μίλτος ἀναμεμιγμένη

Red ochre, I think, and vermillion. Vermillion and ochre mixed up together.

Fr. 11 K-A (= 11 K) Antiatt. p. 87.4:

γυναικάριον   Little woman

Fr. 12 K-A (= 12 K) Antiatt. p. 88.20:

δραπέτευμα   A running away, an escape

Fr. 13 K-A (= 13 K) Antiatt. p. 97.9:

ἐντυλίξαι   To wrap up

EUPOLIS' NANNY-GOATS (Αἶγες), 429–423 B.C.?
PCG V.302–14

Evidence for Eupolis' career includes the statement in the anonymous *De Comoedia* (9 p. 7 Koster) that he was a *didaskalos* in 429 B.C. ("in the archonship of Apollodorus") and a record of his victory at the Dionysia, probably in 424 (Mette V B 1 col. 2.8 = *IG* ii^2 2325.59). It is possible that he is the Eupolis who is listed among those killed in a naval battle in 412/411 (*IG* i^2 950.52). The general Hipponicus was spoken of as alive in *Nanny-Goats* fr. 20; he died ca. 424–422; Geissler dated the *Nanny-Goats* to the period 429 to 423; Storey's suggestion of the Dionysia of 424 is attractive.[51] The *Nanny-Goats* was widely enough known to be cited by Quintilian and Plutarch. Only a few fragments, however, reveal much about the play or chorus, and I include those only:

Fr. 1 K-A (= 1 K) Erotian ς 55:
‡ὡς ἦν ποτ' αὐτῶν δὴ κάμῃ τις,[52] εὐθέως
ἐρεῖ πρὸς αὐτόν "πρίω μοι σελάχιον" τί δὲ ἦν λύκον‡
κεκράξεται φράσει τε πρὸς τὸν αἰπόλον

Because if any of them ever gets sick, he'll say to him, "Buy me a little fish"; but what if it's a wolf? – he'll shout out and show it to the goatherd.

Fr. 3 K-A (= 2 K) Photius κ 506:
σὺ δ' αἰγιάζεις ἐνθαδὶ καθήμενος

You are sitting there, talking about goats.[53]

Fr. 4 K-A (= 3 K) Photius p. 564.17:
καὶ ζῆν μαθόντι μηδὲ τάγυρι μουσικῆς

And he, who learned how to live, doesn't even have a smattering of learning in the arts.

Fr. 8 K-A (= 11 K) Photius α 2839:
ταύτην ἐγὼ 'ζήτουν πάλαι τὴν ἁρμογήν

I've been looking for this [musical] composition for a long time.

Fr. 12 K-A (= 13 K) Photius p. 290.20:
ἐπίσταμαι γὰρ αἰπολεῖν, σκάπτειν, νεᾶν, φυτεύειν

For I know how to tend goats, dig, plow, plant.

Fr. 13 K-A (= 14 K) Plutarch *Quaest. Conv.* 4.1.3 662d:
δοκεῖς μοι διεψεῦσθαι, τὰ θηρία τῶν ἀνθρώπων ἁπλουστέραις
τροφαῖς χρῆσθαι ... ὑποτιθέμενος ... αἱ παρ' Εὐπόλιδος αἶγες
ἀντιμαρτυροῦσιν, ὑμνοῦσαι τὴν τροφὴν ὡς παμμιγῆ καὶ ποικίλην
οὖσαν, οὕτως πως λέγουσαι·
βοσκόμεθ' ὕλης ἀπὸ παντοδαπῆς, ἐλάτης πρίνου κομάρου τε
πτόρθους ἁπαλοὺς ἀποτρώγουσαι, καὶ πρὸς τούτοισιν ἔτ' ἄνθην,
κύτισόν τ' ἠδὲ σφάκον εὐώδη καὶ σμίλακα τὴν πολύμφυλλον,
κότινον, σχῖνον, μελίαν, λεύκην, ἀρίαν, δρῦν, κιττόν, ἐρίκην,

πρόμαλον, ῥάμνον, φλόμον, ἀνθέρικον, κισθόν, φηγόν, θύμα,
θύμβραν
τὰ γὰρ κατηριθμημένα μυρίας δήπου διαφορὰς ἔχει χυμῶν καὶ
ὀδμῶν καὶ δυνάμεων· πλείονα δὲ τῶν εἰρημένων παραλέλειπται.

I think you're mistaken to suppose that animals use nourishment that is simpler than that of human beings; the goats in Eupolis attest to the opposite, singing that their food is blended and varied, saying something like the following:

> "We feed from trees of all sorts, nibbling off young tender shoots of fir, prickly-oak and strawberry-tree, and in addition to these the blossom, tree-medick, and fragrant wild sage and bindweed, which has many leaves, the wild olive tree, lentisk, ash, white poplar, holm oak, oak, ivy, heather, willow, prickly shrubs, mullein, asphodel, rock-rose, Valonia oak, thyme, savory."[54]

So you see, the things they enumerated certainly have a great number of different flavors and smells and powers; and more of the things they said have been omitted.

Fr. 17 K-A (= 17 K) Quintilian *Inst. Orat.* 1.10.17–18:

grammatice quondam ac musice iunctae fuerunt... eosdem utriusque rei praeceptores fuisse cum Sophron ostendit... tum Eupolis, apud quem Prodamus et musicen et litteras docet et Maricas... nihil se ex musice scire nisi litteras confitetur.

The arts of writing and of the Muses were once joined... Sophron showed that the teachers of both subjects were the same people... so too Eupolis, who makes Prodamus teach both literature and music, and who has Maricas confessing that he knows nothing of the arts of the Muses except literature.

Schol. Dion. Thr. *GrGr* I 3 p. 490,25:

πάλαι τοὺς αὐτοὺς γραμματικῆς καὶ μουσικῆς εἶναι διδασκάλους, ὡς
Εὔπολις εἰσάγει ἐν Αἰξί καὶ Ἰσοκράτης ἐν τῷ περὶ ἀντιδόσεως.

The same people were once teachers of writing and of the arts, as Eupolis introduces them in the *Nanny-Goats* and Isocrates in his oration "On the Exchange."

Fr. 18 K-A (= *CGFP* 237) *P.Oxy.* 2738 col. ii:

πυρριχίζων, ἐν δὲ Αἰξὶν Εὐπόλ[ιδος] τὸ μαλακὴν κε[λ]εύ[ειν] τὴν
Ἀθηνᾶν ποεῖν. σκλη[ρ]ῶς ποιοῦντο[ς] τοῦ ἀγροίκου τὸ σχῆμα τῆς
Ἀθηνᾶς ὁ διδ[ά]σκαλος ἐκέλευσεν μαλακῶς αὐτὸ ποιεῖν. ὡς οὖν ὁ

Ἀρ[ισ]τοφ[ά]νη[ς] τῷ Τριτογένεια μόνῳ ἐπιθέτῳ ἠρκέσθη καὶ ὁ Κρατ[ῖ]νος τῷ Γοργο. ρακον. οδοκα ἠρκέσθη τ[ὸ] αὐτὸ δηλοῦντι πρᾶγμα.

The Pyrrhic dance: [an example of this] in the *Nanny-Goats* of Eupolis is the instruction to perform the "Athena" (a dance movement) fluidly. When a rustic was performing the "Athena" movement awkwardly the teacher ordered him to do it fluidly. So, just as Aristophanes did a satisfactory job [in alluding to the pose] with the epithet "Tritogeneia" by itself, Cratinus also did a satisfactory job with [the epithet] "Gorgon-dragon-awaiting," which signifies the same thing.[55]

Fr. 20 K-A (= 19 K) Hesychius ɪ 292:
ἱερεὺς Διονύσου· Εὔπολις Αἰξὶν Ἱππόνικον, σκώπτων ὡς ἐρυθρὸν τῇ ὄψει.

"Priest of Dionysus": Eupolis in the *Nanny-Goats* ridiculing Hipponikos for being red in the face.

Scholia *Frogs* 308:
ὁ τοῦ Διονύσου ἱερεύς. πυρρὸς γὰρ ἦν κατὰ φύσιν . . . Εὔπολις δὲ τὸν τοῦ Διονύσου ἱερέα νομίζετ᾽ αἰγίπυρρον ἀντὶ τοῦ πυρρόν. τὸ γὰρ ἄνθος ἔχειν φησὶ Δημήτριος ἱκανῶς ἐρυθρόν.

"The priest of Dionysus." For he was red by nature . . . Eupolis considers the priest of Dionysus to be "goat-red" (αἰγίπυρρον)[56] instead of "red." For Demetrius says that the flower has sufficient redness.

Fr. 22 K-A (= 14 K) Scholia Hom. Π 353b:
πρόβατα γὰρ πάντα ἐκάλουν τὰ θρέμματα οἱ παλαιοί· καὶ Εὔπολις προβατικὸν χορόν φησι τὸν ἐξ αἰγῶν.

The ancients used to call all creatures "herds" (πρόβατα), and even Eupolis says that a chorus made up of goats was a "herd chorus" (προβατικὸν).

Fr. 326 K-A (= 303 K) Photius β 88 (K-A: "Incertae fabulae"; Bergk attributed this to the *Goats*.)
(Α.) ἄγε δή, πότερα βούλεσθε τὴν ⟨νῦν⟩ διάθεσιν
ᾠδῆς ἀκούειν ἢ τὸν ἀρχαῖον τρόπον;
(Β.) ἀμφότερ᾽ ἐρεῖς, ἐγὼ δ᾽ ἀκούσας τοῖν τρόποιν
ὃν ἂν δοκῇ μοι βαστάσας αἱρήσομαι.

A: Come now, do you want to listen to the modern composition of a song or the old-fashioned mode?

B: You will say both, but I will choose whatever seems best to me after I
     listen to the two modes and consider them carefully.

Fr. 388 K-A (= 353 K) Et. Magn. p. 18.10. (K-A: "Incertae fabulae";
   Bergk attributed this to the *Goats*.)
            ἀλλ' ἀδολεσχεῖν αὐτὸν ἐκδίδαξον, ὦ σοφιστά

But teach him to talk idly, sophist.

MAGNES' *BIRDS* ('Ορνιθες), *FROGS* (Βάτραχοι), AND *FIG-WASPS* (Ψῆνες), 470S–440S B.C.? *PCG* IV.626–631

Magnes is known to have been a victor in 472 BC.[57] Aristotle (*Poetics*
1448a34) thought that Magnes was younger than Epicharmus, who
was active from the late sixth century into the fifth, and that Magnes
was a contemporary of Chionides, a victor in 486. It was thought that
Magnes won eleven victories at the Dionysia, more than any other
comic playwright.[58] We do not know of any victories at the Lenaea,
where comic contests were introduced around 440 B.C., so his career
may have ended by then.

PHERECRATES' *ANT-MEN* (Μυρμηκάνθρωποι), 430S–420S B.C.? *PCG* VII.161–67

The anonymous *De Comoedia* 9 p. 7 (Koster) reports that Pherecrates
won a victory "in the archonship of Theodorus" (ἐπὶ Θεοδώρου,
emended by Dobree from ἐπὶ Θεάτρου), which would be 437 B.C.
This seems to be confirmed by inscriptional evidence; his name has
been restored on the list of victors at the Dionysia, and the date 438–
437 is not inconsistent for the first victory (*IG* ii² 2325.56 = Mette
V B 1 col. 2.5).[59] Two of his victories at the Lenaea are also recorded
(*IG* ii² 2325.122 = Mette V C 1 col. 1.7), the first of which may have
been in the 430s. The only secure date we have is that the *Agrioi* was
performed in 420 ("in the archonship of Aristion," says Athenaeus,
5.218d); other comedies, too, seem to have been produced in the 420s.
We have no direct evidence for the date of his death: Geissler surmises
that he was dead by 400.[60] We do not know when the *Myrmekanthropoi*

was performed, but Pherecrates was evidently most active in the 430s and 420s.

Fr. 117 K-A (= 113 K) Etymologicum genuinum β 308:
(A.) τί ληρεῖς; ἀλλὰ φωνὴν οὐκ ἔχειν
ἰχθύν γε φασὶ τὸ παράπαν. (B.) νὴ τὼ θεώ,
οὐκ ἔστιν ἰχθὺς ἄλλος οὐδεὶς ἢ βόαξ.

A: What are you blabbering about? They say that a fish most certainly does not have a voice. B: By the two goddesses, no other fish does except the boax.

Fr. 118 K-A (= 117 K) Photius α 525 = Suda αι 61:
οἴμοι κακοδαίμων, αἰγὶς αἰγὶς ἔρχεται

Alas, woe is me, a hurricane, a hurricane is coming.

Fr. 119 K-A (= 114 K) Pollux 7.73:
ἀλλ' ὡς τάχιστα τὸν γέρονθ' ἱστὸν ποίει.

But as quickly as you can, set up the spindle as a mast.

Fr. 121 K-A (= 118 K) Photius α 2766 = Suda α 3743:
ὕστερον ἀρᾶται κἀπιθεάζει τῷ πατρί

Later he curses and invokes the gods against his father.
("Prays and beseeches his father"? Norwood tr.)

Fr. 122 K-A (= 119 K) Photius α 2903, 2904 = Suda α 4045:
ξένη γυνὴ γραῦς ἀρτίως ἀφιγμένη

A strange old woman, just now arrived.

Fr. 125 K-A (= 120 K) Athenaeus 8.335a:
μηδέποτ' ἰχθύν, ὦ Δευκαλίων, μηδ' ἢν αἰτῶ παραθῇς μοι

Don't ever offer me fish, Deucalion, not even if I ask for it.

Fr. 126 K-A (= 121 K) Schol. Ar. *Vesp* 674:
ἆρά ποθ' ὑμεῖς(
)καὶ τῆς ὀροφῆς τὸν χοῦν
κατὰ τῆς κεφαλῆς καταμήσονται
λαγαριζόμενοι

Then will you ever... and by scraping they will heap up a mound of earth from the roof onto your head.

PLATO COMICUS' *ANTS* (Μύρμηκες), 425–422 B.C.?
PCG VII.468

Plato's *Hyperbolus* satirized Hyperbolus, who was politically active in the 420s until he was ostracized ca. 417 B.C. Epigraphic evidence puts Plato's first victory at the Dionysia after 414 (*IG* ii² 2325.63 = Mette V B 1 col. ii.12).[61] An argument to Aristophanes' *Frogs* indicates that Plato came in third place with his *Cleophon* in 405. Plato was probably active until about 385 B.C.[62] He was, therefore, nearly an exact contemporary of Aristophanes, whose career began in the 420s and lasted into the fourth century, and we can disregard the statement of Platonios that Plato was a representative of Middle Comedy.[63] Only the title survives for *Ants*, listed in the *Suda* along with other comedies of Plato.

T 1 K-A(= Suda. p 1708)
δράματα δὲ αὐτοῦ κη' ταῦτα· ... Μύρμηκες

His plays are 28 in number, including these: ... *Ants* ...

MISCELLANEOUS DEPICTIONS
OF ANIMAL COSTUMES

A few other figures evidently costumed as animals may be related to comedy, though perhaps not its choruses.

A Vase in Bird Shape

A black-glazed Attic amphoriskos (17.8 cm) from the end of the fifth century, in New York, was molded in the shape of a bird with human features (Figure B.1).[1] Its torso, hands, arms, and legs (which are pulled up) are human, whereas its head is clearly bird-like, with a pronounced beak, and it has wings. Because its date is close to that of Aristophanes' *Birds*, it is reasonable to suppose that it somehow reflects that comedy. Since it is alone, we cannot be sure that it is a member of the chorus; if it is an actor we would expect him to sport a *phallos*, which is missing here.[2] The way the spout of the vessel protrudes from the top of the bird's head reminds a reader that Euelpides compared Peisetaerus to a "blackbird with a bowl pluck" (*Birds* 805–06). This pot is black; the "bowl pluck," however, refers to an upturned bowl-cut, which inverts what we see.[3] Tereus was said to have a pronounced beak (99) and to have lost his wings (103–06), whereas feathers are only visible on this amphoriskos where they have been stamped superficially. More to the point: if this is Tereus, the distinctive hoopoe crest (93–94) has been omitted.

Terracotta Bird Actor

By the end of the fifth century vases and terracotta statuettes depicting actors were beginning to gain in popularity.[4] A terracotta statuette

(18.7 cm high) in the Steinhardt Collection (Plate VIII) potentially depicts Peisetaerus or Euelpides. It was made from a mold and may be Attic or Boeotian, of the fourth century B.C.[5] He is a bearded old man wearing a densely feathered costume that includes a crest, which seems to have two tall, upright feathers. He strides forward and holds his feathered arms from his sides, like wings. Green has remarked on a hole where a *phallos* must have been attached.[6] *Phalloi*, though possible on chorus costumes, were a virtual certainty on actors. The members of the chorus of *Birds* refer twice to their beaks (348 and 364), and the beak is one bird feature that this figurine does not have.[7] Unlike Tereus, who has been plucked clean (*Birds* 284), Peisetaerus, who is an old man (1256), was said by Euelpides to have wings (803–04). Peisetaerus may have looked like this.

Fish-men

On a sixth-century Etruscan, "Pontic" black-figure amphora found in Caere and now in Rome, Museo dei Conservatori, are three elderly figures advancing right toward four Nereids.[8] These three figures each have full human bodies, but the hind-quarters of fish – probably dolphins – are attached to them. There is no *aulos*-player and the vase is not Attic, so we cannot use this as evidence for a chorus or *komos* in Attica. There is little agreement on just who these "Capitoline mermen" are and what they are doing. Lund and Rathje believe they are creatures of Greek mythology rather than local Italic deities.[9] Buschor and Sifakis thought it a mythological scene,[10] but Bowra objected that the figures would have been modeled on Tritons, proposing that it is a dance in which fish-quarters were added.[11] Ridgway suggested that these three bearded men with dolphins attached to their backs represent the chorus of a satyr-play.[12]

Hare-man

On an amphora from Fikellura, Rhodes, from ca. 550–540 B.C., is a figure with a human body, but the head of a hare.[13] The vase is not Attic and, since he stands in isolation, there is no sign that this is a performance. He could be an imaginary creature or perhaps is in a *komos* for some divinity. In Aesopic fables the hare was proverbially stupid and lazy. It was known for its reproductive fertility (Aristotle,

B.1. Black-glazed Attic amphoriskos in the shape of a man wearing a bird costume. End of the fifth century. New York, Metropolitan Museum of Art 1999.68. All rights reserved, The Metropolitan Museum of Art.

HA 579b31ff.) and was consequently given as a love-gift.[14] The hunting was rather stylized: the goal was not to destroy the quarry but to catch it and make it one's own.[15] Usually once caught it would be eaten (references in comedy at Athenaeus 399d; it is prey at Aeschylus, *Agam.* 108–37 and *Eum.* 26; Xen. *Cyneg.* 6.11–17). Although considered unclean in Leviticus 11.6 and Deuteronomy 14.7, the hare had no demonstrable religious or cultic significance in Greece.[16] It would seem that a person wearing a hare-mask would be appropriating its natural powers of fertility.

Apes

A red-figure cup from ca. 520 B.C., found in Vulci, depicts five nude youths wearing ape masks, balancing on a see-saw while one in the middle holds a large skyphos.[17] There is no *aulos*-player, but Brijder speaks of it as a comic act performed for spectators. Apes were associated with lasciviousness, musicality, and dancing, which probably made this an entertaining, informal performance.[18] Brijder suggests that such a performance would caricature and expose human mischief, holding up a mirror to their spectators, who are warned that those who drink too much will behave as ridiculously as apes.[19] Moreover, Brijder proposes that this is a function shared by satyr performances and notes also a relationship was perceived between the two in antiquity: there was a hybrid creature known as the satyr-ape,[20] although there seems to be no evidence for this from archaic or classical Greece. The ape itself, however, was a dualizer in Aristotle' s taxonomy: it shared features of human beings and of quadrupeds (*HA* 502a16–b26). It tends to occupy special places in various schemata of animal categories: among Thai villagers it is inedible and taboo, for it is seen as a lost human being and eating it would be akin to cannibalism.[21] Similarly in Greece they do not seem to have been eaten.[22]

Other Terracotta Figurines of Actors

Several unusual statuettes of actors have survived from Magna Graecia and Sicily.[23] They tend to be 10–20 cm high and are not to be dated from before the third century. There is no literary evidence for animal actors, much less choruses, from New Comedy, so these represent actors of the period, possibly from some popular farce or mime. Although it is not impossible that Attic influence is at work, one suspects that local actors are depicted.[24]

They at least cast light on costume conventions. They lack padding or *phalloi*. Each one relies primarily on a mask and wears a chiton, thus not attempting to create the illusion of a furry or feathered body.

Frog

A statuette in the museum at Reggio Calabria depicts a figure wearing a full head mask of a frog and a chiton that extends only to the knees.[25] The arms appear to have been broken off. It was found in a votive deposit near the theater at Locri. Two statuettes in Karlsruhe have the heads and feet of frogs (though it is possible that they are birds) but wear short chitons.[26]

Pig

A statuette in Palermo, found at Centuripe, depicts a figure wearing a full head mask of a pig, a chiton that extends to his feet, and a mantle on his shoulders.[27]

Owl

A terracotta in Taranto represents a person clad in a long chiton, cinched at the waist, with the head of an owl and wings attached to the back.[28] The arms appear to have been subsumed into the wings on this statuette. The owl makes one think of Athena, of course.

NOTES

1 Ellmann 1988, 497.
2 For fuller discussion, particularly in using ritual sources, see Bowie 1993, 1–17, and Lada-Richards 1999, 10–16.
3 Sparkes 1996, 134. Symposium scenes in particular should not be seen as exact reporting; writes Schmitt Pantel 1992, 19, "L'image est un système de signes et la construction abstraite de l'image est un travail de la pensée dans une société donnée." We rarely know where the vases were excavated; even when we do, we almost never know why or for whom they were manufactured: Rasmussen and Spivey 1991.
4 Van Straten 1995; Hedreen 1992, 1; Carpenter 1997, 1.
5 Green 1991; for further discussions of vase-painting and drama consult Trendall and Webster 1971, 1–13; Hedreen 1992, 6–9, 105–16; Taplin 1993. One cannot even maintain that Old Comedy itself attempted to be illusionistic: see Slater 2002, 3.

I. *KOMOS*, SYMPOSIUM, AND PERFORMANCE

1 Fundamental works on comedy reviewed here include Körte 1893 and 1921; Pickard-Cambridge 1927, 225–91 (= 1962, with Webster's contributions, 132–94); Herter 1947; Pohlenz 1949; Breitholtz 1960; Reckford 1987, 441–98. I have found the following more general surveys of the origins of comedy to be accessible or helpful: Norwood 1931, 5–13; Schmid 1934, 523–38; Bieber 1961; Lesky 1966, 233–40; Simon 1982a, 27–33; Handley 1985, 355–70; Henderson 1993, xi–xxvii; Green 1994, 16–28; Csapo and Slater 1995, 89–101; Rossi 1995, 249–58; Kerkhof 2001, 1–50; Stark 2004, 19–102. An important set of essays on early comedy, including discussions of *komoi* and vase-painting, will be found in Csapo forthcoming.
2 Aristotle reported that the Dorians derived the word κωμῳδοί ("comic actors" or "singers at a *komos*") from κῶμαι ("villages") and not from *komos* (κωμῳδοὺς οὐκ ἀπὸ τοῦ κωμάζειν, *Poetics* 1448a36–7). Most commentators

seem to agree that Aristotle rejects the Dorian tradition on this, but in fact Aristotle's language is not unambiguous: see Bowie 1997, 2 n. 17. Of course, even without Aristotle the archaeological evidence for these types of performances would have made them prime candidates for sources of comedy. A recent discussion is in Kerkhof 2001, 13–17.

3 "Only a fool doesn't enjoy a *komos* after drinking!" (Eur. *Cyclops* 537); at *Frogs* 219 the chorus coin a new word from *komos*: "revelers with hang-overs" (κραιπαλόκωμοι). A thorough collection of evidence is in *RE*, s.v. "Komos," though the insistence there on the "processional" aspect may not have been strictly observed in archaic Greece, when the word occasionally referred to music or merry-making without a procession explicitly intended (see Rossi 1971 and MacDowell 1990, 233). Consult also Herter 1947, 6; Ghiron-Bistagne 1976, 207–38; Reckford 1987, 443 and 539 n. 1; Bron 1988; Frontisi-Ducroux 1992; and Pütz 2003.

4 Literary evidence also points to music. The word κῶμος refers to festive songs at Aristophanes, *Thesmo.* 104 and 988 and to a lyric chorus at Pindar, *Olympian* 4.9 and *Pythian* 5.22; on the latter two consult Heath 1988. For instruments see Vierneisel and Kaeser 1990, 293–97, and Bron 1999. Athenaeus 618c, citing the first-century B.C. grammarian Tryphon, reports that κῶμος was the name of a song played on the *aulos*; see Graf 1999.

5 Illustrated in Bron 1988, whose examples tend to be fifth-century red-figure vases; similarly in the *Plutus* a drunken, garlanded young man is going to a *komos* with a torch (lines 1040–41, 1048).

6 *Ach.* 982–83: ἐπικωμάσας / ἠργάσατο πάντα κακά.

7 Dem. 19.287 (*Emb.*): ἐν ταῖς πομπαῖς ἄνευ τοῦ προσώπου κωμάζει. The mask in question would have been of a satyr, hypothesizes Frontisi-Ducroux 1992. I must, however, point to a problem here: is it possible that κωμάζει, in the light of *Ach.* 982 (cf. the Erinyes as komasts in Aeschylus, *Agamemnon* 1186–93), means something like "corrupt" or "subvert"? Is he at a *pompe* – frequently a distinct event – but treating it like a *komos* by not wearing a mask? That Kyrebion's *komos* was at night is implied, perhaps, by Aeschines' response (at *Emb.* 151) to Demosthenes' criticism of Kyrebion: see Frontisi-Ducroux 1992.

8 Pindar, *Pythian* 5.21, 8.20; see Ghiron-Bistagne 1976, 226–27.

9 Pindar, *Olympian* 4.9.

10 Eur., *Hipp.* 55–6: . . . κῶμος λέλακεν. Ἄρτεμιν τιμῶν θεὰν / ὕμνοισιν . . .

11 A dance contest at a shrine of Heracles in the Tetrakomia of the Phaleron region included komasts: thus *IG* ii² 3103; see Parker 1996, 328–39.

12 The "Law of Evegorus" at Dem. 21.10 (*Meid.*) lists, evidently in order of occurrence, the following events at the City Dionysia: a *pompe*, choruses of boys, *komoi*, comedies, and tragedies. In this list *komoi* may refer not to drunken, carnivalesque processions but to a specific category of competition, presumably men's choruses or dithyrambs. Similarly the heading of *IG* ii² 2318 (= Mette I col. 1.1), a list of victors at the Dionysia, uses *komoi* as an umbrella term for categories of competition; see Pickard-Cambridge 1968,

63 and 102–03; MacDowell 1990, 232–33. These *komoi* might not be directly connected with a symposium, although it was said that Herodes Atticus, centuries later, provided banquets to the Athenians following sacrifices at the Dionysia and that they drank while reclining on mats of ivy in the Kerameikos (Philostratus, *Vita Soph.* 2.15.459).

13 The boundary between *komos* and *pompe* was sometimes poorly marked: several vases show figures who are evidently komasts approaching an altar; moreover, some images that seem to depict *komoi* omit one or more of the markers we would expect (wine cups, musical instruments, revelers in procession): Bron 1988.

14 The robes are mentioned at Dem. 21.22 (*Meid.*). That *phalloi* were carried is stated in Plutarch, *Moralia* 527d, and we learn from *IG* i³ 46.17 (ca. 445 B.C.) that the colony of Brea was required to send a *phallos* to the Dionysia. The *phallophoria* at *Acharnians* 258 is called a *pompe*. See Pickard-Cambridge 1968, 61–62; Ghiron-Bistagne 1976, 208–12; Cole 1993.

15 Perhaps the designation "komast" could, in certain circumstances, be another way of referring to a symposiast: Rossi 1971, 36.

16 Bibliography on the symposium includes Fehr 1971; Rossi 1971; Dentzer 1982; Lissarrague 1990b; Schmitt Pantel 1993, 17–105; important essays are collected in Vetta 1983; Murray 1990, and Slater 1991. Pütz 2003 usefully surveys the evidence from Aristophanes and the comic fragments.

17 The first literary reference to the symposium is in Alcman (fr. 19 Page), and banquet scenes begin to appear on Corinthian vases at the turn of the seventh and sixth centuries: Fehr 1971, 26.

18 Murray 1990, 7, quoting Rossi 1983. See also Dentzer 1982, 447–49.

19 Bowie 1990.

20 Ion of Chios DK 36 A1 (= *FrGH* 392); Mimnermus (fr. 9 W); Xenophanes in DK 21 A1 (= D.L. 9.20). Rösler 1990, 235, suggests that poems on the achievements of the community, showing continuity of past and present, may have been performed at the symposium; Bowie 1986, 29–33, thinks they were too lengthy for practical performance.

21 Murray 1991, 90–94, thinks the symposium reinforced the values of the *syssition* (military mess-hall); see also Steiner 2002.

22 Bremmer 1990, 140. A passion for boys seems to have been substituted for a passion for girls in the sixth century, illustrated by Figure 1.2, for which see n. 30 below.

23 The ritual is described in Plato comicus fr. 71 K-A; see Bielohlawek 1940 for literary sources on the etiquette; further in Pütz 2003, 221–41.

24 Theognis 467–95 advises moderation, a sentiment shared by Xenophanes, who discourages stories about Titans, Giants, or Centaurs (DK 21 B1). Rossi 1971 points to Polyphemus' ignorance of symposium conventions as a sign of his barbarism; see also Pellizer 1990.

25 Miller 1991, 71. An example is Figure 1.2.

26 Schauenburg 1974; Miller 1991, 65 and n. 42.

27 Lissarrague 1990b, 13.

28 Dem. 54.39 (*Conon*); the barbarian god at *Birds* 1259 is a Triballian; see Long 1986, 134–36.

29 Agora P 32413: Camp 1996, 246, no. 22, fig. 7, pl. 72. A comprehensive publication will appear in Lynch forthcoming; I am grateful to Prof. Lynch for allowing me to read her thoughtful entry on the vase. Fisher 2000, 381–83, fig. 10, compares a Theban skyphos of the early fourth century that shows symposiasts wearing puzzling triangular objects on their heads, also illustrated in Boardman 1998, fig. 507. There is evidence for other outdoor symposia: Pütz 2003, 3.

30 Staatliche Museen Kassel, Antikensammlung ALg57. For this vase see Münzen und Medaillen 1975, 64, cat. no. 152; Andreae 1981, 107–111, no. 56; Lissarrague 1990c.

31 Once in the Moccia Collection, Pesaro, this vase is now apparently in a private collection in Switzerland; *Add.²* 18; *Para.* 27.58 quater; Brijder 1991, 458 no. 421, plate 135e; cf. Brijder 1983, 42 n. 209.

32 Dionysus and Ariadne were already important themes on symposiastic ware in the sixth century: see Isler-Kerényi 1993, 7. On the passage in Xenophon see Huss 1999, 440; Steinhart 2004, 7.

33 Fehr 1990; they are discussed further in Stark 2004.

34 A Corinthian bowl, London 61.4–25.45 by the Medallion Painter, ca. 600–575 B.C. See Amyx 1961, 1–15 & pl. 12b; Seeberg 1971, 44, no. 224; Fehr 1990, plate 13b.

35 On a red-figure cup in Brussels A273, ca. 490 B.C., *ARV²* 317.15; see Lissarrague 1990b, 39–40, fig. 26. Some lyrics of Alcaeus and Anacreon were composed in a female voice, yet were surely sung by male symposiasts taking on a female role, suggests Bowie 1986, 16–17.

36 I analyzed in Rothwell 1995b the juxtaposition of Aesopic fables and symposia in the *Wasps*; a similar process is at work here as well. Clearly the boundary between "high" and "low" behavior was a subtle one. For a different view of the fables in *Wasps* see Kloss 2001, 107 n. 221.

37 Athens 1045: black-figure oinochoe by Kleisophos, ca. 530 B.C.; *ABV* 186; Lissarrague 1990b, 96–97, fig. 77.

38 Vierneisel and Kaeser 1990, 283–86, suggest that symposia had elites who wore costumes and could then behave with impropriety. Fehr 1990, 192, sees younger aristocrats participating.

39 Though, as in the *Wasps*, the formal symposium still belonged "largely to the weathier classes": Bowie 1997, 3. Connections between the development of democracy and the rise of the festivals are plotted in Connor 1989. See also Sourvinou-Inwood 1994.

40 Neer 2002, 22. The shift was reflected in iconographical changes: see Dentzer 1982, 108–09. Vickers 1990 extends aristocratic symposia a few decades farther into the fifth century.

41 It was in 486 B.C. that Chionides won his first victory: Suda χ 318. Epigraphical evidence is consistent: *IG* ii² 2325.41 (= Mette V B 1 col. 1,3; cf. Mette I col. 3,8; III B 1 col. 1,2). See Geissler 1969, 10.

The emergence of tragedy is in certain respects murkier than that of comedy: we have no sixth-century depictions of tragic performances, and one important theory even has it that tragedy was forged by the creative act of a single genius, Thespis: Else 1965; Herington 1985, 80–81. Perhaps because the depictions of animal choruses on archaic vases seem to establish such a vigorous claim for ritual origins of some sort, no modern scholar, to my knowledge, has proposed that comedy was the concoction of a creative genius. See below for the case of Susarion, the only possible candidate. This is a pity, however, for a fuller understanding of the development of comedy would include an account of the interplay between traditional contexts for performance and innovations by particular individuals.

42 The "Parian Marble" is an inscription from ca. 260 B.C. (*FGrH* 239 fr. A 39). Testimonia for Susarion are collected in *PCG* VII.661–65. We know nothing substantive about the nature of this chorus, although there is a story in late sources (summarized in Pickard-Cambridge 1962, 186) connected with Susarion that traces the beginnings of comedy to noisy invective delivered one night against wealthy Athenians by rustic peasants; the peasants were asked to repeat this as a performance. When they did so they disguised their identities by smearing their face with wine-lees (τρύξ). For an attempt to identify the *komoi* of *IG* ii² 2318 with the choruses of Susarion, see Ghiron-Bistagne 1976, 258–96, who suggests also that any songs sung by sixth-century *komoidoi* were, in essence, early forms of dithyrambs. Breitholtz 1960, 75–76, objected that the word "chorus" had been restored in the inscription on the basis of a single letter (-ρ-).

43 On the emergence of the actor see Slater 2002, 22–41.

44 Athenians and Megarians both claimed Susarion as a native son. For discussions of the problem see Else 1957, 110–14; Breitholtz 1960, 74–82; Pickard-Cambridge 1962, 186; Piccirilli 1974. Kerkhof 2001, 38–50, supports the view that he was Megarian, but says nothing about the possible nature of this chorus.

45 Helpful surveys of modern scholarship on Dionysus are Henrichs 1984a and 1993. Further studies of Dionysus include: Otto 1965; Detienne 1989a; Versnel 1990, Chpt. 2; Henrichs 1990; Carpenter and Faraone 1993 (a collection of important essays); and Segal 1997. On the importance of Dionysus for drama in particular see Jeanmaire 1978, 220–331 (esp. 302–03 on comedy); Bierl 1990; Riu 1999, reviewed by Bierl 2002. *Komoi* and Dionysus are linked on an oinochoe in New York (*ARV*² 1249, 12; see Bron et al. 1989, 163) in which a depiction of the "Return of Hephaestus" was labeled "Komos" by its painter. "Komos" is the name of a boy satyr, in the company of Dionysus, Ariadne, and Tragoidia, on a red-figure bell krater of 450–425 B.C.: Compiègne 1025; *ARV*² 1055, 76, discussed in Ghiron-Bistagne 1976, 233–38, along with other examples, and Hedreen 1992, 38. Scullion 2002 sees the Dionysiac aspect of drama as a modern construct, and we share points of agreement (see below).

46 *Knights* 536. Deubner 1932, 136–37, suggested that the competitions at Rural Dionysia might have been the place for the genesis of the fantastic choruses of comedy. Seaford 1981 and 1996.

47 For a reading of the *Frogs* as a Dionysiac comedy see Lada-Richards 1999. Green 1994, 85, observes that in the third quarter of the fifth century Dionysus is shown in the company of personifications of Dithyrambos, Tragoidia, and Komoidia.

48 Frontisi-Ducroux 1991; Frickenhaus 1912; see also Wrede 1928; Pickard-Cambridge 1968, 30–34 and figs. 17–21; Henrichs 1993, 34–36.

49 See Foley 1985, 246–54; Henrichs 1993, 13–43.

50 Jameson 1993, 44–64.

51 Foley 1985, 258: "We are left uncertain whether the polis will ever absorb and domesticate Dionysus or control the proliferating and dangerous repercussions of his entry into civic life." His dangerousness is emphasized in Detienne 1979.

52 Henrichs 1990, 258.

53 Herter 1947, 37, thought of the two slaves as a chorus, but it is difficult to see it as a genuine drama, remarks Reckford 1987, 444. On the *phallophoria* see Cole 1993, 26. For a description of the role of Dionysus and wine as restorers of social health in comedy, see Sommerstein 1996, 61–64.

54 We noted above that the mime in Xenophon's *Symposium* was of Ariadne and Dionysus.

55 Lada-Richards 1999, 22. "Dionysus is enchanted by the dancing herds of wild beasts," wrote Pindar (fr. 70b22–23 Maehler).

56 For depictions of Dionysus with animals see *LIMC* III (1986), s.v. "Dionysus" esp. nos. 430–434 for panthers; for literary sources see "fonti letterarie" in the *LIMC* entry and Vierneisel and Kaeser 1990, 401–05. Some scholars call this the "leopard" to avoid confusion with the North American panther: Henrichs 1987, 115 n. 30. On Dionysus in the Return of Hephaestus see Hedreen 1992, 16.

57 Images of the ripping apart of an animal begin around 480 B.C.; see Schöne 1987, 99, 156–61, 192; Henrichs 1987, 98, 104–05.

58 See Dem. 18.259 (*Corona*) for the wearing of fawn-skin. Carpenter 1986, 67–68, 74, cautions that the wearing of fawn-skin may not have had cultic significance but was a sign of common rustic clothing. He further suggests that the presence of the lion is decorative, and that feline imagery in general is simply a device to suggest an eastern origin for Dionysus.

59 Carpenter 1986, 64–67, 83–84, 90; Dionysus wears a *pardalis* in *LIMC* III (1986), s.v. "Dionysos" nos. 151, 312, etc.

60 *Bacchae* 100, 618, 920–22, and 1018. For the animal forms of Dionysus see *LIMC* III (1986), "Dionysos" nos. 154–59 (including mid- to late-fifth-century sculpted heads of him wearing small horns) and p. 414 for references to literary sources for Dionysus' bull shape. Further in Dodds 1960, xviii; Bodson 1978, 149–50.

61 Radermacher 1932, 386.

62 *Clouds* 606 and *Thesmo.* 992, as observed by Pohlenz 1949, 35–36. Then again, comedies with the title *Dionysus* were written by four playwrights; Crates may have written one (*PCG* IV.85, test. 12), Aristophanes wrote a *Dionysos Nauagos*, Aristomenes a *Dionysos Asketes*, Polyzelus and Anaxandrides a *Dionysou gonas*, and Dionysus was a character in five other comedies (including of course the *Frogs*); for further see *PCG* III.2.157 and, on *P.Köln* VI 242A, Bierl 1990, 362–69.

63 Scullion 2002, esp. 112–14 on festivals. He reminds us that in the sixth century Sicyon transferred tragedy from the cult of the hero Adrastus to the cult of Dionysus (Herodotus 5.67), which weakens the case for innate linkage of genre and cult. I sympathize with much that Scullion has written, though in the case of comedy there are the *phalloi* of actors and occasionally of chorus-members, and these point back to ritual and Dionysus. Radermacher 1921, 8–9, doubted whether all the *komoi* on vases were really in the service of Dionysus. See also Schlesier 1993, 89; Friedrich 1996. For a survey of Greek cultic theaters see Nielsen 2002, 69–148.

64 Csapo 2003, 71, argues that what counts is not whether drama is Dionysiac in essence but that at Athens it was Dionysiac in practice.

65 Athens, National Archaeological Museum 1737. See Kavvadias 1893; Dickins 1906/07, 392–95 and pl. 14; Dickins 1911, 311 fig. 2 (a reasonably distinct line drawing); Dickins 1920, 62 and fig. 48; Dietrich 1962, 139–41; Lawler 1964, 67; Stiglitz 1967, 36–46; Sifakis 1971, 123; Lévy and Marcadé 1972; Pollitt 1986, 165, 268, 312 n. 2. The rites are discussed in Loucas-Durie 1992. The statue group is described in Pausanias 8.37.3–5.

66 Nilsson 1967, 214; see Stiglitz 1967, 45–46. We might not expect Damophon, a native of conservative Messene, to decorate a cult statue with masked figures conjured up from his imagination; on Damophon see Themelis 1996.

67 The animals are identified as such in Stiglitz 1967, 36–37, who observes that we would also expect goat, cow, and deer to complete the list of predictable animals. Dickins 1906/07, 393, identified them as, from left to right, pig, ram, ass, a fox or a bear, ram, unknown, horse, dog, fox or wolf, and a ram; he saw them as animals dressed in human clothing, though they are more likely human figures with masks, suggests Dietrich 1962, 139.

68 Lévy and Marcadé 1972, 988–89, fig. 28.

69 Stiglitz 1967, 36 and 38. Steinhart 2004, 25 n. 234, wonders whether these are human beings dancing as animals or animals dancing as human beings.

70 For Artemis as *Potnia Theron* see *LIMC* II (1981), s.v. Artemis, esp. nos. 11–71, with further literature. A wide range of animals were dedicated to Artemis, but nearly all representations of bears have been found at sanctuaries of Artemis: Bevan 1987.

71 Vernant and Frontisi-Ducroux 1988, 196–97, suggest that the world of Artemis was less one of wildness than "a place of margins, border zones where what is 'other' becomes manifest in the contacts made with it, where

the wild and the civilized live side by side, coming into opposition certainly, but thereby mutually infiltrating one another."

72 Xenophon, *Anabasis* 3.2.12; Plutarch, *Moralia* 862b–c; Deubner 1932, 209; Parke 1977, 55. The Spartans sacrificed she-goats (χίμαιραι) before every battle: Xenophon, *Lac. Pol.* 13.8; Plutarch, *Lycurgus* 22.2.

73 Both myths are mentioned in Hesiod but are probably more familiar from Ovid, *Met.* 2.405–507 (Callisto) and *Met.* 3.138–252 (Actaeon); for references to ancient sources see Forbes Irving 1990, 72–74, 80–90, 197–205.

74 Dawkins 1929, esp. 399–407; Scullion 2002, 115, suggests this was the venue of the Spartan *deikeliktai* (see Pickard-Cambridge 1927, 227–31) and was thus a potential source for comedy. Graf 1979b saw the masks as representing barbarian features.

75 Vernant and Frontisi-Ducroux 1988, 199–200.

76 Carter 1987 and 1988; see further discussion of her 1988 paper on p. 103 and p. 108 in the same volume. A note of caution: the name "Artemis" was only explicitly linked with Orthia in the first century A.D.

77 Kahil 1977; Sourvinou-Inwood 1988; Hamilton 1989; Sourvinou-Inwood 1990; Dowden 1992, 102–18; Scanlon 2002, 139–74; Steinhart 2004, 82–84.

78 Vernant and Frontisi-Ducroux 1988, 195–98.

79 A fragmentary red-figure krater of 430–420 B.C., in the collection of H. A. Cahn, Basel, inv. no. HC 503. See Kahil 1977, 93 fig. 3 and 98 fig. c; Kahil 1981; Kahil 1983, 237–38. Simon 1983, 87 and fig. 25, suggested it was a metamorphosis, perhaps illustrating a *Kallisto* by Aeschylus; Reeder 1995, 327–38 and figs. 99–100 (good color plates), also sees the myth. Steinhart 2004, 84, suggests that what is shown is a statue of a bear.

80 Scholion to Theocritus p. 2.21ff. ed. Wendel; text in Pickard-Cambridge 1962, 296; translated by Csapo and Slater 1995, 98–99. For a Hellenistic engraved gem depicting a man wearing stag horns see Steinhart 2004, 30–31 and plate 8.1.

81 For discussions of festive inversion in Athenian comedy, see Carrière 1979; Reckford 1987, Chpt. 1; Bowie 1993, 10–17; von Möllendorff 1995, 73–108; Lada-Richards 1999, 67–68; Edwards 2002. This rests on a larger body of scholarship on ritual, "festive drama," and the carnivalesque in literature, including Barber 1959 and Bakhtin 1968.

82 Scholiast on Dem. 22.69 (*Androt.*); "Law of Evegorus" quoted in Dem. 21.10 (*Meid.*). See Pickard-Cambridge 1968, 27 and 59.

83 Deubner 1932, 93–134; Pickard-Cambridge 1968, 63; Parke 1977, 128; Hedreen 1992, 2, 125–28, 158. See also Versnel 1993, Chpt. 2, on inversion in festivals.

84 Pickard-Cambridge 1968, 1–25; Parke 1977, 107–20; Simon 1983, 92–99; Bowie 1993, 36–38. Bierl 1994 suggests that a carnivalesque pattern modelled on the Anthesteria underlies the *Plutus* of Aristophanes.

85 Dem. 24.26 (*Tim.*); Plutarch, *Moralia* 1098b; Deubner 1932, 152–55; Parke 1977, 29–30.

86 This aspect of comedy is stressed in Reckford 1987, Chpt. 1.

87 For further see Halliwell 1991.

88 Carpenter 1986, 28 and 1997, 5, 119, carves out a role for "whimsy" and distinguishes the "comic" from the "cultic" and "mythic" Dionysus. Contrast this with Henrichs 1987, 112 n. 6, and Lada-Richards 1999, 2, who writes, "a 'stage-Dionysus' cannot be separated from the range of aspects, levels of meaning, and functions which were attached to his mythic, ritual, and cultic counterpart." One might further suggest that the underlying source of most humor lies in the fact that it is almost never "purely" humorous; in fact comedy is at its funniest when it deals, even if indirectly, with serious and explosive issues: see Henderson 1990, 272–75.

89 On padded dancers and Corinthian vases see especially Seeberg 1971; other discussions include Payne 1931, 118–24; Amyx 1988, 651–52; Steinhart 2004, 31–64.

90 Pickard-Cambridge 1962, 169–74; Pickard-Cambridge 1968, 210–13; Taplin 1993, 9–10; Green 1995, 34. A red-figure column-krater in Tarquinia, Museo Nazionale RC8261, ARV^2 260.12, $Add.^2$ 204, seems to depict masked padded dancers from earlier in the fifth century. Moreover, the comic actors known as *phlyakes*, shown on South Italian vases of the fourth and third centuries B.C., wear similar costumes.

91 Seeberg 1971, 1–2.

92 On the Attic vases see Franzius 1973, 24–29; Brijder 1991, 367–99; and especially Brijder 1983, 51–55, 310 s.v. "dancers" and 312 s.v. "komasts."

93 See, for example, an Attic red-figure column-krater of 600–575 B.C., Berlin 1966.17; Trendall and Webster 1971, 20, pl. I,7. The padded dancers disappear from Corinthian and Attic vases around 540 B.C. Schöne 1987, 117, notes that Attic vases continue to show komasts, albeit without exaggerated features, until they dwindle away ca. 480 B.C.; see also Isler-Kerényi 1988, 271, though reservations are expressed by Boardman 1990.

94 Greifenhagen 1929 described Corinthian influence on Attic painting in the first half of the sixth century; Payne 1931 emphasized key differences; the analysis of Franzius 1973, 24, shows the influence at work in her types I–III; see also Brijder, 1983, 51–55.

95 Herter 1947, 22, 35–40, took Aristotle's remark that *comedy* grew "out of the leaders of the phallic songs" (ἀπὸ τῶν τὰ φαλλικὰ [ἐξαρχόντων], *Poetics* 1449a11) to mean that *actors* developed from the leaders of these songs, and he then tried to demonstrate that such phallic processions had existed in Attica; there was thus no need to look farther afield for a source for actors. Others have also argued for a purely Attic origin for comedy, including Greifenhagen 1929; Breitholtz 1960, who attacked evidence for Dorian influence; Giangrande 1963, who allowed for some Dorian influence but saw evidence of native Attic actors. Henderson 1975, 222–28, largely follows Breitholtz.

96 Boardman 1974, 18; Brijder 1983, 17–28; Isler-Kerényi 1988, 274–75.

97 Brijder 1991, 337; Seeberg 1995, 3; Umholtz forthcoming. Isler-Kerényi 1988, 275, suggests that if the Corinthians also painted padded dancers on

alabastra and aryballoi, it was because those pots were appropriate for upper-class athletes.

98 Fehr 1971, 29–30; Dentzer 1982, 85–86 and 438–41; Fehr 1990, 193, n. 66.

99 Brijder 1991, 337; an example is Figure 1.3. Symposiasts also mix with dancers on four or five Corinthian vases; see Seeberg 1995, 2 and n. 20.

100 Amyx 1988, 651–52.

101 Seeberg 1995, 3; cf. Isler-Kerényi 1988, 271–75. Fehr 1990, 191–92, suspects that the proliferation of padded-dancer scenes on vases in the late seventh and early sixth centuries is correlated with the rise of importance of the symposion in aristocratic circles in this period. Neer 2002, 99, notes that vase-painters who insert themselves into symposium scenes are themselves *akletoi* too.

102 Fehr 1990, 192. Steinhart 2004, 53–54, suggests that the dancers are neither aristocrats clad in ridiculous costumes nor impoverished beggars but professional entertainers.

103 These were thought by Dümmler to be Bacchic vegetation daemons; cf. Breitholtz 1960, 10.

104 Schöne 1987, 14; similarly Greifenhagen 1929 saw them as human, but caricatures; Payne 1931 thought the vases represented costumed human cult participants. Reckford 1987, 487, sees them as a proto-chorus: "We may imagine that the fatbellies were originally fertility spirits, impersonated by revellers." He posits such a chorus as Attic, perhaps with influence from Corinth in the sixth century (n. 61).

105 Webster 1954, 584; Hedreen 1992, 130–32; Schöne 1987, 13 n. 51. "The only ritual expressly attested with padded dancers in art is the festive 'bringing-in' of a god, which is also precisely the point of the only myth to which they have a strong affinity, the Return of Hephaistos," writes Seeberg 1995, 10. Reservations about identifying Dionysiac scenes on Corinthian vases are expressed by Carpenter 1986, 15–19 and 88–90, who concedes that there are naked male dancers on vases by the Amasis Painter, but he stresses that these revelers had been painted on drinking cups before Dionysus appeared; combining the dancers with Dionysus was an experiment that was abandoned.

106 See Jucker 1963; Amyx 1988, 653–57; Pemberton 2000.

107 This approach was espoused by Körte 1893 and has been followed by Pickard-Cambridge 1927, 225–84 (= 1962, 162–87); Pohlenz 1949; and now Kerkhof 2001, 1–50, has reaffirmed a role for Dorian farce.

108 *Poetics* 1448a31–49b5. Surviving fragments of Epicharmus do not indicate choral parts, although some of his titles presuppose choruses: see Pickard-Cambridge 1962, 278–81, on Epicharmus' *Komasts*.

109 Louvre E632, ca. 600–575 B.C. (or 560–550 B.C.: Seeberg 1971, no. 226), known as the "Dümmler krater" after its publication in 1885 by Dümmler; see Bieber 1961, fig. 132; Trendall and Webster 1971, 19, pl. I,6; Hampe 1975. Kerkhof 2001, 24–30, accepts it as evidence for Dorian farce. For Breitholtz the Dümmler krater is merely a depiction of a mirthful moment in a potter's shop (Breitholtz 1960, 177–81, as was suggested by Greifenhagen

1929). But this must reckon with the fact that a flute-player is present in the scene: Pohlenz 1949, 39. Hampe 1975, 97–98, suggests that the scene is a forerunner of a farcical mime.

110 On the interaction of elites in different cities see Osborne 1996, 281–91. This was eased by the importance given to *xenia*: see Schmitt Pantel 1993, 40–41, 55, and 226.

111 Murray 1993, 204–05 and 214. This of course is the world of Simonides and Pindar, and it extends to the Western Greeks.

112 Vase-paintings suggesting a symposium context will be examined in the next chapter. It may be that dancers in a private *komos* had no connection with the theater (Breitholtz 1960, 158), but if they were not theatrical performers themselves, their descendants may be, or they could have influenced tastes as theater developed.

113 Herter 1947 made the case for a single, organic origin in Dionysiac ithyphallic *komoi*; he was followed, with qualifications, by Giangrande 1963.

114 Stone 1981, 449; Murphy 1973, who finds Breitholtz to be too sweeping in his rejection of Dorian influences on comedy, points to the variety of types of popular farces and mimes that comic poets may have appropriated.

115 A close parallel to this word is τὸ φαλλικὸν at *Ach.* 261, where it is clearly a "phallic song" (ᾄσομαι τὸ φαλλικὸν) to Phales; further examples in Olson 2002, 147. Of course Aristotle's use of the word could extend to other activities associated with the *phallos*, such as *komoi* or costumes. Leonhardt 1991 idiosyncratically derives tragedy from *phallika*; see the extensive review by Patzer 1995.

116 Semus *FGrH* 396 F 24 (= Athenaeus 622b–d); Herter 1947, esp. 16–22; Pickard-Cambridge 1962, 140–41. Henrichs 1987, 94–99, sees a range of meanings for the *phallos*: it could be a magical symbol with apotropaic powers, a territorial marker, a manifestation of male aggression, or a symbol of sexual arousal for its own sake. Greifenhagen 1929, 102, discussing the Dümmler krater, suggested that an oversized *phallos* might simply indicate that someone is of lower class. Hedreen 1992, 158, suggests that phallic satyrs, especially those who masturbate, were meant to be humorous.

117 Hyperides frag. 50 attests to *ithyphalloi* in the orchestra at Athens.

118 Florence 3897; discussed in Breitholtz 1960, 154–57, fig. 14–15; Pickard-Cambridge 1962, 303, no. 15, pl. IV; Csapo and Slater 1995, pl. 19.

119 It would be interesting to know more about the red-figure fragment from Athens (Acropolis 702; *ARV²* 213.238; *Add.²* 196) on which a man in a long robe wears one false *phallos* over his nose and a second one erect on his forehead, protruding from a crown of ivy; see Herter 1947, 16; Frontisi-Ducroux 1992, 253, fig. on p. 255; Steinhart 2004, 9.

120 For reservations about the value of Semus see Pohlenz 1949, 31–44, and Breitholtz 1960, 114–16. Gelzer 1971, 1516, doubts that the chorus wore a *phallos*.

121 For an example of a dancer with a *phallos* see Pickard-Cambridge 1962, 307, no. 46, a Corinthian aryballos of ca. 600–575 B.C.

122 MacDowell 1971, 270. Pohlenz 1949, 32–34, also argues that the chorus of *Plutus* is exceptional and that if the chorus-members of *Wasps* call attention to their *phalloi*, it is because it is *not* a normal part of their costume. The evidence for actors' and choral *phalloi* is assembled and discussed in Stone 1981, 73–84, 100–03.

123 For further on *phalloi* in the *Wasps* see n. 17 in Chapter 4.

124 Figure IV discussed in Chapter 2.

125 Pohlenz 1949, 33, criticizing Herter, wrote, "Surely no one would seriously imagine that in the *Birds* ducks or partridges would come on stage with a human *phallos*." This must be qualified in the light of the Getty Birds, which are probably cocks. A review of literature is in Giangrande 1963, 6–9.

126 Taplin 1993, 102–03, citing Stone 1981, 81, and Pickard-Cambridge 1968, 220–22.

127 "Satyr" is the more common term, but "silen," the name given them on the François vase, is at least as appropriate: see Hedreen 1992, 10 n. 2. Goat characteristics are generally post-classical.

128 Brommer 1937, 26.

129 Discussions include Seaford 1984, 5–10; Carpenter 1986, 76–97; Schöne 1987, 18–22, 132–42.

130 The literary evidence is examined in Chapter 3. If satyrs performed dithyrambs, which were said by Aristotle to be a source of tragedy, then they played a seminal role in the early phases of tragedy: Webster in Pickard-Cambridge 1962, 20, 34, and 100; consult Seaford 1977/78 for a discussion of the *hyporchema* of Pratinas, which may have been a dithyramb performed by satyrs (on Pratinas see Lloyd-Jones 1990). An alternative view, though, is that satyrs may have been too frivolous to perform the dithyramb, which is a more serious genre: thus Froning 1971, 25–26; cf. Patzer 1962, 52ff.; Hedreen 1992, 123, n. 62. On the date of their appearance see Buschor 1943, 57–58, 80–81; Simon 1982a, 16–18; Seaford 1984, 13. Steinhart 2004, 101–27, takes a somewhat more conservative approach in accepting vase-paintings as images of dramatic performances.

131 Allard Pierson Museum inv. 3356; see below n. 138.

132 Hedreen 1992, 155–70; Schöne 1987, 13, n. 51.

133 Hedreen 1992, 132–34, who cites further examples of padded dancers possibly playing the parts of satyrs. Hampe 1975, 96, felt that the figure in question was not a satyr.

134 See n. 105 above. Examples of padded dancers apparently taking the roles of satyrs in the "Return of Hephaestus" include: Athens 664 (monument no. 38 in Pickard-Cambridge 1962), London BM B42 (no. 39), Paris Musée Rodin 503 (no. 47). Consult also Brommer 1937, 21. Occasionally satyrs and padded dancers mingle with one another on the same vase: see Webster 1954; Pickard-Cambridge 1962, 302, no. 11 (Louvre E876); Carpenter 1986, 20–21, 86, as noted above, is sceptical about equating komasts and padded dancers. Note, too, that although human komasts without exaggerated physical features continue to be painted until ca. 480 B.C., padded

dancers disappear from vase painting around 540 B.C., at which time satyrs begin to predominate. This could mean that satyrs were seen as alternative equivalents to padded dancers.

135 A few scholars (Loeschke 1894, Buschor 1943) equated the padded dancers with satyrs; most, however, consider them independent entities (above all Herter 1947, 11–12 and n. 45 with further earlier bibliography). Franzius, 1973, 5, has pointed to the fact that the character of the dances of satyrs and Corinthian padded dancers are markedly different from one another. A lucid account of the issues at stake is Simon 1982a, 28–30.

136 Berlin Staatliche Museen F 1697, Attic black-figure amphora, ca. 540–530 B.C., by the Painter of Berlin 1686, *ABV* 297.17; *Para.* 128; *Add.*[2] 78; Hedreen 1992 pl. 39a. The obverse side of this vase depicts the Berlin "Knights "chorus, discussed in Chapter 2.

137 Green 1991, 22.

138 Allard Pierson Museum inv. 3356; *ABV* 66.57; *Para.* 27; *Add.*[2] 18; Herter 1947, 8; Pickard-Cambridge 1962, 304, no. 21, plate VIb; Ghiron-Bistagne 1976, fig. 124; Green 1985, 99–100; Brijder 1991, 445, no. 348.

139 Kurtz and Boardman 1986, 58–61.

140 Brijder 1986, 74.

141 Trendall and Webster 1971, 20, though Brijder 1986, 75, objects that feathers would be painted differently.

142 Brijder 1986, 71. Herter 1947, 20, followed by Pickard-Cambridge 1962, 141, thought that the vase depicts *ithyphalloi*, who wore long chitons.

143 Brijder 1986 and 1991. Hedreen 1992, 124 n. 77, although agreeing with the conclusion that a performance of a satyr chorus is plausible by 575–550 B.C., notes that we would expect a more sophisticated depiction of satyrs by this date.

144 Brijder 1986, 80; Buschor 1943, 75, 79–80.

145 New York, Metropolitan Museum of Art 1988.11.3; see *Münzen und Medaillen* 1967, cat. no. 121; Green 1994, fig. 2.8 (once in Sweden: Green 1985, 100).

146 Trendall and Webster 1971, 20. Lynch forthcoming notes that quills are visible.

147 Brijder 1986, 78, and 1991, 398–99. If, however, they are horse ears, there is nothing else satyr-like about the dancers, points out Green (who also raises the possibility that they are deer ears). Price 1990 suggests that these be seen as forerunners to the later Anacreontic vases that depict burlesque performers in effeminate, foreign dress.

148 Christchurch, N. Z., University of Canterbury 41/57; *Para.* 134.31 bis; Pickard-Cambridge 1962, pl. 8a; Trendall 1971, 59, no. 27, pls. 20a, 21a–c, and frontispiece (color); Trendall and Webster 1971, no. I, 10; Boardman 1974, fig. 144; Cohen and Shapiro 1995, 7–8; Steinhart 2004, 10.

149 Green 1985, 101. Two of the men wear corselets that are spotted, as if to represent animal skins, and the corselet of a third has a pattern resembling feathers, note Cohen and Shapiro 1995, 8.

150 Trendall and Webster 1971, 21; they also point out that dolphin- and ostrich-riders may have used stilts.

151 Thebes B. E. 64.342; Trendall and Webster 1971, no. I,13; Green 1985, 102, no. 12 and pls. 15a–b.

152 Fehr 1990, 191; Steinhart 2004, 10.

153 Fedele et al. 1984, 45–46, pl. 43. fig. 14a–c; Green 1991, 22 n. 19.

154 See also Ceccarelli 1998, 82 n. 251.

155 Webster 1970, 93–94.

156 Plato, *Laws* 815a; Xenophon, *Anab.* 6.1.3–13 describes armed dances as performed at a symposium; Lysias 21.1 indicates that these dances were at the Panathenaea. See Steinhart 2004, 11–20, and on the pyrrhic dance in general see especially Ceccarelli 1998.

157 Lawler 1964, 106–08.

158 Würzburg L 344; *ABV* 434.3; *Para.* 296; Brommer 1942, 75, pl. 10; Green 1985, no. 10, fig. 13.

159 Brooklyn Museum 09.35; Green 1985, 101, no. 9, figs. 12a–b.

160 London B 658; Brommer 1942, 75, pl. 8; Haspels 1936, 269 no. 67; *ABV* 586.67; Vermeule 1979, 107, fig. 24, and 236 n. 30; Green 1985, 103, no. 18, fig. 21. The date is suggested by Boardman 1974, 149, fig. 279.

161 Discussions of the problems involved in detecting choruses and dance movements include Green 1985; Hedreen 1992, 105–16; Naerebout 1997, 209–26.

162 Pickard-Cambridge 1962, 157; Green 1994, 28; and even some of the walking warriors are too mysterious to regard as "normal" in any respect.

163 A lekythos by the Beldam Painter shows three women wearing pointed hats; although it was once thought that these were Amazons, the identification was rejected by Beazley: Louvre CA 2925; *ABV* 587.4; *Para.* 292; von Bothmer 1957, 110 no. 200; Green 1985, 105 n. 7.

164 We also hear of the *Lydians* by Magnes (early fifth century, *PCG* V.629–30), and several later comedies: a *Thracians* of Cratinus (ca. 430 B.C., *PCG* IV.159–66); *Persians*, possibly by Pherecrates (late fifth century, *PCG* VII.167–72); Aristophanes' *Babylonians* (426 B.C., *PCG* III.2.62–77); Metagenes' *Thouriopersai* (late fifth/early fourth century, *PCG* VII.6–8); and Theopompus' *Medos* (ca. 378/77 B.C., *PCG* VII.722–23). Cratinus' *Thracians* was, to judge from literary evidence, the "first great endeavor" (Long 1986, 157), but it may have had a tradition behind it stretching into the sixth century.

165 See, for example, Bierl 2001, 98, on comic choruses.

166 Bowie 1993, 13.

167 Long 1986, 129–56; cf. also Hall 1989 on archaic and classical views.

168 The warriors on the Guarini Collection vase were, we noted, (A) bearded men or satyrs, and (B) younger, somewhat effeminate, beardless men. Perhaps this vase or the dance it depicted was meant, on some level, to illustrate a stage in the transition of a young man to adulthood.

169 Henrichs 1993, 32–35; cf. remarks on the relevance of this for dramatic genres by Simon 1982a, 28–29.

170 Kimberley Patton in Csapo forthcoming.

171 Stark 2004 argues against any role for ritual origins and instead sees comedy as generated by the *akletoi* at the symposium. Her concern is with the comic actor and she has little to say about animal costumes.

172 Lissarrague 1990b, 57–58. The choruses of *Acharnians* and *Peace* are "white males" and are conceivably the descendants of Susarion's peasants. Even they, however, may not be fully "ordinary" (see Bowie 1993, 13).

173 One should not insist that the vase-paintings are direct and literal reproductions of what transpired in a symposium (or *komos* or ritual or chorus). Yet if they are not photographic documents, leaving the precise occasion or details of a performance uncertain, but are instead "social statements, constructs, symbols" (Sparkes, Introduction, n. 3 above), the general point still stands.

2. ANIMAL CHORUSES: THE EVIDENCE OF VASE-PAINTING

1 Reich 1903, 480–83, thought the humanly sexual nature would have been so conspicuous that any animal costume would be transparently secondary; see Herter 1947, 9. On similar lines Webster in Pickard-Cambridge 1962, 159–60, saw padded dancers as the ancestors of the comic chorus and the animal *komos* as an extraneous element.

2 Giangrande 1963, 21–23. Sifakis 1971, 84–85, suggested that the factual evidence was too scanty to be conclusive.

3 Körte 1893 and 1921, 1221; Pohlenz 1949 also fell into this school of thought.

4 Pickard-Cambridge 1927, 244–53.

5 Cf. Nagy 1990, 385, on the possibility that undifferentiated choral forms existed before the emergence of comedy and tragedy.

6 Berlin, Staatliche Museen F 1697, by the Painter of Berlin 1686, possibly from Cerveteri (bought at Rome in 1846, says Poppelreuter 1893, 6); *ABV* 297.17; Bieber 1961, 37, fig. 126; Trendall and Webster 1971, 20, pl. I,9; Sifakis 1971, pl. 1; Boardman 1974, 63, fig. 137; Ghiron-Bistagne 1976, fig. 113; Green 1985, 101, no. 3, fig. 6.

7 Boardman 1974, 63; Seeberg 1995, 7.

8 Their beardlessness was observed by Poppelreuter 1893, 6, and by Sifakis 1971, 73, who further points out that the "knights" of Aristophanes' comedy also seem to be young (cf. *Knights* 731). One could argue that the cheek-guards of the helmets have hidden the beards of these riders, but vase-painters were perfectly able to show a beard beneath a helmet when they wanted to.

9 The uplifted arms and open fingers resemble those of a rider on a black-figure Panathenaic vase who has just thrown a javelin at a target: London, BM 1903.2–17.1, *ABV* 411.1 (Kuban group), Boardman 1974, pl. 304.2; Spence 1993, 77 with note 169. The uplifted arm that holds a javelin is a regular feature of the iconography of the cavalryman: see examples in Spence 1993, plates 2, 11, 12, 13. The Berlin vase, however, is from the middle of the sixth century and this sort of competition may have been added later (Kyle 1987, 186–87); moreover, the riders on the London vase do not wear armor. A Panathenaic vase of ca. 510–500 B.C. depicts three horse-riders

in competition (New York, Metropolitan Museum of Art 07.286.80, *ABV* 369.114, Leagros group: Boardman 1974, pl. 300); the Berlin vase might show a parody of a horse race (which had been at the Panathenaea since the sixth century: Kyle 1987, 185), though the Berlin riders are armored. Figures wearing what seem to be Pan-costumes, and in the company of an *aulos*-player, raise their arms and ride one another piggy-back style on a red-figure kalyx-krater of ca. 460–450 B.C.: London, British Museum 1856.12–13.1 (E467); *ARV²* 01.23; Pickard-Cambridge 1968, fig. 42; Green and Handley 1995, 19–20, fig. 4.

10 Pickard-Cambridge 1927, 246; Beazley 1929, 361–67.

11 Hedreen 1992, 136–38 (and pl. 39), suggests that both sides of this vase are choruses at the same festival and that they may both be "comic" choruses.

12 Such, at least, would be a reasonable interpretation by a viewer. On the pitfalls and subjective judgments entailed in reading images from different sides of the same vase in the light of one another see Lissarrague 1994, 12–27.

13 Detienne and Vernant 1974, 193–96; cf. Bodson 1978, 151–57; Burkert 1985, 139 and 221. I suggest that horses are significant primarily as mounts. I see no sign that these stage horses are meant to be anthropomorphized or take on human characteristics, although the disguise is not complete, and if we recall that in Homer Achilles' horses were endowed with speech, the horse would already be inherently suited for anthropomorphizing. Unlike satyrs, who share horse characteristics, the Berlin horses are probably not meant to be hybrids – they are stage "horses." We should note that viewers sometimes wish to see the horse-rider pair, taken together, as a centaur (thus Gerhard, quoted in Poppelreuter 1893, 9), yet the horse-head masks would militate against this. We will find Aristophanes more willing to exploit the possibilities of anthropomorphization in the *Knights*. Although the Lycosura reliefs offer a later example of a horse disguise in an apparently ritual context, I see no obvious link with the Berlin Knights. The Lycosura reliefs show women with partial horse disguises, not mounted by riders, and in the company of other domesticated animals. The animals there are important for themselves, not as mounts.

14 For Areion see Pausanias 8.24.4–5. Poseidon was also father of Pegasus (Hesiod, *Theogony* 278–83). Wiesner 1953, 317, stresses Poseidon's association with primordial equine creatures, whereas Athena seems to enter at a later stage; cf. Burkert 1985, 138. In general on horses see Keller 1913, 218–59; *RE* x s.v. "Pferd." Lore on the procreative powers of horses themselves is found in Aristotle, *HA* esp. 6.22.575b22–577a18, and later writers; see *RE* x s.v. "Pferd" 1334–36.

15 Pausanias 8.42.1–4.

16 Discussed in Chapter 1.

17 At *Lys.* 191–92 Kalonike proposes sacrificing a white horse; on horse sacrifice see Keller 1913, 252–59; Bodson 1978, 152; Henderson 1987, 92–93. An unusual horse sacrifice was excavated in Lefkandi: Popham et al. 1982.

18 For example, Plutarch, *Moralia* 992a–b; see *RE* x s.v. "Pferd" 1438–39.

19 *Cyropedia* 4.3.17. Vilatte 1986; L'Allier 2004. I am grateful to Louis L'Allier for calling my attention to this. Padgett 2000 contrasts the marginalized donkey (and satyr) with the noble horse (and man).

20 Horse races were at Olympia by the mid-seventh century (Pausanias 5.8.7–8) and chariot races are shown on Panathenaic vases by 550 B.C.: Kyle 1987, 185–86. On the Panathenaea see Parke 1977, 33–34, 36; Simon 1983, 55–72.55. Umholtz forthcoming has further evidence of aristocratic equine competitiveness.

21 *Works and Days* 816 and again in an epithet ("horse-breeding Thrace," 507).

22 Rhodes 1981, 138, 143–45; in general see Bugh 1988.

23 Greenhalgh 1973, Chpt. 6, demonstrates the presence of cavalry, which had been doubted by Helbig 1904. See further in Alföldi 1967, 13–47 and Spence 1993, 10–11.

24 Anderson 1961, 128–31; Spence 1993, 165–66; see also Rhodes 1981, 303–04. The cavalry was "an upper-class specialty," notes Raaflaub 1999, 132.

25 This point is now also made in Steinhart 2004, 11.

26 Born and Hansen 1994, figs. 45–46, 49–51 and 65. The spoked wheels on figs. 49–51 support plumes or manes, whereas on the "Knights" vase the wheels stand curiously alone and unadorned.

27 Green 1994, 29, citing Bottini 1989, 1990, 1991.

28 Bottini 1989, 108 fig. 1 for a reconstruction; see also Frielinghaus 1995. Danner 1993, 27–28, suggests that the middle rider wears a *meniskos*, an implement designed to protect statues from bird droppings (see Danner fig. 10). This cannot be discounted, though it would explain only one rider's crest. Panofka 1851 suggested another South Italian connection: Athenaeus 520c–d reported that the Sybarites had taught their horses to dance.

29 See above, Fig. 1.1.

30 Greenhalgh 1973, 126. Nevertheless the roughly contemporary vase in Beazley 1929 (fig. 1) shows a warrior who is apparently Greek and whose skirt is patterned very similarly.

31 Green 1994, 28–29.

32 Fehr 1990, 192.

33 *Knights* 731. Compare also the conservative Hippeis at Athens in 411 B.C. (Thucydides 8.92.6) and the young Pheidippides in *Clouds* 1–90.

34 Vierneisel and Kaeser 1990, 126–29; Spence 1993, 199–200, with Appendices I and II.

35 Spence 1993, 164–230, esp. 194. It is not impossible that the Berlin riders were in some way related to – as a parody, perhaps – a cavalcade of riders that was associated with the Panathenaea, which had been reorganized before the time of this vase. The Parthenon frieze depicts a cavalcade of young riders (see Simon 1983, 59, and Robertson 1975, 48), and vase-paintings show young men throwing spears at a target, also evidently as part of the Panathenaea.

36 The classic study is van Gennep 1960; essays devoted to ancient Greece are in Padilla 1999.

37 I owe these examples to Lonsdale 1981, 45–53.

38 Pindar has young Jason wearing a panther-skin (*Pythian* 4.79–82), though the context is not explicitly ritual; cf. Paris (*Iliad* 3.16–20) and see Bowie 1993, 238; Lada-Richards 1999, 52. In myth human beings on the verge of adulthood are occasionally transformed into animals: for Io, who becomes a cow prior to marriage and motherhood, see Katz 1999; in general Forbes Irving 1990, 50–57. At Ephesus young, unmarried attendants at sacrifices were called *Tauroi* ("Bulls"), but nothing suggests that they are involved in a rite of passage (see below).

39 The bear's role as a mother made it suitable as a *kourotrophos*: Bevan 1987.

40 An account of the two-year routine is in the Aristotelian *Ath. Pol.* 42; for the general subject of the ephebeia see Pélékidis 1962; Vidal-Naquet 1981a and 1986; Parker 1996, 253–55. A helpful survey of initiation and athletics is Scanlon 2002, 64–97. Winkler 1990 suggested that ephebes provided the chorus of tragedy. For discussion of the *ephebeia* in comedy see Bowie 1993, 45–52; Slater 1996 (= 2002, 86–114); Sommerstein 1996; Lada-Richards 1999, 45–122. The role of the symposium in the entry of youths into citizenship is discussed in Schmitt Pantel 1993, 76–90.

41 Thucydides 2.39; Reinmuth 1952, 48.

42 Deubner 1932, 232–34; Parke 1977, 88–92.

43 The earliest source is from Hellanicus (5th century B.C.) *FGrH* 4 F 125 = 323a F 23; for further see Vidal-Naquet 1981a, 255, note 9.

44 See Vidal-Naquet 1981a and 1986; Schnapp 1989.

45 Spence 1993, 164–79.

46 Aristotle, *Politics* 6.4, 1321a9–13; Reinmuth 1952, 45.

47 Basel, Cahn 133; *ARV²* 1626, 1708, near the Thalia Painter; *Para.* 332; Cahn 1973; Shapiro 1989, 108–110.

48 Bugh 1988, 18.

49 For example, scenes of cavalcades, symposia, *komoi*, and athletics were characteristic features of the C Painter: Brijder 1983, 40–42, 109–10, 125–28.

50 Although there is little evidence for the worship of Poseidon in sixth-century Athens, he was seen as the ancestor of the Neleids, the clan that Peisistratus belonged to. A dedication to him on the Acropolis has been dated to 560–550 B.C.: Shapiro 1989, 101–11. As Poseidon Hippios he seems to have shared a cult sanctuary at Kolonos with Athena Hippia; according to one theory this was a cult center for the cavalry, and hence the aristocracy, before hoplite predominance: Siewert 1979; cf. Spence 1993, 188.

51 Rhodes 1981, 564–68.

52 Murray 1991, 86, 97.

53 Murray 1990, 7. Steiner 2002, 372–377, discusses ways in which elitist symposium practices seem to have survived into supposedly democratized public *syssitia* in the fifth century; members of the Hippeis may have played a role in this.

54 Simon 1983a, 59–60, for examples.

55 If the fact that older men carry younger men on this vase suggests some initiatory ritual, one might wonder whether an erotic, pederastic undercurrent

was present. In a famous example from Crete a young initiate was kidnapped by an older lover and kept in the countryside; after two months of hunting and feasting the boy was released and received military garb, an ox, and a drinking cup (Strabo 10.4.21). The Berlin vase perhaps hints that the youths are achieving their manhood. Other viewers may wonder, as I have, whether the objects in the left hands of the riders on the vase are manes or large, erect *phalloi* protruding directly from the riders' groins and resting on the horses' heads. Is this an intentional visual pun or mere coincidence? *Adspice, lector.*

56 Alternatively, one might argue that if hoplite training was important, cavalry training might be appropriate in the context of a rite of passage precisely because it reversed the conventional values of infantry warfare.

57 London, British Museum B 308, from Vulci. *CVA* British Museum (6), III pl. 81 (340), 1; Brit. Mus. Cat. Walters, Vases II 179; Green 1985, 101, no. 5, fig. 8.

58 Ashmolean 1971.903: *Ashmolean Museum. Report of the Visitors 1970–71*, 30; Brown et al. 1975, 30, no. 15, fig. 4, where a date of 525 B.C. is suggested; Green 1985, 101, no. 7, figs. 10a–b, puts it at 510–500 B.C.

59 My thanks to Prof. John Oakley for this observation.

60 Green 1985, 101. Lawler 1964, 71, described the London dancers as having bull masks and hoof-like coverings on their hands, but this seems to be only a guess. Note that Pollux's list of masks includes a "River" along with other special masks for other personifications, such as Mountain, Death, Gadfly, Centaur, Titan, Triton, Polis, and Peitho (4.142). He also describes a dance known as the *morphasmos* in which various animals were imitated: Pollux 4.103, s.v. *morphasmos*, and Athenaeus 629f. These sources are so late that one hesitates to use them as evidence for archaic or classical animal choruses, though Athenaeus' interest suggests that non-theatrical animal dances were appropriate at symposia: Steinhart 2004, 22. He also suggests (p. 23) that the symposiasts on the Agora skyphos (Figure 1.1) wear bull's horns and ears.

61 Bulls, used as a measure when selling slaves, armor, etc., became a kind of currency before coinage; cf. *Iliad* 21.79; further examples at *RE* s.v. "Stier," 2503–04.

62 On the bull in Greek religion see esp. Bodson 1978, 144–51; consult also Keller 1909, 329–72; *RE* s.v. "Stier," 2495–520; Weiss 1984, 70–71.

63 Rosivach 1994; van Straten 1995, 172–79, points out that the number of cattle sacrifices on vase-painting greatly exceeds actual evidence for the practice; painters wanted to portray something ennobling. See also Keller 1909, 355–58; *RE* s.v. "Stier" 2511–15.

64 See Lloyd-Jones and Graf below, n. 76.

65 See above, Chapter 1, n. 60.

66 Keller 1909, 360; *RE* s.v. "Stier," 2507. The epithet also appears in Hesiod, *Shield* 104.

67 Athenaeus 425c (οἱ οἰνοχοῦντες ἤθεοι); Hesychius T 248 (s.v. "ταῦροι"). Consult Bodson 1978, 144–47.

68 Marinatos 1986, 70; cf. fig. 77. For Bronze Age bull figurines see Marinatos 1986, esp. 9–11, 16–17. On the bull in Minoan religion, see Burkert 1985, 36–38, 40; an earlier but still useful study is Malten 1928.

69 Karageorghis 1971; Tatton-Brown 1979, 28; further references in Weiss 1984, 71.

70 Though Nielsen 2002, 75, sees an overall break in continuity between the Bronze Age and the Orientalizing period.

71 Young 1972, 84–97.

72 Young 1972, 84, 90. The earliest identifiable Minotaur dates from 675–650 B.C.: *LIMC* VI (1992), s.v. "Minotauros," no. 16. There is no question of influence from Crete: the image of the Minotaur was essentially extinct in Crete until revived in the fifth century: Woodford 1992, 580.

73 Young 1972, 89–91. Also to be cited here is a terracotta relief found in Rome that shows, in a frieze, a bull-headed figure walking between two panthers (*LIMC* VI [1992], s.v. "Minotauros," no. 49). It has been suggested that this is a masked cult dancer (Schweitzer 1957) and the presence of panthers might support the identification of it as Dionysus as a bull-god (Romanelli 1955), although Dionysus' "bull" features are less pronounced in surviving art than those of river gods.

74 Dietrichs 1974, 100, suggests that the horns alone can stand for the whole animal.

75 Dowden 1992, 110.

76 Lloyd-Jones 1983, 97; Graf 1979b, 33–34. Pyrrhic dances, in which young men danced with armor, were evidently held at the Tauropolia: Ceccarelli 1998, 83.

77 Paris, Louvre F 127 ter, *ARV²* 54.9, *Add.²* 158; Cohen 1978, pl. 68.2; *CVA* 19 pl. 23 (1228) 1. *LIMC* VI (1992), s.v. "Minotauros," no. 3.

78 (a) St. Petersburg, Hermitage 391, *ARV²* 40.15, ca. 520–500 B.C.; Cohen 1978, pl. 63.2; *LIMC* VI (1992), s.v. "Minotauros," no. 1. (b) Munich, Antikensammlung. 2583; *ARV²* 165. 3, ca. 520–500 B.C.; *LIMC* VI (1992), "Minotauros," no. 2. Woodford 1992, 580, contrasts Theseus' use of a sword with the primitive stones of the Minotaur.

79 The earliest literary evidence for the myth is Hesiod fr. 145 MW; Theseus' freeing of victims is mentioned in Sappho fr. 206 LP; the story was the subject of lost tragedies by Euripides. See Gantz 1993, 260–70; Young 1972; *LIMC* VI (1992), s.v. "Minotauros," p. 574.

80 Hundreds of portrayals of Theseus killing the Minotaur have been preserved; see Woodford 1992, 580. On Theseus in this period see Shapiro 1989, 143–49; Neils 1994; Walker 1995, 35–81. Sourvinou-Inwood 1994/95, 235, interprets the myth as embodying the ambiguities of the rule of Minos, whose unjust tyranny is contrasted with Theseus' orderly polis. Bowie 1993, 48, points to the bull's presence in various initiatory experiences in myth: the Minotaur, Jason's ploughing, and Hippolytus' death – but none requires a costume.

81 Weiss 1984, 119; *LIMC* VI (1992), s.v. "Minotauros," no. 34. One might add that if the sixth-century convention in depicting performances was to show a chorus and to omit actors (indeed, their very existence at this date is an open question), then we would not expect Theseus to be present at all. Isler-Kerenyi 1988, 271, notes that stones were also used by other creatures of the primitive world, such as centaurs.

82 This is now a case study in how virtually identical images can have diametrically opposed meanings: Woodford 2003, 209–10, in a chapter on "Misunderstandings and Muddles." Steinhart 2004, 23–25 suggests that they have a cultic, Dionysiac significance that refers neither to river gods nor to the Minotaur.

83 The iconography of Achelous and river gods has been the subject of studies by Isler 1970 and Weiss 1984; the identification of the bull-headed dancers as river gods was proposed by Weiss (p. 119), was accepted by Green 1991, 29, and is weighed by Woodford 1992, 577, and 2003, 209–10. Consult also Hamdorf 1964, 10–16, 80–83; Nilsson 1967, 236–40.

84 Metapontum Stater: Kraay 1976, 179, no. 596; Weiss 1984, 51, pl. 1.3; *LIMC* I (1981), s.v. "Acheloos," no. 75.

85 A series of coins from Selinus, beginning in the fifth century, shows a human figure with bull's horns sprouting out of his head; see Kraay and Hirmer 1966, 230, pl. 82; Isler 1970, 180, 362a; Holloway 1978, 14,1 and 118 (who takes the river god to be Acheloos); *LIMC* I (1981), s.v. "Achelous," 18, nr. 75; Weiss 1984, Catalog II A 2, has further bibliography. It is important to note that Isler (1970, 1990) sees these bull-headed creatures not as representations of local rivers but of Achelous; he may be correct, though in view of the number of local instances I am inclined to agree with Weiss, who suggests that different rivers are intended. In performance they would have been distinguished verbally: Green 1991, 29.

86 Archilochus fr. 287 Page (= Schol. *Iliad* 21.237). Achelous is the most senior of the river gods: *Iliad* 21.194–97.

87 Other literary instance include the *Iliad*, in which the Scamander appears in human form but is said to bellow like a bull (21.237). At *Odyssey* 11.235–57, Poseidon, whose association with the bull we have noted, woos Tyro in the guise of the River God Enipeus. Aelian, *Var. Hist.* 2.33 lists several rivers portrayed in bovine form. Further literary sources are collected in Weiss 1984, 59–61.

88 Weiss 1984, 71–72 and plate 10.1 on an Attic black-figure lekythos in Göttingen depicting a bull's head used as a fountain with water rushing out. Forbes Irving 1990, 43, reminds us that the horn of plenty derived from Achelous.

89 ἄνδρας κουρίζουσι, *Theogony* 346–8; Price 1978, 124, 195; Nilsson 1967, 238.

90 *Iliad* 23.141; Aesch. *Choephoroe* 6; see West 1966, 259–64.

91 Metzger 1972 discusses satyrs shown holding stones and relates these to the practice of striking the soil to summon up subterranean spirits and to

endow the soil with agricultural fertility; he suggests that stones are connected with Dionysus as a rustic fertility god. Figures holding stones appear among padded dancers on a Corinthian aryballos: Seeberg 1971, no. 221.

92 This is not to say that river gods were always benign. Achelous, for example, could be a dangerous threat and was scarcely viewed as the guardian deity that an eponymous river god might have been. Moreover, the dates of these vases (ca. 520–500 B.C. and 510–500 B.C.) approximate the date of a spectacular use of a river's power: when Croton conquered Sybaris in 510 B.C., it was by diverting the course of the Crathis and flooding the site of the city; see Herodotus 5.44–5, 6.21; Diodorus 11.90, 12.9–10; Dunbabin 1948, 364–66.

93 The *Thuriopersai* was never produced, says Athenaeus (270a), but was probably written after 412 B.C.: Baldry 1953, 57–58. The benefits of the rivers were evidently proverbial: the chorus in Euripides' *Trojan Women* speaks of the Crathis as "nurturing and enriching a land of good men" (τρέφων εὔαν-δρόν τ' ὀλβίζων γᾶν, 228–29); in the *Metamorphoses* the rivers Crathis and Sybaris "make hair like amber and gold" (electro similes faciunt auroque capillos, 15.315–16); cf. Aelian *NA* 12.36 on its power to turn things white; Dunbabin 1948, 77–78. On the theme of fertile rivers in comedy see Wilkins 2000a, 118–21.

94 Oracles might direct colonists to a river: see Diodorus 8.23.1; Schmid 1947, 130–37. Lacroix 1953 notes that a disproportionate number are from Sicily and Magna Graecia. De Polignac 1995, 104 n. 35, points out that in the Greek West many rivers flowed parallel to one another and could play a role in determining frontiers. For further examples of tauromorph river deities from the West, primarily on coinage, see *LIMC* IV (1988), s.v. "Gelas," nos. 1–8; *LIMC* VI (1992), s.v. "Krathis," nos. 5–24; *LIMC* I (1981), s.v. "Anapos," no. 2.

95 Weiss 1984, 32; Burkert 1985, 175. Edlund 1987, 58–62, argued that the Greeks of Magna Graecia, in contrast to the Etruscans, incorporated the river into their political structure and subordinated it to the interests of society. Consult also Jones 2005, 40–42.

96 Cahn 1975, 106.

97 Weiss 1984, 53–54 and plate 6.

98 Aelian, *Var. Hist.* 2.33; consult Brackerts 1976, 176.

99 ANS 1957.172.624; Kraay and Hirmer 1966, pl. 66 no. 186R; Kraay 1976, pl. 46 no. 787 (discussion on p. 220); Weiss 1984, plate 2.1b (discussion on pp. 24–26 and compare plates 4.1, 4.2, 4.3); SNG ANS 688–692; *LIMC* VII (1994), s.v. "Selinous I," no. 3. The practice of one god making an offering to another has parallels; see Simon 1953.

100 For the coins see Kraay 1976, no. 788 = Weiss 1984, plate 3.1 (discussion pp. 26–27). A heron is mentioned in Callimachus, *Aetia* fr. 43 Pfeiffer (*P.Oxy.* 2080 vol. xvii) v. 62–67; Kraay 1976, 220.

101 On Apollo *archegetes* consult Schmid 1947, 154–67 ("Apollo in Ktisissagen"); Seibert 1963, 33; Malkin 1986; Malkin 1987, 17–28; Dougherty 1993, 32–41; and bibliography cited in Versnel 1993, 303–09. Cf. Pindar, *Pythian* 9, for

Apollo and Cyrene; Diodorus 12.35, for Apollo and Thurii; see Weiss 1984, 88–89 (= her Cat. I Nr. B 8,) for Apollo *archegetes* on coins from Tauromenium, and Weiss 1984, 43, on Apollo as oikist along with the eponymous Selinus. A parallel with these coins is a silver stater of Croton from the end of the fifth century on which Heracles is depicted as a naked youth making an offering, not unlike Selinus; it is labelled ΟΙΚΣΤΑΣ, leaving little doubt that the scene represents the foundation of Croton: Holloway 1978, 18 I.2, plate 138. Heracles' part in the foundation is attested in Diodorus 4.24.7. Pausanias 4.27.5 describes a sacrifice to Apollo Ismenius and other gods at the foundation of Messene.

102 Weiss 1984, 37–46.

103 British Museum B 509, by the Gela Painter; *ABV* 473; *Para.* 214; Haspels 1936, 214, no. 187; Bieber, 1961, fig. 123; Pickard-Cambridge 1962, no. 26, pl. 9a; Trendall and Webster 1971, pl. I,12; Sifakis 1971, pls. 7–8; Ghiron-Bistagne 1976, fig. 115; Green 1985, no. 8.

104 Trendall and Webster 1971, 22.

105 Green 1985, 109 and 1994, 31.

106 Dunbar 1995, 333.

107 Handley 1985, 364.

108 Taranto 6250 (Trendall and Webster 1971, pl. I,18) and Athens NM 541 (Haspels 1936, 208, 49; Boardman 1974, pl. 235). Although the incised lines below the faces of the London birds trace what is best described as beards, the beards are colored the same red as the protrusions on the crests. Were they meant to be wattles?

109 Trendall and Webster 1971, pl. I,18. Tzachili-Douskou 1981 calls attention to their resemblance to Theran *himatia* resembling sheepskins.

110 Green 1985, 111, points out that similar lines on the leading leg of the dancer on the right would be folds in a garment, but he also finds it tempting to see the lines on the left dancer as a *phallos*. Alternatively, the line may simply indicate a furrow or muscle in the thight, as Prof. Oakley has cautioned me.

111 Green 1985, 108.

112 Taranto 6250: see n. 108 above.

113 Athens NM 541: see n. 108 above. Ivy can be found also on a scene with Herakles on a black-figure lekythos: Agrigento Museum, from Gela; Haspels 1936, 205, 2; Boardman 1974, pl. 234.

114 Berlin F 1830, from Vulci. *CVA* (5) Berlin pls. 43,1–2 and 47,5, ascribes it to the Dot-Ivy Group; Bieber 1961, fig. 124; Pickard-Cambridge 1962, pl. 9b; Sifakis 1971, pl. 6; Green 1985, 11. The *CVA* article suggests that the front bird wears a mask with a nose over his beak; the one on the left has a mouth under his beak (p. 56).

115 Pickard-Cambridge 1962, 152. Compare the noses on satyrs on the black-figure lebes in Cortona and the black-figure amphora in Würzburg, *ABV* 151.22 (Hedreen 1992, pls. 25 and 29). Reich 1903, 483, had remarked on their pig-like snouts.

116 Sifakis 1971, 103–08.

117 Trendall and Webster 1971, 22.

118 Malibu, J. Paul Getty Museum 82.AE.83. Literature includes Green 1985; Taplin 1987; Fowler 1989; Green 1991; Taplin 1993, 101–04; Csapo 1993; Green 1994, 29–30.

119 Green 1985, 111. The smaller circles also resemble a decoration often seen on the clothes of easterners on red-figure vases: Green 1985, 115. On the *perizoma* see Kossatz-Deissmann 1982.

120 Green 1985, 98. Taplin 1987, 102 n. 7 reported that A. D. Trendall, remarking on the provincial style of the painting, expressed doubt on whether it emanated from Athens. For an earlier date, ca. 440–430 B.C., see Steinhart 2004, 22.

121 See *Clouds* Σ^{VE} 889 and Dover 1968, x–xiii and xvi; the case was argued by Taplin 1987; see also Fowler 1989.

122 Green, however, has countered that the differentiation of species may have been achieved verbally or with varied colors; the differentiation by gender is ignored in satyr plays (Green 1991, 27–30); and the presence of the *aulos*-player points to a chorus: "the grammar and syntax of the iconography is quite clear that we are dealing with a chorus" (Green 1994, 179–80 n. 27). Taplin 1993, 70–73, noted that on phlyax vases the *aulos*-player may appear in the fifth century with actors, not just with the chorus; thus it always suggests a performance, but not exclusively a choral performance.

123 Taplin 1987, 96, raises the possibility that the birds on the vase might have belonged to another genre altogether; Csapo 1993, 3, considers whether they belong to some ritual *komos*.

124 Lamberton and Rotroff 1985, 6–7 and pl. 8.

125 Markoe and Serwint 1985, 12 and figs. 12 and 46; further in Dunbar 1995, 330 on *Birds* 483–84.

126 Neils 1992, 29–30, 33. Steinhart 2004, 23 and 73–74, sees a possible association of cocks with the cult of Athena. Vickers 1990, 114, argues that these Panathenaic cocks did not begin to appear until after the Persian Wars.

127 *Birds* 483, 833; Cratinus fr. 279 K-A.

128 Bodson 1978, 100; Dumont 1988, 35.

129 *Phaedo* 118a; Bodson 1978, 97–100. Attitudes toward animals are likely to remain relatively static, so one can use evidence from the Hellenistic or Roman periods to explain phenomena seen in archaic or classical periods. Aristotle is a source for folklore material: Lloyd 1983, 2–4, 17. Nevertheless, I would exercise more caution in the case of the cock: if indeed it was a newcomer in the sixth century B.C., I would hesitate to apply to sixth- or fifth-century B.C. Athens the testimony of Aelian about the cock's role in the cult of Leto or the testimony of Porphyry about the cock's role in the cult of Persephone.

130 Furthermore, there is the possibility that some of the cocks from the earlier sixth or seventh centuries were painted not from reality but as exotic ornaments, following the heraldic style that is found in animal decoration in the wake of the orientalizing period: Kozloff 1981, 111.

131 The social significance of the cock has been the subject of recent work: Bruneau 1965 (with a full compilation of literary and artistic sources); Hoffmann 1974; Hoffmann 1988; Dumont 1988; and especially Csapo 1993, which offers a thorough synthesis.

132 Beazley 1943; Hoffmann 1974; Bentz 1998, 51–53.

133 Aelian, *Var. Hist.* 2.28; see also Lucian 37.37 (*Anach.*); Hoffmann 1974, 199; Fowler 1989; Csapo 1993, 11.

134 *Clouds* 1427–29; *Birds* 757–59, 1347–52; Plato, *Laws* 7.789b; Dumont 1988, 37. Aesopic fables on the vanity of the cock (for example, 12, 20, 270 Chabry = 16, 23, 84 Hausrath) cannot be dated.

135 An aetiological myth, which explained that a young man named "Alektryon" was punished by Ares by being turned into a cock, probably dates from the Hellenistic era: Lucian 22.3 (*Gallus*); Forbes Irving 1990, 228–29; Csapo 1993, 9.

136 Simon 1978, 1415, who also suggested that the cock columns on Panathenaic vases were meant to refer to Zeus, Athena's father.

137 Hoffmann 1974, 203–09; Csapo 1993, 11–27. The "*phallos*-bird" may have the body of a cock (thus Hoffmann 1974, 205 and Csapo, 1993, 21) or, perhaps, a swan (Boardman 1992, 234–35).

138 Dover 1978, 92; Boardman 1974, 167; Hoffmann 1974, 204–10.

139 Kozloff 1981, 111–12, fig. 92, who suggests that alabastra were used by young men, though Boardman 1974, 190, indicates that they were also used by women, aryballoi being the container preferred by men. Another example is a late Corinthian alabastron of ca. 575–550 B.C., Metropolitan Museum of Art 41.162.57; Payne 1931, 319 no. 1225 and pl 36.12; Markoe and Serwint 1985, 18, no. 12. The iconography of these paintings of cocks facing one another provides striking parallels to the Getty Birds; see further Hoffmann 1974, 203.

140 This point has been developed especially in Csapo 1993, who discusses the polarities of triumph and submission implicit in cock depictions.

141 Winkler 1990, 41. For a view of the reverse side see Green 1985, 96 fig. 1. As often, of course, we cannot be certain that either side was necessarily related to the other, especially when one is a scene of arming and departure, conventional in red-figure at this time: Boardman 1989, 220.

142 The crowing of the cock at dawn is first attested in Theognis 860–64, verses which are possibly from the sixth century, and then at Simonides fr. 80b Bergk = 78 *PMG*, and *Wasps* 817; further examples in Thompson 1936, 38. Perhaps as early as 530 B.C. the obverse on coins minted in Himera was a cock, for the cock heralded the advent of day (ἡμέρα) and was the personification of desire (ἵμερος) – puns on the city's name (Kraay 1976, 208).

143 Csapo 1993, 8. Evidence for its association with death seems to be post-classical, although a lekythos by the Athena Painter (ca. 500–490 B.C.) shows a cock on a grave stele: Weicker 1905. Hoffmann 1988, 156–57, relates it to the imagery of competitive aristocracy.

144 Cf. *Ach.* 557–627 and *Lys.* 329ff., though Olson 2002, 219, suggests that the hostility in *Ach.* is between individuals, not chorus halves.

145 Vickers 1990, 114. On the cockfight as a reflection of the values of the *kaloi kagathoi* see Hoffmann 1974, 210–13; Dumont 1988, 37.

146 Vierneisel and Kaeser 1990, 108–110.

147 The evidence for Magnes' plays is discussed in Chapter 4.

148 Only tails and equine ears are missing, though satyrs were sometimes represented without tails: Buschor 1937 and 1943; Price 1972.

149 Green 1985, 119.

150 Taplin 1993, 101–04; for the *hippalektryon* see *LIMC* V (1990), s.v. "Hippalektryon."

151 Lucian, 78.5 (Macleod) (*Dialogues of the Sea Gods*); cf. Oppian, *Hal.* 1.649, who says they inhabited cities along with mortals.

152 New York Met 1989.281.69; Beazley *ARV²* 1622–23.7 bis; *Para.* 326; Hoffmann 1964, no. 25; Greifenhagen 1965; Trendall and Webster 1971, 24, pl. I, 15; Muscarella 1974, no. 57; Settgast 1978, no. 76; Green 1985, 101, no. 6, fig. 9.

153 Greifenhagen 1965, 4, described their armor and the shield emblems, one of which is four dolphins attached to spokes in a wheel-like fashion. The large shields identify the riders as mounted hoplites; mounted cavalry carried smaller shields: Greenhalgh 1973, 122–35. The iconographical language, however, combines that of a cavalcade with that of hoplites; cf. for example the phalanx of hoplites on a black-figure Siana cup of 550–520 B.C. in Taranto (Museo Nazionale inv. 20129); *ABV* 113.70; *Para.* 45; D'Amicis 1997, no. 12.20.

154 Greifenhagen 1965, 6, and Greifenhagen 1974.

155 Sifakis 1967, 36–37, and 1971, 88–89.

156 On the function of the psykter I follow Moore and Philippides 1986, 20–21. It seems less likely that the psykter contained the ice water (Drougou 1975, 28), but if it did the dolphins would have been seen riding through the wine itself. See also Greifenhagen 1965, 6; Vierneisel and Kaeser 1990, 259–64.

157 Dechter Collection: Hamma 1989, 42–43, no. 22; Green 1991, 22 n. 19. On the exterior of the cup is Dionysus, seated among satyrs and vines.

158 Basel, H. A. Cahn Collection 849; Bloesch 1974, 41, no. 244, pl. 39; Green 1985, 103, no. 15, dates it to 490–80.

159 The catalogue notes that the letters A Δ E are of little help in establishing the meaning of the image. We cannot know what part of the word – or words – is written, or whether we have a word-break in these letters, but the letter A is separated by the spears from Δ and E, so it is not impossible that in the letters Δ E we have the beginnings of a form of the word δελφίς ("dolphin") – a "caption" not unlike that on the New York psykter (where it is retrograde).

160 Athens, Kerameikos Inv. 1486 (once 5671); Beazley, *ABV* 518; Brommer 1942, 71; Green 1985, 102, no. 13, figs. 16a–b; Green 1994, 33, fig. 2.12. Full publication in Kunze-Götte et al. 1999, 81.

161 Palermo, Museo Archeologico Regionale, 2816; Trendall 1966/67, 40, fig. 19b–d; Trendall and Webster 1971, 23, pl. I,14; Tusa 1971, 192, fig. 50a–c and pl. (color); Green 1985, 102, no. 14, fig. 17.

162 Paris, Louvre CA 1924, "Preyss Cup"; *ARV*² 1622; *Para.* 259; *Add.*² 130, said to be found in Boeotia ("near the Theseus Painter") Brommer 1942, 71, fig. 3; Ghiron-Bistagne 1976, 259; figs. 111–12; Green 1985, no. 16.

163 Boston 20.18; *ABV* 617, of the Heron Group; Haspels 1936, 108, 144, 164; Bieber 1961, 37, fig. 125; Brommer 1942, 70, figs. 1–2; Pickard-Cambridge 1962, pls. 7b and 8b; Sifakis 1971, pls. 2–4; Trendall and Webster 1971, 22, pl. I, 11; Ghiron-Bistagne 1976, figs. 109–110; Green 1985, 103, no. 17, figs. 20a–b; Csapo and Slater 1995, pl. 20A. Stebbins 1929, 103, discusses the depiction of the dolphin.

164 Other nearly contemporary dolphin-riders survive, but they do not wear armor and are thus less closely related to the series we are examining. They include:

(a) A black-figure lekythos in Baltimore (Johns Hopkins University 60.55.1, ex. Robinson) of ca. 510 B.C., by the Athena Painter: two nude young men ride dolphins on either side of a rocky island that has a satyr on it; *CVA* Baltimore 1(4), p. 51 and pl. 37 (170) 3; Haspels 1936, 151, app. XV, no. 14; Lissarrague 1990b, 117–18, fig. 90.

(b) A black-figure fragment in Istanbul, from Lindos, of a youth riding a dolphin, also by Athena Painter: Haspels 1936, 151, app. XV, no. 15.

(c) A small-neck amphora in Sydney (inv. 70.02) of ca. 480 B.C., with a nude, long-haired youth holding a phiale with an outstretched right arm and riding a dolphin. Shapiro 1989, 60, suggested it was Apollo; Kurtz and Boardman 1995, 85–90, recommended suspending judgment on his identity.

(d) Eros can be found riding a dolphin later in the classical period, a motif that persists for centuries: *LIMC* IV (1988), s.v. "Eros," nos. 157–92; Amelung 1900; Brommer 1942, 67–68; Isler 1985; Lissarrague 1990b, 118–19.

165 Froning 1971, 24–25, noted that the dithyrambic chorus tended to narrate and did not speak in the voice of any one person.

166 What is ostensibly Arion's account of his rescue, but more likely from a dithyramb of the end of the fifth or beginning of the fourth centuries, is sung solo and seems to describe a chorus that imitates a dolphin dance (*PMG* no. 939, 5–10). Bowra 1970, 173–80, suggested that this chorus was costumed as dolphins, in the tradition of Philoxenus (whose *Cyclops* of ca. 400 B.C. may have had a chorus costumed as animals); he is followed by Lonsdale 1993, 98–99. See also Brussich 1976, who sees the "Arion" song as dependent on the description of a dolphin in Eur. *Electra* 435. Webster 1970, 155, thinks it may not necessarily be solo and is inclined to ascribe it to a chorus of "Arions" on dolphins. For Philoxenus' *Cyclops* see Sutton 1983.

167 Webster observed that some vases seem to show such a performance (see Pickard-Cambridge 1962, 34, 96, and 301, nos. 1–3; and Seaford 1994, 267–69), but this has been rejected by Froning 1971, 25, and Herington 1985, 247 n. 33.

168 Bielefeld 1946/47, 49–52. A similar problem arises on the Lysicrates monument (see below), which was ostensibly for a boys' chorus (dithyramb) but depicts satyrs; see Kossatz and Kossatz-Deissmann 1992, 472. Csapo 2003, 87–89, notes that the dolphin-riders apparently dance in a circle and sees them as the chorus of a dithyramb.

169 Trendall and Webster 1971, 23, saw this series more likely as a representation of a pre-comic chorus than of a dithyramb that described dolphin-riders.

170 Csapo and Slater 1995, 96–97, suggested that showing the legs is a concession to reality, an acknowledgment that the dancers used their legs in crossing the stage. If, however, the "dolphins" were props fitted around the dancers' waists, the legs would not have been visible in performance, whereas the illusion would be that the men are straddling their dolphins in the water.

171 Bielefeld 1946/47, 48. Compare the Attic red-figure column krater in Basel, Antikenmuseum BS 415, of three pairs of young men marching in formation toward an altar in what is possibly a tragic chorus: Green 1995, 17, fig. 2.1; Csapo and Slater 1995, pl. 1A.

172 Sifakis 1971, 88.

173 Sifakis 1967 and 1971, 88.

174 Useful surveys of evidence on the dolphin are: Keller 1887, 211–35; Usener 1899, 138–80; Wellmann 1901; Stebbins 1929; Diez 1957, 667–82; Alpers 1961, 3–36; Bodson 1978, 53–57.

175 Aristotle, *HA* 589a31–b11 on the difficulty of classification; cf. Pliny, *NH* 9.19–33 and Aelian, *NA* 2.52. Mary Douglas' *Purity and Danger* (1966) applied this approach to the taboo foods of Leviticus and Deuteronomy and explained them as taxonomical irregularities. See also Douglas 1990.

176 Lloyd 1983, 44–53.

177 For example, Hesiod, *Shield* 211–12, comments on the blow-hole spout. Lloyd 1983, 44–57, observed that "pre-scientific" views on dualizers are repeated in Aristotle.

178 There were no general taboos on animals and food in Greece; the only exceptions were either local or for specific religious groups: Parker 1983, 357–65, and see below Chapter 3 n. 26. Oppian remarked that it was sinful and displeasing to the gods to hunt dolphins (5.416). The only acceptable killings would have been for medicinal purposes: Keller 1909, 409.

179 Aristotle, *HA* 631a10–b5.

180 Stebbins 1929, 84, 108, 117; he rides horses, Hippocamps, Hippalektryons, and bulls, but apparently not dolphins, although he occasionally holds a dolphin by the fin: *LIMC* VII (1994), s.v. "Poseidon," for example: nos. 106, 140, 141, 160, 210.

181 The story appears in *Homeric Hymn to Dionysus* (7.51–53); Ovid, *Met.* 3.582–691; Apollodorus 3.5. Consult Lesky 1947, 102–05; Herter 1980; and Forbes Irving 1990, 316, for more on this myth of transformation.

182 (a) Etruscan black-figure kalpis of ca. 510–500 B.C. Toledo 82.134, *CVA* Toledo (2), pp. 14–16 and pl. 90: one figure has the upper torso of a human being and lower torso of a dolphin; (b) a black-figure Ionic cup of ca. 540 B.C.: Rohde 1955, 102–11; Ridgway 1970, 88; in general see Kossatz and Kossatz-Deissmann 1992; (c) the choragic monument of Lysicrates (*LIMC* III [1986], s.v. "Dionysus," no. 792) has been discussed in Wilson 2000, 219–26.

183 Munich, Antikensammlung 2044, from Vulci; *ABV* 146.21; Boardman 1974, fig. 104.3. Whether this actually depicts the myth of Dionysus and the pirates has been disputed by Simon 1985, 287; the traditional interpretation is defended in Shapiro 1989, 89, and Hedreen 1992, 67.

184 Plutarch was convinced that dolphins formed friendships with no view to their own advantage: *Moralia* 984c–d.

185 The anecdotes and evidence (which, it must be said, are frequently from much later in antiquity) are assembled in Stebbins 1929, 59–86. This is not to say that every account of a dolphin-rider is fictional. It should be noted that such stories are not universal: in China the dolphin does nothing to rescue people: see Pilleri 1979; in Amazonian folk stories the dolphin can take on human appearance, but it becomes a threatening presence that can seduce women: see Slater 1994, 10, 94–95.

186 Herodotus 1.23–24; Arion was later credited with the invention of the dithyramb. On this episode see Bowra 1970; Hooker 1989; Steures 1999. *LIMC* II (1981), s.v. "Arion" finds no secure depictions before the late fourth century.

187 See *LIMC* VI (1992), s.v. "Melikertes"; Pausanias 1.44.7–8; 2.1.8 for the statue; Gebhard 1987 describes the likely sacred precinct for his cult.

188 Aristotle, *HA* 631a9. In fr. 590 R Aristotle mistakenly thinks the hero's name is Taras.

189 Servius on *Aeneid* 3.332.

190 (a) A dolphin fell in love with a boy at Puteoli and carried him to a beach: Pliny, *HN* 9.8.25. (b) A boy of Iasus jumped on a dolphin and was pierced by the dolphin's fin; the dolphin returned the body to shore: Aelian, *NA* 6.15; Pliny, *HN* 9.8.27. (c) The body of Hesiod was carried by dolphins: Plutarch, *Moralia* 162e. (d) A boy of Poroselene was rewarded for saving a dolphin's life: Pausanias 3.25.7. (e) Theseus was said to have ridden a dolphin to visit Poseidon: Bacchylides 17(16).97–100. (f) Enalus of Lesbos leapt into the sea with his lover, though both were rescued by dolphins; he was one of the first colonists on the island, and they built a temple to Poseidon: Myrsilus of Methymna (*FGrH* 477 F 14). (g) Koiranus had saved some dolphins from fishermen; they in turn saved him when shipwrecked near Naxos and, later, assembled near the seashore when his body was burned in a funeral pyre: Archilochus 192 Page = 117 Diehl; Plutarch, *Moralia* 985a;

Aelian 8.3. Further in Pliny, *HN* 9.8.25–28; Stebbins 1929, 73–77. Brommer 1942, 68, mentions a Kastalios.

191 Burkert 1983, 196.

192 Usener 1899, 149, took the locale as proof of a Dionysiac connection. Could dolphins have rescued Dionysus in Aristophanes' *Dionysus Shipwrecked* (*Dionysos Nauagos*, PCG III.2.157), of which only one fragment survives?

193 Bowra 1970, 121–34, lists five: Koiranos, Enalos, Melicertes, Palaemon, and Phalanthos/Taras.

194 They are φιλόμουσοι, *PMG* 939, line 7, and φίλαυλος, Eur., *Electra* 435; *Frogs* 1317; cf. Pindar, fr. 140b15–17 (Maehler); Davies 1978, 75, and Borthwick 1994, 31 and 36. Like horses, the dolphin could be bewitched by the *aulos* and syrinx, says Pliny, *NH* 11.137.

195 Villa Giulia, inv. 64 608; see Simon and Hirmer 1976, 78–79, pl. 61; Lissarrague 1990b, 119–20, fig. 93; Csapo 2003, 82, fig. 4.4.

196 Burkert 1983, 196.

197 See above; Beazley in Haspels 1936, 151–52, App. 15 255 no. 14f.; Zimmermann 1992, 86.

198 Froning 1971, 47; *LIMC* VII (1993), s.v. "Theseus," nos. 223, 224.

199 Usener 1899, 162, attempted to connect "Phalanthos" with *phallos*, and hence with Dionysus.

200 Sources include Ephorus *FGrH* 70 F 216; Antiochus of Syracuse *FGrH* 555 F 13; Pausanias 10.13.10; for discussions of the myth and history of the foundation of Tarentum see Bérard 1957, 162–75; Vidal-Naquet 1981b; Malkin 1987, 47–51, 216–21; Dougherty 1993, 35, 49–50, 73–74; Malkin 1994, 115–42; Kingsley 1995; Antonetti 1996. Consult also *RE* s.v. "Phalantos" [*sic*] and *LIMC* VII (1994), s.v. "Phalanthos."

201 Bielefeld 1946/47, 52, noted that Phalanthus was not alone ("after being thrown overboard *they* finally arrived at Italy," *iactati tandem in Italiam deferuntur*, Justin 3.4.11: note the plural), an account that follows Antiochus of Syracuse, ca. 420 B.C., as excerpted by Pompeius Trogus.

202 Bielefeld 1946/47, 48–54.

203 ANS 1967.152.17, a silver didrachm; Ravel 1947, no. 68; *LIMC* VII (1994), s.v. "Phalanthos," no. 4; Kraay and Hirmer 1966 fig. 294. The series of coins is discussed in Lacroix 1964, 97–100; Cahn 1975, 98–114; Fischer-Bossert 1999, 45–48 and 410–23.

204 Ravel 1947, no. 132; *LIMC* VII (1994), s.v. "Phalanthos," no. 3.

205 Ravel 1947, nos. 231, 232, etc.; Holloway 1978, 10.2 and 97; *LIMC* VII (1994), s.v. "Phalanthos" nos. 11, 13, 14, "weitere Kombinationen."

206 The image could also have been inspired by statues of him and a dolphin at Tarentum (Justin 3.4; Probus on *Georgics* 2.197) and Delphi (Pausanias 10.13.10), where they were shown as warriors. The dates of these are uncertain.

207 Geagan 1970, 44–46, fig. 16a. The stern of the ship ends in two swan heads, which may be an allusion to Hyacinthus, whose cult Phalanthus was thought to have introduced to Tarentum. Hyacinthus may appear on early Tarentine coinage: Kraay 1976, 175, no. 663.

Another Penteskouphia plaque (Berlin Antikensammlung, Compartment VII, no. 779) shows a dolphin being ridden, although the rider is visible only from the waist down and the plaque is poorly preserved. I also note a poorly preserved Attic chous from 400–390 B.C. (London, BM 98.2–27.1) that shows what seems to be a man on a fish, rowing it. This has been suggested to be a caricature of Taras (by Taplin 1993, 9). There is no *aulos*-player and we cannot know whether this is in fact a chorus. Also similar is a vase of ca. 360 B.C. (now lost) in which a bearded phlyax actor, without armor, reclines atop a fish: Bieber 1961, 136 and fig. 496; Trendall 1967, no. 144.

208 Pausanias 10.10.6; cf. Ephorus *FGrH* 70 F 216, who notes that they waged war against the barbarians.

209 On Apollo and colonization see above, n. 101. Evidence for various dolphins involved in foundations is in Keller 1887, 216–21.

210 Versnel 1993, 306.

211 Versnel 1993, 302–10. Some emigrants may have been ousted out of fear of pollution (p. 311); Apollo keeps the impure in the outer world (p. 299).

212 See Dumont 1975, 57–85; Robbins 1978. Bodson 1978, 56, saw Apollo as most prominent in sacred symbolism of the dolphin. Dionysus, too, is concerned with the division between order/society and nature/wild, though in different ways: Versnel 1993, Chpt. 2.

213 *Homeric Hymn to Apollo* 397–421, 493–6; see Dumont 1975. A variant has a dolphin as a guide for the ship: Plutarch, *Moralia* 984a. The association of Apollo with dolphins, as well as with music, is illustrated by an amphora in the Vatican showing Apollo, holding a lyre, being carried over the waves on a winged tripod; he is escorted by dolphins (*ARV*² 209.166; Boardman 1975, fig. 157).

214 Graf 1979a, 6, pointed out that there was no clear connection between Apollo Delphinius and colonists setting out, though homecomings are a recurrent feature in myths associated with Delphinius, including Theseus, Argonauts (pp. 13–14, 18–19).

215 On Apollo's ephebic role see Burkert 1975, 19; Graf 1979a, 13–19; Jameson 1980; Graf 1985, 221–26; Versnel 1993, 313–29, 328–29.

216 Apollonius of Rhodes, 4.1765–72; Graf 1979a, 18–19.

217 Graf 1979a, 19, who cites Wachsmuth 1967, 168, 176.

218 On Deucalion see Apollonius *FGrH* 365 F 4; Graf 1979a, 19 n. 145 & 146, gives references, incl. Burkert 1983, 240.

219 And Versnel 1993, 314, noted that Apollo was the counterpart to Achilles: youthful, baptized in fire, educated by Cheiron, clothed as a girl.

220 Graf 1979a, 21.

221 Versnel 1993, 316; certainly their name, "Partheniai," smacks of a reversal of sexual identity, though it seems to reflect their parentage: Vidal-Naquet 1981b, 195.

222 *Ath. Pol.* 42.5, though it also was worn by travelers, cavalry, and soldiers: Xenophon, *Mem.* 7.4.4; Antiphanes fr. 17 K-A; see Sommerstein 1996, 57.

223 Jameson 1980, 232, discussed the role of Apollo in receiving ephebes into the community of assembled warriors.

224 Versnel 1993, 328–31.

225 A similar alternation can be found on terracotta figures of reclining banqueters from the late sixth century found at Tarentum and related to Phalanthus and Taras: see Kingsley 1995, 207 and 211.

226 Slater 1976; Davies 1978; Lissarrague 1990b, 107–22. The banqueters reclining and holding wine cups were votive offerings to Phalanthus, suggesting a shared sympotic impulse; see Kingsley 1995.

227 Louvre G92: *ARV* 2 134.3; Greifenhagen 1965, 6; Lissarrague 1990b, 74, fig. 55. An interesting discussion of dolphins, dancing, and drinking is in Csapo 2003, 79–85, esp. on komasts and dolphins, 85–87.

228 Drougou 1975, 28–38; Lissarrague 1990b, 114–15.

229 Lissarrague 1990b, 115 and 116.

230 It is hard not to remark on the functional and visual similarity of the dolphin-riders to the pyrrhic dance, in which a nude dancer carried weapons and performed movements for attacking an enemy. This was part of the training for young boys, with an educational and civilizing function (cf. Plato, *Laws* 7.796c and 7.815a; Athenaeus 628e–f). There were competitions at the Panathenaea, where boys would learn to use arms and wear the *chlamys*, a cloak worn by ephebes (*Ath. Pol.* 42.5; see Ceccarelli 1998, 16–45), and at performances at symposia (Ceccarelli 1998, 58–60). Xenophon describes them at a reception (*Anabasis* 6.1.1–13). Visual representations of pyrrhic dancers, which began ca. 520 B.C., could take on Dionysiac features and showed an *aulos*-player. Several dancers on black-figure lekythoi by the Athena Painter (including [a] one in Baltimore: Lawler 1964, figs. 41 & 42; [b] Taranto inv. 4573: Haspels 1936, 257, 56; Poursat 1968, no. 11; D'Amicis 1997, no. 9.1) bear striking compositional similarities to the nude dolphin-riders by the Athena Painter (see above), which in turn closely resemble the armed dolphin-riders in Athens by the Theseus Painter (Figure 2.4). For others see Poursat 1968, nos. 13–15, and Ceccarelli 1998, plates 3–5. On the pyrrhic dance see also Lissarrague 1990b, 116; Lonsdale 1993, 137–68; and especially Ceccarelli 1998, who sees similarities between the dolphin-riders and pyrrhic dancers (p. 82 n. 253).

231 Military cloaks, suggest Trendall and Webster 1971, 22.

232 Ghiron-Bistagne 1976, 261.

233 Sifakis 1971, 91.

234 Bieber 1961, 37.

235 Trendall and Webster 1971.

236 Sifakis 1971, 91–92, cites Bieber's view that he is a "dancing dwarf," but notes that dwarves are rare before the Hellenistic time; Reinach 1922, 486, sees him as a pygmy, and pygmies do appear on Attic vases, engaged in battle with cranes – cf. the François vase (ca. 575 B.C.); Webster (in Pickard-Cambridge 1962, 159) considers him as an antagonist. Smith 1881, 314, discussing a small figure on a now-lost vase from the Hamilton collection,

reports the following: "At the meeting of the Society on Oct. 21st, Prof. Constantinides informed me that in modern Greek puppet shows a character almost exactly corresponding in appearance to the smaller figure in the Tischbein vase occurs, and is called χοραγός (?)." In ancient Athens the χορηγός was normally the citizen chosen to underwrite a chorus, although in a few instances the word seems to apply to the "leader" of the chorus (like κορυφαῖος): cf. *Lys.* 1315; Eur. *Helen* 1454 (of Phoinicia, "the chorus-leader of dolphins"). The notion that the short man with either goat horns or unusual hair is somehow the leader of the chorus can not be proved but is appealing. We might wonder, too, whether this short man functions as do the "Choregoi" on the Fleischman vase discussed in Taplin 1993, esp. 55–66. Gilula 1995 raises the possibility that they were the ancestors of the *choragi* of Roman comedy who furnished costumes and props to a theatrical troupe. I am not aware of specific evidence for any such "prop-master" for the Greek stage of the early fifth century, but perhaps there was a person like this, a sort of "master of ceremonies" who helped orchestrate movements on stage, for whom literary evidence has been lost. Gilula suggests the "Choregoi" vase shows a rehearsal, but, as often in depictions of comedy, we see with the ostrich-riders not just the narrative event but the theatrical functionaries, such as the *aulos*-player, that accompany it.

237 Pickard-Cambridge 1962, 153.

238 For what Greek folklore there is consult Keller 1913, 174; Steier 1932, 339–47; Thompson 1936, 270–73. Most references to ostriches are from much later in antiquity. Herodotus mentions ostrich-skins used as shields by the Makai (4.175), which certainly indicates that ostriches were hunted, and he cites the presence of ostriches in the land of the nomads (4.192). In Aristophanes a feather on Lamachus' helmet comes from an ostrich (*Ach.* 1106); a priest invokes the "Great Ostrich Mother" goddess (*Birds* 874–75), assimilating the ostrich to the goddess Cybele. Sommerstein 1987, 256–57, points out that both were called μεγάλαι and that Cybele, like one variety of ostrich in antiquity, came from Asia.

239 Noted in Brommer 1942, 66. The ostrich is completely absent from Bodson 1978.

240 Aristotle, *PA* 697b14–26, cf. 658a13 on eyelashes; Thompson 1936, 270ff.; Lloyd 1983, 47 n. 189, points out that swine are dualizers because some are cloven-hoofed and others are solid-hoofed: Aristotle, *HA* 499b11–14; *GA* 774b17–20.

241 Deut. 14.15; Levit. 11.16; *Hist. Aug. Heliog.* 30.2: Elagabalus cooked the brains of six hundred ostrich heads (cf. 28.4, where Jews were commanded to eat them).

242 Athenaeus 200f; Steier 1932, 345.

243 Oppian, *Cynegetica* 3.482; at 3.490–91 he reports that an ostrich can carry a youth.

244 *Münzen und Gemmen* 22.36; Keller 1913, 173.

245 Brommer 1942, 68–74.

246 Young men riding ostriches might be reminiscent of the *adynata* that occasionally appear in colony-foundation oracles (Vian 1963, 77–94; Dougherty 1993, 50); these *adynata* typically show that nonsense is a path to the truth. Just as Phalanthus and the Partheniai were saved by dolphins to found Tarentum, so too this band of young men was saved by ostriches to accomplish some outlandish task.

247 Serpell 1996, 45.

248 Leach 1964; for critiques see Halverson 1976 and Serpell 1990. Harris 1985 emphasizes practical and economic factors over symbolic ones – consult, for example, his chapter on the "abominable pig" that is taboo in Leviticus. See also Parker 1983, 61 n. 101 and 357–65. Serpell 1996, 66–68.

249 Tambiah 1969. For another approach, see Lévi-Strauss 1966, 204–10, who posited four categories for animals, depending on their relationship with human society: (a) metaphorical human beings, those separate from human society but intrinsically social, e.g. birds; (b) metonymical human beings, those part of human society, but low in it, e.g. dogs; (c) metaphorical inhuman beings, those disjoined from human society, intrinsically un-social, e.g. racehorses; and (d) metonymical inhuman beings, those part of society, treated as an object in the economic system, e.g. cattle.

250 Hippoc. *Regimen* 2.46 (6.544–6 L.).

251 Van Straten 1995; Rosivach 1994.

252 This point was made by Radermacher in 1932.

253 Parker 1996, 85–86; Walker 1995, 35–81.

254 Steinhart 2004, however, is more open to possible cultic origins for animal masquerades.

255 Suggested by Ridgway 1970, 91; for the name "Simo" for dolphins see Pliny, *NH* 9.25; see further Stebbins 1929, 5; for satyrs riding dolphins, which appears on a red-figure lekythos, see Amelung 1900.

256 Gerhard, cited in Poppelreuter 1893, 9.

257 *LIMC* V (1990), s.v. "Hippalektryon," 431, where no. 83 is a painting on a plate of ca. 520–510 B.C. of a young boy riding a cock. We also find sphinxes, sirens, sea-monsters and tritons, especially on the C Painter: Brijder 1983, 119. One can, it has been suggested to me, add the *phallos*-bird to this list; consult Boardman 1992 for a survey of these.

258 Zacharia 2003 sees an imperial subtext in references to the Greek West in the fragments of Sophocles.

259 Carpenter 1991, 160; Shapiro 1989, 143–50, who points out that the process had begun even earlier. Theseus was also connected with Apollo Delphinius: Shapiro 1989, 61.

260 Steinhart 2004, 21, suggests that the dolphin-riders reflect the early sea empire.

261 Förtsch 1997, 61.

262 Neer 2002, 22. Comparable is the argument that archaic poets such as Sappho, Alcaeus, and Anakreon blurred the distinction between male and

female, and Greek and Lydian, to reinforce a distinction between aristocrat and commoner: Morris 1996, 35.

263 The ritual role of the comic chorus is emphasized in Bierl 2001, 96–101. Adrados 1975, 53, speaks of comic material as "derived from the ancient agricultural and animalistic cults."

264 Seeberg 1995, 6: "The padded *komos* apparently depended on the chieftain class that commissioned festivals and also much of the great poetry of the time."

265 We might remember that of the few actual examples of *phallika* that we can find, the *ithyphalloi* conducted not bawdy festivity but a relatively formal ceremony.

266 Edwards 2002, 35.

3. ANIMALS AND SATYRS IN CLASSICAL GREECE: AN EXCURSUS

1 Lonsdale 1990, whose Appendix D cites 41 lion similes. See also Schnapp-Gourbeillon 1981.

2 Lonsdale 1990, 109. Of course the similes would not be effective if human beings were not capable of equal savagery.

3 Heath 1999, 47. Aeschylean animal imagery is collected in Dumortier 1975, 134–55; Petrounias 1976 discusses the use of birds in the motif of punishment (pp. 129–40) and the symbolism of hunting (pp. 140–52).

4 The *Oresteia* has far more animal metaphors than the other four Aeschylean plays (Earp 1948, 104; cited by Heath 1999, 17). I regret that I only discovered Heath 2005 at the copy-editing stage of this book, for it has much of great interest. The *Bacchae* has a disproportionately large animal presence: fifteen of sixty-three Euripidean instances of θήρ are in the *Bacchae*; eight of thirty-seven instances of *drakon*; seven of twenty-six instances of *leon*.

5 A doe is mangled by a wolf (90), a bird is flushed out (178), a nightingale has a piteous voice (337), a beast tracks its quarry (1058), beasts eat a meal (1073), children are eaten by dogs (1078), and a beast hunts dogs (1173). Dogs can also be tame and companionable, and Hecuba's final metamorphosis need not be a sign of violent bestiality, suggests Burnett 1994.

6 Thucydides, notes Smith 1992, 32–39, names only seven different animals, for a total of forty-two entries; thirty of these entries are of the horse.

7 Smith 1992, 98–106.

8 Moreover, when Herodotus describes peoples who live in areas remote from Greece, he tends to characterize them in ways that associate them more with animals. The Auses, for example, copulate with their women in common "like animals" (κτηνηδόν, 4.180.5), and the Troglodytes communicate by speaking like bats (4.183.4): Smith 1992, 132–36.

9 Smith 1992, 58–76. The Greeks feared animals, writes Padel 1992, 143, because "they are part of the unpredictable physical fabric through which gods express their power."

10 Wilkins 2000a, xvii, noted that comedy does not linger over the violence of sacrifice but continues beyond, even to the point of chopping up food.

11 One finds a eunuch likened to a monkey (120), the army compared to locusts (150), smelly children likened to cats (256), voters compared to cuckoos (598), and another half dozen similar comparisons.

12 I have counted 195 different animals named in all of Aristophanes, for a total of 959 entries. Of these approximately one quarter, the largest single category, refer to animals as food.

13 Secondary literature I have consulted includes: Uxkull-Gyllenband 1924; Havelock 1957; Cole 1967 (repr. with afterword 1990); Edelstein 1967; Guthrie 1971, 226–48; Dodds 1973; den Boer 1977; Vidal-Naquet 1978; Kahn 1981; Renehan 1981; O'Brien 1985; Hussey 1985; Blundell 1986; Piette 1987; Tulin 1993.

14 In this period, of course, νόμος began to be distinguished from φύσις, with νόμος referring to "norms" or "conventions" established by human beings and φύσις referring to that which exists in "nature" or the innate qualities of a person or institution. See Heinimann 1945, 78–85 and 95–108; Guthrie 1971; Kerferd 1981, 111–30; Ostwald 1986, 250–73.

15 In addition to Critias the phrase appears in Eur., *Suppliants* 202; Hippocratic *Vet. Med.* 3.29; Moschion 6.4; Isocrates, *Paneg.* 28, *Bus.* 25, *Antid.* 254; Ditt. *Syll.* 704; Diodorus Siculus 1.8.1. Cf. Aeschylus, *Palamedes* frag. 181a *TrGF*: θηρσίν θ' ὅμοιον.

16 *PCG* VII.106–14, frags. 5–20 K-A; see Long 1986, 18–19, and Dobrov 1997, 115–17.

17 The progressivist view had, in one respect, been anticipated by prior Greek aetiological myths attributing steps in civilization to culture heroes or "first inventors" (πρῶτοι εὑρέται): Prometheus gave fire to humankind, Dionysus gave wine, Triptolemus brought agriculture, and so forth. This view is scarcely more "historical" than other myths, but it does understand human culture to have evolved out of an animal-like life, and evidence for interest in it before the emergence of fifth-century rationalism is meager: see Kleingünther 1933. For discussions of the question of authorship of the *Prom.*, consult Griffith 1977 and Saïd 1985, 27–80.

18 Cole 1967, 186–88; Blundell 1986, 177; Diodorus' account of early life, which may be dependent on Democritus, also assumes that the impetus for early human advances was mechanical, and even physical or biological.

19 For discussions of Hesiod's account see Gatz 1967, 28–51; West 1978, 172–204. Notably, the Greeks omitted animals from Flood and Creation Myths, observes Kitchell 1993.

20 Even Hesiod's sequence of ages is not consistently pessimistic in that the age of heroes seems to interrupt the decline. Similarly he saw Zeus as an improvement on Uranus: den Boer 1977, 7.

21 On these themes and comedies, see Schmid 1946, 83–84 and 124–32; Baldry 1952; Gatz 1967, 114–22; Carrière 1979, 238–50; Coulter 1995, 281–86; Ceccarelli 1996; Ruffell 2000. On the *Demes* see Storey 2003, 111–74.

22 Empedocles DK 31 B130; Xenophon, *Mem.* 2.7.13 notes that the sheep and dog would talk to their master; Plato, *Politicus* 272b–c; an Aesopic version appears in the prologue to Babrius (5–13); for further references see Gatz 1967, 165–71; Dierauer 1977, 3; Carrière 1979, 258; Osborne 1990; Gera 2003, 18–67.

23 Callimachus, *Iambi* 2 (fr. 192 Pf.); trans. Nisetich 2001, 100. See also Beta 2004, 82–94, who discusses the assignment of animal vocal features to human beings.

24 The issue of sacrifice has generated much attention from modern scholars. Svenbro 1989 gives a full bibliography; see also Burkert 1983; Foley 1985; Obbink 1988 and 1993; Detienne 1989b; Durand and Schnapp 1989; Peirce 1993.

25 Accounts of this Pythagorean doctrine include Kirk and Raven 1957, 217–31; Guthrie 1962, 182–212; Sorabji 1993, 170–94, esp. 172–74.

26 Burkert 1972, 97–131. Empedocles pictured a father killing his own son (DK 31 B136–137). There were also dietary taboos held by Orphics and others against eating meat: Burkert 1985, 301–04. The Greeks may to have had a taboo against eating animals that might eat men: Parker 1983, 357–64. In Eskimo myth one finds the motif of alternating existences: a person might be an animal at one time or a human at another: Dierauer 1977, 2.

27 Piette 1987, 7.

28 Piette 1987, 8.

29 ἀποικίζει αὐτοὺς σὺν τῶν ἐπιγόνων τινὶ ἡγεμόνι: *Oec.* 7.34; cf. *Oec.* 7.38 and *Cyr.* 5.1.24. My thanks to Louis L'Allier for calling these passages to my attention.

30 See Diogenes Laertius 6.63 (on the *kosmopolites*) and 6.72. Discussions include Vidal-Naquet 1978, 135; Sorabji 1993, 158–61.

31 This view is attributed to Diogenes the Cynic in Dio Chrysostom, *Orations* 6.25–29, 10.16; Dawson 1992, 143–46, has suggested that Dio's portrait misrepresents Cynic doctrine; if this is so, my interest is more in Dio's portrait than in Diogenes the Cynic. See also Diogenes Laertius 6.22 on Cynic admiration for the adaptability of the mouse.

32 *Gryllus* or *Whether Beasts are Rational* (*Moralia*, 986f–992a). For reviews of Plutarch's attitude toward animals see Dierauer 1977, 279–93 (with a discussion of Plutarch's indebtedness to Cynic ideas about animals); Sorabji 1993, 160–61; Newmyer 1997.

33 Boardman 1975, 215.

34 Weiss 1984, 102–04.

35 Weiss 1984, 105.

36 Trendall and Webster 1971, on II.6; Griffith 1983, 198–99. She also continues to be shown as a cow or a cow with a woman's face.

37 Schiffler 1976, 27–30, 168–70.

38 This list differs from that of Sifakis 1971, 77, in that I have included the satyr comedies, the *Cyclopes*, and the *Griffins*. I have omitted the two *Amazons* by Cephisodorus and Epicrates; the Amazons may have ridden

horses but the surviving fragments offer nothing of interest about animal-human concerns. (Aristophanes' *Knights*, by contrast, includes anthropomorphized horses.) Athenaeus VII.286a–b attributed the *Cyclopes* to either Callias or Diocles (*PCG* V.20).

Other titles indicate a role for centaurs, though with the title in the singular we cannot assume it refers to the chorus. We know of comedies with the title *Centaur* by Ophelio (*PCG* VII.98), Lynceus (*PCG* V.616–17), Theognetus (*PCG* VII.696), Timocles (*PCG* VII.770–71; an alternative title is *Dexamenos*); Nicochares (*PCG* VII.44; alternatively given as *Centaurs*, in plural); Aristophanes (*PCG* III.2.158–63; alternative title *Dramata*); and we should not overlook Pherecrates' *Cheiron* (*PCG* VII.178–86).

39 The *Dionysalexandros* had a satyr chorus (*PCG* IV.140, test. I.42). The phrase ἐν Σατύροις in *P.Oxy.* 1801 (*CGFP* 343) 17, could be the title of another comedy. Handley 1985, 364, suggested that the chorus of Magnes' *Barbitistai* ("Lyre-players") were musical satyrs. On the "Pronomos" vase the playwright's name is Demetrios; Trendall and Webster 1971, 29, suggest it may be the comic poet of that name. The "Return of Hephaestus," which typically included satyrs on vase-painting, was a theme in comedy: cf. Epicharmus' *Komasts or Hephaestus*, for which see Pickard-Cambridge 1962, 264 and Hedreen 1992, 24 n.7. On the overlap of the genres consult Guggisberg 1947, 36–44; Pickard-Cambridge 1962, 171; Wilson 1973, 126–27; Sutton 1980, 136–37; Handley 1982, 109–17; Green 1985, 111; Katsouris 1999; Dobrov forthcoming; Shaw 2005.

40 Lissarrague 1990a, 235. General treatments of the satyr-play include Rossi 1972; Sutton 1980; Seaford 1984, 1–48; Seidensticker 1989; Krumeich et al. 1999.

41 The date is evidently fixed by the fact that Athenian victory-lists go back to 502/501 B.C.: Sutton 1980, 6 n. 14; see also Pickard-Cambridge 1968, 72.

42 Horace, *Ars Poetica* 220–24; he conceives this in terms of delaying a drunken spectator. For Seidensticker 1989 the satyr-play offers an uncomplicated, optimistic view of life; Sutton 1980, 85: "the purpose of classical satyr play was to supply comic relief after tragedy." The satyr-play thus debunks the tragedies that preceded it: Sutton 1974, 192; Sutton 1980, 167–91.

43 Chamaileon on Thespis (fr. 38) and Zenobius (5.40); see Rossi 1972, 267–68 [= 1989, 233–34]; Seaford 1984, 11–12.

44 Seaford 1984, 31.

45 Vitruvius (5.6.9) noted that the setting of satyr-plays had trees, caves, and mountains; cf. Rossi 1972, 261–63, who suggests (n. 81) that comedy may have had a rustic character at one point but had lost it by the time of the classical festivals.

46 Fr. 47a.808–09 *TrGF*.

47 Seaford 1984, 18.

48 Rossi 1972, 278–79.

49 Examples of this *topos* in satyr-plays are collected and studied in Kleingünther 1933, 91–93; Snell 1956, 8; Ussher 1978, 17–19; and above all Seaford 1976, 209–21 and 1984, 36–42.
50 Sutton 1980, 137.
51 This fragment may not belong to a satyr play: see Krumeich 1999, 172.
52 Brommer 1959, 48–49, figs. 42–46, nos. 187–199a. Fire may also have been revealed in Sophocles' *Kophoi* (fr. 362 *TrGF*) and in Aristias (fr. 8 *TrGF*).
53 Fr. 5 *TrGF*; see Seaford 1984, 36–37.
54 The possible identity of the interlocutor (Daedalus, Hephaestus, Sisyphus?) is discussed at Krumeich et al. 1999, 140, n. 40.
55 Price 1972, 244.
56 Lloyd-Jones 1957, 548, suggests he was in Aeschylus' *Theoroi*. Metal-working may have figured in satyr-plays by Sophocles: *Daidalos* and *Kophoi* (fr. 364 *TrGF*).
57 For example, a krater from near Caltanisetta of ca. 480–470 B.C. shows them as artisans at the forge of Hephaestus: *Para.* 354, no. 39bis; Boardman 1975, fig. 174; Gempeler 1969; see also Simon 1982b, 136–38. On a squat lekythos of ca. 500–480 B.C., University of Chicago, Smart Museum of Art, Warren-Tarbell 23, are satyrs who may be working at a forge (Price 1972) or on a piece of wood (Ferrari et al. 1998, 42–43). The figure on the left has been thought to be a dancer in a bird costume with a large beak and a receding forehead (Price 1972), and the possibility that the satyrs are accompanied by a figure in animal costume would highlight the common interest of both in human culture. A more recent view, however, is that the "bird" is actually a standing female whose face has worn away, leaving only the black silhouette of her hair (Ferrari et al. 1998).
58 Whereas treading on grapes was done by human workmen on an early black-figure vintage scene, it was later done by satyrs: see Sparkes 1976; Brijder 1983, 188. Pliny reported that Staphylos, a son of Silenus, invented wine mixed with water – a civilized improvement over undiluted wine (*NH* 7.199).
59 The "new toys" of Aeschylus' *Theoroi* were perhaps javelins – athletic gear, suggests Snell 1956, 8.
60 Seaford 1984, 35.
61 Brommer 1959, 60–63, nos. 108–15; see also Simon 1982b, 129–31. On one vase a satyr with well-groomed hair has his penis bound up like an athlete's (Leiden, Rijksmuseum van Oudheden PC 80; *ARV*2 183.7; Lissarrague 1993, 210, fig. 14.)
62 Fr. 372 Nauck².
63 Lloyd-Jones 1957, 541–56; Stieber 1994.
64 Boston 62.613, a red-figure kylix by the Antiphon Painter, ca. 475 B.C. *ARV²* 1701, 342.19bis; *Add.²* 219; *Para.* 362; Beazley Archive Pottery Database no. 275647.

65 In fr. 382 Nauck². Sutton 1980, 68; this is not included in Krumeich et al. 1999, 474.

66 Berlin F 2418; *CVA* Berlin 2, pl. 147; Lissarrague 1993, 218. Athenaeus, who reports that Athena gave the *aulos* to Marsyas (184a), records an alternative tradition, namely, that Marsyas had invented it (Metrodorus in the *Trojan History*, DK 70 B3). *Trag. adesp.* 381 *TrGF* is from a play in which Athena invented the *aulos* and then gave it to a satyr.

67 Fr. 269c *TrGF*; Carden 1974, 81; Seaford 1984, 36 n. 96. Sutton 1980, 157n. suggests, however, that it may have been not newly invented but simply newly made.

68 Fr. 314 *TrGF*, esp. lines 284–331. In the second half of the *Ichneutai* it seems that Apollo received the newly invented lyre from Hermes; this might have provided the aetiology for the satyrs' use of stringed instruments, such as the cithara, which were seen as more civilized than the *syrinx* (in Ovid, *Met.* 11.146–71, Apollo's lyre defeats Pan's pipes). Satyrs have obtained a drum (the *tympanum*) at *Bacchae* 120–34. Guggisberg 1947, 35, pointed out that satyrs, in their variety of roles as workers, sing songs to accompany their work. Orpheus, who was traditionally regarded as a *protos heuretes* of music, was the subject in a satyr-play. The fifth-century poet Aristias wrote an *Orpheus*, which was possibly a satyr-play, and several early fifth-century vase-paintings show Orpheus with Silenus or the satyrs (Brommer 1959, 57, fig. 53, and nos. 94–96).

69 New York Met 25.78.66; *ARV*² 1172.8; Buschor 1943, 28, 71–3; Bieber 1961, 6, fig. 17; Froning 1971, 25–26.

70 The children include Dionysus (Aeschylus' *Dionysou Trophoi*, of which we have the title only, and Sophocles' *Dionysiskos*, fr. 171 *TrGF*), Hermes (Sophocles' *Ichneutai*, fr. 314 *TrGF*), Heracles (possibly in Sophocles' *Heracleiskos* and Achaeus' *Linus*, fr. 26 *TrGF*), Maron (Euripides' *Cyclops* 142), and Perseus (Aeschylus' *Diktyoulkoi*, fr. 47a *TrGF*). See Seaford, 1976, 213–14.

71 Pearson 1917, on frr. 150ff.; Sutton 1980, 36–38.

72 Sophocles fr. 1130 *TrGF* (*P. Oxy.* 1083, the *Oeneus* or *Schoeneus*); Sutton 1980, 57ff.

73 On a cup by the Brygos Painter of ca. 490–480 B.C. (London E 65, *ARV*² 370.13); Buschor 1943, 103–04; Simon 1982b, 125–129 on a fight with Iris and Hera; see Scharffenberger 1995 on *Birds*.

74 Brommer 1959, 43–45, figs. 35, 36, 38; Simon 1982b, esp. 146–47; Lissarrague 1993, 216–17.

75 Bérard and Bron 1989, 134 and 139; Lissarrague 1993, 212.

76 Boardman 1975, 216–222; Cook 1997, 161.

77 In several vase-paintings we also seem to find human beings assimilated to satyrs, dancing like them; moreover the friezes on vases tend to imply a continuum between men and satyrs: Bérard and Bron 1989, 137, fig. 187 and 141–42, fig. 194. Perhaps the chief point is that there is an occasional dissolution of boundaries; it is possible to pass back and forth between human and bestial conditions. This continuum can be compared with the ambiguities

of Dionysus himself, who "abolishes differences": Bérard and Bron 1989, 137–38, figs. 188 and 189.

78 Hesiod fr. 123 MW, although disparaging satyrs as "worthless," gives them a divine genealogy. In Sophocles' *Oeneus* they identified themselves as "sons of nymphs, servants of Bacchus, and companions of the gods" (lines 7–8).

79 Herodotus 8.138; Aristotle fr. 44 Rose; Theopompus 115 *FGrH* 75c: Silenus is "by nature more obscure than a god, but more powerful than a human being, since he is also immortal." In Plutarch, *Sulla* 27.2, a silen is captured and brought to Sulla, but can only make a sound like a cross between the neigh of a horse or the bleat of goat.

80 Examples are collected in Lissarrague 1988, including a vase-painting in which a satyr plays a pipe for a chorus of three dancing goats (fig. 7).

81 Lissarrague 1993, 212. Silenus says in Sophocles' *Ichneutai* that they are "nothing but bodies and tongues and phalluses" (fr. 314.150–51 *TrGF*).

82 Seaford 1984, 30. Their boorish behavior is "a cautionary model of anti-social irresponsibility," says Padgett 2000, 44.

83 Munich 2645, *ARV²* 371.15; Lissarrague 1993, 212.

84 Berlin 1966.1, an Attic black-figure amphora, late sixth century, *ABV* 285.1; in Lissarrague 1993, 208.

85 Seaford 1984, 42. Such is the range of activities and artefacts, however, that one must wonder whether they were still felt to be ritual.

86 Lissarrague 1993, 219; cf. Sutton 1980, 137; Stieber 1994, 91.

87 Aeschylus, *Prometheus Pyrkaios* fr. 116 Lloyd-Jones = fr. 206 *TrGF*.

88 Brommer 1959, 72–73 on no. 17; Simon 1982b, 145–46.

89 Translation from Silk and Stern 1981, 69. Similarly Plato, *Laws* 815c, wrote that ritual dances of Pans, nymphs, silens, and satyrs were unfit for the polis.

90 Seaford 1984, 33.

91 Lissarrague 1993, 219 and 1990a, 235–36.

92 Lissarrague 1993, 212.

93 Collinge 1989, 90: "It is not surprising that the dramatic satyr, despite being a fantasy creature, does not challenge authority, since its existence is circumscribed by so much orthodoxy, creating, as it were, an establishment fantasy."

94 Seaford 1984, 30.

95 On centaurs see Schiffler 1976; Padgett 2003; *LIMC* III (1986), s.v. "Cheiron" and *LIMC* VI (1992), s.v. "Kentauroi et Kentaurides." For an interpretation see du Bois 1982, 25–32, 49–70. It would be interesting to know how Cheiron and the centaurs were treated in the comedies that seem to have had centaurs as choruses.

96 "Healer, prophet, teacher, he is in many respects a type of the poet himself," writes Robbins 1978, 93, in a study of *Pythian* 9, which connects Cheiron with the foundation of Cyrene. Mackie 1997 suggests that whereas Cheiron teaches Achilles medicine, music, and hunting, Phoenix teaches him "community skills" such as speaking and debating; this closely corresponds to the difference I see between satyr and animal choruses.

97 Although they, too, were subject to the "humanization" trend of the fifth century: Schiffler 1976, 169.

98 Sutton 1980, 114–20, in favor of 424 B.C.; Paganelli 1979, *passim* and 138, in favor of 414/413 B.C.; Seaford 1982, 163–72, in favor of 408 B.C. Krumeich 1999, 431–32, is non-committal. It may reflect Euripides' reservations about the Peloponnesian War when the satyrs cast the fall of Troy as an opportunity to rape Helen, minimizing the significance of the victory (lines 179–81); see Konstan 1990a, 220–21.

99 Paganelli 1979, 119–25.

100 The Greeks trapped in Polyphemus' cave at the foot of Mt. Etna may have reminded Athenians of their fellow-citizens imprisoned in Syracuse in the years after 413: Seaford 1984, 55.

101 Although Odysseus calls Polyphemus a "man" or "male" (ἀνήρ, 591, 605), he never calls him a "human being" (ἄνθρωπος).

102 The sequence he follows – roasting, then boiling – would have been recognized as a civilized one, suggests Seaford 1984, 152.

103 Seaford 1984, 52 n. 157.

104 Arrowsmith 1956, 8; Ussher 1978, 187. Despite his apparent sophistication, though, Polyphemus knows nothing of wine or of Dionysus and has to be instructed in matters of the *komos* and symposium: Rossi 1971.

105 Plato, *Gorgias* 483a–484c: Callicles compared the strong individual to a lion whose taming by society would be an unjust transgression of *physis*. For discussion see Heinimann 1945, 140–41; Guthrie 1971, 101–07. His position resembles "Socrates" in the *Clouds*: the role of necessity in natural processes, the replacement of Zeus with "Vortex" at *Clouds* 381: see Turato 1979, 79, and O'Regan 1992, 49–66.

106 Konstan 1990b, 216–19.

107 Seaford reads μόναδες with Schmidt 1975; Konstan 1990a, 217 n. 20, and the mss. read νόμαδες, "nomads."

108 Seaford 1984, 54.

109 Nilsson 1967, 212–16; Erbse 1980.

110 Konstan 1991, 12; see also Saïd 1988.

111 See Wilkins 2000a, 1–23, who sees the body in comedy as more prone to permeability, unlike tragedy, in which the interest is on the surface whole of the person.

112 Rothwell 1995a.

113 Segal 1963, 28. Thiercy 1987, pointing to the absence of direct address by the chorus to the audience in the plays with non-human choruses, speculated that an Athenian audience would not have identified with a chorus of animals (or clouds, or the like). He points out though that one should perhaps not underestimate the ability of an audience to identify imaginatively with any anthropomorphized creature.

114 Sorabji 1993.

115 See Philemon frr. 2, 93, 96; Menander fr. 844. See Dierauer 1977, 178–79.

116 Segal 1963, 45.

4. THE LITERARY FRAGMENTS AND ARISTOPHANES' *KNIGHTS*, *WASPS*, AND *FROGS*

1 For an amusing experiment in how a few random fragments of Aristophanes' *Frogs* might be reassembled and misinterpreted by a hypothetical student, see Dover 2000.

2 Athenaeus claimed even to have written a (now lost) treatise on the *Fishes* of Archippus (329c). Discussions of comic fragments from the *Deipnosophists* may be found in Nesselrath 1990, 65–79; Arnott 2000; and Sidwell 2000.

3 See now Davidson 1997 and Wilkins 2000a.

4 Although it is not impossible that the papyrus itself came from a work of culinary selections. Willis 1991, 337, suggests that Athenaeus' failure to quote the *Comoedia Dukiana* may be because the comedy was no longer extant in his day; and Athenaeus himself may have been relying on selections already excerpted by earlier grammatical and lexicographical treatises. We cannot be confident that Athenaeus had the complete texts of the comedies he quoted. See Nesselrath 1990, 65–79.

5 The differences between this list and that of Sifakis 1971, 76, are these: the title of Magnes' play (Ψῆνες) should probably be translated as *Fig-Wasps* (not *Gall-Flies*); K-A ascribe a *Birds* to Crates II; Crates' *Beasts* may be dated to the early 420s; the *Ants* of Plato perhaps belong to 425–422; the goats of Eupolis' play are feminine; the *Frogs* of Callias may be earlier than the period 430–426; Aristophanes' *Birds* was omitted from Sifakis' list; I include the *Comoedia Dukiana*, which may be from Archippus' *Fishes*. We know nothing, apart from the suggestive title, of the *Ornithokomoi* ("Bird-revels"? "Poultry Keepers"?) of Anaxilas (*PCG* II.291). There is also a possibility that the playwright Carcinus wrote a comedy with the title *Mice*: see Rothwell 1994; for the standard view see Olson 2000.

6 I acknowledge that what follows is a hypothetical exercise. The relative absence of animal choruses from vase-painting after ca. 480 B.C. may have less to do with performances of animal choruses than with the vicissitudes of survival and the interests of the painters; vase-painting for all genres of drama is rare in mid-century: Taplin 1993, 6–11. Förtsch 1997 posited a process whereby the visual arts were overshadowed in the middle of the fifth century by drama and thought that we should not expect visual representations of drama on art in this period.

7 When animals had no or very little role in myth, ritual, or literature, comic playwrights would have been relying more on their direct observation of the animals' behavior in nature – or their anecdotal impressions.

Interestingly the Getty Birds, which are among the very, very few performing animals to be depicted in the late fifth century, are also domesticated animals: cocks.

8 Discussed in Chapter 3.

9 Reckford 1987, 236.

10 Bowie 1993, 97.

11 On wasps, consult Keller 1913, 431–35; *RE* s.v. "Wespe"; Davies and Kathirithamby 1986, 75–83.

12 Aristotle, *HA* 554b22–25, 622b21 and 628a12–24, and Pliny, *NH* 11.71ff. It was also thought that wasps bred in the carcasses of horses (Aelian, *NA* 1.28; further refs. at Page 1981, 22).

13 Aelian, *NA* 5.15–16. For further examples of the wasp's irascibility, see Davies and Kathirithamby 1986, 75–76.

14 The image is a *hapax* usage, notes Taillardat 1965, 460.

15 See Davies 1990, who suggested that the substitution of the donkey for the ram is inspired by a black-figure portrayal of the Return of Hephaestus in which a satyr rides underneath the donkey.

16 Though one son's preference for figs – like a fig-wasp's? – is curious; see below on Magnes' play.

17 The evidence for members of the chorus wearing a *phallos* in Old Comedy is weak (as discussed in Chapter 1), but in *Wasps* they make unmistakable allusions to their virility at lines 1062 and 1066 – allusions that make best sense if they wore a visible *phallos* that would, like the *phalloi* of actors, dangle in front. The descriptions of their "stinger" (*kentron*), however, are precise enough to warrant the assumption of a specific, separate wasp "stinger" as part of the costume. It evidently projected from the rear: see ὀσφύος at 225, and at 1075 members of the chorus speak of themselves as "we who have this kind of rump (ὀρροπύγιον)," which must refer to a stinger, since its natural position is behind, not in front. (The ὀρροπύγιον is certainly something on the posterior; cf. Henderson 1975, 201, §448.) It may also have had a sharp point.

It seems easiest to assume that there were two separate appendages. Of course it is possible there was a single appendage that could swing back and forth, serving both purposes (cf. *Thesmo.* 643–54, where the *phallos* can evidently be tucked between the legs).

What seems to me less likely, however, is the suggestion that what were called *kentra* were simply *phalloi* being manipulated as wasp stingers (Newiger 1957, 79–80). If so, the verb ἐντατέον ("must be braced, 408"; see Sommerstein 2001, 266, for the reading), from ἐντείνω, used by Aristotle of the *phallos* (*Probl.* 4.22), would have had a sexual connotation when used of the stinger at 408; furthermore, Philocleon would be using the language of pederasty when he tells the chorus to sting their enemies in the anus (πρωκτός, 431).

Nevertheless something that was not simply a *phallos* but designed to look like a stinger, projecting from the rear, was part of the costume (Sifakis 1971, 127 n. 9). Moreover, whatever the chorus had is something that men like Bdelycleon, Xanthias, and even Philocleon lacked (MacDowell 1971, 11 nn. 2 & 3) – and it is far more certain that actors in comedy had a *phallos* than did choral members. Sommerstein 1983, 183, suggested that having a stinger that could protrude forward ("extend stings!" 423) would make it easier for the chorus to attack, though a stinger in the rear might offer the comic potential of a quick, backward sprint-and-stab maneuver.

Consult Reckford 1987, 236 and 238 on the sexual nature of the wasps' sting and its role in compensating for lost potency.

18 If the wasp-jurors were "wasp-waisted," they would have had tightly cinched mid-sections. At *Plutus* 561 Penia ("Poverty") has been explaining that she produces "lean, wasplike" men for Athens; Chremylus takes it that the "leanness" is due to starvation, but it could also refer to their segmented bodies.

19 Stripes: MacDowell 1971, 11. Mask: Newiger 1957, 79; Dearden 1976, 120. Little can be said about their dance, though we might note that when they enter they are stumbling across the stage and do so not in trochaic tetrameters but in iambic tetrameters, a slower, more plodding meter; see MacDowell 1971, 24, and 162. They conduct their skirmishing in trochaic tetrameters, which are livelier but have reduced metra and give the impression that they are getting out of breath: MacDowell 1971, 28–29, and 190; Zimmermann 1984, 93–100. Any concerns about their nimbleness might be allayed at the end, where they claim that this is the first comedy to end with a dancing chorus (1537).

20 Greek text as in MacDowell 1971.

21 Wasps drink "thyme" (θύμος) but the Athenians drink "spirit" (θυμός). They are here reminiscing about their battles with the Persians in 490 and 480 B.C.

22 *Oxy-* here has a "literal and metaphorical sense" (MacDowell 971, 190), both "quick" and "sharp."

23 Of twenty-eight instances of these two words in the works of Aristophanes, thirteen are in *Wasps*: Konstan 1995, 19.

24 In the final scene of the play, however, their differences are set aside as Philocleon and the chorus appear to join in a dance. His mania for jury-duty cured, he is now a rejuvenated performer, suggested Slater 1996, 49.

25 Edmunds 1987 on the invocation of the Persian Wars in the *Knights*.

26 Perhaps the chorus have become *too* uncritical now and are as blindly devoted to Bdelycleon as they were to Philocleon; if so, they are not wasps but sheep, which is what the Athenian people had been compared to earlier (32), suggested Sommerstein 1983, 244. Note, further, that in Bdelycleon's view one point in favor of the dog on trial was that it took care of sheep (955).

27 It is attractive to identify the *enkentrides* of *Wasps* 427 with the stylus used on the wax tablet for the conviction of defendants, but there is no contemporary evidence for this meaning, noted MacDowell 1971, 192. Philocleon used his fingernail anyway (107).

28 Sommerstein 1983, 169–70; Beta 2004, 68 n. 114.

29 Bowie 1993, 97. Cf. Schmid 1946, 271 and Borthwick 1990.

30 He is likened, explicitly or implicitly, to a monster (4), limpet (105), honey bee (107 and 366) and bumble bee (107 – βομβουλιός, a solitary [μοναδικός], non-social species of the bee, says Aristotle, *HA* 623b13), jack-daw (129), mouse (140), foal (189), sparrow (207), gnat (352), ferret (363),

and rooster (794). See especially Whitman 1964, 162–65 and Silk 2000, 252–55.

31 Bowie 1993, 78–98.

32 The fig is a recurrent item in the agricultural fantasies of the *Peace* (575, 1145, 1249, 1324), and at 1359 it seems to be part of a sexual double-entendre; see Olson 1998, 191, on *Peace* 558–59.

33 Text as in Sommerstein 1981.

34 Leo 1878, 139; *RE*, s.v. "Magnes."

35 Aristotle, *Rhetoric* 3.1.3 (1403b23) reports that the earliest tragic poets acted in their plays; for early comic actors, see Ghiron-Bistagne 1976, 136–38. We have the terracotta statuette of an actor with a frog mask, in Reggio Calabria: Todisco 2002, 123 and pl. XVIII.3; see Appendix B below.

36 Spyropoulos 1988, 192–94; Slater 2002, 31. However, Sommerstein 2001, 244, pointed out that *Frogs* 13–15 ascribes to playwrights actions that were surely performed by actors.

37 Although this clearly does not apply to dyeing one's face in frog color.

38 Herodotus 1.193.4–5, although he mistakenly applies the procedure to Babylonian dates. Other ancient explanations are found in Aristotle, *HA* 557b25–30, and Theophrastus, *HP* 2.8.1; for full accounts see Georgi 1982; Davies and Kathirithamby 1986, 81–82.

39 Kock, Com. Adesp. 12; at *PCG* VIII.506 it is not accepted as comic but ascribed to Mac. Prov. VI.74. On the obscene meaning see Henderson 1975, 118 and 216–17.

40 One might speculate that a ritual occasion for figs was invoked. Fig fertilization took place in mid-May and was celebrated at Athens in the Thargelia when scapegoats (*pharmakoi*) wearing "male" and white "female" figs were beaten with fig branches; their expulsion eliminated evil from the ripening of crops. Hipponax frr. 5–10 West gives some details from Colophon; for further see Deubner 1932, 179–98; Parke 1977, 146–47; Simon 1983, 77. The fig, and possibly the fig-wasp, may thus have had an important symbolic role in notions of agricultural fertility at Athens, but nothing indicates that the fig-wasp had any part in the Thargelia.

41 Useful collections of information on the bee include Bodson 1978, 20–43; Davies and Kathirithamby 1986, 47–75.

42 Discussion in Bodson 1978, 25–43. On the "bee maidens" of the *Homeric Hymn to Hermes* 552–56, see Larson 1995.

43 *Frogs* 1274 (= Aeschylus fr. 87); Bodson 1978, 47–43; Dover 1993, 346–47.

44 Mnaseas, a mythographer of the third century B.C., fr. 5 Müller, *FHG* III, p. 150 (= Schol. on Pindar, Pythian 4.104); see Bodson 1978, 32–33.

45 A gem depicts a woman-headed insect who is holding a lyre; the body is either that of a bee or cicada: Ransome 1937, 103. Philostratus (*Imagines* 2.8.6) claimed that the Muses assumed the appearance of bees when guiding the Athenians to Ionia. See *LIMC* II (1981), s.v. "Artemis" no. 71 for "la déesse-abeille."

46 Bacchylides 10.10; Pindar, *Pythian* 10.54; Aristophanes, *Birds* 748–51; Plato, *Ion* 533e. Davies and Kathirithamby 1986, 70–72, who cite Waszink 1974.

47 Schmid 1946, 172 n. 9.

48 Aristotle, *HA* 488a10. On the ant, consult Keller 1913, 416–21; Davies and Kathirithamby 1986.

49 Fr. 155 K-A. On musical sinuosities in contemporary music, see Borthwick 1968, 69–73. The dithyrambist Philoxenus was nicknamed "Myrmex" (*Suda* s.v. "Philoxenus").

50 Hesiod, *Works and Days* 778 and West 1978, 355.

51 Forbes Irving 1990, 315.

52 Eubulus fr. 19 K-A; Plato, *Rep.* 5.450b.

53 Hesiod fr. 205 MW; cf. Schol. *Iliad* 1.180; in Ovid's version Aegina was devastated by a plague and then repopulated by men created from ants: *Met.* 7.614–60.

54 Aeacus may have come originally from Thessaly; moreover, another etymology had it that Zeus transformed himself into an ant and fathered Myrmidon, the ancestor of the Myrmidons: *RE*, s.v. "Myrmidones."

55 Schmid 1946, 104–05; these may also be the words of the chorus, threatening the audience if they do not grant a victory, thought Zielinski 1931, 69, though Whittaker 1935, 183–84, believed it was a *pnigos* spoken before the entire chorus had entered from the *parodos*, when the *myrmekanthropoi* were still in the first stages of creation.

56 Schmid 1946, 105, saw a possible Pythagorean prohibition here, and fr. 117 anthropomorphizes fish in that one of them can communicate. Alternatively it may reflect boredom with a fish diet during the flood: Norwood 1931, 161.

57 Anon. *De Com.* 9 p. 7 Koster (= *PCG* VII 102, Pherekrates T 2a).

58 Zielinski 1931, 68–9, n. 24, objected that this sort of joining of myths was unprecedented. Henderson 2000, 136, notes that *Ant-Men* would be Pherecrates' only mythical comedy, and that "the fragments suggest something more fantastical than mythical."

59 Whittaker 1935, 182; Norwood 1931, 161, who speculates that fr. 122 refers to Pyrrha on her arrival at Aegina.

60 Dover 1966, 41.

61 For example, Herodotus 3.108.

62 *Homeric Hymn to Aphrodite* 4.

63 Plato, *Symposium* 188b.

64 Aristotle, *Politics* 1253a29.

65 Carnivores: Plato, *Menexenus* 237d. *Theria* include the stag (*Odyssey* 10.171), the spider's prey (Aristotle, *HA* 623a27), sharks (Herodotus 6.44); θῆρες in epic and drama include especially the lion (*Iliad* 15.586 etc.), wild boar (Soph. *Trach.* 1097), Cerberus (Soph. *OC* 1569), hind (Soph. *Electra* 572), vermin killed by birds (Aristophanes *Birds* 1064).

66 *Knights* 273. An exception: Antiphon the Sophist speaks of human beings as the most divine of all *theria* (*Peri homonoias* DK 87 B48).

67 Oddly, Athenaeus says that the speaker of fr. 17 spoke in opposition to the speaker of fr. 16. This is not a conclusion one would draw from the fragments themselves. Although Athenaeus may have known more about the context than we do, it is also possible that he was himself misled by earlier excerpters: Nesselrath 1990, 65–79. Carrière 1979, 258–59, suggested that the speakers of frs. 16 and 17 were the same person, stressing food in one passage and hot baths in another. See also Ceccarelli 2000, 454, and Ruffell 2000, 481.

68 Because these animals are obviously sources of food, Zielinski 1931, 32, suggested the *theria* of the play were bulls. If one had to choose, however, it seems more likely that *theria* would be wild, hunted animals than domesticated ones.

69 The disappearance of slavery was a theme found elsewhere in comedy and myth. Pherecrates' *Agrioi* fr. 10 K-A; Aristophanes, *Eccl.* 651, by contrast, creates a utopia that is dependent on slave labor. For further discussion see Carrière 1979, 258–59, and Ruffell 2000, 485. Farioli 1999, 21–27 stressed the imperialism of the beasts. Schmid 1946, 91, thought the fragments were about the troublesome need for domestic servants and a solution conceived of by a comic playwright in an age of sophistic suggestions for improvement of the world. Thus it is not simply a mythical pattern.

70 Deubner 1932, 152–54; Parke 1977, 29–30. Burkert 1985, 231–32, sees a link between the festival of Kronos and a reversion to a time when oppression and labor did not yet hold sway.

71 Meineke thought that one of the speakers was recommending a "life in accordance with the laws of nature" ("vitam . . . legibus naturae convenientem," cited in *PCG* IV.91).

72 Ceccarelli 2000, 455 n. 10, suggested that fr. 19 K-A ("keep your hands off us") was a conscious echo of Empedocles DK 31 B141.

73 On the Pythagorean prohibition against eating fish, see Diogenes Laertius 8.1.34; Plutarch, *Moralia* 728d–30f.

74 Carrière 1979, 258.

75 Wilkins 2000b, 347–48, comments that this play appears to have opened up the question of a fundamental re-ordering of society in a way that even *Birds* did not. It may be worth recording here that Cobet 1840, 191, ingeniously tried to make the *Heortai* of Plato comicus, of ca. 413 B.C., into an animal comedy along the lines of the *Beasts* by emending a few key pronouns. Fr. 27 K-A reads: "In the future, we shouldn't (ἔδει ἡμᾶς) kill any four-footed creatures except for pigs"; Cobet suggested ἔδει ὑμᾶς, "you shouldn't kill," thus spoken by animals who attacked the cruelty of human beings. Cobet pointed to other fragments (e.g., frs. 34 and 36 K-A) that would make sense in this light. The chorus was composed of (personified) festivals of Athens, so these would be actors, not a chorus, playing the parts of animals. The suggestion was rejected by Kaibel (see on Plato fr. 34 K-A) but accepted by Giannini 1959, 200–01. The protest against the eating of animals would make sense coming from animals, but it also makes sense coming from a

Pythagorean or from any number of others, and we have no idea what the context is.

76 Wilkins 2000b, 346, suggested that fish and human beings found common enemies in Melanthius and the fishmonger, for they were hated by the fish for selling and consuming and hated by people because of their "implicitly anti-democratic sympathies," which put their interests ahead of the common good of the Athenians. Davidson 1997, 11–35, elaborated on the degree to which fish were considered a delicacy in classical Athens.

77 Wilkins 2000b, 303.

78 Thus Plato, *Timaeus* 92b, and even Plutarch, *Moralia* 975b, although the dolphin generally escaped such prejudices: Bodson 1978, 53–57. We do not know what the costumes would have looked like, but one possible model is the amphora in Rome on which are depicted "fish-men" who have fish-fins attached to their otherwise human bodies (see Appendix B). Radermacher 1921, 5–7, cites, as an example of the sort of *komos* that led to comedy, the use of fish in a *komos* conducted by young men of Naxos (Aristotle fr. 558 Rose); he compares such improvisations with Archippus' comedy, but there is not enough evidence to suggest any relationship. Lawler 1941 recorded fish dances and dance movements known in the ancient world and found that such dances were often important in cults of Artemis (though none bear specifically on Archippus' *Fishes*). For Artemis and evidence for sacred fish, see Bodson 1978, 45–57.

79 Kaibel 1889, 50.

80 Parallels are to be found in Eupolis, fr. 401 K-A (= Schol. *Knights* 941a), where the scholiast says that Eupolis used prose. Cf. *Birds* 864–88, 1035–59 passim, 1661–66; *Ach.* 43, 61, 237, 241; *Thesmo.* 295–311. On prose in poetry see Kassel 1981, 5 and 21.

81 There may also be proper names (Thalassa, Porphyra) alluded to in fr. 25: thus Meineke 1840 (vol. II), 207.

82 Unless there was meant to be a pun on κλεῖδες, a word for the roast shoulder bones of the tunny fish: cf. Aristophon fr. 7.2 K-A. One might note, however, that not all of the names correspond *exactly* to the names of the fish. The red mullet, for example, is the τρίγλη, or in diminutive either τριγλίς or τριγλίον; our fragment has τριγλίαι as if from τριγλία. Moreover we know of prostitutes with names like "Sand-smelt," "Red mullet," and "Cuttlefish": Davidson 1997, 10.

83 Wilkins 2000b, 346.

84 Schmid 1946, 156–57.

85 Kaibel 1889, 50, suggested that it was intentionally ambiguous.

86 Schmid 1946, 156–57; for parallels between *Birds* and *Fishes*, see also Csapo 1994, 40–41. Farioli 1999 saw the animal comedies as pessimistic reflections of contemporary fifth-century violence.

87 Athenaeus 287a; the voice of the *boax* is also cited in Pherecrates, *Myrmekanthropoi* fr. 117 K-A (see above); Thompson 1947, 36.

88 Athenaeus 284c; Thompson 1947, 293–4. The reference to *galeoi* of fr. 15 may allude to the Galeoi, priests in Sicily: Bodson 1978, 65–66.

89 The *editio princeps* is Willis 1991. The various fish called the *silouros* are discussed in Thompson 1947, 43–48 and 233–37; we do not know which one is intended here, but Willis suggested that it is the sheatfish or European catfish (*Silurus glanis*), a remarkably large creature.

90 Willis 1991, 335.

91 This is not to deny that these, or other, puns are present. The *Comoedia Dukiana* exploits terms "to capitalize (*ad nauseam*) on the comic conceit of fish anthropomorphized and socially organized in a *polis*": Csapo 1994, 43–44.

92 Willis 1991, 337; the case for Archippus is argued in detail by Csapo 1994.

93 *PCG* 8.477. Notes Willis 1991, 352: "The finger-sucking child Harpochrates...seems not to be mentioned by name in extant Greek sources before Eudoxus of Cnidus (fr. 292.23 Lass.), the fourth-century B.C. astronomer." Austin, noting that Cratinus fr. 336 would be a fitting introduction to the *Comoedia Dukiana*, suggests that it belongs to the *Gigantes* of Cratinus Junior: Willis 1991, 336.

94 Or, the sheat may be suffering the consequences of having abandoned itself to pleasure: thus Parsons in Willis 1991, 342.

95 Consult: Keller 1909, 296–309; *RE* s.v. "Ziege."

96 *Odyssey* 14.530; *Works and Days* 516; Theognis 55–56.

97 The sacrifice of a goat (*tragos*) on the occasion of the city-foundation at *Birds* 902, 959, 1056–57, has a comic ring to it: one would expect, perhaps, a bull: see Dunbar 1995, 506, on *Birds* 856.

98 Diodorus 1.88.1 describes their "great propensity for copulation"; on the application of goat features to Pan see *RE* s.v. "Phallos" 1698.

99 Cf. Pausanias 7.26.3 on the temple at Aigeira, which was dedicated to Artemis where a goat sat down: Burkert 1985, 151.

100 Xenophon, *Lac. Pol.* 13.8; *Hell.* 4.2.20.

101 Chapter 1, n. 72.

102 Zenobius Athous 1.8 p. 350 Miller; Parke 1977, 138 (citing Suda, Ἔμβαρος; App. Prov. 2,54; Eust. *Il.* 268, 24ff.); Burkert 1985, 263.

103 Pausanias 9.8.2 and 2.35.1. There really is no association of the goat with Dionysiac cult in Eupolis' comedy. The reference to a "priest of Dionysus" in fr. 20 is meaningless without a context. Dionysus is addressed in fr. 6 K-A (= Athenaeus 426e), but the context is a discussion of mixing wine and water, and "Dionysus" may be less the god than the wine.

104 See Burkert 1966, 89–102: "The memory of sacrifice stands at the center of the Dionysiac performance" (p. 102); see also Winkler 1990, 58–62 for a conjecture about the relevance of goats to tragedy.

105 The τράγος is always the male goat; αἴξ is usually feminine. Their gender in Eupolis' comedy is guaranteed by the feminine participles in fr. 13.2 and

fr. 24 K-A; see Dover 2000, xvii, and Storey 2003, 68. Storey 2003, 305–06, suggests that the chorus of *Nanny-Goats* may have been costumed as Pans, which were of course human-goat hybrid creatures.

106 Of course if Plutarch had found the passage already excerpted and did not have the entire play, he would not have known the context of these lines; see Teodorson 1990, *ad loc.*

107 Wilkins 2000b, 348.

108 Schmid 1946, 117–18.

109 Indeed, real goats refuse to eat several plants on the list; Eupolis may have chosen the words for sound effects, suggested Rackham 2000. For the purposes of the play, however, we are evidently meant to think they are all delectable.

110 Four of the items in their list (fragrant wild sage, tree medick, asphodel, mullein) are also cited in Cratinus fr. 363 as the products of spontaneous (αὐτομάτη) generation, so presumably these foods were thought of as Golden Age produce.

111 Pherecrates frr. 13 and 14 K-A; see Schmid 1946, 117–18; Ceccarelli 2000, 458.

112 Hence animal choruses do not generally extol the creations of nature but are more interested in the creations of human beings or, at least, the use human beings put to natural products.

113 One might adduce the suggestive discussion of the *Poleis* of Eupolis in Rosen 1997; in that comedy the fact that the chorus-members were female is shown to be significant, but nothing else in the fragments of *Goats* tells us how gender may have figured in this play. The only other demonstrably female animal chorus is the *Bees* or *Melittai* of Diocles, for which we have no fragments. One could say here that the realms of the "other" (animal, woman) converge, yet what may be more notable is how rare this is. The notion that animals, and by extension the world of nature, have their autonomous qualities is a theme in New Comedy.

114 Lawler 1964, 70 and 78–79, speculated that "the lively, skipping, sportive actions of the animal itself must naturally have invited imitation in the dance." Perhaps the goats of Eupolis' comedy followed suit. Possibly the chorus sounded like goats, though goats' voices were thought to be similar to the thin, bleating voices of epileptics: Plutarch, *Moralia* 290a; Hippocrates, *Sacred Disease* 4.21.

115 The interesting parallels are developed in Storey 2003, 69–71, who suggested that the play may have capitalized on the comic theme of a rustic farmer who has settled in the city.

116 Borthwick 1970, 330–31.

117 Bergk 1838, 334; cf. discussion of Eupolis fr. 326 K-A in *PCG* V.485.

118 Dover 2000, xvii.

119 Perhaps Magnes' birds, like the birds on that vase, were cocks and had traits of satyrs.

120 Ovid, *Met.* 6.93–97, tells of Antigone, daughter of Laomedon, who is turned into a white stork for having tried to compete with Juno. See Forbes Irving 1990, 225.

121 *Birds* 1139.

122 *Kleine Pauly*, s.v. "Storch"; Dunbar 1995, 656–57.

123 *NA* 8.20; Aelian also stressed that the stork's care for its parent was not by a law of man but by nature (3.23). Scholia on *Birds* 1355 mention depictions of Storks on scepters as symbols of justice. In fable it cares for its father (Babrius 13); an adulterous storch is punished (Perry 713).

124 Proposed by Süvern 1827, 83, and followed by many since, for example, Schmid 1946, 215.

125 The use of ἀπεσημηνάμην in fr. 447 finds a parallel in Xenophon, *Hellenica* 2.3.21, where it is used of confiscation of property by the Thirty.

126 Demianczuk, cited in *PCG* III.2.240, on fr. 445.

127 For the chief sources and variants of the myth see Forbes Irving 1990, 248–49, and discussion, 99–107; Burkert 1983, 179–85; for the treatment of the myth in Sophocles and Aristophanes, consult Dobrov 2001, 105–32. Barker 2004 suggests that the song of the nightingale in the *Birds* was in fact an *aulos* playing disconcerting "New Music" and that an *auletris* appeared instead of the expected female bird figure.

128 Horace wrote that Thespis, who was credited with the invention of tragedy, had smeared his face with wine-lees and that Aeschylus had invented the mask (*Ars Poetica* 275–80); the *Suda* reported that Thespis disguised his face with white lead when acting. Masks were attested on vase-painting for tragedy only by 470–460 B.C.: Pickard-Cambridge 1968, 180 (with fig. 32), 190 and 191.

129 Hoffmann 1973 suggested that three molded frogs that served as feet for a bowl by Sotades of ca. 450 B.C. constitute a small chorus and illustrate the same interest we see in comedy.

130 Ovid, *Met.* 15.375; Pliny, *NH* 32.42.122.

131 Allison 1983, 16.

132 Noise: Aristophanes, *Frogs* 226–27; *Batrachomyomachia* 187–92. Magic and forecasts: ps.-Theophrastus, *sign. temp.* 15; Aratus 946; Aristotle, *Probl.* 862a10–16; Virgil, *Georgics* 1.378.

133 Bodson 1978, 59–61. The association that the frogs in the *Frogs* claim to have with Dionysus seems not to be attested anywhere else; moreover, it consists largely of the fact that, as marsh-dwellers, they would have been present at the sanctuary of Dionysus "in the Marshes" at Athens.

134 Ovid, *Met.* 6.317–81. The myth may be traced back to the *Lykiaka* of Menecrates of Xanthos, of the fourth century B.C. (*FGrH* 769 F2), see Forbes Irving 1990, 313–14.

135 Ovid, *Met.* 15.375. The view that they are "chthonic" – that is, closely bound up with divinities beneath the earth (for which see Deonna 1951 and Bodson

1978, 59–61) – is not well supported by evidence from classical Greece, as noted by Bowie 1993, 235 n. 42. The association of frogs and the underworld was, however, taken to greater lengths in Celtic France: remains of a chariot buried at Châlon-sur-Marne, as part of a ritual burial offering, contained a hundred frogs in a pot. "The amphibious nature of these beasts may have endowed them with a special symbolism associated with life and death": Green 1992, 125.

136 They are water animals in Aristotle, *HA* 487a28. As an oviparous quadruped the frog shares the company of the tortoise: *HA* 511a1.

137 In invoking the *komos* of Chytroi (*Frogs* 218), the second day of the Anthesteria, the frogs may also be invoking "a liminal time of transition between one ceremony and another, and between the death-shadowed second day of the Choes and the life-celebrating Chytroi": Reckford 1987, 412. Bodson 1978, 61, suggests that the frogs, in conjunction with the children of Leto, symbolize the power of the fertility of the goddesses.

138 Russo 1994, 212, pointed out that the title *Mustai* ("Initiates") might be more descriptive for this play, but that Phrynichus had just used that title in 407 B.C. Perhaps the audience of the *Frogs* would have felt it to be the "same" chorus, transformed from frogs into holy Initiates, mirroring a dialectic between the physical and spiritual, suggests Hubbard 1991, 202. On the phenomenon of the secondary chorus see Dover 1993, 55, and Wilson 2000, 343 n. 169.

139 Dover 1993, 219, points out that "Brekekekex koax koax" matches the rhythm of the croak of the Marsh Frog (*rana ridibunda*), but that the consonants (especially the initial βρ- and final -ξ) are conventional ways of indicating quasi-verbal sounds. "Initial βρ- appears in many Greek words denoting the production of sound, e.g. βρέμειν, βρυχᾶσθαι," etc.; the final -ξ resembles the bird sound (-τοροτίξ) of *Birds* 260. (We might add to this the fish sound of the βόαξ in Pherecrates' *Ant-men*, fr. 117 K-A). The actual sound of frogs would, therefore, be understood to be: "ekekeke koak koak" (see also Dover 1968, 151, on *Clouds* 390). But for an ear-witness account of two frog choruses, one chanting βρεκεκεκέξ and the other κοάξ κοάξ, in antiphonal response, see Wansbrough 1993. Consult also Baldwin 1988.

140 *Frogs* Σ^VE 209. For an articulate defense of the position that the frogs are invisible, see Allison 1983.

141 Stanford 1958, 95.

142 Allison 1983, 12–13, suggested that in view of the fact that Magnes and Callias had produced frog comedies, Aristophanes, never one to be thought old-fashioned, might just have made his chorus invisible for the sake of innovation. This could be right, but since we really know nothing about the animal choruses of Magnes and Callias, we are not in a position to say anything about Aristophanes' innovations.

143 If anything off stage is audible it would be a chorus of twenty four, suggests Allison; Dover 1993, 57, offers counter-examples; cf. MacDowell 1972, 4.

Sifakis 1971, 94, reminds us that dialogue would be difficult with off-stage frogs.

144 Marshall 1996.

145 Allison 1983, 15. The chorus of initiates explicitly refers to the "cheapness" (*euteleia*) of their costumes at *Frogs* 404–08; further discussion in Dover 1993, 62–63 and Sommerstein 1996,192.

146 There was no need for two separate sets of twenty-four choristers; the chorus would have had time to exit, change out of frog costumes, and return as initiates, suggests MacDowell 1972.

147 Dover 1993, 57; Wilson 2000, 343 n. 169, points out that the evidence for the *synchoregia* is for the Dionysia but that the *Frogs* was performed at the Lenaea.

148 Text and colometry as in Dover 1993.

149 For the Anthesteria see Deubner 1932, 93–123, and Parke 1977, 107–20. Lada-Richards 1999, 126–28, suggested that the evening of the Choes is intended. On the location of the sanctuary of Dionysus in the Marshes, see Hooker 1960 and Slater 1986.

150 Sommerstein 1996, 177–8 on 227.

151 Silk 2000, 190–95, which revises and supersedes Silk 1980, 136–37.

152 Defradas 1969, pointing, for example, to the preposterous effect of the long compound word πομφολυφοπαφλάσμασιν (249).

153 Demand 1970. On the *Muses* of Phrynichus see Harvey 2000.

154 Wills 1969, who also gave a lucid summary of earlier scholarship, especially on the question of the "basis" of the competition (volume, rhythm, violence, or beauty?). I am inclined to agree with Sommerstein 1996, 176, that it begins when Dionysus is challenged to match their tempo (this seems to me the best way of understanding Charon's remark at 205 that the frogs will make it easy for Dionysus to row) but ends when Dionysus shouts them down and they lose their voice. MacDowell, too, pointed to the "persistence" of frogs, who can croak throughout the night (*Batrachomyomachia* 187–92).

155 Dover 1993, 56 n. 2. Their lyrics may not be as noble as those of Pindar, but, as Campbell noted, "For the most part the Frogs' language is elevated: it is Dionysus who lowers the tone" (Campbell 1984).

156 Some scholars have thought the frogs were related to Apollo the prophet, but as Bodson 1978, 60, has pointed out, this passage shows that the more important connection is with Apollo the musician.

157 Dover 1993, 225: in the *Homeric Hymn to Hermes* 47, the god used δόνακες καλάμοιο, "stalks of reed," in creating his lyre; thus the *donax* evidently refers to the stalk and the *kalamos* to the plant as a whole.

158 On the comic effect of the incongruity, see Campbell 1984.

159 Habash 2002, 6. Dionysus and the frogs are probably singing in unison at 250, 256, and 260: thus Sommerstein 1996, 178. Dover has them croak in alternation.

160 Saïd 1988, 82: Dionysus in the *Frogs* is more animal-like than the animals. See also Segal 1986.

161 Lada-Richards 1999, 17–44.

162 Lada-Richards 1999, 118–19.

163 Cf. *Ach.* 6–8, 299–302; Sommerstein 1981, 3–4.

164 On the politics of this comedy, see Edmunds 1987.

165 In 425 B.C. two hundred cavalry, under Nicias, helped secure a victory in an Athenian landing on Corinthian territory; see Thucydides 4.24–44. On the intertwining of military *syssition* and social *symposion* in classical Athens, see Steiner 2002, esp. 372–73 on the Hippeis.

166 Those inclined to accept the presence of horses (or men costumed as such) include: Zielinski 1931; Poppelreuter 1893; Schmid 1946, 235; Webster in Pickard-Cambridge 1962, 154; Sifakis 1971, 99–100. Sommerstein 1981, 4, noting the lack of a demonstrative pronoun in line 595, thought none was onstage. Bieber 1961, 37, suggested that one half of the chorus was mounted on the other.

167 Text as in Sommerstein 1981.

168 An ally of Cleon, hence someone pursued by the Knights.

169 The horses appear to be assimilated to sailors or hoplites; rather than operate by stealth and manoeuvre they work cooperatively – rowing together and digging in. Aristophanes may have wanted to de-emphasize cavalry techniques that were exclusively aristocratic in order to show that there was common ground with the *demos*. For such unifying imagery in the play, see Edmunds 1987.

170 At *Knights* 604 it is the horses, not the riders (*pace* Bowie 1993, 57), who are "younger."

171 Bowie 1993, 52–58. He also suggests that if they were shown to be riding a horse, they might evoke centaurs, creatures spanning the divide between nature and culture.

172 Nesselrath 1990, 327.

173 Ceccarelli 2000, 467, n. 31. Goossens 1935, 413, pointed to Aristophanes' *Storks* and Cratinus' *Cheirones* as parallels for a fantastic chorus interested in observance of a moral order.

174 This is not to say that every animal noise was pleasant: buzzing wasps were like annoying "bumble-bee pipers" (*Ach.* 864–66), the crow was thought to be raucous (*Birds* 609), the noises of the dolphin seemed shrill to Aristotle, (*HA* 535b33–536a4), goats sounded like epileptics (Hippocrates, *Sacred Disease* 4.21), and frogs kept people awake (*Frogs* 226–27).

175 Perhaps this comedy was an early one of Magnes and did not yet reflect any trend toward socializing animals.

176 Wilkins 2000b, 347–48.

177 Schmid 1946, 104–05.

178 Several of these animals have chthonic associations – frogs were associated with the underworld (Bodson 1978, 59), dolphins were known to have transported the body of dead youths, cocks appeared on funerary stele, and the nightingale mourned for her dead son – yet the evidence that these associations were at all common in the fifth century B.C. is slender.

179 Edwards 2002, 40–43.

180 Compare Csapo 2003, 95, on the New Music of the late fifth century. Steinhart 2004, 22, raises the possibility that late-fifth-century animal choruses were archaizing.

5. ARISTOPHANES' *BIRDS* AND THE RISE OF CIVILIZATION

1 This approach to the comedy has never been explored in detail, though it has been suggested: de Carli 1971, 50–54; Hubbard 1991, 163 n. 21; Romer 1997, 51.

2 Newiger 1975, 275.

3 *Prom.* 452. The *Homeric Hymn* 20 (to Hephaestus, ca. 400 B.C.) speaks of human beings "dwelling in caves in mountains, like wild beasts" (4).

4 The cohesion reminds us of Democritus, who saw creatures associating with their own kind (DK 68 B164); nature and culture thus blend, suggested Piette 1987, 7. This may be echoed in Lucretius' account of early men wandering in groups (*volgivago*, 5.932), albeit like animals.

5 A related notion is that Eden could be found in a distant place, and *Birds* 145 refers to the "Red Sea," alluding to the ends of the earth where there is a land of perfect happiness. Dunbar 1995, 180, notes that the recent publication of Herodotus' *Histories* would have strengthened such impressions.

6 This resembles the peaceful, self-sufficient existence of *Laws* 679a. Compare also the self-sufficiency of Dicaearchus, for whom nature is on the side of the Golden Race: Dicaearchus frr. 47–66 Wehrli; Guthrie 1957, 74–76.

7 Pozzi 1991, 150 n. 77 (also Pozzi 1985/86); Whitman 1964, 167, 176–78, sees the birds in a "happy innocence" and describes the song of the nightingale as "pastoral." Moulton 1981, 101, in his discussion of the extensive pastoral elements in *Peace*, where the "dear Seasons" are invoked (ˏὯραι φίλαι, 1168), recognized a pastoral tendency in the *Birds*, but (with Arrowsmith 1973) believed that the "pastoral fantasy of the *Birds* . . . though it be adorned with shimmering lyrics . . . is swiftly transformed into Peisetaerus' ambiguous 'utopia.'"

8 Dunbar 1995, 185, notes that a likely influence here is the idea of gardens as the scene of many matings in myth and legend.

9 Auger 1979, 82.

10 On *Birds* and *Philoctetes* see Craik 1990; on the *Birds* set see Dunbar 1995, 16–19.

11 De Carli 1971, 50, suggested that their vulnerability was already implicit in the fact that they had "gaping mouths" (165).

12 Dunbar 1995, 277–78, pointed to the comic incongruity in the fact that birds are hardly natural prey for wolves!

13 The three songs cited by Pozzi were all sung *before* the city was completed.

14 Thus the products of "nature" and of "culture" are merged; a part of the social order is embedded in nature. With their new wings the men will put *physis* to work to help *nomos*.

15 *Birds* 369–74; Dunbar 1995, 649.

16 Similarly at 316 Tereus had invoked both justice (δίκαιον) and self-interest (ὠφελήσιμον) among other reasons for listening to the men. The argument smacks of contemporary sophists.

17 Perhaps foreshadowing the use of ἀθροίζεσθαι in descriptions of human gathering in Plato's *Prot.* 322b6, Polybius 6.5.7, and Diodorus 1.8.2.

18 Konstan 1990b, 195 and 200. Turato 1971/72, 119–23, distinguishes an Edenic world of nature, celebrated primarily in the lyric parts of the two parabases, from a society of birds that is governed by ancestral laws (θεσμοὺς ἀρχαίους, *Birds* 331), founded on concord (ὁμόφρονας λόγους, 631), and respecting the sanctity of oaths (332, 461), trust (456), and concern for the common good (457). This society strives to blend both *nomos* and *physis*, all the while obeying the ancestral laws, proposes Turato. Dunbar 1995, 264, suggests that the ὅρκος ὀρνίθων might well suggest the ephebic oath of loyalty (Tod 1947, ii no. 204), which, though of the fourth century, has linguistic features from earlier; cf. Siewert 1977, 102–11. The family plays virtually no role in the *Birds*. Diodorus (and thus, perhaps, also Democritus) had stressed the importance of larger social groups (*systemata*) but not the family, whereas Plato, had seen the family as a more important kernel. See Cole 1967, 107, 112–20.

19 Their harmony and sharing is brought out by the large number of συν-compounds that they use, observed Perkell 1993, 7.

20 Reckford 1987, 333, wrote of the "disruption of the garden by the machine"; there were pastoral passages, but was it ever such a garden? Indeed, the military language (e.g. ταξίαρχος, 353; the chorus leader calls them "hoplites" at 402, as does Peisetaerus at 448) hints at a pre-existing, non-Edenic social organization.

21 The notion of an earlier bird order is reinforced by the pattern of the Hesiodic succession myth that underlies the play: Hofmann 1976, 85–90 and 177–96. Peisetaerus also "proves" the birds' earlier origins by citing the Aesopic fable of the lark who could not bury her dead father because the earth did not yet exist. Hubbard 1997, 32, accurately describes the parabasis as a "fusion of Hesiod's *Theogony*, Orphism, pre-Socratic cosmogony, and sheer nonsense."

22 Similarly the simple existence in Plato, *Laws* 3 is led by survivors of a destructive cataclysm (677a–b) who must start again from scratch to rebuild civilization.

23 Cataudella 1940, 59–61, thought Prodicus' account deprived men of divine providence and showed that the birds could offer benefits. When the chorus leader says that the audience will "hear correctly" (ἀκούσαντες...ὀρθῶς, 692) about the world's origins, he seems to be echoing Prodicus' catchword, "correctness" (ὀρθότης), suggests Hofmann 1976, 181; cf. Dunbar 1995, 433.

24 Dobrov 1993, 229. Their knowledge may be a false one, as Hubbard 1991, 7, suggests, but what matters is that they have persuaded themselves that it is true.

25 Dunbar 1995, 281, sees an allusion to the well-fortified naval power Syracuse.

26 The role of *chreia* was stressed in Diodorus 1.8.9, who saw men as coming to one another's defense out of expediency (cf. 1.8.2), as well as Thucydides, notes de Romilly 1966, 154–57 and 160–91. One can compare the way "Poverty" pointed to *chreia* as a powerful motivation for action (*Plutus* 507–34). By contrast, in the account of Tzetzes mutual defense was not just a response to pressure but an expression of *philallelia*: Cole 1967, 35–36.

27 "For security": ἀσφαλείας οὔνεκα, *Birds* 293, cf. Polybius in discussing the evolution of walls: ἀσφαλείας χάριν (6.7.4). In *Laws* 680b Plato has the earliest people live in caves on the crests of hills, though their lives tended not to be subject to violence (679c). Henry 1977 suggested that part of the joke in the *Birds* was that members of the chorus were up on the crest of the *skene*.

28 *Prot.* 322b5. The *Prom.* is silent about hunting or warfare; thus the *Birds* is giving this greater emphasis. By tradition Palamedes had been the inventor of military skills; he was said by Gorgias to have discovered τάξεις πολεμικὰς (Gorgias DK 82 B11a, c. 30; cf. Aeschylus fr. 182 *TrGF*: καὶ ταξίαρχας καὶ στρατάρχας . . . ἔταξα); consult Kleingünther 1933, 78–83.

29 Tereus, of course, is no "king among birds"; he needs to persuade with his personal authority and influence; cf. Dunbar 1995, 200.

30 At *Birds* 500–01 he sanctions kingship by noting that the kite was the first king and had introduced to mankind the new practice of grovelling before kites; Dunbar 1995, 343 pointed to the use of καταδείκνυμι as "introduce a new custom to mankind."

31 Hubbard 1997, 28.

32 Ewbank 1980, 254–55.

33 Bowie 1993, 151–77; Hamilton 1985.

34 Havelock 1957, 113–14, who suggested that this was later reflected in the *Laws*, where Plato imagined that a stronger man (*kreitton*) produced a social order. Plato tended to see paternal authority as the pattern, leading to *patrioi nomoi*: see *Laws* 680b–e. Polybius thought that a man of strength would necessarily rule and lead (6.5.7) and that this would lead to monarchy (6.5.9); see Cole 1967, 111–12.

35 The passage rings of Callicles, and Hornblower 1987, 180 n. 87, suggested that Democritus may not have thought that this was right. Indeed Democritus thought that the importance of the powerful was that they helped the poor and promoted harmony among citizens (DK 68 B255), balancing the claims of individual superiority with those of the collectivity, notes Cole 1967, 111.

36 On this consult de Romilly 1966, 163; Hunter 1982, 17–49.

37 *Theogony* 521–616 and *Works and Days* 42–89; consult Griffith 1977, 17, and 1983, 2; Said 1985, 115–30; West 1990, 51–72. He is omitted by Democritus, Thucydides, and the chorus of *Antigone*. Later Cynics (see Dio of Prusa 6.25, 29–30; Plutarch, *Moralia* 956b) condemned the gifts of Prometheus, but we see none of this in the fifth century: Cole 1967, 150.

38 Havelock 1957, 54–57; Griffith 1983, 219.

39 There are several points at which the *Birds* seems to reflect the *Prom.* Herington 1963 collected allusions in the *Birds* to the *Prom.*, especially in the final scenes. Some of Herington's parallels, for example, that Iris corresponds to Hermes of *Prom.*, seem fanciful to Rau 1967, 176; see also Turato 1971/72, 142 n. Dunbar 1995 notes echoes of *Prom.* at *Birds* 199–200 (influenced by the wording of *Prom.* 443–44), 654 (possible echo of *Prom.* 128), 685–87 (an allusion to men "molded from clay" *Prom.* 547; see also Griffith 1983, 2, and 1977, 12), 1197 (aeolic forms), and 1547 (echoes *Prom.* 975; cf. Griffith 1977, 11). Prometheus' speech culminated in the statement that all skills come to mortals from Prometheus (*Prom.* 506), and the birds end their list of offerings with a sweeping inclusion "health-and-wealth, happiness, life, peace, youth, laughter, dances, festivities – and birds' milk" (*Birds* 731–34). On the "scepter" (σκῆπτρον, 1535, 1600; cf. *Prom.* 171, 761), see Griffith 1977, 296 n. 20; consult further Bacon 1928, 117–19; Davison 1949, 66 n. 2; Flintoff 1983.

40 *Birds* 1494–1552.

41 Dunbar 1995, 693, pointed out that this was clearly a stage *after* that of the *Prom.*: he has returned to be with the gods.

42 The claim they had made at 615–18 – that they would live in bushes, saplings, and olive trees – is completely forgotten as the play progresses.

43 Mastromarco 1977 pointed out that the description of the wall closely parallels that of the Themistoclean wall in Thucydides 1.93; this raises the possibility that Book 1 of Thucydides was circulating by 414 B.C. (though Dunbar 1995, 596, on 1127 considers this too early a date). At least the parallel implies that the wall was familiar, not just the exotic thing it was initially said to be at *Birds* 552, where it is described as built of "kiln-burnt" bricks, reminiscent of the walls of Babylon (Herodotus 1.179). Nevertheless, noted Dunbar 1995, 595, the description at 1125–31 doubles some of Herodotus' dimensions.

44 Perhaps the specialized duties of the birds in building the wall at 1136ff. reflect the distribution of various technical arts to people of different abilities at *Prot.* 322c5, suggests de Carli 1971, 51. Another division of labor is described in the building of the siege wall at Melos: see Thuc. 5.114. Consult Dunbar 1995, 601–05, on the textual problems in assigning tasks to individual birds in this passage.

45 χελιδόνος ἐν οἰκοδομίᾳ, DK 68 B154. Aristotle seems to have been "correcting" Democritus by claiming that it was birds who learned from human beings (*HA* 612b18–21; see Cole 1967, 53 n. 18). Vitruvius, who saw architecture as a prerequisite for any further developments in civilization, also imagined that the earliest men imitated the nests of birds (*De arch.* 24.6–8). Pliny puts a heurematist stamp on it: Toxius invents mud buildings from the example of swallows' nests (*NH* 7.194; Cole 1967, 50 n. 7; Dunbar 1995, 602, on *Birds* 1148–53).

46 DK 59 A102. Xenophon, *Mem.* 1.4.11 and 14, gives it a teleological twist: the gods gave hands to human beings to be the principal agents of our

superior happiness. Diodorus (1.8.9) and Vitruvius (34.2–6), possibly following Democritus, cite the role of hands in enabling growth of the arts; see Cole 1967, 40–41.

47 Trag. adesp. 46 TrGF. At Birds 359 talons are used as fighting weapons for the birds; at 759 the expected "put up your hands if you're going to fight" is, in a cock-fighting context, replaced by "put up your spur (πλῆκτρον)."

48 Human beings are also blind, deaf, and helpless at Prom. 447–48.

49 Henrichs 1975, 112 n. 67; on the arbitrariness of language, see also Heinimann 1945, 51–53.

50 Eur., Suppl. 203–04 and Prot. 322a6.

51 Thucydides says little but at 1.3.2 describes the spread of Greek occurring tribe by tribe in Greece: Cole 1967, 221.

52 This opening scene might represent an attempt at communication by sign language, which represented a preliminary step in speech: Cole 1967, 63.

53 Learning over time was a motif in some accounts of the development of human culture: Xenophanes DK 21 B18; Philemon fr. 136 K-A; Moschion fr. 6.18 Snell; Athenio, Samothracians fr. 1.29 K-A.

54 Dobrov 2001, 125.

55 Text as in Dunbar. Dunbar 1995, 215, suggests a similar transition for the bird call ἰτώ to the Greek verb ἴτω and observes that the unresolved dochmiacs of line 230 perhaps suggest a birds poking and prodding about (1995, 210); subsequent lines hint at a bird flying off, hopping, rapid flight, wading, skimming. Conversely, human speech may take on an alliterative, bird-like cadence, as Bowie 1993, 173, n. 103, remarks on Birds 57ff. (e.g., τὸν ἔποπα "παῖ" καλεῖς). Compare the nonsense syllables on a vase (τοτοτο τοτο) seemingly indicating music: Lissarrague 1990b, 127.

56 Similar are the accounts of the initially varied and distinct sounds naturally uttered (Diodorus 1.8.2; Vitruvius 33.24; Lucretius 5.1028–9, cf. 1078–90 on birds' noises); see Cole 1967, 60.

57 Hermes (Homeric Hymn to Hermes 108–37) or Hephaestus (Harpocr. s.v. λαμπάς); see Griffith 1983, 1 n. 2.

58 Cole 1967, 15–16. Diodorus 1.13.1 inserts a discoverer – Hephaestus – though he too accepts material explanations for fire's first occurrence. The title of a work by Democritus (Αἰτίαι περὶ πυρὸς καὶ τῶν ἐν πυρί, DK 68 B11e) implies interest in the discovery of fire.

59 "Πυρφόρος occurs only twice elsewhere in Aristophanes, and then in quotations from the tragedians," observes Herington 1963, 241. See Dunbar 1995, 629, on the striking phrase "fire-carrying eagles" (πυρφόροισιν αἰετοῖς, 1248).

60 In Lucretius (5.101–27) and Vitruvius (33.28–34.2) the discovery of fire immediately led to social covenants.

61 Bacchae 272–85 ; Kleingünther 1933, 18–19, 35–37, 38. Diodorus attributed it to Isis and Osiris (1.14.1; consult Henrichs 1984b); for Dionysus see Diodorus 1.38.3–6.

62 The chorus of the *Antigone* remarks on the ways men snare animals (342–50), and Prometheus says he taught about sacrifice (*Prom.* 493–99). In the fragment of the *Samothracians* of Athenio that we examined in Chapter 4, a cook portrayed the culinary art as the basis for civilized *poleis*.

63 Dunbar 1995, 185.

64 One might say the diet is Hesiodic, but it is also strongly reminiscent of the sustenance of the pre-agricultural peoples in *Laws* 679a. Tereus, however, still eats sardines and soup (75–79), as well as myrtle and gnats (82).

65 An exception to the trend: in the second parabasis myrtle is praised as a food (1100).

66 Nestle 1936, 151–70: "Was hier Aristophanes den Vögeln zuschreibt, das war bei Prodikos das Werk der Horen"; see Ambrose 1983, 135–56; Henrichs 1984b, 140–45.

67 Of course birds threaten destruction as well: eating seed in the fields (579) or plucking the eyes of sheep (583).

68 Using the crane to know when to sow (*Works and Days* 448–51), swallow announcing spring (568–69), weather and shipowners (619–29); see Sommerstein 1987 on *Birds* 586.

69 This is, of course, a particularly un-materialistic explanation for a materialist philosopher. Cole 1967, 105 n. 19 noted that as a rule *mantike* was omitted from the Hellenistic *Kulturentstehungslehren*, though it appears in the list of the *Epinomis* (974e–76c) at 975c.

70 *Prom.* 484–92. Dodds 1973, 5, took the emphasis on divination as a sign of the essentially archaic character of Prometheus' speech. Theseus' list of civilized accomplishments included prophecy from fires, entrails, and birds: Eur., *Suppl.* 213.

71 See Democritus DK 68 B14; for Prodicus' *Horai*, see DK 84 B1. Manilius saw astronomy as the final step in human culture (1.66–112): cf. Cole 1967, 7. Consult also Ambrose 1983, 135–56.

72 Greeks did not systematically name four seasons; cf. Dunbar 1995, 450.

73 Havelock 1957, 71, pointed out that commercial exchange is an item appearing new in Eur.' *Suppl.*; Plato, *Republic* 369c–372e develops, for a few pages, the notion of material necessity in the commercial exchange economy. Sea voyages and trade provide what the land lacks.

74 The *Birds* shows little interest in the building of ships. It had been the avoidance of a summons-server ship that motivated the Athenians – an escapist touch. Moreover, it would have been far-fetched to claim that birds contributed to ship-building. Elsewhere, however, ship-building was thought to set men farther down the path of civilization (see *Prom.* 467–68 and *Antigone* 334–37) or, in later pessimistic views, the path to degeneration. Critias DK 88 B2 credited Carians with inventing ships.

75 *Birds* 592–93. The notion that mining brings prosperity may be an allusion to the wealth of Nicias, who consulted a diviner about silver mining: Plutarch, *Nicias* 4; Gill 1975, 69–72.

76 Lucretius 5.1241–65. The "Golden Age" view was that metallurgy led to decline in civilization: Guthrie 1957, 76; Griffith 1983, 176. Dunbar 1995, 399, pointed out that the motif of birds revealing hidden treasure also occurs in folklore of other cultures.

77 A series of promises to the judges (1105–13) include further bird contributions. These are, on closer inspection, merely a series of puns, yet they contribute to the impression of the utility of birds.

78 Dunbar 1995, 465–66.

79 Democritus DK 68 A75 and B30; Guthrie 1965, 478–83; Cole 1967, 202–05; Henrichs 1975, 96–106.

80 Critias DK 88 B25.12. Whether this should be ascribed to Critias or Euripides is a matter of long-standing debate; see, for example, Dihle 1977 (for Euripides), discussed by Winiarczyk 1987; Davies 1989 (undecided on authorship); further literature in Winiarczyk 1989.

81 Prodicus DK 84 B5; Henrichs 1975, 93–123; Guthrie 1971, 238–47.

82 Hornblower 1987, 182–84.

83 *Birds* 694–703, cf. 477–78; note, too, the instructions at 562–63 to sacrifice first to birds, then to gods. At 1570–71 Poseidon complains that the Triballian has been voted into his ambassadorial position. Olympus is scarcely an all-knowing hierarchy. Perkell 1993, 11, believes that the gods are "hamstrung by a democracy ruled by mediocrity" and that, despite the reverential portrait in their songs, the birds have no true insight into the divine.

84 Text as in Dunbar.

85 Similarly, the birds' claim to divinity rests in part on the usefulness of what they give to men (seasonal indicators, etc.), reflecting Prodicus' teachings, notes Hubbard 1997, 32–33.

86 Note that Peisetaerus is πυκνότατον (429); cf. πυκνός (Critias DK 88 B25.12). At 862–88 Peisetaerus and a priest pray in alternation to gods and a series of birds who have been re-inaugurated as gods.

87 "City-dwelling instincts," translates Hornblower 1987, 130.

88 The *Prom.* has little to say one way or the other; Havelock (1957, 62, 79–81) found signs of interest in social cohesion, but this element has been overstressed, thinks Conacher 1977, 195 n. 9. Said 1985, 284–86, sees Zeus as disconnected from *eunomia* in this tragedy.

89 As noted by de Carli 1971, 51. Anhalt 1993, 110–13, found that *eunomia* in Solon may not be a divine force but a desired social goal that can be attained only by human action. Although *eunomia* can have overtones of aristocratic government, Ostwald 1969, 80, noted that, although it is not particularly democratic, it is at least not specifically associated with Sparta. The term is also discussed in Grossmann 1950, 30–89. Zimmermann 1983, 96–70, found these to be oligarchic slogans that are nevertheless associated with Athena; in this he follows Newiger 1957, 92–103 and Newiger 1983. De Romilly 1966, 172 n. 90, pointed to Diodotus' favorable view of *euboulia* as "wise counsel" (Thucydides 3.42.1, 48.2). Griffith 1983, 303, suggested that the introduction of justice and other civic virtues may have occurred in the

Prometheus Lyomenos and cites *Birds* 1539–40 as a parallel. Note, too, that the birds claim for their city "Wisdom, Desire, Immortal Graces, and Peace" (1320–21).

90 This is comparable to the unequal distribution of gifts in the *Prot.*

91 At least at 1433 the informer is told that he should go off to "decent occupations" (ἔργα σώφρονα), so the principle of *sophrosyne* is present.

92 DK 87 B44A col. 5.16; Plato, *Laws* 680b, which in turn quotes *Odyssey* 9.112–15 on the Cyclopes, held up the family as the first, natural society, where the rule of the parent prevails and where activities are based not on cooperation but on laws pronounced to wives and children. On the other hand there were no families in the Golden Age of Plato's *Politicus*, 272a. A role for the family in social development occurs in Aristotle, *Politics* 1252a24-b34; Lucretius 5.1021–23; Diodorus 1.8.4. See Cole 1967, 107, 112–20.

93 He remarks that parents expect gratitude from their children (6.6.2–3). This is related to a more general concern on Polybius' part about violations of what in the fifth and fourth century were unwritten *nomoi*: returning benefactions, helping friends, respecting parents, and revering gods. The unwritten code to honor parents appears in different contexts, for example, Aristotle, *Rhet.* 1.1374a18–25; Anaximenes, *Rhet. ad Alex.* 1.1421b35–22a2; Xenophon, *Mem.* 4.4.19–24; Eur., *Hecuba* 800–01: Cole 1967, 113–14. Dunbar 1995, 469, adds Aeschylus, *Suppl.* 707–09, and *Frogs* 145–51.

94 Dunbar 1995, 657 suggests that storks were thought to show parental and filial piety because they were large and dignified and placed their nests in conspicuous places so that their family-rearing was unusually visible. We saw in Chapter 4 that a speaker in Aristophanes' *Storks* seems to reprimand another character for not offering his father something to wear (fr. 445 K-A). The fable of the stork (*Birds* 471–75) also shows concern for the father: discussed in Hofmann 1976, 165–66.

95 Diogenes Laertius 1.55. Arrowsmith 1973, 159, sees father-beating as the sole natural practice and the fact that the storks' laws were written on *kurbeis* as evidence of their artificiality. Yet I suggest that anything based on animal behavior should be regarded as *physis*.

96 A *nomos* that is inherent in *physis* (cf. Xen. *Mem.* 4.4): Turato 1971–72, 126–27, whose discussion of the issue seems to me most illuminating.

97 Democritus DK 68 B259; cf. DK 68 B257, B258.

98 Lewis 1990 on Lewis-Meiggs 30 B 8–28.

99 We might compare the similar position in the *Anonymus Iamblichi*, in which things generated by *nomos* are ingrained in nature (6.1).

100 As noted by Stewart 1967, 358, who contrasts Peisetaerus with the men transformed in the *Odyssey* by Circe ; their animal shapes limit their abilities. It was only centuries later that Plutarch, as we saw, transformed one of those men, Gryllus, into an articulate defender of the animal life.

101 Tellingly, the account in Eur, *Suppliants*, in which mortals are beholden to a divinity, is largely ignored.

102 Cole 1967, 47.

103 Reckford 1987, 333, alludes to the model of the Archaeology.

104 Most evidence points to a date in the fourth century for the "publication" of Thucydides' history; see Hornblower 1995. My point is simply that Aristophanes and Thucydides share a conception of power.

105 Turato 1971–72, 118, who also remarks that the description of Peisetaerus' plan as "incredible" (ἄπιστα, 417) echoes Thucydides 6.31.1 (ἄπιστον).

106 Arrowsmith 1973, 128–29, who gives a brilliant analysis of the imperialist instinct underlying the *Birds*.

107 A lucid account is Ostwald 1986, 305–12.

108 *Birds* 14 and 1077, noted in Romer 1994, 359.

109 A. Andrewes in Lewis et al. 1992, 446.

110 Henderson 1997, 143.

111 Hunter 1982; Ceccarelli 1996; Kallet-Marx 1993, 21–35.

112 Henderson 1997, 136.

113 Thuc. 1.93; Mastromarco 1977.

114 For more see Sommerstein 1987, 1, n. 3. The resemblance to the new city is noted in Auger 1979, 86; Corsini 1985, 66.

115 Alink 1983, 323. Alink points to the cock's habit of beating fathers (755–56), but ignores the alternative stork habit of caring for parents (1355–57).

116 Tereus says that Peisetaerus is "kin" of Procne (ξυγγενεῖ, 368), though this simply means that both are Athenians. The young man is sent to the Thracian front to serve the *polis*, not the family. In contrast to the father-beating episode in *Clouds*, family considerations are minimized.

117 Human beings are energetically finding everything bird-like in their own habits and beings (1283–1307).

118 Seen from the outside, much of what happens in the comedy is verbal artifice, a theme developed by Whitman 1964, 167–99. The manipulation of language gives an opening to the self-authentication of Peisetaerus.

119 Turato 1971/72, 125–26. Epstein 1981, 28, seems to see Peisetaerus as arriving at an appreciation of the standards of a polis by making an excursion into nature worship. Riu 1999, 155–64, believed that the *Birds* represented a Dionysiac "disfoundation," with the city barbarized by animal citizens; this is an interesting proposition, though I see it more as a parody with subversive potential.

120 In this light line 210 (λῦσον δὲ νόμους), which means "Send forth the melodies," perhaps puns on the meaning "Undo the laws."

121 Turato 1971/72, 122; Reckford 1987, 337, notes that the parabasis odes (737–52, 769–84) and the epirrheme and antepirrheme (753–68, 785–800) juxtapose the sublime and the low; salvation must "include our lower selves," by which Reckford would mean *eros* and *physis*.

122 Sommerstein 1987, 246.

123 Alink 1983, 323, dismissed these, thinking of them as purely human laws.

124 The antinomian remarks appear only in the parabasis, where the birds perhaps do not adhere as closely to their dramatic role.

125 Paduano 1973/74, 131, objected that this is merely the same of repressive theology.

126 On this see Zimmermann 1983, 67; Reckford 1987, 338; Henderson 1997, 140–41. Saïd 1985, 12–21, suggested that the *Prom.* be understood in the light of an opposition between Prometheus the sophist and Zeus the tyrant; Peisetaerus could be explained as embodying both qualities simultaneously. West 1990, 63, saw the *Prom.* as an illustration of the right of the stronger.

127 *Birds* 1708. The anti-democratic outbursts, such as contempt for voting urns (1032, 1052), are discussed by Bowie, 1993, 170–71; see also Romer 1994, 360–61. His name may have been meant to recall that of the sixth-century tyrant Peisistratus, thinks Reckford 1987, 333. Schareika 1978, 104, however, saw the new city as an idealized Athenian democracy, with the Olympians as its enemies.

128 This aspect of his behavior may stem from satyr-plays, in which assaults on Iris are known: see Scharffenberger 1995. An attack on Iris and Hera is depicted on a vase of ca. 490–480 B.C.: Simon 1982b, 125–29.

129 Hussey 1985, 124, noted that self-discipline was not much apparent in Pericles' speech (there is only the threat of external punishment, 2.37.2); Alcibiades illustrates this vice.

130 Paduano 1973/74, 143–44. Peisetaerus explicitly invokes the law of the stronger in addressing Iris: "[you], in turn, must obey your superiors" ἀκροατέον ὑμῖν ἐν μέρει τῶν κρειττόνων (1228). Had he not been likened to a blackbird, we would wish to think of him as an aggressive cock, a creature that was in vogue contemporary with the ideology of power in the late fifth century, suggests Dumont 1988, 37.

131 Auger 1979, 82–84, also sees in him the rebirth of the cannibal Tereus, though it is not clear that Tereus' savage past survives his shift into comedy: see Dobrov 2001, 220.

132 Hubbard 1997, 36. Wilkins 2000a, 23, points out that Aristophanes slightly sidesteps the issue by concentrating on the presentation of the meal, with the degrading use of sauce.

133 Cf. Aristotle: "Anyone too self-sufficient for a *polis* is either a beast or a god" (*Politics* 1253a29; cf. *EN* 1097b5–21). In some respects the conventional wisdom – that Peisetaerus is an urban creature and the birds are creatures of nature – is backwards: the birds are the social creatures, and Peisetaerus is the one who has transcended the need for the *polis*.

134 Westlake 1954, 93, observed that "the father-beater doubtless left the stage amid sympathetic cheers." Perkell 1993, 2–5, noted that he can appeal to a "higher moral sense." See also Turato 1971/72, 126–30.

135 Dunbar 1995, 12 and 694.

136 Andocides *On the Mysteries* 34, 38, 52, 59; Thucydides 6.28; Ostwald 1986, 526, 537–50; see Henderson 1997, 145, and MacDowell 1995, 224–25.

137 Craik 1987, 33, who also believed that the wedding to Basileia parodies the marriage to Basilinna in the Anthesteria, and that the significance is more religious than political.

138 Wilkins 2000a, 345, pointed out that, unlike the *Beasts* of Crates or the *Fishes* of Archippus, members of the chorus were in no danger of being eaten themselves.

139 Democritus thought that education could transform nature (DK 69 B33); see Hussey 1985, 120.

140 Auger 1979, 88, saw that Peisetaerus does support orderly institutions, such as marriage and sacrifice, but saw this as being merely form that lacks content.

141 Slater 2002, 149. Dunbar 1995, 316: "Whether Ar. intended Peis. to be now revealed as a 'sophistic' character, blatantly deceiving the simple birds by cunning, unsound arguments, or conceived him simply as a typical Athenian, resourceful, energetic and bold . . . is a difficult question," though she answers (p. 12) that the audience would likely see him as a sympathetic character. Henderson 1997, 142: "Few would have seen anything sinister or ominous in Peisetaerus' success."

142 That these are indeed Peisetaerus' lines – something that is not a matter of certainty – was advanced by Fraenkel 1962, 61–65.

143 Strauss 1966, 163.

144 Konstan 1990b, 183 n. 1. Cf. Whitman 1964, 177, "No true Greek could live without a city, even if he was returning to nature." Zimmermann 1983, 67–68, also saw the pastoral theme as being dropped. Peisetaerus ultimately represents something else. It is pertinent that the word ἄνθρωπος occurs two and a half times more frequently in this play than others: Griffith 1987, 62 n. 16.

145 The word "anti-dicasts" has seemed to some to indicate a political faction, but Dunbar 1995, 169, pointed out that he may simply be alluding to the obvious fact that the lawcourts were held in the city so that countrymen were less likely to volunteer for jury service.

146 Pozzi 1991, 150.

147 Reckford 1987, 332–33.

148 Green 1985, 117–18, discusses affinities between *Birds* and satyr-plays.

149 See the discussion in Chapter 4.

150 Not a single one of the cultural accomplishments associated with satyrs is mentioned in Thucydides' "Archaeology" as part of the formation of society.

APPENDIX A: TESTIMONIA AND FRAGMENTS OF LOST COMEDIES

1 Information on these playwrights may also be found in the "Biographical Appendix" in Harvey and Wilkins 2000, 507–20.

2 On Antiphanes see Nesselrath 1990, 193.

3 Geissler 1969, 66.

4 Dogfish or shark: Thompson 1947, 39–42; Olson and Sens 2000, 97–98.

5 Boax or Box: Thompson 1947, 36–37.

6 Thompson 1947, 224–25; Olson and Sens 2000, 124–25.

7 Thompson 1947, 187–88.

8 Gilt-head or Dorade: Thompson 1947, 292–94; Olson and Sens 2000, 64–65.

9 Thompson 1947, 221–22; Olson and Sens 2000, 192.

10 Dogfish or shark: Thompson 1947, 39–42; Olson and Sens 2000, 97–98.

11 Thompson 1947, 140.

12 The Keryx, a general term for whelk: Thompson 1947, 113; Olson and Sens 2000, 43. Keryx, Thalassa, and Porphyra could be proper names.

13 Purple shellfish or Murex: Thompson 1947, 209–18.

14 Either an Egyptian fish, said to be sacred because it gave forewarning of the inundation (Aelian, *NA* 10.19), or fish of the Black Sea who dwell around Lake Maiotis (the Sea of Azov: Pliny 32.146 and Athenaeus 312a). See Thompson 1947, 155.

15 A synonym of *korakinos* (a term that covers several kinds of fishes); included with fishes of the Nile in this fragment (thus Thompson), though also from the Black Sea (thus Archestratus fr. 39, Athenaeus117a): Thompson 1947, 226; Olson and Sens 2000, 165.

16 Perhaps the *Silurus glanis* or sheatfish, a large catfish: Thompson 1947, 43–48.

17 Herring: Thompson 1947, 77.

18 Atherine or Sand-smelt: Thompson 1947, 3–4.

19 Cuttlefish: Thompson 1947, 231–22; Olson and Sens 2000, 206.

20 Red Mullet: Thompson 1947, 264–68; Olson and Sens 2000, 173.

21 These may correspond to the *korakinoi*, various imprecise types of fish: Thompson 1947, 122–25; Olson and Sens 2000, 93.

22 The *batrachos* was an Angler or Fishing-frog: Thompson 1947, 28–29; Olson and Sens 2000, 194.

23 Geissler 1969, 71; cf. Schmid 1946, 215 n. 4.

24 On the difficulties of identifying the several men with this name in classical Athens, see MacDowell 1962, 208–210.

25 This has been interpreted variously. "If you prosecute one corrupt man, twelve testify against you, bribed by other corrupt men who think their own welfare is at stake" (Herwerden 1878); ". . . testify against the others . . ." (Fritzsche 1835, 60); see *PCG ad loc.*

26 By Capps 1899, 396.

27 Pickard-Cambridge 1968, 121; Mette *ad loc.*; Dittmer 1923, 39–42; Schmid 1946, 93; Geissler 1969, 14.

28 Fifth place, in 434, Antiochides, follows. See Schwarze 1971, 91.

29 By Oellacher 1916, 116.

30 By Capps 1907, 199.

31 Giannini 1959, 195–96, and Geissler 1969, xiii and 40.

32 The *editio princeps* is Willis 1991.

33 *Maiotai*: fish from Lake Maiotis (Sea of Azov) in Scythia, but the word could also refer to human inhabitants of the region. Perhaps an Egyptian fish in Archippus fr. 26: Thompson 1947, 155.

34 *Labrakes*: bass: Thompson 1947, 140; Olson and Sens 2000, 182.

35 *Petrerikon* and *sagenikon* are comic coinages: perhaps these fish live "among the rocks" and "among the nets."

36 *Choiroi*: Egyptian fish; they were avoided by crocodiles because of their sharp armature (Strabo 17.823) and were able to make creaking noises (Aristotle fr. 272R = Athenaeus 331d): Thompson 1947, 291.

37 A pun on Samothracian, suggests *PCG ad loc.*

38 *Solen* (literally a "tube" or "pipe"): razorfish or razorshell. It was tube-shaped, lived in the sand, and was plentiful in the Aegean: Thompson 1947, 257–58.

39 Eusebius (Jerome) on Ol. 82.2 (= 451/50 B.C.); see *PCG* IV.84 T 7.

40 [Κρά]της· V B 1 col. 1.16 Mette; Pickard-Cambridge 1968, 112–20.

41 Cratinus, *Ploutoi* fr. 171.22 K-A, may contain an allusion to the removal of Pericles from power in 429, but a range of years between 437 and 429 is possible: see Geissler 1969, x, for further discussion.

42 See Geissler 1969, xii; a date in the 430s is also possible.

43 Geissler 1969, xii.

44 Norwood and Schmid assume that Crates was dead by the time Aristophanes was writing, but Bonnano 1972, 28 n. 1 believes that this is not a necessary conclusion from the imperfect tenses. See also Schmid 1946, 90–91; Roux 1976; text and notes in Carrière 1979, 256–63.

45 On line 2: Carrière (1979, 260) gives line 2 to speaker B, noting that ἀλλά can express surprise in an interruption (Denniston 1954, 274); see also Bonnano 1972, 89, and Tammaro 1984/85. On line 5, for τὶς some editors read τὶ.

46 This may have come from the comedy's *agon*: Whittaker 1935, 186; Gelzer 1960, 185.

47 A hospital? See *PCG ad loc.*, disputed by Carrière 1979, 263.

48 Another possibility (following Ruffell 2000, 483) is that the water addresses the bottle of myrrh, "Get up!"

49 Whittaker 1935,187; Gelzer 1960, 185.

50 One could also imagine reversing the order of the fragments, with speaker A responding to the question posed by speaker B.

51 Geissler 1969, 29; Storey 2003, 65–67.

52 I adopt here Austin's emendation; manuscripts read: ὡς ἡ ποτ' αὐτὸν ἦν κάμη τις...

53 Meineke 1840, 116, assigned this to the *Goats*.

54 These verses are in anapestic tetrameters and, as such, are likely to be from the parabasis: Whittaker 1935, 189. I am indebted to the "Aegological Note" of Rackham 2000.

55 This papyrus fragment is a commentary on an unknown Old Comedy. For discussion of the dance movements here see Borthwick 1970; "Gorgon-dragon-awaiting" presupposes Γοργοδρακοντοδοκα.

56 The *aigipuros* is a plant, the rest-harrow (*Ononis antiquorum*), with pink or purplish flowers.

57 Magnes' victory in 472 is recorded in *IG* ii² 2318, col. i (Mette I col. 4.2 "Fasti"). For the assumption that his career had ended by 440, see Oellacher 1916, 83.

58 Anon. *De com.* (*Proleg. De com.* III) 9 p. 7 Koster.

59 Hermippus, the poet named immediately after Pherecrates, won a victory in 436 (*IG* ii² 2318 col. iv); see Capps 1943. This fragment would seem to answer doubts voiced about Dobree's emendation in Schmid 1946, 100 n. 1; consult also Geissler 1969, viii and 5.

60 Geissler 1969, 42.

61 But his first victory may have been in 421/420 B.C.: Luppe 1970 and Rosen 1989.

62 Geissler 1969, 74.

63 Nesselrath 1990, 34–37 and Rosen 1996 regard him as a poet of Old Comedy. That no fragments have survived may mean that *Ants* was one of his less important works, from earlier in his career, and may thus have been produced between 425 and 422 B.C.: Giannini 1959, 196, followed by Geissler 1969, xiii. On his career and fragments see also Scuppa 1956 and Rossi 1981.

APPENDIX B: MISCELLANEOUS DEPICTIONS OF ANIMAL COSTUMES

1 New York, Metropolitan Museum of Art 1999.68; Picon and Mertens 1999/2000.

2 In addition to the vases discussed here, there is a late archaic aryballic lekythos cited in Dugas 1946, 172–78, pl. ix and figs. 1ff., on which is a bird-in-arms; it may not be a member of a chorus, for there are no human features, but may be an imaginative depiction of the name of the lark, κορυδαλλός, "the bird in helmet," suggests Dugas.

3 Stone 1981, 357–58; Dunbar 1995, 488.

4 Green 1994, 34–38, 47. A Hellenistic terracotta figure of an actor evidently wearing a bird mask is in Cambridge, Fitzwilliam GR.1.2002; see Nicholson 1968.

5 Muscarella 1974, no. 49; Settgast 1978, no. 89.

6 Green 1985, 112.

7 Stone 1981, 383–84. The beaks on the Getty Birds favor their being from the *Birds*.

8 Musei Capitolini no. 91.

9 Lund and Rathje 1988, 360, fig. 6

10 Buschor 1941, 30; Sifakis 1971, 90.

11 Bowra 1970, 176. On the iconography of Triton see Brijder 1983, 119.

12 Ridgway 1970, 86–95, esp. 91.

13 Louvre A330 (S445); *CVA* fasc. I II Dc pl. 2 11; Cook 1933–34; Ghiron-Bistagne 1976, 262, fig. 116.

14 Dover 1978, 92, for examples on vase-painting.

15 Burkert 1983, 75.

16 *Kleine Pauly*, s.v. "Hase" (W. Richter).

17 Vulci 64224; *Para.* 330: "an imitation of the Euergides Painter"; Hoffmann 1977; Brijder 1988.
18 Aelian, *NA* 5.26, 6.10, 7.19, 15.14, 17.25; McDermott 1938, 137.
19 Brijder 1988, 68.
20 Pliny, *HN* 8.80.216 (*satyrus*), perhaps the orangutan.
21 Tambiah 1969, 441. In contrast, Speakers of Kachin, in Burma, do not see the monkey as close to mankind and sometimes eat it, notes Leach 1964, 60.
22 *Kleine Pauly*, s.v. "Affe."
23 For these and more see Todisco 2002, 122–24.
24 Dearden 1990; Green 1994, 65.
25 Reggio Calabria 24722; Todisco 2002, pl. XLVIII.3.
26 Karlsruhe, Badisches Landesmuseum 654, 655; Todisco 2002, figs. 44 and 45.
27 Palermo 959 [3922]; Todisco 2002, pl. XLIX.1 (a poor photograph).
28 Taranto 208357; Todisco 2002, 123 and pl. XLVIII.2. There is a second example at the museum as well.

BIBLIOGRAPHY

Adrados 1975. Adrados, Francisco R. *Festival, Comedy and Tragedy. The Greek Origins of Theatre.* Leiden, 1975.

Alföldi 1967. Alföldi, A. *Die Herrschaft der Reiterei in Griechenland und Rom nach dem Sturz der Könige.* Antike Kunst Beiheft 4. Bern, 1967.

Alink 1983. Alink, M. *De Vogels van Aristophanes: een structuuranalyse en interpretatie.* Amsterdam, 1983.

L'Allier 2004. L'Allier, Louis. *Le bonheur des moutons. Étude sur l'homme et l'animal dans la hiérarchie de Xénophon.* Montreal, 2004.

Allison 1983. Allison, Richard H. "Amphibian Ambiguities: Aristophanes and his Frogs," *Greece and Rome* 30 (1983), 8–20.

Alpers 1961. Alpers, Antony. *Dolphins. The Myth and the Mammal.* Boston, 1961.

Ambrose 1983. Ambrose, Z. Philip. "Socrates and Prodicus in the *Clouds*" in *Essays in Ancient Greek Philosophy.* Edd. J. P. Anton and A. Preuss. Vol. II. Albany, NY, 1983, pp. 129–40.

Amelung 1900. Amelung, W. "Satyrs Ritt durch die Wellen" in *Strena Helbigiana.* Leipzig, 1900, pp. 1–9.

d'Amicis 1997. d'Amicis, Amelia, ed. *Catalogo del Museo Nazionale Archeologico di Taranto.* I.3: *Atleti e guerrieri.* Taranto, 1997.

Amyx 1961. Amyx, D. A. "The Medallion Painter," *AJA* 65 (1961), 1–15.

Amyx 1988. ___. *Corinthian Vase-Painting of the Archaic Period.* Berkeley, 1988.

Anderson 1961. Anderson, J. K. *Ancient Greek Horsemanship.* Berkeley, 1961.

Andreae 1981. Andreae, B. "Kalpis" in *Funde aus der Antike. Sammlung Paul Dierichs.* Ed. P. Gercke. Kassel, 1981, 107–11, no. 56.

Anhalt 1993. Anhalt, Emily Katz. *Solon the Singer. Politics and Poetics.* Lanham, MD, 1993.

Antonetti 1996. Antonetti, Claudia. "Phalanthos 'entre Corinthe et Sicyone'," *Dialogues d'histoire ancienne* 22 (1996), 65–78.

Arnott 2000. Arnott, W. G. "On Editing Comic Fragments from Literary and Lexicographical Sources," in Harvey and Wilkins 2000, pp. 1–13.

Arrowsmith 1956. Arrowsmith, William, tr. *Euripides: Cyclops.* Chicago, 1956.

Arrowsmith 1973. ——. "Aristophanes' Birds: The Fantasy Politics of Eros," *Arion* 1 (1973), 119–67.

Auger 1979. Auger, Danièle. "Le theâtre d'Aristophane: le myth, l'utopie, et les femmes" in *Aristophane: les femmes et la cité*. Edd. J. Bonnamour and H. Delvault. Fontenay-aux-Roses, 1979, pp. 71–101.

Bacon 1928. Bacon, J. R. "Three Notes on Aeschylus, *Prometheus Vinctus*," *CR* 42 (1928), 115–20.

Bakhtin 1968. Bakhtin, M. *Rabelais and his World*. Tr. H. Iswolsky. Cambridge, MA, 1968.

Baldry 1953. Baldry, H. C. "The Idler's Paradise in Attic Comedy," *G&R* 22 (1953), 49–60.

Baldwin 1988. Baldwin, Barry. "The Frogs' Chorus in Aristophanes," *Eranos* 86 (1988), 67–76.

Barker 2004. Barker, Andrew. "Transforming the Nightingale: Aspects of Athenian Musical Discourse in the Late Fifth Century" in *Music and the Muses. The Culture of 'Mousike' in the Classical Athenian City*. Edd. Penelope Murray and Peter Wilson. Oxford, 2004, pp. 185–204.

Barber 1959. Barber, C. L. *Shakespeare's Festive Comedy*. Princeton, 1959.

Beazley 1929. Beazley, John. "Some Inscriptions on Vases – II," *AJA* 33 (1929), 361–67.

Beazley 1943. ——. "Panathenaica," *AJA* 47 (1943), 441–65.

Bentz 1998. Bentz, Martin. *Panathenaische Preisamphoren. Eine athenische Gattung und ihre Funktion vom 6. – 4. Jahrhundert v. Chr.* Basel, 1998.

Bérard 1957. Bérard, J. *La colonisation grecque de l'Italie méridionale et de la Sicile dans l'antiquité*. Paris, 1957.

Bérard and Bron 1989. Bérard, Claude and Christiane Bron. "Satyric Revels" in *A City of Images. Iconography and Society in Ancient Greece*. Edd. C. Bérard et al. Tr. Deborah Lyons. Princeton, 1989, pp. 131–49.

Bergk 1838. Bergk, T. *Commentationum de reliquiis comoediae Atticae antiquae libri duo*. Leipzig, 1838.

Beta 2004. Beta, Simone. *Il linguaggio nelle commedie di Aristofane. Parola positiva e negative nella commedia antica*. Rome, 2004.

Bevan 1987. Bevan, Elinor. "The Goddess Artemis and the Dedication of Bears in Sanctuaries," *Annual of the British School at Athens* 82 (1987), 17–21.

Bieber 1961. Bieber, Margarete. *The History of the Greek and Roman Theater*. 2nd ed. Princeton, 1961.

Bielefeld 1946/47. Beilefeld, Erwin. "Ein Delphinreiter-Chor," *JdI* (1946/47), 48–54.

Bierl 1990. Bierl, Anton. "Dionysus, Wine, and Tragic Poetry: A Metatheatrical Reading of P.Köln VI 242A = TrGF II F 646a," *GRBS* 31 (1990), 353–91.

Bierl 1994. ——. "Karion, die Karer und der Plutos des Aristophanes als Inszenierung eines anthesterienartigen Ausnahmefestes" in *Orchestra*.

Drama – Mythos – Buhne. Festschrift für H. Flashar. Edd. A. Bierl and P. von Möllendorff. Stuttgart/Leipzig, 1994, 30–43.

Bierl 2001. ___. *Der Chor in der alten Komödie. Ritual und Performativität.* Munich/Leipzig, 2001.

Bierl 2002. ___. Review of Riu, *Dionysism in Comedy. Gnomon* (2002), 196–203.

Bielohlawek 1940. Bielohlawek, K. "Gastmahls- u. Symposionlehren bei gr. Dichtern," *Wiener Studien* 58 (1940), 11–30.

Bloesch 1974. Bloesch, Hansjörg, ed. *Das Tier in der Antike.* Exhibition Catalogue. Zurich, 1974.

Blundell 1986. Blundell, Sue. *The Origins of Civilization in Greek and Roman Thought.* London, 1986.

Boardman 1974. Boardman, John. *Athenian Black Figure Vases.* London, 1974.

Boardman 1975. ___. *Athenian Red Figure Vases. The Archaic Period.* London, 1975.

Boardman 1989. ___. *Athenian Red Figure Vases. The Classical Period.* London, 1989.

Boardman 1990. ___. "Chariot, Trapeze, or Lyre," *Oxford Journal of Archaeology* 9 (1990), 367–68.

Boardman 1992. ___. "The Phallos-Bird in Archaic and Classical Greek Art," *Revue Archéologique* (1992), 227–42.

Boardman 1998. ___. *Early Greek Vase Painting.* London, 1998.

Bodson 1978. Bodson, Liliane. *ΊΕΡΑ ΖΩΙΑ. Contribution à la l'étude de la place de l'animal dans la religion grecque ancienne.* Brussels, 1978.

den Boer 1977. den Boer, W. *Progress in the Greece of Thucydides.* Amsterdam, 1977.

Bonanno 1972. Bonnano, Maria Grazia. *Studi su Cratete comico.* Padua, 1972.

Born and Hansen 1994. Born, Hermann and Svend Hansen. *Frühgriechische Bronzehelme.* Band III. Sammlung Axel Guttmann. Mainz, 1994.

Borthwick 1968. Borthwick, E. K. "Notes on the Plutarch De Musica and the Cheiron of Pherecrates," *Hermes* 96 (1968), 60–73.

Borthwick 1970. ___. "P.Oxy. 2738: Athena and the Pyrrhic Dance," *Hermes* 98 (1970), 318–31.

Borthwick 1990. ___. "Bees and Drones in Aristophanes, Aelian and Euripides," *BICS* 37 (1990), 57–62.

Borthwick 1994. ___. "New Interpretations of Aristophanes *Frogs* 1249–1328," *Phoenix* 48 (1994), 21–41.

von Bothmer 1957. von Bothmer, Dietrich. *Amazons in Greek Art.* Oxford, 1957.

Bottini 1989. Bottini, A. "Apulische-korinthische Helme" in *Antike Helme.* Ed. H. Pflug. Mainz, 1989, pp. 107–36.

Bottini 1990. ___. "Gli elmi apulo-corinzi: proposata di classificazione," *AION* 12 (1990), 23–38.

Bottini 1991. ___. *Gli strumenti della guerra in Basilicata fra VIII e III secolo a. C.* Bari, 1991.

Bowie 1993. Bowie, A. M. *Aristophanes. Myth, Ritual and Comedy*. Cambridge, 1993.

Bowie 1997. ___. "Thinking with Drinking: Wine and the Symposium in Aristophanes," *JHS* 117 (1997), 1–21.

Bowie 1986. Bowie, E. L. "Early Greek Elegy, Symposium and Public Festival," *JHS* 106 (1986), 13–35.

Bowie 1990. ___. "*Miles Ludens?* The Problem of Martial Exhortation in Early Greek Elegy," in Murray 1990, pp. 221–29.

Bowra 1970. Bowra, C. M. "Arion and the Dolphin" in *On Greek Margins*. Oxford, 1970, pp. 164–81 (= *Museum Helveticum* 20 [1963], 121–34).

Brackerts 1976. Brackerts, Ursula. *Zum Problem der Schützgottheiten griechischer Städte*. Berlin, 1976.

Breitholtz 1960. Breitholtz, Leenart. *Die dorische Farce im griechischen Mutterland vor dem 5. Jahrhundert. Hypothese oder Realität?* Stockholm, 1960.

Bremmer 1990. Bremmer, Jan. "Adolescents, *Symposion*, and Pederasty," in Murray 1990, pp. 135–45.

Brijder 1983. Brijder, H. A. G. *Siana Cups I and Komast Cups*. Allard Pierson Series 4. Amsterdam, 1983.

Brijder 1986. ___. "A Pre-dramatic Performance of a Satyr Chorus by the Heidelberg Painter" in *Enthousiasmos. Essays on Greek and Related Pottery Presented to J. M. Hemelrijk*. Edd. H. A. G. Brijder, A. A. Drukker, and C. W. Neeft. Amsterdam, 1986, pp. 69–82.

Brijder 1988. ___. "Apish Performances in the 6th Cent. BC," *Proceedings of the 3rd Symposium on Ancient Greek and Related Pottery, Copenhagen, Aug. 31–Sept. 4, 1987*. Copenhagen, 1988, 62–70.

Brijder 1991. ___. *Siana Cups II: The Heidelberg Painter*. Allard Pierson Series 8. Amsterdam, 1991.

Brommer 1937. Brommer, Frank. *Satyroi*. Würzburg, 1937.

Brommer 1942. ___. "Delphinreiter. Vasenbilder früher Komödien," *AA* (1942), 65–75.

Brommer 1959. ___. *Satyrspiele. Bilder griechischer Vasen*. 2nd ed. Berlin, 1959.

Bron 1988. Bron, Christiane, "Le lieu du comos" in *Proceedings of the 3rd Symposium on Ancient Greek and Related Pottery*. Edd. J. Christiansen and T. Melander. Copenhagen, 1988, pp. 71–79.

Bron 1999. ___. "La musique du comos" in *Proceedings of the XVth International Congress of Classical Archaeology, Amsterdam, July 12–17, 1998*. Ed. R. Docter and F. Moormann. Allard Pierson Series 12. Amsterdam, 1999, 98–100.

Brown et al. 1975. Brown, A. C., H. W. Catling, and M. Vickers. "Recent Acquisitions by the Ashmolean Museum, Oxford," *Archaeological Reports for 1974–75*. No. 21 (1975), 30.

Bruneau 1965. Bruneau, Philippe. "Le motif des coqs affrontés dans l'imagerie antique," *BCH* 89 (1965), 90–121.

Brussich 1976. Brussich, Guerrino F. "La danze dei delfini in Euripides, nello pseudo-Arione e in Livio Andronico," *QUCC* 21 (1976), 53–56.

Bugh 1988. Bugh, G. R. *The Horsemen of Athens*. Princeton, 1988.

Burkert 1966. Burkert, Walter. "Greek Tragedy and Sacrificial Ritual," *GRBS* 7 (1966), 87–121.

Burkert 1972. ___. *Lore and Science in Ancient Pythagoreanism*. Tr. Edwin L. Minar, Jr. Cambridge, MA, 1972.

Burkert 1975. ___. "Apellai und Apollon," *RhM* 118 (1975), 1–21.

Burkert 1983. ___. *Homo Necans*. Tr. Peter Bing. Berkeley, 1983.

Burkert 1985. ___. *Greek Religion*. Tr. John Raffan. Cambridge, 1985.

Burnett 1994. Burnett, Anne Pippin. "Hekabe the Dog," *Arethusa* 27 (1994), 151–64.

Buschor 1937. Buschor, Ernst. *Feldmäuse*. SBAW. Munich, 1937.

Buschor 1941. ___. *Meermänner*. SBAW. Munich, 1941.

Buschor 1943. ___. *Satyrtänze und frühes Drama*. SBAW. Munich, 1943.

Cahn 1973. Cahn, H. A. "Dokimasia," *RA* (1973), 3–22.

Cahn 1975. ___. "Early Tarentine Coinage" in *Kleine Schriften zur Münzenkunde und Archäologie*. Ed. H.C. Ackermann. Mainz, 1975, pp. 98–114 (= *Essays . . . Stanley Robinson* [1968], 59–74).

Camp 1996. Camp, John McK. "Excavations in the Athenian Agora: 1994 and 1995," *Hesperia* 65 (1996), 231–61.

Campbell 1984. Campbell, David A. "The Frogs in the *Frogs*," *JHS* 104 (1984), 163–65.

Capps 1899. Capps, Edward. "II. – The Catalogues of Victors at the Dionysia and Lenaea, CIA. II 977," *AJP* 20 (1899), 388–405.

Capps 1907. ___. "III. – Epigraphical Problems in the History of Attic Comedy," *AJP* 28 (1907), 179–99.

Capps 1943. ___. "A New Fragment of the List of Victors at the City Dionysia," *Hesperia* 12 (1943), 1–11.

Carden 1974. Carden, Richard. *Papyrus Fragments of Sophocles*. Berlin and New York, 1974.

de Carli 1971. de Carli, E. *Aristofane e la sofistica*. Florence, 1971.

Carpenter 1986. Carpenter, T. H. *Dionysian Imagery in Archaic Greek Art. Its Development in Black-figure Vase Painting*. Oxford, 1986.

Carpenter 1991. ___. *Art and Myth in Ancient Greece*. London, 1991.

Carpenter 1997. ___. *Dionysian Imagery in Fifth-Century Athens*. Oxford, 1997.

Carpenter and Faraone 1993. Carpenter, T. H. and C. Faraone, edd. *Masks of Dionysus*. Cornell, 1993.

Carrière 1979. Carrière, Jean Claude. *Le carnaval et la politique. Une introduction à la comédie grecque suivie d'un choix de fragments*. Paris, 1979.

Carter 1987. Carter, Jane B. "The Masks of Ortheia," *AJA* 91 (1987), 355–83.

Carter 1988. ___. "Masks and Poetry in Early Sparta" in *Early Greek Cult Practice*. Edd. R. Hägg, N. Marinatos, and G. Nordquist. Stockholm, 1988, pp. 89–98.

Cataudella 1940. Cataudella, Quintino. *La poesia di Aristofane*. Bari, 1934.

Ceccarelli 1996. Ceccarelli, Paola. "L'Athènes de Périclès: un 'pays de cocagne'? L'idéologie démocratique et l'αὐτόματος βίος dans la comédie ancienne," *QUCC* 54 (1996), 109–59.

Ceccarelli 1998. ___. *La pirrica nell'antichità greco romana: studi sulla danza armata.* Pisa and Rome, 1998.

Ceccarelli 2000. ___. "Live among the Savages and Escape from the City in Old Comedy," in Harvey and Wilkins 2000, pp. 453–472 (= "Le monde sauvage et la cité dans la comédie ancienne," *Études de lettres* [Lausanne] 1 [1992], 23–37).

Cobet 1840. Cobet, C. G. *Observationes criticae in Platonis comici reliquias.* Amsterdam, 1840.

Cohen 1978. Cohen, Beth. *Attic Bilingual Vases.* New York, 1978.

Cohen and Shapiro 1995. Cohen, Beth and H. A. Shapiro, edd. *Mother City and Colony. Classical Athenian and South Italian Vases in New Zealand and Australia.* Christchurch, N.Z., 1995.

Cole 1967. Cole, Thomas. *Democritus and the Sources of Greek Anthropology.* Cleveland, 1967. (repr. with addenda, Atlanta, GA, 1990)

Cole 1993. Cole, Susan Guettel. "Procession and Celebration at the Dionysia" in *Theater and Society in the Classical World.* Ed. R. Scodel. Ann Arbor, 1993, pp. 25–38.

Collinge 1958/59. Collinge, N. E. "Some Reflections on Satyr-plays," *PCPS* 5 (1958/59), 28–35.

Collinge 1989. Collinge, Anna. "The Case of Satyrs" in *Images of Authority. Papers Presented to Joyce Reynolds.* Edd. M. M. Mackenzie and C. Roueché. Cambridge, 1989, pp. 82–103.

Conacher 1977. Conacher, J. D. "Prometheus as Founder of the Arts," *GRBS* 18 (1977), 189–206.

Connor 1989. Connor, W. R. "The City Dionysia and Athenian Democracy," *Classica et Medievalia* 40 (1989), 7–32.

Cook 1997. Cook, R. M. *Greek Painted Pottery.* 3rd ed. London, 1997.

Corsini 1985. Corsini, Eugenio. "Gli *Uccelli* di Aristofane: utopia o satira politica?" in *La Città ideale nella tradizione classica e biblio-cristiana.* Ed. E. R. Uglione. Torino, 1985, pp. 57–136.

Coulter 1995. Coulter, James. Review of Bowie, *Aristophanes: Myth and Ritual. CP* 90 (1995), 281–86.

Craik 1987. Craik, Elizabeth. "'One for the Pot': Aristophanes' *Birds* and the Anthesteria," *Eranos* 85 (1987), 25–34.

Craik 1990. ___. "The Staging of Sophokles' *Philoktetes* and Aristophanes' *Birds*" in *Owls to Athens.* Ed. E. M. Craik. Oxford, 1990, pp. 81–84.

Csapo 1993. Csapo, E. "Deep Ambivalence: Notes on a Greek Cockfight," *Phoenix* 47 (1993), 1–28, 115–24.

Csapo 1994. ___. "The Authorship of the Comoedia Dukiana," *ZPE* 100 (1994), 39–44.

Csapo 2003. ___. "The Dolphins of Dionysus" in *Poetry, Theory, Praxis. The Social Life of Myth, Word and Image in Ancient Greece. Essays in Honour of W. J. Slater.* Edd. E. Csapo and M., Miller. Oxford, 2003, pp. 69–98.

Csapo forthcoming. ___. ed. *The Origins of Theater in Ancient Greece and Beyond.* Cambridge, Forthcoming.

Csapo and Slater 1995. Csapo, E. and W. J. Slater. *The Context of Ancient Drama.* Ann Arbor, 1995.

Danner 1993. Danner, Peter. "Meniskoi und Obeloi. Zum Schutz von Statuen und Bauwerken vor den Vögeln," *Jahreshefte des österreichischen archäologischen Institutes in Wien* 62 (1993), 19–28.

Davidson 1997. Davidson, James. *Courtesans and Fishcakes. The Consuming Passions of Classical Athens.* London, 1997.

Davies 1989. Davies, Malcolm. "Sisyphus and the Invention of Religion ('Critias' *TrGF* 1 (43) F 19 = B25 DK)," *BICS* 36 (1989), 16–32.

Davies and Kathirithamby 1986. Davies, Malcolm and J. Kathirithamby. *Greek Insects.* Oxford, 1986.

Davies 1978. Davies, Mark I. "Sailing, Rowing, and Sporting in One's Cups on the Wine-dark Sea. ἅλαδε, μύσται" in *Athens Comes of Age. From Solon to Salamis.* Princeton, 1978, pp. 72–92.

Davies 1990. ___. "Asses and Rams: Dionysiac Release in Aristophanes' *Wasps* and Attic Vase-Painting," *Metis* (1990), 169–81.

Davison 1949. Davison, J. A. "The Date of the Prometheia," *TAPA* 80 (1949), 66–93.

Dawkins 1929. Dawkins, R. M., ed. *The Sanctuary of Artemis Orthia.* London, 1929.

Dawson 1992. Dawson, Doyne. *Cities of the Gods.* Oxford, 1992.

Dearden 1976. Dearden, C. W. *The Stage of Aristophanes.* London, 1976.

Defradas 1969. Defradas, Jean. "'Le Chant des Grenouilles: Aristophane Critique Musical," *REA* 71 (1969), 23–37.

Demand 1970. Demand, Nancy. "The Identity of the Frogs," *CP* 65 (1970) 83–87.

Demianczuk 1912. Demianczuk, J. *Supplementum comicum.* Cracow, 1912.

Denniston 1954. Denniston, J. D. *The Greek Particles.* 2nd ed. Oxford, 1954.

Dentzer 1982. Dentzer, J.-M. *Le Motif du banquet couché dans le Proche-Orient et le monde grec du VIIème au IVème siècle avant J.-C.* Paris, 1982.

Deonna 1951. Deonna, W. "L'ex-voto de Cypsélos à Delphes: le symbolisme du palmier et des grenouilles," *Revue de l'histoire des religions* 139 (1951), 162–207 and 140 (1952), 5–58.

Detienne 1979. Detienne, M. *Dionysus Slain.* Tr. M. and L. Muellner. Baltimore, 1979.

Detienne 1989a. ___. *Dionysus at Large.* Tr. A. Goldhammer. Cambridge, MA, 1989.

Detienne 1989b. ___. "Culinary Practices and the Spirit of Sacrifice" in *The Cuisine of Sacrifice among the Greeks*. Edd. M. Detienne and J.-P. Vernant. Tr. P. Wissing. Chicago, 1989, pp. 1–20. [*La cuisine du sacrifice en pays grec.* Paris 1979]

Detienne and Vernant 1974. Detienne, M. and J.-P. Vernant. *Les ruses de l'intelligence*. Paris, 1974.

Deubner 1932. Deubner, Ludwig. *Attische Feste*. Berlin, 1932.

Dickins 1906/07. Dickins, Guy. "Damophon's Style." *Annual of the British School at Athens* 13 (1906/07), 392–95.

Dickins 1911. ___. "The Sandal in the Palazzo dei Conservatori," *JHS* 31 (1911), 308–14.

Dickins 1920. ___. *Hellenistic Sculpture*. Oxford, 1920.

Dierauer 1977. Dierauer, Urs. *Tier und Mensch im Denken der Antike*. Amsterdam, 1977.

Dietrich 1962. Dietrich, Bernard. "Demeter, Erinys, Artemis," *Hermes* 90 (1962), 129–48.

Dietrich 1974. ___. *The Origins of Greek Religion*. Berlin and New York, 1974.

Diez 1957. Diez, E. "Delphin" in *Reallexikon für Antike und Christentum* 3 (1957), 667–82.

Dihle 1977. Dihle, A. "Das Satyrspiel 'Sisyphos'," *Hermes* 105 (1977), 28–42.

Dittmer 1923. Dittmer, William A. *The Fragments of Athenian Comic Didascaliae Found in Rome*. Diss. Princeton, 1923.

Dobrov 1993. Dobrov, Gregory. "The Tragic and the Comic Tereus," *AJP* 114 (1993), 189–234.

Dobrov 1995. ___. ed. *Beyond Aristophanes. Transition and Diversity in Greek Comedy*. American Classical Studies, 38. Atlanta, 1995.

Dobrov 1997. ___. ed. *The City as Comedy. Society and Representation in Athenian Drama*. Chapel Hill, NC, 1997.

Dobrov 2001. ___. *Figures of Play. Greek Drama and Metafictional Poetics*. Oxford, 2001.

Dobrov forthcoming. ___. "Aristophanes and the Satyr Chorus," *CJ* forthcoming.

Dodds 1960. Dodds, E. R. *Euripides: Bacchae*. 2nd ed. Oxford, 1960.

Dodds 1973. ___. "The Ancient Concept of Progress" in *The Ancient Concept of Progress and Other Essays*. Oxford, 1971, pp. 1–25.

Dougherty 1993. Dougherty, Carol. *The Poetics of Colonization: From City to Text in Archaic Greece*. Oxford, 1993.

Douglas 1966. Douglas, Mary. *Purity and Danger. An Analysis of the Concepts of Pollution and Taboo*. London, 1966. Repr. 1991.

Douglas 1990. ___. "The Pangolin Revisited: A New Approach to Animal Symbolism" in *Signifying Animals. Human Meaning & the Natural World*. Ed. R. Willis. London, 1990, pp. 25–36.

Dover 1966. Dover, K. J. "Aristophanes' Speech in Plato's *Symposium*," *JHS* 86 (1966), 41–50.

Dover 1968. ___. ed. *Aristophanes: Clouds*. Oxford, 1968.

Dover 1978. ___. *Greek Homosexuality*. New York, 1978.

Dover 1993. ___. ed. *Aristophanes: Frogs*. Oxford, 1993.

Dover 2000. ___. "Foreword: Frogments," in Harvey and Wilkins 2000, pp. xvii–x.

Dowden 1992. Dowden, Ken. *The Uses of Greek Mythology*. London, 1992.

Drougou 1975. Drougou, Stella. *Der attische Psykter*. Beiträge zur Archäologie 9. Würzburg, 1975.

duBois 1982. duBois, Page. *Centaurs and Amazons. Women and the Pre-History of the Great Chain of Being*. Ann Arbor, 1982.

Dugas 1946. Dugas, Ch. "Lécythe aryballisque athénien," *BCH* 70 (1946), 172–78.

Dumont 1975. Dumont, Jacques. "Les dauphins d'Apollon," *Quaderni di Storia* 1 (1975), 57–85.

Dumont 1988. ___. "Les combats de coq furent-ils un sport?" *Pallas* 34 (1988), 33–44.

Dumortier 1975. Dumortier, Jean. *Les images dans la poésie d'Eschyle*. Paris, 1975.

Dunbabin 1948. Dunbabin, T. J. *The Western Greeks*. Oxford, 1948.

Dunbar 1995. Dunbar, Nan V., ed. *Aristophanes: Birds*. Oxford, 1995.

Durand and Schnapp 1989. Durand, J.-L. and A. Schnapp, "Sacrificial Slaughter and Initiatory Hunt" in *A City of Images. Iconography and Society in Ancient Greece*. Edd. C. Bérard et al. Tr. Deborah Lyons. Princeton, 1989, pp. 53–70.

Earp 1948. Earp, F. *The Style of Aeschylus*. Cambridge, 1948.

Edelstein 1967. Edelstein, Ludwig. *The Idea of Progress in Classical Antiquity*. Baltimore, 1967.

Edlund 1987. Edlund, I. *The Gods and the Place: Location and Function of Sanctuaries in the Countryside of Etruria and Magna Graecia (700–400 B.C.)*. Stockholm, 1987.

Edmunds 1987. Edmunds, Lowell. *Cleon, Knights and Aristophanes' Politics*. Lanham, MD, 1987.

Edwards 2002. Edwards, Antony. "Historicizing the Popular Grotesque: Bakhtin's *Rabelais and His World* and Attic Old Comedy" in *Bakhtin and the Classics*. Ed. R. Bracht Branham. Evanston, IL., 2002, pp. 27–55.

Ellmann 1988. Ellmann, Richard. *Oscar Wilde*. New York, 1988.

Else 1957. Else, Gerald. *Aristotle's Poetics: The Argument*. Leiden, 1957.

Else 1965. ___. *The Origin and Early Form of Greek Tragedy*. New York, 1965.

Epstein 1981. Epstein, Paul D. "The Marriage of Peisthetairos to *Basileia* in the *Birds* of Aristophanes," *Dionysius* 5 (1981), 5–28.

Erbse 1980. Erbse, Hartmut. "Homerische Götter in Vogelgestalt," *Hermes* 108 (1980), 259–74.

Ewbank 1980. Ewbank, Joseph. *Fable and Proverb in Aristophanes*. Diss. Univ. of North Carolina, 1980.

Farioli 1999. Farioli, Marcella. "Due zoocrazie comiche: Les *Bestie* di Cratete e i *Pesci* di Archippo," *Aevum Antiquum* 12 (1999), 17–59. (Also in *Mundus alter. Utopie e distopie nella commedia greca antica*. Milan, 2001.)

Fedele et al. 1984. Fedele, B. et al. *Antichità della collezione Guarini*. Galatina, 1984.

Fehr 1971. Fehr, Burkhard. *Orientalische und griechische Gelage*. Bonn, 1971.

Fehr 1990. ___. "Entertainers at the *Symposion*: The *Akletoi* in the Archaic Period," in Murray 1990, pp. 185–96.

Ferrari et al. 1998. Ferrari, G., C. M., Nielsen and K. Olson, edd. *The Classical Collection. The David and Alfred Smart Museum of Art, The University of Chicago*. Chicago, 1998.

Fischer-Bossert 1999. Fischer-Bossert, W. *Chronologie der Didrachmenprägung von Tarent*. Berlin and New York, 1999.

Fisher 2000. Fisher, Nick. "Symposiasts, Fish-Eaters and Flatterers: Social Mobility and Moral Concerns in Old Comedy," in Harvey and Wilkins 2000, pp. 355–96.

Flintoff 1983. Flintoff, E. "Aristophanes and the *Prometheus Bound*," *CQ* 33 (1983), 1–5.

Foley 1985. Foley, Helene P. *Ritual Irony. Poetry and Sacrifice in Euripides*. Ithaca, NY, 1985.

Forbes Irving 1990. Forbes Irving, P. M. C. *Metamorphosis in Greek Myths*. Oxford, 1990.

Förtsch 1997. Förtsch, Reinhard. "Die Nichtdarstellung des Spektakulären: Griechische Buldkunst und griechische Drama im 5. und frühen 4. Jh. v. Chr.," *Hephaistos* 15 (1997), 47–68.

Fowler 1989. Fowler, Don. "Taplin on Cocks," *CQ* 39 (1989), 257–59.

Fraenkel 1962. Fraenkel, Eduard. *Beobachtungen zu Aristophanes*. Rome, 1962.

Franzius 1973. Franzius, Georgia. *Tänzer und Tänze in der archaischen Vasenmalerei*. Göttingen, 1973.

Friedrich 1996. Friedrich, Rainer. 1996. "Everything to Do with Dionysos? Ritualism, the Dionysiac, and the Tragic" in *Tragedy and the Tragic. Greek Theatre and Beyond*. Ed. M. S. Silk. Oxford, 1996, pp. 257–83.

Frickenhaus 1912. Frickenhaus, A. *Lenäenvasen*. Winckelmannsprogramm 77. Berlin, 1912.

Frielinghaus 1995. Frielinghaus, Heide. *Einheimische in der apulischen Vasenmalerei: Ikonographie im Spannungsfeld zwischen Produzenten und Rezipienten*. Berlin, 1995.

Froning 1971. Froning, Heide. *Dithyrambos und Vasenmalerei in Athen*. Beiträge zur Archäologie 2. Würzburg, 1971.

Frontisi-Ducroux 1991. Frontisi-Ducroux, Françoise. *Le Dieu-masque. Une figure du Dionysos d'Athènes*. Paris and Rome, 1991.

Frontisi-Ducroux 1992. ___. "Un Scandale à Athènes: faire le *comos* sans masque," *Dialogues d'histoire ancienne* 18 (1992), 245–56.

Gantz 1993. Gantz, Timothy. *Early Greek Myth*. Baltimore, 1993.

Gatz 1967. Gatz, Bodo. *Weltalter, goldene Zeit und sinnverwandte Vorstellungen.* Hildesheim, 1967.

Geagan 1970. Geagan, H. "Mythological Themes on the Plaques from Pentes-kouphia," *AA* (1970), 31–48.

Gebhard 1987. Gebhard, Elizabeth R. "The Early Sanctuary of Poseidon at Isth-mia," *AJA* 91 (1987), 475–76.

Geissler 1969. Geissler, Paul. *Chronologie der altattischen Komödie.* Berlin, 1969. [Repr. of 1925 ed., with addenda.]

Gelzer 1960. Gelzer, Thomas. *Der epirrhematische Agon bei Aristophanes.* Munich, 1960.

Gelzer 1971. ___. *Aristophanes der Komiker.* Stuttgart, 1971. [= RE Supplement XII, 1392–1570]

Gempeler 1969. Gempeler, R. D. "Die Schmiede des Hephäst – eine Satyrspiel-szene des Harrowmalers," *AK* 12 (1969), 16–21, pls. 13–14.

van Gennep 1960. van Gennep, A. *The Rites of Passage.* Trs. M. Vizedoni and G. Caffee. London, 1960. [Originally published 1909.]

Georgi 1982. Georgi, Laura. "Pollination Ecology of the Date Palm and Fig Tree: Herodotus 1.193.4–5," *CP* 77 (1982), 224–28.

Gera 2003. Gera, Deborah Levine. *Ancient Greek Ideas on Speech, Language, and Civilization.* Oxford, 2003.

Ghiron-Bistagne 1976. Ghiron-Bistagne, Paulette. *Recherches sur les acteurs dans la Grèce antique.* Paris, 1976.

Giangrande 1963. Giangrande, G. "The Origin of Attic Comedy," *Eranos* 61 (1963), 1–24.

Giannini 1959. Giannini, Alessandro. "Platone comico: questioni cronologiche e tematiche," *Dioniso* 22 (1959), 189–204.

Gill 1975. Gill, David. "*Birds* 593–595: A Note," *HSCP* 79 (1975), 69–72.

Gilula 1995. Gilula, D. "The *Choregoi* Vase – Comic Yes, But Angels?" *ZPE* 109 (1995), 5–10.

Goossens 1935. Goossens, R. "Les 'Ploutoi' de Kratinos," *REA* 37 (1935), 405–34.

Graf 1979a. Graf, Fritz. "Apollon Delphinios," *Museum Helveticum* 36 (1979), 2–22.

Graf 1979b. ___. "Das Götterbild aus dem Taurerland," *Antike Welt* 10 (1979), 33–41.

Graf 1985. ___. *Nordionische Culte: Religionsgeschichtliche und epigraphische Unter-suchungen zu den Kulten von Chios, Erythrai, Klazomenai und Phokaia.* Rome, 1985.

Graf 1999. ___. "Komos" in *Der neue Pauly.* Leiden, 1999.

Green 1985. Green, J. R. "A Representation of the *Birds* of Aristophanes," *Greek Vases in the J. Paul Getty Museum* 2 (1985), 95–118.

Green 1989. ___. "Theatre Production: 1971–1986," *Lustrum* 31 (1989), 7–95.

Green 1991. ___. "On Seeing and Depicting the Theatre in Classical Athens," *GRBS* 32 (1991), 15–50.

Green 1994. ——. *Theatre in Ancient Greek Society*. London, 1994.

Green and Handley 1995. Green, J. R. and Eric Handley. *Images of the Greek Theater*. Austin, TX, 1995.

Green 1992. Green, Miranda. *Animals in Celtic Life and Myth*. London, 1992.

Greenhalgh 1973. Greenhalgh, P. A. L. *Early Greek Warfare. Horsemen and Chariots in the Homeric and Archaic Ages*. Cambridge, 1973.

Greifenhagen 1929. Greifenhagen, A. *Eine attische schwarzfigurige Vasengattung und die Darstellung des Komos im VI. Jahrhundert*. Diss. Königsberg, 1929.

Greifenhagen 1965. ——. "Delphinreiter auf einem Psykter des Oltos," *Pantheon* 23 (1965), 1–7.

Greifenhagen 1974. ——. "Red-figured Psykter with Dolphin Riders by Oltos" in *Ancient Art. The Norbert Schimmel Collection*. Ed. O. W. Muscarella. Mainz, 1974, no. 57.

Griffith 1977. Griffith, Mark. *The Authenticity of the Prometheus Bound*. Cambridge, 1977.

Griffith 1983. ——. ed. *Aeschylus: Prometheus Bound*. Cambridge, 1983.

Griffith 1987. Griffith, R. Drew. "The Hoopoe's Name (A Note on *Birds* 48)," *QUCC* 26 (1987), 59–63.

Grossmann 1950. Grossmann, G. *Politische Schlagwörter aus der Zeit des Peloponnesischen Krieges*. Basel, 1950.

Guggisberg 1947. Guggisberg, Peter. *Das Satyrspiel*. Diss. Zurich, 1947.

Guthrie 1957. Guthrie, W. K. C. *In the Beginning. Some Greek Views on the Origins of Life and the Early State of Man*. London, 1957.

Guthrie 1962, 1965, 1975. ——. *A History of Greek Philosophy*. Cambridge, vol. 1, 1962; vol. 2, 1965; vol. 4, 1975.

Guthrie 1971. ——. *The Sophists*. Cambridge, 1971. (= vol. 3, pt. 1 of preceding.)

Habash 2002. Habash, Martha. "Dionysos' Roles in Aristophanes' *Frogs*," *Mnemosyne* 55 (2002), 1–17.

Hall 1989. Hall, Edith. *Inventing the Barbarian. Greek Self-Definition through Tragedy*. Oxford, 1989.

Halliwell 1991. Halliwell, S. "The Uses of Laughter in Greek Culture," *CQ* 41 (1991), 279–96.

Halverson 1976. Halverson, J. "Animal Categories and Terms of Abuse," *Man* 11 (1976), 505–16.

Hamdorf 1964. Hamdorf, F. W. *Griechische Kultpersonifikationen der vorhellenistischen Zeit*. Mainz, 1964.

Hamilton 1985. Hamilton, Richard. "The Well-Equipped Traveller: *Birds* 42," *GRBS* 26 (1985), 235–39.

Hamilton 1989. ——. "Alkman and the Athenian Arkteia," *Hesperia* 58 (1989), 449–72.

Hamma 1989. Hamma, K., ed. *The Dechter Collection of Greek Vases*. San Bernardino, CA, 1989.

Hampe 1975. Hampe, Roland. "Dickbauchtänzer und Diebe auf Korinthischem Krater," *JdI* 90 (1975), 85–99.

Handley 1985. Handley, E. G. "Comedy" in *The Cambridge History of Classical Literature. Vol. 1: Greek Literature.* Edd. P. E. Easterling and B. M. W. Knox. Cambridge, 1985, pp. 355–425.

Harris 1985. Harris, Marvin. *The Sacred Cow and the Abominable Pig. Riddles of Food and Culture.* New York, 1985. [original title: *Good to Eat*]

Harvey 2000. Harvey, David. "Phrynichos and His Muses" in Harvey and Wilkins 2000, pp. 91–124.

Harvey and Wilkins 2000. Harvey, David and John Wilkins. *The Rivals of Aristophanes. Studies in Athenian Old Comedy.* London and Swansea, 2000.

Haspels 1936. Haspels, C. H. Emelie. *Attic Black-figured Lekythoi.* Paris, 1936.

Havelock 1957. Havelock, Eric. *The Liberal Temper in Greek Politics.* New Haven, 1957.

Heath 1988. Heath, M. "Receiving the κῶμος: The Context and Performance of Epinician," *AJP* 109 (1988), 180–95.

Heath 1999. Heath, John. "Disentangling the Beast: Humans and Other Animals in Aeschylus' *Oresteia,*" *JHS* 119 (1999), 17–47.

Heath 2005. Heath, John. *The Talking Greeks: Speech, Animals and the Other in Homer, Aeschylus, and Plato.* Cambridge, 2005.

Hedreen 1992. Hedreen, Guy. *Silens in Attic Black-figure Vase-painting. Myth and Performance.* Ann Arbor, 1992.

Heinimann 1945. Heinimann, F. *Nomos und Physis.* Basel, 1945.

Helbig 1904. Helbig, W. *Les Ἱππεῖς Athéniens.* Paris, 1904.

Henderson 1975. Henderson, Jeffrey. *The Maculate Muse.* New Haven, 1975. (2nd ed. with addenda, Oxford, 1991)

Henderson 1987. ——. *Aristophanes: Lysistrata.* Oxford, 1987.

Henderson 1990. ——. "The *Demos* and the Comic Competition" in Winkler and Zeitlin 1990, pp. 271–313.

Henderson 1993. ——. Introduction to F. M. Cornford, *The Origin of Attic Comedy.* Ann Arbor, 1993.

Henderson 1997. ——. "Mass versus Elite and the Comic Heroism of Peisetairos" in Dobrov 1997, pp. 135–48.

Henderson 2000. ——. "Pherekrates and the Women of Old Comedy" in Harvey and Wilkins 2000, pp. 135–50.

Henrichs 1975. Henrichs, Albert. "Two Doxographical Notes: Democritus and Prodicus on Religion," *HSCP* 79 (1975), 93–123.

Henrichs 1984a. ——. "Loss of Self, Suffering, Violence: The Modern View of Dionysus from Nietzsche to Girard," *HSCP* 88 (1984), 205–40.

Henrichs 1984b. ——. "The Sophists and Hellenistic Religion: Prodicus as the Spiritual Father of the Isis Aretalogies," *HSCP* 88 (1984), 139–58.

Henrichs 1987. ___. "Myth Visualized: Dionysos and His Circle in Sixth-Century Attic Vase-Painting" in *Papers on the Amasis Painter and His World*. Malibu, California, 1987.

Henrichs 1990. ___. "Between Country and City: Cultic Dimensions of Dionysus in Athens and Attica" in *Cabinet of the Muses*. Edd. M. Griffith and D. J. Mastronarde. Atlanta, 1990, pp. 257–77.

Henrichs 1993. ___. "'He Has a God in Him': Human and Divine in the Modern Perception of Dionysus" in Carpenter and Faraone 1993, pp. 13–43.

Henry 1977. Henry, A. S. "Aristophanes *Birds* 268–93," *CQ* 72 (1977), 52–53.

Herington 1963. Herington, C. J. "A Study in the *Prometheia*, Part II: *Birds* and *Prometheia*," *Phoenix* 17 (1963), 236–43.

Herington 1985. Herington, C. J. *Poetry into Drama: Early Tragedy and the Greek Poetic Tradition*. Berkeley, 1985.

Herter 1947. Herter, Hans. *Vom dionysischen Tanz zum komischen Spiel*. Iserlohn, 1947.

Herter 1980. ___. "Die Delphine des Dionysus," *Archaiognosia* 1 (1980), 101–34.

Hoffmann 1964. Hoffmann, H., ed. *Norbert Schimmel Collection*. Mainz, 1964.

Hoffmann 1973. ___. "Frösche des Sotades. βρεκεκεκὲξ κοὰξ κοὰξ" in *Zur griechischen Kunst. Hansjörg Bloesch zum sechzigsten Geburtstag*. Edd. H. P. Isler and G. Seiterle. Bern, 1973, pp. 20–22.

Hoffmann 1974. ___. "Hahnenkampf in Athen. Zur Ikonologie einer attischen Bildformel," *RA* (1974), 195–220.

Hoffmann 1977. ___. *Sexual and Asexual Pursuit*. Royal Anthropological Institute of Great Britain and Ireland, Occ. Paper no. 34. London, 1977.

Hoffmann 1988. Hoffmann, H. "Why Did the Greeks Need Imagery? An Anthropological Approach to the Study of Greek Vase Painting," *Hephaistos* 9 (1988), 143–62.

Hofmann 1976. Hofmann, Heinz. *Mythos und Komödie. Untersuchungen zu den Vögeln des Aristophanes*. Hildesheim, 1976.

Holloway 1978. Holloway, R. Ross. *Art and Coinage in Magna Graecia*. Bellinzona, 1978.

Hooker 1960. Hooker, G. T. W. "The Topography of the *Frogs*," *JHS* 80 (1960), 112–17.

Hooker 1989. Hooker, J. T. "Arion and the Dolphin," *G&R* 36 (1989), 141–46.

Hornblower 1987. Hornblower, S. *Thucydides*. Baltimore, 1987.

Hornblower 1995. ___. "The Fourth-Century and Hellenistic Reception of Thucydides," *JHS* 115 (1995), 47–68.

Hubbard 1991. Hubbard, Thomas K. *The Mask of Comedy. Aristophanes and the Intertextual Parabasis*. Ithaca, 1991.

Hubbard 1997. ___. "Utopianism and the Sophistic City in Aristophanes" in Dobrov 1997, pp. 23–50.

Hunter 1982. Hunter, Virginia. *Past and Process in Herodotus and Thucydides*. Princeton, 1982.

Huss 1999. Huss, Bernhard, ed. *Xenophons Symposion*. Stuttgart, 1999.

Hussey 1985. Hussey, Edward. "Thucydidean History and Democritean Theory" in *CRUX. Essays in Greek History Presented to G. E. M. de Ste. Croix*. Edd. P. A. Cartledge and F. D. Harvey. London, 1985, pp. 118–38.

Isler 1970. Isler, Hans Peter. *Acheloos*. Bern 1970.

Isler 1990. ___. Review of Weiss, *Griechische Flussgottheiten. Gnomon* 62 (1990), 661–63.

Isler 1985. ___. "Eros auf dem Delphin?" in *Lebendige Altertumswissenschaft. Festgabe Hermann Vetters*. Edd. E. von Ploeckinger and M. Bietak. Vienna, 1985, pp. 74–76.

Isler-Kerényi 1988. Isler-Kerényi, Cornelia. "Dickbäuche, Komasten, dionysische Tänzer?" in *Proceedings of the 3rd Symposium on Ancient Greek and Related Pottery*. Edd. J. Christiansen and T. Melander. Zutphen, 1988, pp. 269–77.

Isler-Kerényi 1993. ___. "Dionysos und Solon," *Antike Kunst* 36 (1993), 3–10.

Jameson 1980. Jameson, Michael. "Apollo Lykeios in Athens," *Archaiognosia* 1 (1980), 213–36.

Jameson 1993. ___. "The Asexuality of Dionysus" in Carpenter and Faraone 1993, pp. 44–64.

Jeanmaire 1978. Jeanmaire, Henri. *Dionysos: histoire du culte de Bacchus: l'orgiasme dans l'antiquité et les temps modernes*. Paris, 1978.

Jones 2005. Jones, Prudence. *Reading Rivers in Roman Literature and Culture*. Lanham, MD, 2005.

Jucker 1963. Jucker, Ines. "Frauenfest in Korinth," *AK* 6 (1963), 47–61.

Kahil 1977. Kahil, L. "L'Artémis de Brauron: rites et mystère," *Antike Kunst* 20 (1977), 86–98.

Kahil 1981. ___. "Le 'cratérisque' d'Artémis et le Brauronion de l'Acropole," *Hesperia* 50 (1981), 253–63.

Kahil 1983. ___. "Mythological Repertoire of Brauron" in *Ancient Greek Art and Iconography*. Ed. W. Moon. Madison, WI, 1983, pp. 231–44.

Kahn 1981. Kahn, Ch. H. "The Origins of Social Contract Theory" in *The Sophists and their Legacy*. Ed. G. B. Kerferd. Wiesbaden, 1981, 92–108.

Kaibel 1889. Kaibel, G. "Zur attischen Komödie," *Hermes* 24 (1889), 35–66.

Kallet-Marx 1993. Kallet-Marx, Lisa. *Money, Expense and Naval Power in Thucydides' History 1–5.24*. Berkeley, 1993.

Karageorghis 1971. Karageorghis, V. "Notes on Some Cypriote Priests Wearing Bull-Masks," *Harvard Theological Review* 64 (1971), 261–70.

Kassel 1981. Kassel, R. *Dichtkunst und Versifikation bei den Griechen*. Rheinland-Westfalen Akademie, Vortr. G 250, 1981.

Katsouris 1999. Katsouris, A. G. "Comedy and Satyr Drama," *Dodone. Philosophike Schole Panepistemiou Ioanninon* 28 (1999), 181–207.

Katz 1999. Katz, Ph. B. 1999. "Io in the *Pometheus Bound*: A Coming of Age Paradigm for the Athenian Community" in *Rites of Passage in Ancient Greece*. Ed. Mark W. Padilla. Lewisburg, PA, 1999, pp. 129–47.

Kavvadias 1893. Kavvadias, P. *Fouilles de Lycosoura. I. Les sculptures de Damophon.* Athens, 1893.

Keller 1887. Keller, O. *Thiere des classischen Altertums.* Innsbruck, 1887.

Keller 1909 and 1913. Keller, O. *Die antike Tierwelt.* Leipzig. vol. I, 1909; vol. II, 1913.

Kerferd 1981. Kerferd, G. B. *The Sophistic Movement.* Cambridge, 1981.

Kerkhof 2001. Kerkhof, Rainer. *Dorische Posse, Epicharm und attische Komödie.* Munich and Leipzig, 2001.

Kingsley 1995. Kingsley, Bonnie M. "The Reclining Heroes of Taras and Their Cult," *California Studies in Classical Antiquity* 12 (1995), 201–20.

Kirk and Raven 1957. Kirk, G. S. and J. E. Raven. *The Presocratic Philosophers.* Cambridge, 1957.

Kitchell 1993. Kitchell, K. "The View from Deucalion's Ark: New Windows on Antiquity," *CJ* 88 (1993), 341–57.

Kleingünther 1933. Kleingünther, Adolf. ΠΡΩΤΟΣ ΕΥΡΕΤΗΣ. *Untersuchungen zur Geschichte einer Fragestellung.* Leipzig, 1933.

Kloss 2001. Kloss, Gerrit. *Erscheinungsformen komischen Sprechens bei Aristophanes.* Berlin and New York, 2001.

Konstan 1990a. Konstan, David. "An Anthropology of Euripides' *Kyklops*" in Winkler and Zeitlin, 1990, pp. 207–27. (An earlier version appeared in *Ramus* 10 [1981], 87–103).

Konstan 1990b. ___. "Aristophanes' *Birds* and the City in the Air," *Arethusa* 23 (1990), 183–207. (Also Konstan 1995, pp. 29–44 and in Dobrov 1997, pp. 3–22.)

Konstan 1991. ___. "What is Greek about Greek Mythology?" *Kernos* 4 (1991), 11–30.

Konstan 1995. ___. *Greek Comedy and Ideology.* Oxford, 1995.

Körte 1893. Körte, Alfred. "Archäologische Studien zur alten Komödie," *JdI* 8 (1893), 61–93.

Körte 1921. ___. "Komödie," *RE* 11 (1921), 1207–75.

Kossatz and Kossatz-Deissmann 1992. Kossatz, Tilman and Anneliese Kossatz-Deissmann. "Martin von Wagner, Dionysos und die Seeräuber" in *Kotinos. Festschrift für Erika Simon.* Edd. Heide Froning, T. Hölscher, and H. Mielsch. Mainz, 1992, pp. 469–78.

Kossatz-Deissmann 1982. Kossatz-Deissmann, Anneliese. "Zur Herkunft des Perizoma im Satyrspiel," *JdI* 97 (1982), 65–90.

Koster 1969. Koster, W. J. W. *Scholia in Aristophanem.* Pars 1, Fasc. II. Scholia Vetera et Scholia Tricliniana in Aristophanis Equites. Ed. D. M. Jones and N. G. Wilson. Groningen and Amsterdam, 1969.

Koster 1974. *Scholia Recentiora in Nubes. Scholia in Aristophanem,* Pars I, Fasc. III.2. Groningen, 1974.

Kozloff 1981. Kozloff, Arielle, P., ed. *Animals in Ancient Art from the Leo Mildenberg Collection.* Cleveland Museum of Art and Indiana University Press, 1981.

Kraay 1976. Kraay, Colin M. *Archaic and Classical Greek Coins*. London, 1976.

Kraay and Hirmer 1966. Kraay, Colin M. and M. Hirmer. *Greek Coins*. London, 1966.

Krumeich et al. 1999. Krumeich, Ralf, Nikolaus Pechstein, and Bernd Seidensticker, edd. *Das griechische Satyrspiel*. Darmstadt, 1999.

Kunze-Götte et al. 1999. Kunze-Götte, Erika, Karin Tancke, and Klaus Vierneisel. *Kerameikos 7.2. Die Nekropole von der Mitte des 6. bis zum Ende des 5. Jahrhunderts. Die Beigaben*. Deutsches archäologisches Institut. Munich, 1999.

Kurtz and Boardman 1986. Kurtz, D. C. and J. Boardman. "Booners," *Greek Vases in the J. Paul Getty Museum* 3 (1986), 35–70.

Kurtz and Boardman 1995.—. "An Athenian Red-Figure Neck-Amphora by the Athena-Bowdoin Painter" in *Classical Art in the Nicholson Museum, Sydney*. Ed. A. Cambitoglou, asst. ed. E. G. D. Robinson. Mainz, 1995, pp. 85–90.

Kyle 1987. Kyle, Donald. *Athletics in Ancient Athens*. Leiden, 1987.

Lacroix 1953. Lacroix, L. "Fleuves et nymphes éponymes sur les monnaies grecques," *Revue belge de numismatique et de sigillographie* 99 (1953), 5–21.

Lacroix 1964. —. *Monnaies et Colonisation dans L'Occident Grec*. Brussels, 1964.

Lada-Richards 1999. Lada-Richards, Ismene. *Initiating Dionysus. Ritual and Theatre in Aristophanes' Frogs*. Oxford, 1999.

Lamberton and Rotroff 1985. Lamberton, Robert D. and Susan I. Rotroff. *Birds of the Athenian Agora*. Princeton, 1985.

Larson 1995. Larson, Jennifer. "The Corycian Nymphs and the Bee Maidens of the *Homeric Hymn to Hermes*," *GRBS* 36 (1995), 341–57.

Lawler 1941. Lawler, Lillian. "ΙΧΘΥΕΣ ΧΟΡΕΥΤΑΙ," *CP* 36 (1941), 142–55.

Lawler 1964. —. *The Dance in Ancient Greece*. Middletown, CT, 1964.

Leach 1964. Leach, E. "Anthropological Aspects of Language: Animal Categories and Verbal Abuse" in *New Directions in the Study of Language*. Ed. E. Lenneberg. Cambridge, MA, 1964, pp. 23–63.

Leo 1878. Leo, Friedrich. "Ein Sieg des Magnes," *RhM* 33 (1878), 139.

Leonhardt 1991. Leonhardt, Jürgen. *Phalloslied und Dithyrambos. Aristoteles über den Ursprung des griechischen Dramas*. Heidelberg, 1991.

Lesky 1947. Lesky, Albin. *Thalatta*. Vienna, 1947.

Lesky 1966. —. *A History of Greek Literature*. Trs. J. Willis and C. de Heer. New York, 1966.

Lévi-Strauss 1966. Lévi-Strauss, Claude. *The Savage Mind*. Chicago, 1966. [= *La Pensée sauvage*. Paris, 1962.]

Lévy and Marcadé 1972. Lévy, E. and J. Marcadé. "Au musée de Lycosoura," *BCH* 96 (1972), 967–1004.

Lewis 1990. Lewis, D. M. "The Political Background of Democritus" in *Owls to Athens. Essays K. J. Dover*. Ed. E. M. Craik. Oxford, 1990, pp. 151–54.

Lewis et al. 1992. Lewis, D. M. et al., edd. *Cambridge Ancient History. Vol. V: The Fifth Century B.C.* 2nd ed. Cambridge, 1992.

Lissarrague 1988. Lissarrague, François. "Les satyres et le monde animal" in *Proceedings of the 3rd Symposium on Ancient Greek and Related Pottery*. Copenhagen, Aug. 31–Sept. 4, 1987. Copenhagen, 1988, pp. 335–51.

Lissarrague 1990a. ___. "Why Satyrs are Good to Represent" in Winkler and Zeitlin 1990, pp. 228–36.

Lissarrague 1990b. ___. *The Aesthetics of the Greek Banquet*. Tr. A. Szegedy-Maszak. Princeton, 1990.

Lissarrague 1990c. François Lissarrague, "Around the *Krater*: An Aspect of Banquet Imagery," in Murray 1990, pp. 196–209.

Lissarrague 1993. ___. "On the Wildness of Satyrs" in Carpenter and Faraone 1993, pp. 207–20.

Lissarrague. 1994. ___. "*Epiktetos egraphsen*: The Writing on the Cup" in *Art and Text in Ancient Greek Culture*. Edd. S. Goldhill and R. Osborne. Cambridge, 1994, pp. 12–27.

Lloyd 1983. Lloyd, G. E. R. *Science, Folklore and Ideology. Studies in the Life Sciences in Ancient Greece*. Cambridge, 1983.

Lloyd-Jones 1957. Lloyd-Jones, H. Appendix to H. W. Smyth, tr., *Aeschylus*. Vol. II. Cambridge and London, 1957.

Lloyd-Jones 1983. ___. "Artemis and Iphigeneia," *JHS* 103 (1983), 87–102.

Lloyd-Jones 1990. ___. "Problems of Early Greek Tragedy: Pratinas and Phrynichus" in *Greek Epic, Lyric and Tragedy*. Oxford, 1990, pp. 225–37.

Lloyd-Jones 1996.—. ed. *Sophocles Vol. 3: Fragments*. Loeb Classical Library. Cambridge and London, 1996.

Loeschke 1894. Loeschke, G. "Korinthische Vase mit der Rückführung des Hephaestos," *AM* 19 (1894), 510–25.

Long 1986. Long, Timothy. *Barbarians in Greek Comedy*. Carbondale, IL, 1986.

Lonsdale 1981. Lonsdale, S. *Animals and the Origins of Dance*. New York, 1981.

Lonsdale 1990. ___. *Creatures of Speech. Lion, Herding, and Hunting Similes in the Iliad*. Stuttgart, 1990.

Lonsdale 1993. ___. *Dance and Ritual Play in Greek Religion*. Baltimore, 1993.

Lund and Rathje 1988. Lund, John and Annette Rathje. "Italic Gods and Deities on Pontic Vases" in *Proceedings of the 3rd Symposium on Ancient Greek and Related Pottery Copenhagen, Aug. 31–Sept. 4, 1987*. Edd. J. Christiensen and T. Melander. Copenhagen, 1988, pp. 353–66.

Loucas-Durie 1992. Loucas-Durie, Eveline. "L'element orgiastique dans la religion arcadienne," *Kernos* 5 (1992), 87–96.

Luppe 1970. Luppe, W. "Zur Datierung einiger Dramatiker in der Eusebius Hieronymus Chronik," *Philologus* 114 (1970), 1–8.

Lynch forthcoming. Lynch, Kathleen. *The Symposium in Context: Pottery from a Late Archaic House near the Classical Athenian Agora*. Hesperia Supplement Series. American School of Classical Studies, Athens. Forthcoming.

MacDowell 1962. MacDowell, D. M., ed. *Andokides: On the Mysteries*. Oxford, 1962.

MacDowell 1971. ——. ed. *Aristophanes: Wasps*. Oxford, 1971.

MacDowell 1972. ——. "The Frogs' Chorus," *CR* 22 (1972), 3–5.

MacDowell 1990. ——. ed. and tr. *Demosthenes: Against Meidias*. Oxford, 1990.

MacDowell 1995. ——. *Aristophanes and Athens. An Introduction to the Plays*. Oxford, 1995.

Mackie 1997. Mackie, C. J. "Achilles' Teachers: Chiron and Phoenix in the *Iliad*," *G&R* 44 (1997), 1–10.

Malkin 1986. Malkin, Irad. "Apollo Archegetes and Sicily," *Annali della Scuola Normale Superiore di Pisa, Cl. di Lettere* 16 (1986), 959–72.

Malkin 1987. ——. *Religion and Colonization in Ancient Greece*. Leiden, 1987.

Malkin 1994. ——. *Myth and Territory in the Spartan Mediterranean*. Cambridge, 1994.

Malten 1928. L. Malten, "Der Stier in Kult und mythischem Bild," *Archäologisches Jahrbuch* 43 (1928), 90–138.

Marinatos 1986. Marinatos, N. *Minoan Sacrificial Ritual: Cult Practice and Symbolism*. Acta Instituti Atheniensis Regni Sueciae. Stockholm, 1986.

Markoe and Serwint 1985. Markoe, Glenn E. and Nancy J. Serwint. *Animal Style on Greek and Etruscan Vases*. Robert Hull Fleming Museum, University of Vermont, 1985.

Marshall 1996. Marshall, C. W. "Amphibian Ambiguities Answered," *Échoes de Monde Classique / Classical Views* 40 (1996), 251–65.

Mastromarco 1977. Mastromarco, G. "Le mura di Temistocle e le mura di Nubiculia," *Quaderni di Storia* 3 (1977), 41–50.

Meineke 1840–57. Meineke, A. *Fragmenta Comicorum Graecorum*. 5 vols. Berlin, 1840–57.

Mette 1977. Mette, Hans Joachim. *Urkunden dramatischer Aufführungen in Griechenland*. Berlin and New York, 1977.

Metzger 1972. Metzger, Henri. "Satyrs lanceurs de pierres," *Revue Archéologique* (1972), 31–34.

Miller 1991. Miller, Margaret. "Foreigners at the Greek Symposium?" in Slater 1991, pp. 59–81.

Möllendorff 1995. Möllendorff, Peter von. *Grundlagen einer Ästhetik der Alten Komödie. Untersuchungen zu Aristophanes und Michail Bachtin*. Classica Monacensia, Band 9. Tübingen, 1995.

Moore and Philippides 1986. Moore, Mary B. and Mary Zelia Pease Philippides. *Attic Black-Figured Pottery. The Athenian Agora. Vol. XXII*. Princeton, 1986.

Morris 1996. Morris, Ian. "The Strong Principle of Equality and the Archaic Origins of Greek Democracy" in *Demokratia: A Conversation on Democracies, Ancient and Modern*. Edd. J. Ober and C. Hedrick. Princeton, 1996, pp. 19–48.

Moulton 1981. Moulton, Carroll. *Aristophanic Poetry*. Göttingen, 1981.

Münzen und Medaillen 1967. Münzen und Medaillen A. G., Basel. *Kunstwerke der Antike. Auktion 34*. May 6, 1967.

Münzen und Medaillen 1975. ——. *Kunstwerke der Antike. Auktion* 51. March 14–15, 1975.

Murphy 1973. Murphy, C. T. "Popular Comedy in Aristophanes," *AJP* 93 (1973), 169–89.

Murray 1990. Murray, Oswyn, ed. *Sympotica. A Symposium on the Symposion.* Oxford, 1990.

Murray 1991. ——. "War and the Symposium" in Slater 1991, pp. 83–103.

Murray 1993. ——. *Early Greece.* 2nd ed. Cambridge, MA, 1993.

Muscarella 1974. Muscarella, O. W., ed. *Ancient Art. The Norbert Schimmel Collection.* Mainz, 1974.

Naerebout 1997. Naerebout, F. G. *Attractive Performances: Ancient Greek Dance.* Gieben, 1997.

Nagy 1990. Nagy, Gregory. *Pindar's Homer.* Baltimore, 1990.

Neer 2002. Neer, Richard. *Style and Politics in Athenian Vase-Painting: The Craft of Democracy, ca. 530–460 B.C.* Cambridge, 2002.

Neils 1992. Neils, Jennifer. "Panathenaic Amphoras: Their Meaning, Makers and Markets" in *Goddess and Polis: The Panathenaic Festival in Ancient Athens.* Ed. J. Neils. Hood Museum of Art, Dartmouth College, and Princeton Univ. Press, 1992, pp. 29–51.

Neils 1994. ——. "Theseus" in *LIMC* VIII (1994), 922–955.

Nesselrath 1990. Nesselrath, Heinz-Günther. *Die attische Mittlere Komödie. Ihre Stellung in der antike Literaturkritik und Literaturgeschichte.* Berlin and New York, 1990.

Nestle 1936. Nestle, W. "Die Horen des Prodikos," *Hermes* 71 (1936), 151–70.

Newiger 1957. Newiger, Hans-Joachim. *Metapher und Allegorie. Studien zu Aristophanes.* Munich, 1957.

Newiger 1975. ——. "Die Vögel und ihre Stellung im Gesamtwerk des Aristophanes" in *Aristophanes und die alte Komödie.* Ed. H.-J. Newiger. Darmstadt, 1975, pp. 266–82.

Newiger 1983. ——. "Gedanken zu Aristophanes' 'Vögeln'" in *Aretes Mneme for K. I. Vourveris.* Athens, 1983, pp. 45–57.

Newmyer 1997. Newmyer, Stephen. "Just Beasts? Plutarch and Modern Science on the Sense of Fair Play in Animals," *Classical Outlook* 74 (1997), 85–88.

Nicholson 1968. Nicholson, Felicity. *Ancient Life in Miniature. An Exhibition of Classical Terracottas from Private Collections in England.* Birmingham, 1968.

Nielsen 2002. Nielsen, Inge. *Cultic Theatres and Ritual Drama.* Aarhus Studies in Mediterranean Antiquity IV. Aarhus, 2002.

Nilsson 1961 and 1967. Nilsson, M. P. *Geschichte der griechischen Religion.* Vol. I, 3rd ed. Munich, 1967; Vol. II, 2nd ed., 1961.

Nisetich 2001. Nisetich, Frank. *The Poems of Callimachus.* Oxford, 2001.

Norwood 1931. Norwood, Gilbert. *Greek Comedy.* London, 1931.

O'Brien 1985. O'Brien, M. J. "Xenophanes, Aeschylus and the Doctrine of Primeval Brutishness," *CQ* 79 (1985), 264–77.

Obbink 1988. Obbink, Dirk. "The Origin of Greek Sacrifice: Theophrastus on Religion and Cultural History" in *Theophrastan Studies*. Vol. III. Edd. W. W. Fortenbaugh and R. W. Sharples. New Brunswick, 1988, pp. 272–95.

Obbink 1993. ___. "Dionysus Poured Out: Ancient and Modern Theories of Sacrifice and Cultural Formation" in Carpenter and Faraone 1993, pp. 65–86.

Oellacher 1916. Oellacher, Hans. "Zur Chronologie der altattischen Komödie," *WS* 38 (1916), 81–93.

Olson 1998. Olson, S. D., ed. *Aristophanes: Peace*. Oxford, 1998.

Olson 2000. ___. "We Didn't Know Whether to Laugh or Cry: The Case of Karkinos" in Harvey and Wilkins 2000, pp. 65–74.

Olson 2002. ___. ed. *Aristophanes: Acharnians*. Oxford, 2002.

Olson and Sens 2000. Olson, S. D. and Alexander Sens. *Archestratos of Gela. Greek Culture and Cuisine in the Fourth Century BCE*. Oxford, 2000.

O'Regan 1992. O'Regan, Daphne. *Rhetoric, Comedy, and the Violence of Language in Aristophanes' Clouds*. Oxford, 1992.

Osborne 1990. Osborne, Catherine. "Boundaries in Nature: Eating with Animals in the Fifth Century B.C.," *BICS* 37 (1990), 15–29.

Osborne 1996. Osborne, Robin. *Greece in the Making, 1200–479 B.C.* New York, 1996.

Ostwald 1969. Ostwald, Martin. *Nomos and the Beginnings of Athenian Democracy*. Oxford, 1969.

Ostwald 1986. ___. *From Popular Sovereignty to the Sovereignty of Law. Law, Society and Politics in Fifth-Century Athens*. Berkeley, 1996.

Otto 1965. Otto, Walter F. *Dionysus, Myth and Cult*. Tr. R. B. Palmer. Bloomington, IN, 1965.

Padel 1992. Padel, Ruth. *In and Out of Mind. Greek Images of the Tragic Self*. Princeton, 1992.

Padgett 2000. Padgett, J. Michael. "The Stable Hands of Dionysos: Satyrs and Donkeys as Symbols of Social Marginalization in Attic Vase Painting" in *Not the Classical Ideal*. Ed. Beth Cohen. Leiden, 2000, pp. 43–70.

Padgett 2003. ___. *The Centaur's Smile: The Human Animal in Early Greek Art*. New Haven, 2003.

Padilla 1999. Padilla, Mark, ed. *Rites of Passage in Ancient Greece: Literature, Religion, Society*. Lewisburg, 1999.

Paduano 1973/74. Paduano, G. "La Città degli uccelli e le ambivalenze del nuovo sistem etico-politico," *Studi classici e orientali* 22–23 (1973/74), 115–44.

Paganelli 1979. Paganelli, Leonardo. *Echi storico-politici nel "Ciclope" Euripideo*. Padua, 1979.

Page 1981. Page, D. *Further Greek Epigrams*. Cambridge, 1981.

Panofka 1851. Panofka, A. *Abhandlungen der Berl. Akademie*. Berlin, 1851.

Parke 1977. Parke, H. W. *Festivals of the Athenians*. Ithaca, NY, 1977.

Parker 1983. Parker, Robert. *Miasma. Pollution and Purification in Early Greek Religion*. Oxford, 1983.

303

Parker 1996. ___. *Athenian Religion: A History*. Oxford, 1996.

Patzer 1962. Patzer, H. *Die Anfänge der griechischen Tragödie*. Wiesbaden, 1962.

Patzer 1995. ___. Review of Leonhardt. Phalloslied und Dithyrambos. *Gnomon* 67 (1995), 289–310.

Payne 1931. Payne, H. G. *Necrocorinthia. A Study of Corinthian Art in the Archaic Period*. Oxford, 1931.

Pearson 1917. Pearson, A. C. *The Fragments of Sophocles*. 1917; repr. Amsterdam, 1963.

Peirce 1984. Peirce, Sarah M. "Death, Revelry and Thysia," *Classical Antiquity* 12 (1993), 219–66.

Pélékidis 1962. Pélékidis, C. *Histoire de l' éphébie attique des origins à 31 avant Jésus-Christ*. Paris, 1962.

Pellizer 1990. Pellizer, Ezio. "Outlines of a Morphology of Sympotic Entertainment," in Murray 2000, pp. 177–84.

Pemberton 2000. Pemberton, Elizabeth G. "Wine, Women and Song: Gender Roles in Cult," *Kernos* 13 (2000), 85–106.

Perkell 1993. Perkell, Christine. "On the Two Voices of the Birds in *Birds*," *Ramus* 22 (1993), 1–18.

Petrounias 1976. Petrounias, E. *Funktion und Thematik der Bilder bei Aischylos*. Göttingen, 1976.

Pfeiffer 1949 and 1953. Pfeiffer, R. ed. *Callimachus*. Vol. I: Fragmenta. Oxford, 1949. Vol. II: Hymni et Epigrammata. Oxford, 1953.

Piccirilli 1974. Piccirilli, Luigi, "Susarione e la rivendicazione megarese dell' origine dell commedia greca (Arist., *Poet.*, 3, p. 1448a29–48b2)," *Annali della Scuola Normale Superiore, Pisa* ser. iii 4 (1974), 1289–99.

Pickard-Cambridge 1927. Pickard-Cambridge, A. W. *Dithyramb, Tragedy, and Comedy*. 1st ed. Oxford, 1927.

Pickard-Cambridge 1962. ___. *Dithyramb, Tragedy, and Comedy*. 2nd ed. Rev. by T. B. L. Webster. Oxford, 1962.

Pickard-Cambridge 1968. ___. *The Dramatic Festivals of Athens*. 2nd ed. Rev. by John Gould and D. M. Lewis. Oxford, 1968.

Picon and Mertens 1999/2000. Picon, C. and J. Mertens. "Recent Acquisitions: Amphoriskos," *Bulletin of the Metropolitan Museum of Art* 57 (1999/2000), 8–9.

Piette 1987. Piette, Albert. "Les penseurs grecs à la recherche de l'homme primitif," *Revue belge de Philologie et d'Histoire* 45 (1987), 5–20.

Pilleri 1979. Pilleri, G. "The Chinese River Dolphin (*Lipotes vexillifer*) in Poetry, Literature and Legend," *Investigations on Cetacea* 10 (1979), 335–49.

Pohlenz 1949. Pohlenz, Max. "Die Entstehung der attischen Komödie," *Nachrichten der Akademie der Wissenschaften in Göttingen, Phil.-Hist. Klasse. 1949*, 2, 31–44. (= *Kleine Schriften*, vol. 2. Hildesheim, 1965, pp. 497–510)

de Polignac 1995. de Polignac, François. *Cults, Territory, and the Origins of the Greek City-State*. Tr. Janet Lloyd. Chicago, 1995. [*La Naissance de la cité grecque*, Paris, 1984]

Pollitt 1986. Pollitt, J. J. *Art in the Hellenistic Age*. Cambridge, 1986.

Popham et al. 1982. Popham, M., E. Touloupa, and H. L. Sackett. "The Hero of Lefkandi," *Antiquity* 56 (1982), 169–74.

Poppelreuter 1893. Poppelreuter, J. *De comoediae atticae primordiis particulae duae*. Diss. Berlin, 1893.

Poursat 1968. Poursat, J. C. "Les représentations de danse armée dans la céramique attique," *BCH* 92 (1968), 550–615.

Pozzi 1985/86. Pozzi, Dora. "The Pastoral Ideal in the *Birds* of Aristophanes," *CJ* 81 (1985/86), 119–29.

Pozzi 1991. ___. "The Polis in Crisis" in *Myth and the Polis*. Edd. D. Pozzi and J. M. Wickersham. Ithaca, 1991, pp. 26–63.

Price 1990. Price, Sarah D. "Anakreontic Vases Reconsidered," *GRBS* 31 (1990), 133–75.

Price 1972. Price, Theodora Hadzisteliou. "Bird-Dancer and Satyr-Craftsmen on an Attic Vase," *GRBS* 13 (1972), 239–246.

Price 1978. ___. *Kourotrophos. Cults and Representations of the Greek Nursing Deities*. Leiden, 1978.

Pütz 2003. Pütz, Babette. *The Symposium and Komos in Aristophanes*. Drama Beiheft 22. Stuttgart and Weimar, 2003.

Raaflaub 1999. Raaflaub, Kurt. "Archaic and Classical Greece" in *War and Society in the Ancient and Medieval Worlds*. Edd. Kurt Raaflaub and Nathan Rosenstein. Washington, DC, 1999, pp. 129–161.

Rackham 2000. Rackham, Oliver. "Aegological Note on Eupolis Fr. 13," in Harvey and Wilkins 2000, pp. 349–50.

Radermacher 1921. Radermacher, L., ed. *Aristophanes' Frösche*. Wien, 1921. Repr. 1967.

Radermacher 1932. ___, ed. "Kalenden-Masken und Komödien-Masken," *Philologus* 87 (1932), 382–87.

Ransome 1937. Ransome, Hilda. *The Sacred Bee in Ancient Times and Folklore*. London, 1937.

Rasmussen and Spivey 1991. Rasmussen, Tom and Nigel Spivey, edd. *Looking at Greek Vases*. Cambridge, 1991.

Rau 1967. Rau, Peter. *Paratragodia. Untersuchungen einer kömischen Form des Aristophanes*. Zetemata 45. Munich, 1967.

Ravel 1947. Ravel, O. E. *Descriptive Catalog of the Collection of Tarentine Coins formed by M. P. Vlasto*. London, 1947.

Reckford 1987. Reckford, Kenneth. *Aristophanes' Old-and-New Comedy*. Chapel Hill, 1987.

Reeder 1995. Reeder, Ellen, ed. *Pandora. Women in Classical Greece*. Baltimore and Princeton, 1995.

Reich 1903. Reich, H. *Der Mimus. Ein litterar-entwicklungsgeschichtlicher Versuch*. Berlin, 1903.

Reinach 1922. Reinach, S. *Répertoire des vases peints*. Vol. 1. Paris, 1922.

Reinmuth 1952. Reinmuth, O. W. "The Genesis of the Athenian Ephebeia," *TAPA* 83 (1952), 34–50.

Renehan 1981. Renehan, Robert. "The Greek Anthropocentric View of Man," *HSCP* 85 (1981), 239–59.

Rhodes 1981. Rhodes, P. J. *A Commentary on the Aristotelian Athenaion Politeia.* Oxford, 1981.

Ridgway 1970. Ridgway, Brunilde S. "Dolphins and Dolphin-Riders," *Archaeology* 23 (1970), 86–95.

Riu 1999. Riu, Xavier. *Dionysism and Comedy.* Lanham, MD, 1999.

Robbins 1978. Robbins, E. "Cyrene and Cheiron: The Myth of Pindar's Ninth Pythian," *Phoenix* 32 (1978), 91–104.

Robertson 1975. Robertson, M. *The Parthenon Frieze.* London, 1975.

Rohde 1955. Rohde, Elisabeth. "Vorlage und Bestimmung einiger unveröffentlicher Vasen," *JdI* 70 (1955), 94–126.

Romanelli 1955. Romanelli, Pietro. "Terracotte architettoniche del Foro Romano," *Bolletino d'Arte* 40 (1955), 203–07.

Romer 1994. Romer, Frank. "Atheism, Impiety and the *Limos Melios* in Aristophanes' *Birds*," *AJP* 115 (1994), 351–65.

Romer 1997. ___. "Good Intentions and the ὁδὸς ἡ ἐς κόρακας," in Dobrov 1997, pp. 51–74.

de Romilly 1966. de Romilly, Jacqueline. "Thucydide et l'idée de progrès," *Annali della scuola normale superiore di Pisa. Classe di lettere e filosofia* 35 (1966), 143–91.

Rosen 1988. Rosen, Ralph. *Old Comedy and the Iambographic Tradition.* Atlanta, GA, 1988.

Rosen 1989. ___. "Trouble in the Early Career of Plato Comicus: Another Look at P.Oxy. 2737.44–51 (PCG III 2,590)," *ZPE* 76 (1989), 223–28.

Rosen 1995. ___. "Plato Comicus and the Evolution of Greek Comedy" in Dobrov, 1995, pp. 119–37.

Rosen 1997. ___. "The Gendered Polis in Eupolis' *Cities*," in Dobrov 1997, pp. 149–76.

Rosivach 1994. Rosivach, Vincent J. *The System of Sacrifice in Fourth-Century Athens.* Atlanta, GA, 1994.

Rösler 1990. Rösler, Wolfgang. "*Mnemosyne* in the *Symposion*," in Murray 1990, pp. 230–37.

Rossi 1971. Rossi, Luigi Enrico. "Il Ciclope di Euripides come κῶμος 'mancato,'" *Maia* 23 (1971), 10–38.

Rossi 1972. ___. "Il drama satiresco attico. Forma, fortuna e funzione di un genere letterario antico," *Dialoghi di Archeologia* 6 (1972), 248–302. [Repr. as "Das attische Satyrspiel. Form, Erfolg und Funktion einer antiken literarischen Gattung" in *Satyrspiel*. Ed. Bernd Seidensticker. Darmstadt, 1989, pp. 222–51.]

Rossi 1983. Rossi, L. E. "Il simposio greco arcaico e classico come spettacolo a se stesso" in *Atti del VII Convegno di studio. Spettacoli conviviali dall'antichità classica alle corti italiane del '400.* Viterbo, 1983, pp. 41–50.

Rossi 1995. ——. *Letteratura Greca.* Milan, 1995.

Rossi 1981. Rossi, Patrizia. "Sull' Esordio di Platone comico," *Homonoia* 3 (1981), 81–90.

Rothwell 1994. Rothwell, Kenneth S., Jr. "Was Carcinus I a Tragic Playwright?" *CP* 89 (1994) 241–45.

Rothwell 1995a. ——. "Aristophanes' *Wasps* and the Sociopolitics of Aesop's Fables," *Classical Journal* 93 (1995), 233–54.

Rothwell 1995b. ——. "The Continuity of the Chorus in Fourth-Century Attic Comedy" in Dobrov 1995, pp. 99–118. (An earlier version appeared in *Greek, Roman and Byzantine Studies* 33 [1992], 209–225.)

Roux 1976. Roux, Georges. "Un maître disparu de l'ancienne comédie: le poète Cratès, jugé par Aristophane," *Revue de Philologie* 50 (1976), 256–65.

Ruffell 2000. Ruffell, Ian. "The World Turned Upside Down: Utopia and Utopianism in the Fragments of Old Comedy," in Harvey and Wilkins 2000, pp. 473–506.

Russo 1994. Russo, C. F. *Aristophanes: An Author for the Stage.* Tr. K. Wren. London, 1994. [Italian original: 1962]

Saïd 1985. Saïd, Suzanne. *Sophiste et tyran ou le problème du Prométhée Enchaîné.* Paris, 1985.

Saïd 1988. ——. "Pas si bête ou Le jeu de la bêtise dans la comédie ancienne," *Le temps de la réflexion* 9 (1988), 73–92.

Scanlon 2002. Scanlon, Thomas F. *Eros and Greek Athletics.* Oxford, 2002.

Schareika 1978. Schareika, H. *Der Realismus der aristophanischen Komödie. Exemplarische Analysen zur Funktion des Komischen in den Werken des Aristophanes.* Bern, 1979

Scharffenberger 1995. Scharffenberger, E. "Peisetaerus' 'Satyric' Teatment of Iris: Aristophanes *Birds* 1253–6," *JHS* 115 (1995), 172–73.

Schauenburg 1974. Schauenburg, K. "Achilleus als Barbar; ein antikes Missverständnis," *Antike und Abendland* 20 (1974), 88–96.

Schibli 1983. Schibli, Hermann. "Fragments of a Weasel and Mouse War," *ZPE* 53 (1983), 1–25.

Schiffler 1976. Schiffler, Birgitt. *Die Typologie des Kentauren in der antiken Kunst vom 10. bis zum Ende des 4. Jhs. v. Chr.* Archäologische Studien 4. Frankfurt and Bern, 1976.

Schlesier 1993. Schlesier, Renate. "Mixtures of Masks: Maenads as Tragic Models," in Carpenter and Faraone 1993, pp. 89–114.

Schmid 1934 and 1946. Schmid, Wilhelm. *Geschichte der griechischen Literatur.* I.2. Munich, 1934. I.4, 1946.

Schmid 1947. Schmid, P. *Studien zur griechischen Ktisissagen*. Diss. Freiburg in der Schweiz, 1947.

Schmidt 1975. Schmidt, Volkmar. "Zu Euripides, Kyklops 120 und 707," *Maia* 27 (1975), 291–92.

Schmitt Pantel 1993. Schmitt Pantel, Pauline. *La cité au banquet. Histoire des repas publics dans les cités grecques*. Rome, 1992.

Schnapp 1989. Schnapp, Alain. "Eros the Hunter" in *A City of Images. Iconography and Society in Ancient Greece*. Edd. C. Bérard et al. Tr. Deborah Lyons. Princeton, 1989, pp. 71–87.

Schnapp-Gourbeillon 1981. Schnapp-Gourbeillon, Annie. *Lions, héros, masques. Les représentations animales chez Homère*. Paris, 1981.

Schöne 1987. Schöne, Angelika. *Der Thiasos. Eine ikonographische Untersuchung über das Gefolge des Dionysos in der attischen Vasenmalerei des 6. und 5. Jhs. v. Chr.* Göteborg, 1987.

Schwarze 1971. Schwarze, Joachim. *Die Beurteilung des Perikles*. Munich, 1971.

Schweitzer 1957. Schweitzer, Bernhard. "Stiermenschen" in *Charites. Studien zur Altertumswissenschaft*. Bonn, 1957, pp. 175–81.

Scullion 2002. Scullion, Scott. "'Nothing to Do with Dionysus': Tragedy Misconceived as Ritual," *CQ* 52 (2002), 102–37.

Scuppa 1956. Scuppa, A. *Platonis comici fragmenta*. Camerini, 1956.

Seaford 1976. Seaford, Richard. "On the Origins of Satyric Drama," *Maia* 28 (1976), 209–21.

Seaford 1977/78. ___. "The 'Hyporchema' of Pratinas," *Maia* 29 (1977/78), 81–94.

Seaford 1981. ___. "Dionysiac Drama and the Dionysiac Mysteries," *CQ* 31 (1981), 252–75.

Seaford 1982. ___. "The Date of Euripides' *Cyclops*," *JHS* 102 (1982), 161–72.

Seaford 1984. ___. ed. *Euripides: Cyclops*. Oxford, 1984.

Seaford 1994. ___. *Reciprocity and Ritual: Homer and Tragedy in the Developing City-State*. Oxford, 1994.

Seaford 1996. ___. "Something to Do with Dionysos – Tragedy and the Dionysiac: Response to Friedrich" in *Tragedy and the Tragic. Greek Theatre and Beyond*. Ed. M. S. Silk. Oxford, 1996, pp. 284–94.

Seeberg 1971. Seeberg, Axel. *Corinthian Komos Vases*. BICS Supp. 27. London, 1971.

Seeberg 1995. ___. "From Padded Dancers to Comedy" in *Stage Directions. Essays in Ancient Drama in Honour of E. W. Handley*. Ed. A. Griffiths. London, 1995, pp. 1–12.

Segal 1961. Segal, Charles. "The Character and Cults of Dionysus and the Unity of the *Frogs*," *HSCP* 65 (1961), 207–42.

Segal 1963. ___. "Nature and the World of Man in Greek Literature," *Arion* 2 (1963), 19–53.

Segal 1997. ___. *Dionysiac Poetics and Euripides' Bacchae*. Expanded edition. Princeton, 1997. Orig. publ. 1982.

Seibert 1963. Seibert, J. *Metropolis und Apoikie*. Bonn, 1963.

Seidensticker 1989. Seidensticker, Bernd. "Das Satyrspiel" in *Satyrspiel*. Ed. B. Seidensticker. Darmstadt, 1989, pp. 332–61. (n.b. Bibliography, pp. 405ff.)

Serpell 1990. Serpell, James. "All the King's Horses," *Anthrozoos* 3 (1990), 223–26.

Serpell 1996. ___. *In the Company of Animals. A Study of Human-Animal Relationships*. Rev. ed. Cambridge, 1996.

Settgast 1978. Settgast, J., ed. *Von Troja bis Amarna. The Norbert Schimmel Collection, New York*. Mainz, 1978.

Shapiro 1989. Shapiro, H. A. *Art and Cult under the Tyrants in Athens*. Mainz, 1989.

Shaw 2005. Shaw, Carl A. *Greek Comedy and the Evolution of Satyr Drama*. Diss. Univ. of Pennsylvania, 2005.

Sidwell 2000. Sidwell, Keith. "Athenaeus, Lucian, and Fifth-century Comedy" in *Athenaeus and his World*. Edd. D. Braund and J. Wilkins. Exeter, 2000, pp. 136–52.

Siewert 1977. Siewert, P. "The Ephebic Oath in Fifth-Century Athens," *JHS* 97 (1977), 102–11.

Siewert 1979. ___. "Poseidon Hippios am Kolonos und die athenischen Hippeis" in *Arktouros. Hellenic Studies Presented to B.M.W. Knox*. Edd. G. Bowersock, W. Burkert, and M. Putnam. Berlin and New York, 1979, pp. 280–89.

Sifakis 1967. Sifakis, G. *Studies in Hellenistic Drama*. London, 1967.

Sifakis 1971. ___. *Parabasis and Animal Choruses*. London, 1971.

Silk 1980. Silk, Michael. "Aristophanes as a Lyric Poet" in *Aristophanes: Essays in Interpretation*. Yale Classical Studies, vol. 25. Ed. Jeffrey Henderson. Cambridge, 1980, pp. 99–151.

Silk 2000. Silk, Michael. *Aristophanes and the Definition of Comedy*. Oxford, 2000.

Silk and Stern 1981. Silk, M. and J. P. Stern. *Nietzsche on Tragedy*. Cambridge, 1981.

Simon 1953. Simon, Erika. *Opfernde Götter*. Berlin 1953.

Simon 1978. ___. "Zeus" in *RE* Suppl. 15 (1978), 1415.

Simon 1982a. ___. *The Ancient Theatre*. Tr. C. E. Vafopoulou-Richardson. London and New York, 1982.

Simon 1982b. ___. "Satyrplays on Vases in the Time of Aeschylus" in *The Eye of Greece*. Edd. D.C. Kurtz and B. A. Sparkes. Cambridge, 1982, pp. 123–48. (Also publ. as "Satyrspielbilder aus der Zeit des Aischylos" in *Satyrspiel*. Ed. B. Seidensticker. Darmstadt, 1989, pp. 362–403.)

Simon 1983. ___. *Festivals of Attica. An Archaeological Commentary*. Madison, WI, 1983.

Simon 1985. ___. *Die Götter der Griechen*. 3rd ed. Munich, 1985.

Simon and Hirmer 1976. Simon, E., and M. Hirmer and A. Hirmer. *Die griechischen Vasen*. Munich, 1976.

Slater 1994. Slater, Candace. *Dance of the Dolphin. Transformation and Disenchantment in the Amazonian Imagination*. Chicago, 1994.

Slater 1986. Slater, Niall. "The Lenaean Theater," *ZPE* 66 (1986), 255–65.

Slater 1996. ——. "Bringing Up Father: *Paideia* and *Ephebeia* in the *Wasps*" in *Education in Greek Fiction*. Edd. Alan H. Sommerstein and C. Atherton. Bari, 1997, pp. 27–52.

Slater 2002. ——. *Spectator Politics. Metatheatre and Performance in Aristophanes*. Philadelphia, 2002.

Slater 1976. Slater, W. J. "Symposium at Sea," *HSCP* 80 (1976), 161–70.

Slater 1991. ——, ed. *Dining in a Classical Context*. Ann Arbor, 1991.

Smith 1881. Smith, Cecil. "Actors with Bird-Masks on Vases," *JHS* 2 (1881), 309–14.

Smith 1992. Smith, Stephen M. *Herodotus' Use of Animals: A Literary, Ethnographic, and Zoological Study*. Diss. Ohio State Univ., 1992.

Snell 1956. Snell, B. "Aischylos' Isthmiastai," *Hermes* 84 (1956), 1–11.

Sommerstein 1980. Sommerstein, Alan, H., ed. *Aristophanes: Acharnians*. Warminster, 1980.

Sommerstein 1981. ——. *Aristophanes: Knights*. Warminster, 1981.

Sommerstein 1983. ——. *Aristophanes: Wasps*. Warminster, 1983.

Sommerstein 1987. ——. *Aristophanes: Birds*. Warminster, 1987.

Sommerstein 1996. ——. *Aristophanes: Frogs*. Warminster, 1996.

Sommerstein 2001. ——. *Aristophanes: Wealth*. Warminster, 2001.

Sorabji 1993. Sorabji, Richard. *Animal Minds and Human Morals*. Ithaca, NY, 1993.

Sourvinou-Inwood 1988. Sourvinou-Inwood, Christiane. *Studies in Girls' Transitions. Aspects of the Arkteia and Age Representation in Attic Iconography*. Athens, 1988.

Sourvinou-Inwood 1990. ——. "Ancient Rites and Modern Constructs: On the Brauronian Bears Again," *BICS* 37 (1990), 1–14.

Sourvinou-Inwood 1994. ——. "Something to do with Athens: Tragedy and Ritual" in *Ritual, Finance, Politics. Athenian Democratic Accounts Presented to David Lewis*. Edd. R. Osborne and Simon Hornblower. Oxford, 1994, pp. 269–90.

Sourvinou-Inwood 1994/95. ——. "Le minotaure et les autres. Images et perceptions," *Metis* 9/10 (1994/95), 227–35.

Sparkes 1976. Sparkes, Brian A. "Treading the Grapes," *Bulletin Antieke Beschaving* 51 (1976), 47–56.

Sparkes 1996. ——. *The Red and the Black. Studies in Greek Pottery*. London, 1996.

Spence 1993. Spence, I. G. *The Cavalry of Classical Greece. A Social and Military History*. Oxford, 1993.

Spyropoulos 1988. Spyropoulos, E. S. "Κωμικοί ζωομορφοί χοροί" in "Ἀριστοφάνης. Σάτιρα. Θέατρο. ποίηση." Thessalonika, 1988, pp. 177–216.

(= "Μάγνης ὁ κωμικὸς καὶ ἡ θέση του στὴν ἱστορία τῆς ἀρχαίας ἀττικῆς κωμῳδίας," *Hellenika* 28 [1975], 247–74.)

Stanford 1958. Stanford, W. B., ed. *Aristophanes: Frogs.* London, 1958.

Stark 2004. Stark, Isolde. *Der hämische Muse. Spott als soziale und mentale Kontrolle in der griechischen Komödie.* Zetemata Vol. 121. Munich, 2004.

Stebbins 1929. Stebbins, Eunice Burr. *The Dolphin in the Literature and Art of Greece and Rome.* Diss. Johns Hopkins, 1927. Published Menasha, WI, 1929.

Steier 1932. Steier. "Strauss" in *RE* 4 (1932), 339–47.

Steiner 2002. Steiner, Ann. "Private and Public: Links between *Symposion* and *Syssition* in Fifth-Century Athens," *Classical Antiquity* 21 (2002), 347–80.

Steinhart 2004. Steinhart, Matthias. *Die Kunst der Nachahmung. Darstellungen mimetischer Vorführungen in der griechischen Bildkunst archaischer und klassischer Zeit.* Mainz, 2004.

Steures 1999. Steures, D.C. "Arion's Misunderstood Votive Offering" in *Proceedings of the XVth International Congress of Classical Archaeology, Amsterdam, July 12–17, 1998.* Edd. R. Docter and E. Moormann. Allard Pierson Series 12. Amsterdam 1999, pp. 397–99.

Stewart 1967. Stewart, D. J. "The Poet as Bird in Aristophanes and Horace," *CJ* 52 (1967), 357–61.

Stieber 1994. Stieber, Mary. "Aeschylus' *Theoroi* and Realism in Greek Art," *TAPA* 124 (1994), 85–119.

Stiglitz 1967. Stiglitz, Roman. *Die grossen Göttinnen Arkadiens. Der Kultname* ΜΕΓΑΛΑΙ ΘΕΑΙ *und seine Grundlagen.* Sonderschriften, Österreichischen Archäologischen Institut in Wien. Vienna, 1967.

Stone 1981. Stone, Laura M. *Costume in Aristophanic Comedy.* New York, 1981.

Storey 2003. Storey, Ian C. *Eupolis. Poet of Old Comedy.* Oxford, 2003.

van Straten 1995. van Straten, F. T. *Hiera Kala.* Leiden, 1995.

Strauss 1966. Strauss, Leo. *Socrates and Aristophanes.* New York, 1966.

Sutton 1974. Sutton, Dana F. "Sophocles' Dionysiscus," *Eos* 62 (1974), 205–11.

Sutton 1980. ___. *The Greek Satyr Play.* Meisenheim, 1980.

Sutton 1981. ___. "Aeschylus' *Theoroi or Isthmiastai* : A Reconsideration," *GRBS* 22 (1981), 335–38.

Sutton 1983. ___. "Dithyramb as Δρᾶμα: Philoxenus of Cythera's *Cyclops or Galatea*," *QUCC* 13 (1983), 37–43.

Süvern 1827. Süvern J. W. *Über Aristophanes Vögel.* Berlin, 1827.

Svenbro 1989. Svenbro, Jesper. "A Bibliography of Greek Sacrifice" in *The Cuisine of Sacrifice.* Edd. M. Detienne and J.-P. Vernant. Chicago, 1989, pp. 204–17.

Szegedy-Maszak 1978. Szegedy-Maszak, Andrew. "Legends of the Greek Lawgivers," *GRBS* 19 (1978), 199–209.

Taillardat 1965. Taillardat, J. *Les images d'Aristophane.* 2nd ed. Paris, 1965.

Tambiah 1969. Tambiah, S. J. "Animals are Good to Think and Good to Prohibit," *Ethnology* 8 (1969), 423–59.

Tammaro 1984/85. Tammaro, V. "Crates fr. 16, 1ss. K-A," *Museum Criticum* 19/20 (1984/85), 43–44.

Taplin 1987. Taplin, Oliver. "Phallology, Phylakes, Iconography and Aristophanes," *PCPS* 33 (1987), 92–104.

Taplin 1993. ___. *Comic Angels and Other Approaches to Greek Drama through Vase-Paintings*. Oxford, 1993.

Tatton-Brown 1979. Tatton-Brown, Veronica. *Cyprus BC: 7000 Years of History*. London, 1979.

Teodorson 1990. Teodorson, S. *A Commentary on Plutarch's Table Talk*. Vol. II. Göteborg, 1990.

Themelis 1996. Themelis, Petros. "Damophon" in *Personal Styles in Greek Sculpture*. Yale Classical Studies, Vol. 30. Edd. O. Palagia and J. J. Pollitt. Cambridge, 1996, pp. 154–185.

Thiercy 1987. Thiercy, Pascal. "Il ruolo del pubblico nella commedia di Aristofane (Le rôle du public dans la comédie d'Aristophane)," *Dioniso* 57 (1987), 169–85.

Thompson 1936. Thompson, D'Arcy W. *A Glossary of Greek Birds*. 2nd ed. Oxford, 1936.

Thompson, 1947. ___. *A Glossary of Greek Fishes*. Oxford, 1947.

Tod 1947. Tod, M. N. *Greek Historical Inscriptions*. 2nd ed. Oxford, 1947.

Todisco 2002. Todisco, Luigi. *Teatro e spettacolo in Magna Grecia e in Sicilia*. Milan, 2002.

Trendall 1966/67. Trendall, A. D. "Western Sicily," *Archaeological Reports* 13 (1966/67), 40.

Trendall and Webster 1971. Trendall, A. D. and T. B. L. Webster. *Illustrations of Greek Drama*. London, 1971.

Tulin 1993. Tulin, Alexander. "Xenophanes Fr. 18 D.-K. and the Origins of the Idea of Progress," *Hermes* 121 (1993), 129–38.

Turato 1971/72. Turato, Fabio. "Le leggi non scritte negli 'Uccelli' di Aristofane," *Atti e memorie dell' Accademia Pataviana di Scienze, Lettere* 84 pt. 3 (1971–72), 113–43.

Turato 1979. ___. *La crisi della città e l'ideologia del selvaggio nell' atene del v. sec. a. C.* Rome, 1979.

Tusa 1971. Tusa, V., ed. *Odeon ed altri monumenti archeologici. = Odeon and other Archaeological Monuments*. Palermo, 1971.

Tzachili-Douskou 1981. Tzachili-Douskou, Iris. "Τα ποικιλα θηραικα ιματια και η τοιχογραφια του στολου μια ιδιομορφη τεχνικη στα υφαντα της θηρας," *Archaiologika Analekta ex Athenon* 14 (1981), 251–65.

Umholtz forthcoming. Umholtz, Gretchen. "Democratic Dining and Aristocratic Display in Classical Athens: Alcibiades' Paintings in the Propylaia," *Mouseion* forthcoming.

Usener 1899. Usener, Hermann. *Die Sintfluthsagen*. Bonn, 1899.

Ussher 1978. Ussher, R. G., ed. *Euripides: Cyclops*. Rome, 1978.

Uxkull-Gyllenband 1924. Uxkull-Gyllenband, W. *Griechische Kultur-Entstehungslehren*. Berlin, 1924.

Vermeule 1979. Vermeule, Emily. *Aspects of Death in Early Greek Art and Poetry*. Berkeley, 1979.

Vernant and Frontisi-Ducroux 1988. Vernant, J.-P. and Françoise Frontisi-Ducroux. "Features of the Mask in Ancient Greece" in *Myth and Tragedy in Ancient Greece*. Edd. J.-P. Vernant and P. Vidal-Naquet. Tr. Janet Lloyd. New York, 1988, pp. 189–206.

Versnel 1990. Versnel, H. S. *Inconsistencies in Greek and Roman Religion, I. Ter Unus: Isis, Dionysos, Hermes: Three Studies in Henotheism*. Leiden, 1990.

Versnel 1993. ——. *Inconsistencies in Greek and Roman Religion. II. Transition and Reversal in Myth and Ritual*. Leiden, 1993.

Vetta 1983. Vetta, M., ed. *Poesia e simposio nella Grecia antica*. Rome, 1983.

Vian 1963. Vian, F. *Les origines de Thèbes: Cadmos et les Spartes*. Paris, 1963.

Vickers 1990. Vickers, M. "Attic *Symposia* after the Persian Wars" in Murray. 1990, pp. 105–21.

Vidal-Naquet 1978. Vidal-Naquet, P. "Plato's Myth of the Statesman, the Ambiguities of the Golden Age and of History," *JHS* 98 (1978), 132–41.

Vidal-Naquet 1981a. ——. "The Black Hunter and the Origin of the Athenian *Ephebeia*" in *Myth, Religion and Society*. Ed. R. L. Gordon. Cambridge and Paris, 1981, pp. 147–62.

Vidal-Naquet 1981b. ——. "Slavery and the Rule of Women in Myth, Tradition and Utopia" in *Myth, Religion and Society*. Ed. R. L. Gordon. Cambridge and Paris, 1981, pp. 187–200.

Vidal-Naquet 1986. ——. "The Black Hunter Revisited," *PCPS* 32 (1986), 126–44.

Vierneisel and Kaeser 1990. Vierneisel, Klaus and Bert Kaeser, edd. *Kunst der Schale, Kultur des Trinkens*. An Exhibition at the Antikensammlung, Munich. Munich, 1990.

Vilatte 1986. Vilatte S. "La femme, l'esclave, le cheval et le chien. Les emblèmes du kalos kagathos Ischomaque," *Dialogues d'histoire ancienne* 12 (1986), 271–94.

Wachsmuth 1967. Wachsmuth, D. πόμπιμος ὁ Δαίμων. *Untersuchungen zu den antiken Sakralhandlungen bei Seereisen*. Diss. Berlin, 1967.

Walker 1995. Walker, Henry. *Theseus and Athens*. Oxford, 1995.

Wansbrough 1993. Wansbrough, Henry. "Two Choruses of Frogs?" *JHS* 113 (1993), 162.

Waszink 1974. Waszink, J. H. *Biene und Honig als Symbol des Dichters und der Dichtung in der griech.-röm. Antike*. Opladen, 1974.

Webster 1954. Webster, T. B. L. "Greek Comic Costume: Its History and Diffusion," *Bulletin of the John Rylands Library* 36 (1954), 563–88.

Webster 1970. ——. *The Greek Chorus*. London, 1970.

Weicker 1905. Weicker, G. "Hähne auf Grabstelen," *AM* (1905), 207–12.

Weiss 1984. Weiss, Carina. *Griechische Flussgottheiten in vorhellenistischer Zeit. Ikono-graphie und Bedeutung.* Beiträge zur Archäologie 17. Würzburg, 1984.

Wellman 1901. Wellman, M. "Delphin" in *RE* 4 (1901), 2504–10.

West 1966. West, M. L., ed. *Hesiod: Theogony.* Oxford, 1966.

West 1978. ___. *Hesiod: Works and Days.* Oxford, 1978.

West 1990. ___. *Studies in Aeschylus.* Stuttgart, 1990.

Westlake 1954. Westlake, H. D. "Overseas Service for the Father-Beater," *CR* 68 (1954), 90–94.

Whittaker 1935. Whittaker, M. "The Comic Fragments in their Relation to the Structure of Old Attic Comedy," *CQ* 29 (1935), 181–91.

Whitman 1964. Whitman, Cedric. *Aristophanes and the Comic Hero.* Cambridge, MA, 1964.

Wiesner 1953. Wiesner, J. Review of Delebecque and Yalouris. *Gnomon* 25 (1953), 314–19.

Wilkins 2000a. Wilkins, John. *The Boastful Chef. The Discourse of Food in Ancient Greek Comedy.* Oxford, 2000.

Wilkins 2000b. ___. "Edible Choruses," in Harvey and Wilkins 2000, pp. 341–54.

Williams 1991. Williams, Dyfri. "The Invention of the Red-Figure Technique and the Race between Vase-painting and Free Painting" in *Looking at Greek Vases.* Edd. T. Rasmussen and N. Spivey. Cambridge, 1991, pp. 103–18.

Willis 1991. Willis, W. H. "Comoedia Dukiana," *GRBS* 32 (1991), 331–53.

Wills 1969. Wills, Garry. "Why are the Frogs in the *Frogs*?" *Hermes* 97 (1969), 306–17.

Wilson 1973. Wilson, Allan M. "Not Callias, but Ecphantides? An Alternative Interpretation of *I.G.* v.1097," *CR* 87 (1973), 126–27.

Wilson 2000. Wilson, Peter. *The Athenian Institution of the Choregia. The Chorus, the City and the Stage.* Cambridge, 2000.

Winiarczyk 1987. Winiarczyk, Marek. "Nochmals das Satyrspiel 'Sisyphos'," *WS* 100 (1987), 35–45.

Winiarczyk 1989. Winiarczyk, Marek. "Bibliographie zum antiken Atheismus," *Elenchos* 10 (1989), 103–192.

Winkler 1990. Winkler, J. "The Ephebes' Song" in Winkler and Zeitlin 1990, pp. 20–62. (An earlier version appeared in *Representations* 11 [1985], 26–62.)

Winkler and Zeitlin 1990. Winkler, J. and F. Zeitlin, edd. *Nothing to Do with Dionysus? Athenian Drama in Its Social Context.* Princeton, 1990.

Woodford 1992. Woodford, Susan. "Minotaurus" in *LIMC* VI (1992), 574–81.

Woodford 2003. ___. *Images of Myths in Classical Antiquity.* Cambridge, 2003.

Wrede 1928. Wrede, W. "Der Maskengott," *AM* 53 (1928), 66–95.

Young 1972. Young, Ellen. *The Slaying of the Minotaur. Evidence in Art and Literature for the Development of the Myth.* Diss. Bryn Mawr College, 1972.

Zacharia 2003. Zacharia, Katerina. "Sophocles and the West: The Evidence of the Fragments" in *Shards from Kolonos: Studies in Sophoclean Fragments.* Ed. A. H. Sommerstein. Bari, 2003, pp. 57–76.

Zielinski 1931. Zielinski, Thaddaeus. "Die Märchenkomödie in Athen" in *Iresione*. Vol. 1. Leopoli, 1931, pp. 8–75. (Orig. publ. St. Petersburg, 1885.)

Zimmermann 1983. Zimmermann, B. "Utopisches und Utopie in den Komödien des Aristophanes," *Würzburger Jahrbücher für die Altertumswissenschaft* 9 (1983), 57–77.

Zimmermann 1984–87. ___. *Untersuchungen zur Form und dramatischen Technik der Aristophanischen Komödien*. 3 vols. Königstein, 1984, 1986; Frankfurt, 1987.

Zimmermann 1992. ___. *Dithyrambos. Geschichte einer Gattung*. Göttingen, 1992.

INDEX

Cinesias, 175, 178
Circe, 90
city foundation, 50–52, 58, 77, 145, 158,
    174
(*see also* ktistes)
Cleisthenes of Sicyon, 13, 24
Cleisthenes of Athens, 43
Cleon, 20, 114, 142, 150, 177, 179
colonization, 77
Colophon, foundation of, 9
Comoedia Dukiana, 104, 128–30, 144,
    194–97
Corinth, 14, 24
Corinthian vases, 14, 21–25, 40, 55, 56
courtrooms, Athenian, 114–15
Crates II, *Birds*, 87, 104, 199
Crates, *Beasts*, 87, 104, 106, 107, 123–26,
    131, 142, 148, 163, 199
Crathis, River, 50
Cratinus
    Cheirones, 88, 91
    Dionysalexandros, 91
    Ploutoi, 30, 197
    Satyrs, 91
Creon, 158
Crete
    and bull, 47
Critias, 86
    DK 88 B2, 86
    DK 88 B25 (*Sisyphus*), 86, 154, 167, 168
Cyclopes, 91, 100, 108
Cynics, 90, 101
Cyprus, and bull-masks, 47

Daedalus, 94, 97
Damophon, 219
Delphi, 51, 65, 66, 68
Demeter, 17–18, 39, 163
    and Lycosura, 17–18
    and "melissai", 120
    Tauropolos, 47
democracy, 43, 66, 77
    and symposium, 14, 71
Democritus, 57, 87, 89, 134, 146, 167, 170,
    171, 174, 178
    DK 68 A138, 165
    DK 68 B26, 162
    DK 68 B33, 168
    DK 68 B154, 160

DK 68 B266, 170
DK 68 B267, 158
DK 68 B278, 169
Demos, in *Knights*, 142
Demosthenes, orator, 7, 35
Demosthenes, slave in *Knights*, 142
Despoina (*see also* Demeter), 17, 39, 44
Deucalion, 69, 122, 145
Dicaeopolis, 84, 179
Diocles, *Bees*, 104, 106, 120–21, 199–200
Diogenes, 90
dioiketes, Ptolemaic, 129
Dionysia, 7, 8, 15, 17, 20, 26, 34, 52, 57,
    78, 92, 115, 117, 130, 150, 214
Dionysius, boy dolphin-rider, 65
Dionysius Chalkous, 70
Dionysus, 5, 12, 15–17, 20, 28, 34, 53, 58,
    66, 79, 94, 96, 97, 130, 136,
    137–41, 163
    and animals, 16–17, 47, 48, 64, 65, 75,
    141, 232
    and drama, 24, 25, 149
Dirce, 47
dithyramb, 29, 62, 65, 72, 140
dokimasia, 42, 43
dolphin-riders, 31, 71, 76, 77, 79
Dorian comedy, 14, 22, 24, 35, 77
Dümmler krater, 24, 27

Ecphantides, *Satyrs*, 91
ekkyklema, 153
Egyptian cats, 83
Elea, colonization of, 9
Eleusinian Mysteries, 136
Embarus, and Artemis, 130
Empedocles, 88
    DK 31 B130, 125
ephebes and ephebeia, 18, 41–44, 45, 56,
    65, 68–70, 76, 116, 144, 149, 196,
    244
Epicharmus, 24, 204
Epicrates, *Amazons*, 249
Epimetheus, 161, 184
Eros, 155, 167
Eskimo myth of animal existence, 249
euboulia, 168, 171, 179
Eubulus, 71
Eucleides, 127, 188, 190
Euelpides, 153–55, 172, 180, 207, 208